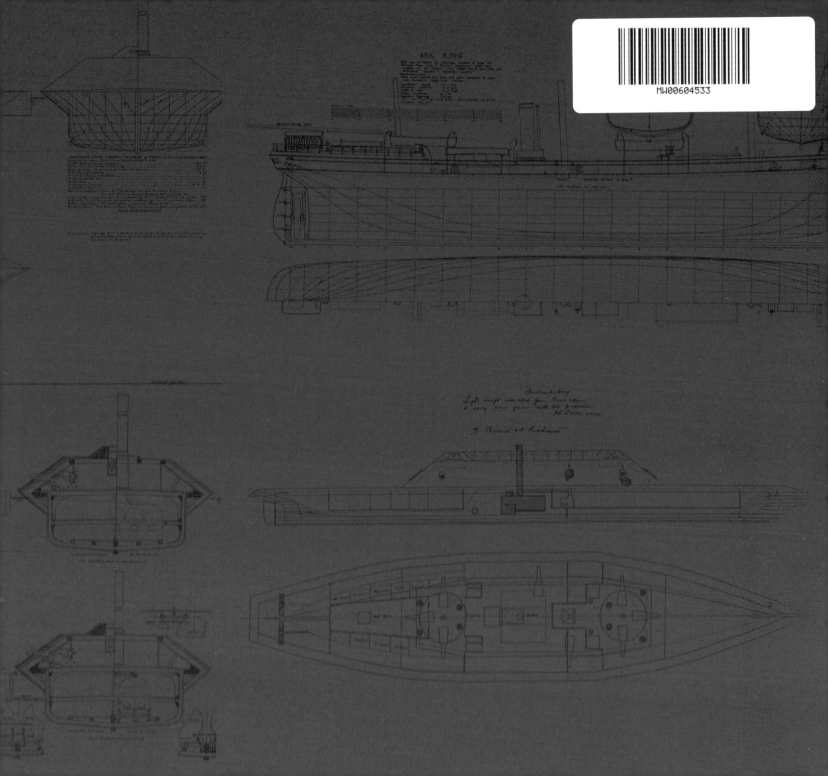

DONALD L. CANNEY

THE
CONFEDERATE
STEAM NAVY

1861-1865

Schiffer Publishing Ltd

4880 Lower Valley Road • Atglen, PA 19310

Designed by Molly Shields
Cover designed by Brenda McCallum
Type set in Krasivyi/Times New Roman

ISBN: 978-0-7643-4824-2
Printed in China

Published by Schiffer Publishing, Ltd.
4880 Lower Valley Road
Atglen, PA 19310
Phone: (610) 593-1777; Fax: (610) 593-2002
E-mail: Info@schifferbooks.com

For our complete selection of fine books on this and related
subjects, please visit our website at www.schifferbooks.com.
You may also write for a free catalog.

This book may be purchased from the publisher. Please try
your bookstore first.

We are always looking for people to write books on new and
related subjects. If you have an idea for a book, please contact
us at proposals@schifferbooks.com.

Schiffer Publishing's titles are available at special discounts
for bulk purchases for sales promotions or premiums. Special
editions, including personalized covers, corporate imprints,
and excerpts can be created in large quantities for special
needs. For more information, contact the publisher.

Contents

ACKNOWLEDGMENTS

A great number of institutions and individuals have been of assistance in researching this book. I thank the staffs of the National Archives in Washington DC as well as College Park, Maryland, in particular those at the Architectural and Cartographic Branch at Archives 2. At the Naval Historical Center, I thank the staff at the library as well as the Photographic Branch.

I appreciate the assistance of the staffs at, among other places, the Virginia Historical Society, Museum of the Confederacy, Duke University library, University of North Carolina library, Alabama Department of Archives and History, Emory University library, East Carolina University library, and Ohio State University Thompson library. Overseas, the staff at Merseyside Maritime Museum in Liverpool, and Glasgow University library were uniformly helpful, even on short notice.

I owe much to many individuals for their support and advice. First, to Kevin Foster, formerly of the National Park Service, who is a wealth of information, in particular on blockade runners, but not less on other maritime aspects of the War Between the States. Second, I thank Bob Holcombe, formerly at the National Civil War Naval Museum at Columbus, Georgia, for his knowledge of Confederate ironclads and willingness to answer my sometimes clueless questions, as well as for use of his many scale drawings of Confederate ironclads.

Thanks also to Andrew Bowcock for permission to use his plans of the *Alabama*, and Michael Crisafulli for his excellent plans of the *H.L. Hunley*.

As always I am thankful for the support from Dr. Robert Browning, Coast Guard Historian and my former supervisor, as well as Chuck Haberlein, now retired from the Naval Historical Center's Photo Section.

On a more personal basis, I thank the Jones, Lichtensteigers, Gaups, Crawfords, Tim and Les Canney, and my wife Janice and son Brendan for their support.

INTRODUCTION

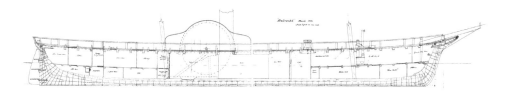

Traditionally, the study of the Civil War navy has long been overshadowed by that of the land war. In recent years technology has aided in growing interest in the maritime aspect of the subject. The advent of the side-scan radar and other deep-sea apparatus has resulted in uncovering long lost wrecks from that internecine conflict: notably that of the Confederate cruiser *Alabama,* off France, and that of the original submarine *H.L. Hunley*, long lost in Charleston harbor where she lay after sinking the first victim of sub warfare in 1864.

Thus, we have seen re-kindled arguments about various aspects of that war: the effectiveness of the Union blockade, the efficacy of the Confederate commerce raiders, the naval policies of Secretary of the Navy Stephen Mallory, and so forth.

Up until now, there has not been a serious effort to study the ships of the Confederate States Navy, as a group. There have only been annotated lists and catalogs, such as those written by Paul Silverstone (*Civil War Navies* and *Warships of the Civil War Navies*), the "official" versions done by the U.S. Naval History office in the 1970s, as well as the listing in the *Official Records of the Union and Confederate Navies in the War of the Rebellion*, Series II. At the other end of the spectrum there are many studies of individual vessels and other aspects of the war – strategic, tactical and logistical – as well as biographical accounts of leading figures on both sides.

Determining the scope of this work has been a challenge. I have used the phrase "steam navy" as the key to narrow my focus. Steam power was necessary for any navy of the period, leaving sailing vessels to play very secondary roles. This eliminates many vessels that were purely support or auxiliary craft, as well as the many sailing blockade runners. On the other hand, I have a short section on the floating batteries, and have, necessarily, included the hand-powered *H.L. Hunley* and its predecessors.

The term 'navy' is somewhat indefinite also. I have included the Mississippi River Defense Force, which was under the auspices of the Confederate Army, and a few blockade runners. While the majority of these were essentially fast merchant vessels, a few were under the command of Confederate naval officers. Not included here are the naval forces under various states in the Confederacy.

A second daunting factor in any book about the Confederate Navy is the location of original source material. While the majority of the Union navy's official wartime documentation is concentrated in the National Archives, Confederate naval documents are scattered. Though much is in the National Archives, the selection is not particularly systematic or complete. The balance of the material is literally scattered from coast to coast. And of course, there are documents relating to Confederate activities in Europe in various depositories in the United Kingdom and France.

My objective in all of this is to make a systematic account of the development of Confederate naval ships during the war and, where possible, show how the South adopted modern technology in the pursuit of their national goals. The concept is a logical continuation of my earlier books on the Union navy, entitled *The Old Steam Navy*, published in the 1990s.

This is not an operational history. However, I have included sketches of critical engagements or incidents selected to emphasize the practical, operational, impact of technology as it was used by the Confederate Navy and its officers and men.

French ironclad Gloire. The first sea-going iron-armored warship, launched in 1859. The British responded with the Warrior and both influenced ironclad developments in the Civil War. Illustrated London News

MID-NINETEENTH CENTURY NAVAL TECHNOLOGY

AND THE EARLY CONFEDERATE RESPONSE

The outbreak of the Civil War fell in the midst of an era of massive changes in naval technology brought on by the Industrial Revolution. By the 1860s, iron was replacing wood for shipbuilding, and was being adopted for protection; steam was making great inroads on sail power, and ordnance was turning from smooth bore guns and solid shot, to rifled guns and explosive shell projectiles.

The use of iron both for ship construction and protective plating was one response to the increasing dependence on explosive shells and rifled ordnance, as well as heavier projectiles. Explosive projectiles were devastating to wooden-hulled ships and rifled projectiles were increasingly dangerous against wooden hulls.

In Europe, the Crimean War had emphasized these trends with the appearance and effectiveness of British and French iron-protected floating batteries, particularly at the siege of Kinburn in 1855. As can be seen from period illustrations, these vessels were slab-sided and designed to be towed to stationary positions before going into action. Both French and British versions were wooden hulled, about 180-feet in length, with batteries of fourteen or more guns. Four-inch thick iron plates formed the bulwarks, backed by twenty inches of oak.[1] They were not designed for seakeeping or to participate in the line of battle, but proved to be effective against fortifications.

Building a true armored self-propelled war vessel was the next step in the evolution of armored warships, and by the end of the decade both the British and French were building steam powered ironclads: the French navy's *Gloire* was launched in 1859, and the Royal Navy's *Warrior,* in 1861. Both vessels were ocean going steamers, armed with shell guns and protected by over four inches of iron on their sides. Interestingly, neither vessel had a ram. (The French warships *Magenta* and *Solferino,* launched in mid-1861, were the first to have that device).[2]

These developments were not unnoticed across the Atlantic. In fact, American interest in iron-armored warships antedated that of the British and French, but had generated little tangible result. As early as 1842, inventor Robert L. Stevens, of New Jersey, had begun work on such a vessel, encouraged by a congressional appropriation. His "battery" was to have an iron hull and over four inches of armor, inclined at forty-five degrees to deflect shot. It dispensed entirely with sailing rig and had a ram bow. Unfortunately, Stevens severely underestimated the complexity and cost of the project. Furthermore, the work was hampered by redesigns

Crimean War-era floating battery. The nearly vertical sides were made of wood with iron plating; they were given a light sailing rig and small steam engine. The latter was insufficient for seakeeping and they were towed into position to bombard enemy fortifications. Wikimedia Commons

necessitated by advances in technology made during the two decades before the Civil War. Despite continued government subsidies, it was far from complete by the outbreak of the conflict. An official inquiry reported that the projected 400-foot vessel would not be of practical use for coastal or river warfare and recommended against it acquisition by the navy. The vessel, in fact, was never finished.[3]

There was much American interest in the Crimean war and official observers were sent to report on the conflict, including the use of ironclad batteries. The observers' report was published under the auspices of the Secretary of the Army, who was, at that time, Jefferson Davis.

By the outbreak of the Civil War, the U.S. Navy had built its last sail-only warship in 1854, and over half of its fleet was steam powered, though for economy's sake all the ships still retained a full sailing rig. Only one vessel, the

USS *Michigan*, stationed on the Great Lakes, had an iron hull, and none of the sixty some active American warships were iron-armored.[4]

By 1861, the Union navy was on a par with other nation's fleets in two areas: steam propulsion and ordnance. Their steam power plants were in the same league as those of other naval powers and the service boasted the Dahlgren smoothbore shell gun, a formidable piece of ordnance. Additionally, around the outbreak of the conflict they adopted the rifled guns invented by Robert Parrott.[5] Thus, in two of three technological areas, the navy of Abraham Lincoln was relatively modern.

However, when news of the French and English ironclads reached America, it was obvious that a new era had begun, and that the U.S. Navy was suddenly vulnerable. Any adversary prescient enough to quickly equip itself with iron armored warships would have the upper hand – or at least would until the USN responded in kind.

The naval leadership in the newly formed Confederate States of America was indeed aware of the opportunities presented by this situation. The question became whether they could implement a successful plan to take the advantage desired, which leads to the question of whether the seceded states possessed the literal nuts and bolts necessary to build a fleet that would out match that of the U.S. Navy.

Unfortunately, the South's quotient of bravado was not matched by the reality on the ground. The industrial capacity of the Northern states far exceeded that of the South. It has been estimated that less than a tenth of American manufactured goods were produced in the newly confederated states and that New York City alone exceeded the south in manufacturing capability. More critical was the fact that the south had no capability of manufacturing machine tools: the tools that produced the machinery to turn out manufactured goods. This industrial deficit was to become a major factor in the defeat of the Confederacy. In naval terms, the contrast was equally stark. If navy yards are considered, there were five major yards in the north: Portsmouth, New Hampshire, Boston, Brooklyn, Philadelphia, and Washington, D.C. (Plus there was a small facility at Sackett's Harbor on the Great Lakes.) In the southern states there were two, Norfolk and Pensacola, and the latter was incapable of heavy work, concentrating only on engine repair. Before the war, only nine naval steam vessels had been built in the south, and only two of their engines had been southern-built – both at Tredegar Iron Works in Richmond.

The Stevens battery. This is a highly speculative view. This experimental ironclad was begun in 1842, gained some government funding, but was never completed. At over 400-feet long, U.S. Navy authorities determined that it would not be suitable for completion or useful for the war. Naval Historical Center

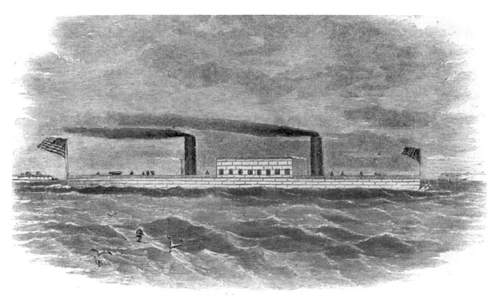

THE STEVENS BOMB-PROOF BATTERY AS IT WILL APPEAR WHEN COMPLETED.

By the same token, Tredegar was, at the outset of the war, the only Southern foundry capable of producing heavy ordnance and iron plate suitable for armor. There were several smaller foundries but these were equipped for only light work.[6]

In terms of natural resources, the south was well supplied with timber and coal. However, the supply of iron ore was severely reduced early in the war when the Union gained control of Kentucky, Tennessee and western Virginia. This limited the South's iron ore supply to the deposits in northern Alabama and Georgia. However, a rickety and minimal rail system prevented effective transportation between the sources and the manufacturing facilities. There were approximately 8,800-miles of railroads in the South, compared to around 23,000 in the North. There was also no standardization of track gauge, meaning that cargoes often had to be manually transshipped from freight cars of one track width to those of another width to continue a protracted journey. These supply and transportation problems would hamper the manufacture of iron products throughout the war.[7]

Three other key elements played into the Confederate naval effort at the outset of the war: the availability of personnel, ordnance and ships. Of the first there was sufficient, of the second there was a temporary glut, of the third there were nearly none.

For a section of the nation that had relatively little maritime activity or tradition, the South never had a shortage of naval officers. The core group within this number were those who "went south"

and resigned their Union navy commissions, to take up arms against that service. The most important men of this group were those in the top three grades: Captain, Commander and Lieutenant. (At that time these were the only officer ranks in the USN). Of 571 men in these grades, 126 resigned: about twenty-two percent. Over one hundred of these had ten to fifty years' service in the "old navy." And, of course these men fell in all categories, from incompetent upward, but included such men as Franklin Buchanan, Josiah Tatnall, Raphael Semmes, and John Newland Maffitt. On the other hand, it did not include David G. Farragut, a native of Virginia. In all pay grades, from sailmakers up, including third assistants and upward in the Marine Corps, 321 resigned of a total of 1,563 – again about one fifth.[8] As the war progressed, the Confederate navy's major personnel shortages were internal, resulting from competition for personnel by the Confederate army.

No shortages were apparent in terms of ordnance, at least early on. There was in effect a windfall, a result of the Confederate take-over of various federal facilities, along with their stores of powder and ordnance. The largest of these was the navy yard at Portsmouth (called Gosport in those days), Virginia. On April 20, 1861, the Union forces abandoned the yard, but botched the attempt to destroy the facility, leaving untouched about 1,200 cannon, of which around 300 were the latest Dahlgren smoothbores.[9] To give some scale to this loss, 1,200 pieces of ordnance more than exceeded the total number of guns mounted on all of the Navy's ships in and out of commission at the time. Though the Confederacy would establish cannon-making facilities and purchase many guns abroad, this original supply was a quite adequate beginning.

Finally there were the basic building blocks of any navy: ships. In February 1861, when the Confederate congress created a navy department, the government had no vessels or fleet. When war came two months later, these non-existent vessels would face the Union's sixty ships, about a third of which were less than five years old, and, in pre-ironclad days, were on a par with the best European warships.

The Confederate navy's acquisitions began with seizures of Federal vessels remaining in Southern waters: revenue cutters and coast survey vessels, for instance. A few Union naval vessels were left in burnt and sinking condition at Norfolk navy yard; and one sidewheel steamer was undergoing major reconstruction at Pensacola yard. Some of the smaller vessels were initially taken by various state navies, then transferred to the central government. A second group, if found to be suitable for use or conversion to war purposes, was purchased. A third group was constructed by the navy department. Most were built by contract at privately owned southern shipyards, while others were acquired from European builders using purchase methods designed to avoid neutrality issues in the builders's countries.

• • •

A single individual was destined to play the key role in the Confederate response to the U.S. Navy in 1861. Stephen R. Mallory was appointed Confederate naval secretary on February 21, the day following the official establishment of the navy department. Mallory was in many ways an appropriate man for the position. He was born in 1813 and spent his younger years at Key West, where he became inspector of customs when not yet twenty years old. He became well known in legal circles in Key West and no doubt obtained a certain type of maritime knowledge at that city, given its reputation with shipwrecks and wreck salvors. In 1851, he was elected senator from Florida and was later chairman of the Senate's Naval Affairs Committee. While on this committee

he became familiar with the trends in naval technology, and had advocated continuing congressional funding for the Stevens Battery in 1853. He was noted for insisting that the navy keep pace with European naval technology and supported the building of the 1854 steam frigates, which included USS *Merrimack*. Unfortunately Mallory had also been part of a naval review board created to remove the "deadwood" of old naval officers from the service. The board's methods caused an uproar and a portion of the defrocked officers were later reinstated by Congress. Many officers later in the Confederate navy – notably Matthew Fontaine Maury – had been affected negatively by the board, and this was to result in strained relations between them and Mallory.[10]

It is also noteworthy that Mallory was a cousin to the shipbuilding and whaling Mallory family of Mystic, Connecticut. Shortly after his appointment as naval secretary, Mallory wrote the family inquiring about details of steamship construction and specifics on some of the vessels built by the family company. In answer, they supplied information quite easily obtained from public sources, then politely avoided relating further details.[11]

• • •

When Stephen R. Mallory took office as Secretary of the Navy the breach between nations had been officially declared, but war was still unthinkable to many. Seven states had seceded and the flashpoints were becoming obvious: Federal entities within the seceded states: navy yards, arsenals, forts, customs houses and revenue vessels. Open hostilities were still two months away, awaiting the firing on Fort Sumter by Confederate forces.

In a flurry of activity, Mallory strove to create a viable naval force, spending these early days building the nascent organization. The earliest results in terms of vessel acquisition came on March 12,

about three weeks after his appointment, with a recommendation for building or purchasing ten steam gunboats "for coast defense," five of 750-tons and another five of 1,000-tons each. He requested $1-million for this plus $100,000 for contingencies. He also estimated $168,000 to enlist 500 sailors at $18 per month. The only specific vessel mentioned was the seized USN steamer *Fulton*, at Pensacola, for which he requested $250,000 for her completion.[12]

The next day, Mallory wrote to Raphael Semmes, who had earlier resigned his U.S. naval commission, and who was "touring" New England and New York making purchases of munitions for the armed forces of the new nation. Mallory wrote: "I have received reliable information, that two, or more steamers, of a class desired for immediate service, may be purchased at, or near New York; steamers of speed, light draught, and strength sufficient for at least one heavy gun ... designed to navigate ... the coast from Charleston to the St. Mary's, and from Key West, to the Rio Grande, for coast defense; that their speed should be sufficient ... to engage, or evade an engagement." He suggested they should each carry a single eight- or ten-inch gun plus two thirty-two-pounders. After a survey of New York waters, particularly Long Island Sound, Semmes concluded that such vessels were not available. (It is instructive that Mallory's letter to his shipbuilding cousins in Connecticut was dated two days after his missive to Semmes.)[13]

While Mallory continued his outreach in search of vessels of war, the amalgamation of the several states into the Confederacy resulted in an immediate acquisition of a core of relatively small ships: On March 15, the "navies" of several of the southern states were turned over to the Confederacy. (This group did not include the Virginia navy, which was not transferred until after that state's secession in April). A total of ten vessels were turned over, five of them ex-revenue cutters, plus one ex-slaver, all sailing vessels. The other four were steamers, including the old *Fulton*.

Seven of these vessels carried one gun each, the *Fulton* had three guns, and the *McClelland*, another revenue cutter, was variously credited with one, three or five guns. With these vessels, the Confederate navy had eleven (or fifteen) guns on ten vessels spread from Charleston to Galveston.[14]

The most important Confederate port was New Orleans, both because of its foreign trade and for its access to mid-American markets. On March 17, Mallory sent a committee to the city in search of vessels suitable for conversion, or failing that, to contract for gunboat construction. Arriving in early April, they surveyed the local yards and learned that they were capable of constructing and repairing riverboats, but none had ever built a warship. Two vessels were purchased for conversion: the *Habana*, which later became the cruiser *Sumter*, and the *Marquis de la Habana*, later to be the *McRae*. A smaller vessel, the *Florida* was fitted out for the lakes.[15]

These initiatives were in place when the Confederates fired on Ft. Sumter on April 12. Less than a week later, Jefferson Davis announced his government would sanction "privately armed vessels" operating on the high seas. This was an attempt to strike at the Union's merchant fleet, but privateering had been prohibited by international agreement in 1856. The United States, however, had not been a signatory to the treaty, and the Confederate States of America did not exist at the time. Within days, Southerners had applied for letters of marque, and a few were at sea by mid-May.[16] But the Southern privateers seemed many times to have an excess of swagger and had little impact on the course of the war at sea.

Two seemingly unrelated events occurred on April 19 and 20, both of which would have national and international repercussions. The first of these was Abraham Lincoln's proclamation of the blockade of the Southern coast. This would become the major task of the Union navy for the duration of the conflict. Maintaining it would become a priority because of the international ramifications that would append should the blockade be broken at any point. For the South, the blockade would spur extreme measures to break its "noose" and prevent their trade from being strangled.

The event of the twentieth was to have more indirect consequences: the burning of Norfolk navy yard by the abandoning federal forces. The loss to the federal navy ordnance supply was immense, as has been mentioned, and the number of warships lost in the conflagration was significant, though most were obsolete sailing men-of-war. The most modern vessel, the steam frigate *Merrimack* went down in flames – but only to the waterline. Her hull and engines would be the starting point for building an ironclad capable of attacking with impunity, every wooden vessel she encountered.

If the Union was targeting Southern merchants with the blockade, Mallory reasoned, the quid pro quo was to be the commerce raider, but his search for appropriate sea-going vessels in the south, the north, and Canada had yielded only the relatively small steamer *Sumter*, which was being refitted and would sail in June. Meanwhile, Mallory determined that the only source of such ships was Europe and had obtained congressional approval to spend $600,000 for that purpose. Consequently, in late May, Commander James D. Bulloch, an ex-U.S. naval officer, was sent to England to obtain six cruising ships, whether by purchase or construction.[17] Bulloch's arrival at Liverpool marked the genesis of the raiders *Florida* and *Alabama*, et al, which were to terrorize the American merchant marine throughout the war.

Europe was to be the source for another type of warship. Mallory wrote to the chairman of the naval affairs committee of the Confederate Congress on May 10: "I regard possession of an iron armored ship as a matter of the first necessity. Such a vessel at this time could traverse the entire coast of the United States, prevent all blockades, and encounter, with a fair prospect of success, their entire Navy

… inequality of numbers may be compensated by invulnerability." Mallory was intent on buying one of the already built European ironclads, but inquiries to this effect were fruitless as the European powers were not anxious to part with their newest technology.

The next best thing was to have a sea-going ironclad built in Europe. In pursuit of this, Mallory detailed Lt. James H. North for the task, writing to him on May 17: "… we require a few ships of this description," referring to the French *Gloire*. North also sailed to Europe that month.[18]

Mallory's search for an ironclad then took an unexpected turn. The remains of the steam frigate *Merrimack* were inspected and her lower hull and machinery were found to be viable. Sometime in June, the decision was made to re-construct the vessel into an iron-armored warship. The *Merrimack* emerged as the CSS *Virginia*, the most celebrated of the Confederate ironclads.

The *Virginia* was the first of many: by the end of 1861, the Confederacy had six ironclads under construction and a seventh (*Manassas*) operational. The majority of the armored steamers were to follow the general pattern set by *Virginia*.

The final initiative of 1861 was rather the opposite of the ironclad. As early as February 1861, the idea of a fleet of small, one- or two-gunned wooden steam gunboats was suggested. Matthew Fontaine Maury wrote that large numbers of these, each about 110-feet long, could theoretically overwhelm the Union navy's large frigates. The Confederate Congress agreed and authorized two million dollars for building no less than one hundred of them.[19] Several of these, along with other conventional gunboats, were begun in 1861, adding to the growing Confederate fleet.

I will, in the following chapters, discuss the various categories of vessels outlined above in detail. The only types not mentioned above are the blockade runners, torpedo vessels – both surface and submerged – and the wartime converted riverboats. All will be covered in the ensuing chapters.

IRONCLADS, 1861:

FIRST IN THE WATER

The first of the South's ironclads, all begun in 1861, were a disparate group, and understandably so, due to the exigencies of the situation as well as the novelty of their concept. There were seven begun that year: *Manassas, Virginia, Baltic, Arkansas, Tennessee, Louisiana* and *Mississippi.* Four of the seven saw combat and two were destroyed before completion. Three were conversions of existing vessels: one of a tug, one of a riverboat, and *Virginia* of a seagoing steam frigate. Their batteries were equally varied: from *Manassas,* carrying one gun, to the *Mississippi*, capable of mounting over twenty. Chronologically, the first of the seven under construction was probably *Virginia* (ex-*Merrimack*), with the conversion under way late in June or early-July 1861. The *Manassas* began life as a privateer venture at New Orleans, thus her conversion had to have been begun sometime after Jefferson Davis's May 6 proclamation sanctioning privateering and her trial trip on September 9, 1861.[20]

While the South launched headlong into implementing practical ironclads, it appears the Union navy was somewhat late in responding. The navy department advertised for bids for building ironclads in August 1861, resulting in contracts and the laying down of John Ericsson's *Monitor* and the small broadside ironclad *Galena* in October. Meanwhile, the U.S. Army laid down the *Cairo*

and six other partially ironclad sister ships at Mound City, Illinois, in August, and launched them in October. The *Benton*, converted from a catamaran river snagboat, was acquired in November 1861.[21]

Manassas

The *Manassas* was, in an era of eccentricity in warship design, unique, and never to be repeated. Its construction exemplifies the lengths to which new technology was being applied to otherwise ordinary vessels to meet the exigencies of the war. The vessel was nearly the antithesis of the warship when originally constructed. She was built by J.O. Curtis of Medford, Massachusetts, as a tug and ice boat (the latter an archaic term for icebreaker) in 1855.

Originally named *Enoch Train*, after a prominent merchant and shipbuilder of Boston and New York, the vessel was 128-feet in length with a twenty-eight-foot beam and 12½-foot depth of hold (distance between the keel and main deck), at 385-tons burthen. (It should be noted that there was another *Enoch Train* in this era, a full rigged ship built for the transatlantic trade in the early-1850s). She had two masts and was built for heavy work with an inclined two-cylinder engine and two boilers, all built by Harrison Loring of Boston. The cylinders were thirty-six inches in diameter by thirty-two-inch stroke, probably of the direct

Confederate ram Manassas, sketched while in dock under construction. A powerful New York tug and iceboat, it was cut down and given an armored ram bow. Official Records

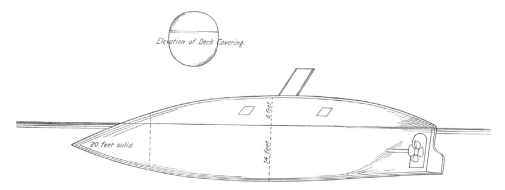

The ram Manassas in a post-war drawing. Note the single gun forward gunport and funnel. Naval Historical Center

acting variety, driving one screw propeller. Her hull was strongly built of white oak, "cross-fastened with iron and tree-nails" and with bows strengthened for ice work.[22]

She had been brought to New Orleans in 1859 to be used to tow vessels from the mouth of the Mississippi to New Orleans. When war threatened, John A. Stevenson, commission agent and official of the New Orleans pilots' association, recognized the possibilities inherent in the vessel, and began converting her into a rather strange-looking object, using the facilities of John Hughes's shipyard at Algiers, across the river from New Orleans. The upper works of the tug were first removed. A convex-curved structure of twelve inches of wood was built over the entire remaining main deck. Added to the bow was a twenty-foot ram built of seventeen-and-one-half inch iron – to deflect shot. Her primary offensive weapon was to be the ram bow, as her only other gun was a fixed, non-training, smoothbore firing directly forward, with a port shutter which automatically closed when the gun was run in. Early on, this was a sixty-four-pounder; it was later replaced with a thirty-two-pounder. The only other apertures were a pilothouse mounted aft, and two hatches. Sources disagree on whether she had one or two funnels. Only about two and a half feet of the upper part of the vessel's hull was above water, giving her a whale-like appearance. The locals nicknamed her "Turtle" and "Nondescript."[23]

When completed the vessel, now renamed *Manassas*, was 145-feet by thirty-three feet and reportedly had an arrangement to spew scalding steam over her deck to repel boarders. Since her construction had been independent of any government, she was registered as a privateer, with Stevenson as captain and a crew of eighty-six.[24]

With regard to the number of smokestacks: Various sources claim she had one, or two, or stacks which retracted when necessary. There are

even contradictions on the same page of some works: J. Thomas Scharf states, "two chimneys" on page 265 of his *The Confederate Navy*, while the illustration of the vessel directly across the page clearly shows only a single funnel. Lt. Alexander Warley, her final commanding officer, wrote in his official report in August 1862 of her "smokestack" being riddled. One day earlier, Warley wrote to a newspaper editor – for publication – that her "smokestacks" were riddled. The controversy extended to the next century: In 1904, a former assistant engineer who claimed to have been on board both the *Enoch Train* and the *Manassas* insisted with some heat that she only ever had one stack. There is also a possibility that she had two stacks placed so closely together – side by side – that they appeared from many angles to be only one. Another writer said she had two funnels until one went by the board when she rammed the *Brooklyn*.[25] As no original photographs or plans of the *Manassas* or of the

Boston tug have been found we are left with no "smoking" answer.

The vessel may have been powerful as a tug, but the addition of substantial weight and beam apparently was deleterious to her speed. She "could not stem a strong current," according to one writer.[26] This was a great disadvantage given the usual currents prevalent on the Mississippi. These factors would prevent effective use of her ram in combat situations.

Manassas remained in private hands until October 11, 1861, when Confederate navy Commodore George N. Hollins directed that the vessel be seized and put under naval command. Shortly thereafter Hollins began his squadron's attack on the Union blockading squadron at the Head of the Passes below New Orleans.

The vessel's operational life was short: from the battle at the Head of the Passes, October 12, 1861, to her destruction on April 24, 1862 when Commodore Farragut's fleet passed the forts below

New Orleans. During the latter, she ran aground and burned.

Manassas in Action

At the Head of the Passes: Very early on October 12, Commodore Hollins brought his flotilla down the river, intending to have *Manassas* ram the first suitable Union blockader, then close in with fire rafts and the other vessels of his flotilla. The blockaders were all at anchor, with the steam sloop *Richmond* coaling. Inexplicably, *Manassas* managed to pass two or three of the Union vessels and close on the *Richmond* before much notice was taken of the strange "indescribable object." *Manassas* first caromed off the coaling barge then rammed into the *Richmond* just below the port side fore channels. After the collision, *Richmond* and *Water Witch* fired wildly, to little effect, missing the hull of the low-lying ex-privateer. The damage caused by the ram was light: three planks crushed and a hole about five inches in circumference two feet below the waterline "causing a considerable leak." The shock value of what had happened was much greater: *Richmond* and the remainder of the blockaders retreated downstream, exchanging fire with Hollins's fleet. *Manassas,* according to her commander, had her funnels (?) shot off and one of her cylinders "ruined" by the force of the collision. She drifted without power until towed back upstream.[27]

At New Orleans: Unlike the earlier engagement, *Manassas*'s adversaries above Forts Jackson and St. Philip were under way. In the melee, *Manassas* first attempted to strike a "large ship" but was frustrated by that vessel's speed. Second, she aimed for the side-wheel steamer *Mississippi,* and attempted to strike her on the paddle wheel, but instead struck her on the port quarter, "cutting four strakes of plank, seven feet long and … four inches deep, and the heads of fifty copper bolts." Her next target was the steam sloop *Brooklyn*, which she hit on her starboard beam, nearly amidships. When the *Brooklyn*'s carpenter returned from surveying the damage his report was: "All right, sir; no harm done." *Brooklyn*'s chain armor on her side and coalbunkers had prevented serious damage; at least it appeared so at the time. Later, when *Brooklyn*'s bunkers were emptied it was found that the damage was more significant. The collision had, however, dismounted the *Manassas*'s single gun. Subsequently, the thin-clad vessel was caught by two of the Union steamers and "shot through as if she had been made of thin plank." wrote her commander, Lt. Warley. *Manassas* then went aground and her crew escaped.[28]

Manassas's claim to fame was that she was the first ironclad steamer to go into combat. She was, however, seriously flawed. Her plating was simply too thin to deal with the standard broadside weapons of the Union navy, mostly thirty-two-pounders and nine-inch Dahlgren smoothbores. The mount of the single gun could not withstand the shock of ramming and the gun's limited field of fire made it of little use. Similarly, her machinery was easily dislocated by the shock of ramming. As for her ram, the *Manassas*'s slowness was doubly problematic: her would-be targets could easily escape her, and when she did make contact, her momentum was insufficient to cause serious damage.

Virginia

The *Virginia*, more popularly recognizable as the *Merrimack* of the alliterative "Monitor and Merrimack" duo, was by far the most influential of the Confederate ironclads and has gained well-deserved notice in thousands of historians' words and hundreds of illustrations. For this volume I will simply give a technical description of the vessel and salient facts concerning her career.

The origin of her design is somewhat hazy. In the tradition of history, the coat tails of fame become crowded with hangers-on, some legitimate, many not. Two men vied for preeminence in her creation: John M. Brooke and John Luke Porter, the former a veteran naval officer and sometime inventor, the latter an experienced naval constructor. The official version, written by Secretary Mallory in response to a post-battle inquiry, stated: "He [Brooke] entered upon this duty at once and a few days thereafter submitted … rough drawings of a casemated vessel, with submerged ends and inclined iron-plated sides. The ends of the vessel and the eaves of the casemate … were to be submerged two feet; and a light bulwark or false bow was … to divide the water … and serve as a tank to regulate the ship's draft."[29] Generally, this was the plan adopted for converting the hull of the steam frigate *Merrimack* to an ironclad.

Naval Constructor Porter subsequently maintained that he had also submitted a model of a proposed ironclad, which featured an inclined casemate, submerged "eaves" and ends with a "rough breakwater" forward, and that Mallory had ignored this in his report. Brooke later obtained a Confederate patent for this concept, which Porter never opposed.[30]

At any rate, Mallory ordered Porter to make detailed plans of this design, in mid-June 1861, and directed that inquiries be made at Tredegar Ironworks for suitable engines for the proposed ship. No immediate help was found at Tredegar

and Brooke and Chief Engineer William P. Williamson then went to Portsmouth (Gosport) navy yard and examined the *Merrimack*, which had been out of the water since May 30, and determined that the design in hand could successfully be applied to the remains of the steam frigate.[31]

The *Merrimack* had been built at Charlestown Navy Yard, at Boston, and commissioned in 1856, the first of the most advanced steam frigates built by the U.S. Navy. She was 256-feet 10½-inches in length and fifty-feet two inches in beam, and had a draft of almost twenty-four feet as originally armed with forty guns. Her two cylinders were seventy-two-inches in diameter with stroke of thirty-six-inches, in a back-acting configuration. That is, each cylinder was mounted horizontally and cross-wise in the hull. In part because of the large size of the pistons, there were two piston rods per cylinder. The rods straddled (above and below) the crankshaft and operated a crosshead to which the crank was attached. The crank, in turn, drove the crankshaft and propeller. This arrangement allowed a large-cylindered engine in a restricted space: the width of the ship's lower hull. This was a common naval engine configuration of this era, where cylinders were large and unwieldy, often over three-feet in diameter, and engines were to be placed as far below the waterline as possible to prevent combat damage. *Merrimack*'s engines required a space fifteen-feet long and over twenty-eight feet wide; this in addition to the four boilers, which added at least another twenty-eight-feet in length to the machinery spaces, for a total of about sixty-feet.[32] Ironically, in the frigate's design stage, a board recommended engines designed by John Ericsson – who designed the *Monitor* – for the *Merrimack*. For unknown reasons, this idea was not carried out, though plans of this engine still exist.[33]

The boilers were of the vertical water tube type patented by navy steam engineer Daniel B. Martin and were standard for the navy of this era.

U.S. STEAM FRIGATE MERRIMAC, 1856,

From a Lithograph made in London on the occasion of the visit of the *Merrimac* to Southampton. Loaned by Mr. Charles Schroeder, of Portsmouth, Virginia, who was a third assistant engineer on the *Merrimac* during her European cruise in 1856.

U.S. steam frigate Merrimack. Built in 1856, it had a powerful battery of forty guns, but was saddled with unreliable machinery. She was under repair at Norfolk when Confederate forces took the navy yard – and was subsequently burned and scuttled. Her remaining hull became the basis for the ironclad Virginia. Naval Historical Center

Longitudinal section of the Merrimack. She had been burned to the waterline and that which remained, from the keel upwards about twenty feet, was the foundation for the casemate and guns of the CSS Virginia. Note the location of the engines and boiler, which were re-used in place. The steamer's lowest, or orlop deck, was extended aft to the boilers and forward to the engines and was altered to become the crew's berth deck. The next deck up became the gundeck for the ironclad. National Archives

These were arranged around a single fire room about nine-feet wide. A serious drawback to these vertical water tube boilers was that cleaning and maintenance was time consuming: in horizontal tube boilers, the water could be drained only as far down as necessary to reach any problem areas; whereas the vertical type boilers would have to be completely drained for such maintenance. The engines were low-pressure with jet-type condensers. (Condensing engines were necessary for sea-going vessels to provide fresh – as opposed to salt – water for the boilers.) Exhaust was into a single eight-foot diameter funnel, which was some seventy feet tall (from boiler to top), and designed to lower to rail-level if necessary.[34]

Finally, the engine drove a single, two-bladed, seventeen-foot four-inch diameter screw propeller, weighing about 19,000-pounds. The propeller hub was on sliding harp or yoke that moved vertically, and the entire entity could be raised or lowered by a process similar to raising the anchor: by the crew operating the capstan. Thus, when under sail alone, the prop would be raised and there would be no propeller drag.[35]

The *Merrimack* may have had a steam engine, but she was still essentially a sailing frigate, lengthened to accommodate the engines. Thus, the wooden hull was extremely substantially built: it had been found that wooden hulls, particularly those carrying a large number of guns on the upper decks, would tend to sag at the ends due to the vast weights involved, a condition called hogging. This of course, weakened the hull. Even in the early sailing frigates such as *Constitution*, with a hull about 175-feet long, hogging was endemic. Consequently, on *Merrimack*, the wood framing, in itself massive, was strengthened by a web-work of iron straps crisscrossing the hull diagonally, running from the bilge to the upper deck, and adding longitudinal strength.[36]

The ship's frame itself was typical of mid-century American navy practice: made of live oak with each frame measuring thirteen by seventeen inches at the keel, and the keel measured eighteen inches. The hull was constructed with copper and iron bolts, each 1½- to two-inches in diameter, and often over a foot long. These bolts weighed an aggregate of over 360,000 pounds.[37]

The vessel had four decks, the upper two carrying the battery. The third was the berth deck; the lowest was the orlop deck that was not a continuous structure, but was interrupted by the engine and machinery space. The orlop deck and hold were below the waterline.

The strength of this hull was sufficient for the battery weighing in excess of 175-tons, engines and machinery, 600-tons of coal, a crew of over 500 with provisions, and the three mast sailing rig. The latter included 58,000 square feet of heavy canvas. Her main and fore masts were over 200-feet long and over three feet in diameter at the deck, and her largest yards were 110-feet long.[38]

The weakest element of this vessel was clearly not in her structure or sailing rig, these were essentially the most advanced version yet of the sailing frigate, as a class. However, the steam engine was the problem: the ship proved very slow and, with age, grew in unreliability. At the outset there were predictions of 9½-knots, but in practice 6.1-knots was the best average achieved under steam alone; 10.5-knots with sail and a good quartering breeze. She used 3,400-pounds of coal per hour, and the slip of her screw – a measure of efficiency, the higher the percentage, the less efficient the prop – was over thirty-eight percent.[39] By the time the frigate was put out of commission at Norfolk in 1859, the engines had deteriorated to the point that the navy had condemned them. When it became evident that the navy yard was to be abandoned to the Confederates, *Merrimack*'s engines were in pieces scattered in shops across the yard. Though a senior engineer had been brought in and a temporary fix was made on her machinery, the ship was still at the dock when the yard was burned.[40]

In any event, this was the ship left burned to the waterline and sunk at Portsmouth in 1861. It was a mixed blessing: a solidly built hull and a barely viable steam engine. The "blessing" aspect was again in play when the decision was made to build an iron casemate in place of her hull above the waterline: the fire and water had simplified the matter by having already removed everything down to that very line.

After a general clean up and cutting away the partially burned structure, naval constructor Porter began by calculating the weight he estimated for the completed vessel and the resulting displacement. This figure was easy in some respects, where there were "givens," such as number of proposed crew (320), provisions, and coal to be stored, etc. Much had to be estimated, such as the exact weight of the remaining hull, bulkheads and so on. This worked out to nineteen feet up from the keel. On running this line, he found it impinged on her propeller by a foot, so altered the line to a slight angle, making her depth of hold twenty feet aft, and retaining nineteen feet at the head. This was not quite satisfactory and he eventually resorted to adding iron kentledge ballast to bring her down to where the eaves were submerged.[41]

Inboard, the vessel's orlop deck was extended somewhat, bringing it directly to the boilers forward and to the engine spaces aft. Thus, the old orlop deck became the berth deck (though interrupted) for the ironclad. The few original plans do not detail how the captain's cabin, galley, and other spaces were arranged on that deck. There was no need to change the original storage spaces in the hold, below the orlop deck.[42]

Once the old berth deck was demolished, work began on the ironclad's casemate. This structure was some thirty-feet from the stem and fifty-five from the stern and about 180-feet long at its base, tapering to 154-feet at the top deck,

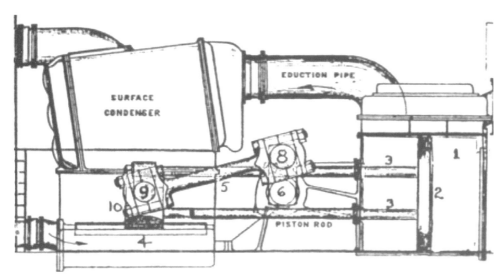

Diagram of a typical horizontal return connecting rod or "back acting" marine engine, of the type that powered the original Merrimack, and retained in the Virginia. There were two cylinders (1) and pistons (2). Double piston rods (3) operated athwartship and "straddled" the propeller shaft (6); the rods operated crossheads (10) that in turn moved the connecting rod (8 and 9). The connecting rod rotated the crankshaft (6) and therefore the propeller shaft. This back-acting arrangement was developed to make an otherwise too-wide engine able to fit into the confines of the width of a ship's hull. Wikimedia Commons

giving an angle of thirty-six degrees for the sides. The gun deck, placed several feet higher than the edge of the casemate, was 167-feet long. The top deck (over the casemate) was about eleven-feet wide at midship, and narrowed to around six-feet at the ends, though the inexactness of the original plans make it possible that these two dimensions were fourteen- and eleven-feet, respectively. The casemate sides would take the brunt of any enemy projectile and Porter resorted to pine, oak and iron, in that order for these. White pine "rafters" one-foot square ran from the knuckle to the upper deck, and oak knees connected them to the hull frames, and were bolted solidly together, side by side. Topping this solid wall was another five-inch layer of yellow pine, and that was covered with four inches of oak. The curved ends of the casemate were also made with a combination of square and tapered twelve-inch rafters, and was layered in the same manner as the sides.[43]

The iron plating was originally to have been made of three layers of one-inch plate. However, Brooke suggested a test should be made on a specially constructed target. This was accordingly set up at Jamestown Island, where plates were placed at thirty-six degrees and fired at by an eight-inch Columbiad at 300-yards. The results were unsettling: solid shot broke the plates and penetrated the pinewood backing to about four inches. Brooke then changed the target to two, two-inch thick layers, and the wood backing from pine to oak. The results were better: only the outer layer was smashed; while the second one was cracked, and the wood was not penetrated. Brooke ordered the change in October 1861.[44] The iron plates, made at Tredegar, were seven or eight inches wide, with the under layer installed horizontally; the outer layer, vertically. Bolts, about 1¼-inches in diameter and some twenty-six-inches long secured the entire thickness of wood and iron.[45]

Once the casemate's walls were complete, work began on the gun deck, then the upper deck, with their various hatchways and apertures. The narrow upper deck was composed of a wooden framework attaching it to the sides and a latticework grating of two-inch square iron rods, riveted together. At the fore end was the cone-shaped pilothouse, which was a single iron casting, twelve-inches thick and with four loopholes. Porter later wrote, however, that the pilothouse was never used in battle, and that the commanding officer stood on a "peak" (Porter's word) on the gundeck peering out a hatchway of the top deck. The distance between the gun and upper deck was over seven feet, so the commander may have climbed part way up the ladder for his observations, or possibly some sort of platform had been erected for this purpose on the deck. The wheel itself was located under or near the hatch forward of the funnel.[46]

Fore and aft of the casemate, the upper (weather) decks may have been based on the original ship's orlop deck. As constructor Porter is one of the few sources of information on the vessel's construction, we are left with his description: "[the]… beams were solid and bolted together, on this an iron deck four inches thick was laid. This deck was submerged two feet under water. They were plated with iron armor one inch

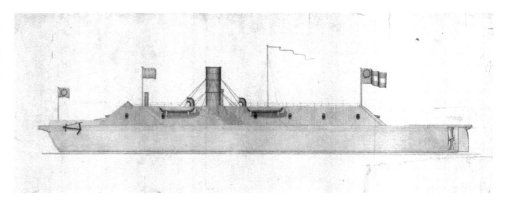

thick and then armored with pig iron five inches thick for ballast." These decks were probably made of the twelve by twelve beams as used on the "rafters," then covered with four inches of iron. The vertical side surfaces of this deck were then plated with one-inch iron. Atop the wood-and-iron fore deck was the v-shaped "breakwater" about four and a half feet high, all of layered wood. Within this enclosure was the pig-iron kentledge necessary to bring the ship deep enough to cover the casemate's eaves.[47]

One of the puzzles of this ship is the fact that this breakwater sometimes appears in illustrations, sometimes not. If it were indeed over four-feet high, it would have obviously been exposed above the waterline.

No such breakwater was on the stern, and the original plan was to have the rudder chains running beneath the iron on the stern deck, thence through pipes into the casemate to the wheel. Brooke objected to this, fearing that if the iron were hit and indented, this would jam the chains and they could not be repaired. Consequently, they were run over the deck, then into the casemate.[48] It did not seem to occur to anyone that repairing a broken chain on an exposed deck might be rather difficult in heat of battle, and, in fact, exposed chains were a key reason for the

disabling of the ironclad *Tennessee* at Mobile Bay in 1864.

Probably the most significant portion of the vessel not yet mentioned, is the ram. Porter later wrote that when the project began, "there was no mention of a prow, and after she had been in progress for some time, I determined to put one on her." Porter also said it was, "intended more to look at than for use." It weighed about 1,500 pounds, extended about two feet from the stem, and was of cast iron.[49]

Exactly when the idea for a ram was brought up is still unclear, but it was in place on the ship by late-February, when Mallory mentioned it in a letter to Franklin Buchanan.[50] It is possible that the activities of the CSS *Manassas* off the Head of the Passes the previous November might have had an influence on its adoption for the *Virginia.*

Though the *Virginia*'s ram would prove deadly, the primary offensive weapons were the cannon behind the formidable casemate. Ten guns were mounted in the casemate, and there were fourteen gunports. The extra gunports were to allow the forward and aft guns to also pivot and fire on each beam. The broadside ports' arrangement was asymmetrical with the port forward gunport farther forward than its starboard counterpart,

and the aft two on the port side are farther astern than those on the opposite side. Only two guns, the second on each broadside, were directly across from each other. The odd arrangement was to give as much athwartship space as possible for each gun. By the same token, no guns were mounted beside the hatchways and funnel.[51]

Six of the guns on broadside were nine-inch Dahlgren smoothbores; the other two were 6.4-inch Brooke rifles. The fore and aft pivots were seven-inch Brooke rifles.

The crowding on the gundeck was obvious from a few significant dimensions: at deck level, it was slightly less than thirty-feet; at the level of the gun tubes, it was about twenty-two-feet across at midships. The Dahlgren's gun tube was ten-feet in length; the 6.4-inch Brookes was about a foot again longer. Had any two Brookes been directly opposite each other, the guns would have collided when they were run in. If both guns had fired simultaneously the results were unthinkable; hence the odd arrangement of guns and gunports. It should be noted that some experts think the width of the upper deck was fourteen feet rather than eleven, in which case the width of the casemate at midship could have been twenty-four feet, rather than twenty-two.[52] Further, if the guns' muzzles were as far out as the gunport shutters, then another two feet could be added on each side, because of the thickness of the casemate sides. Of course, the guns would have been run out the ports for firing. However, there would still be limited range for recoil. There may have been standing orders that both center guns be not fired at once.

It is fortunate that the Confederates had a *Merrimack*-class frigate, which was designed for an all-Dahlgren battery, with the concomitant weights: each of the six nine-inch gun tubes on *Virginia* weighed 9,500-pounds plus carriage; and the seven-inch Brookes weighed 15,300-pounds for the tubes alone.[53] There was something over 100,000-pounds in gun tubes on the gundeck of *Virginia*.

Each of the gunports was circular on top and bottom and, two-feet wide and about three-feet high, with the base two feet from the deck. To allow some degree of training, the ports were wider – about four-feet – on the inside of the casemate. The gunport shutters were of four-inch iron, made at Tredegar. Their exact design is not certain, but it is thought they operated scissor-like with the "points" upward. They operated by chains run from the tops of the points into the casemate.[54]

A few miscellaneous items round out the picture of *Virginia*. She had two, possibly four, ship's boats mounted on chocks (not davits), one (or two) ventilators on her top deck, and a galley stack forward of her funnel. Period illustrations show these variations, and after-battle reports confirm "all" of her boats were destroyed during the engagements.[55]

Virginia at Hampton Roads: March 8-9, 1862

Between 2:20 and 4:00pm on March 8, *Virginia* destroyed two of the Union navy's major warships, that resulted in a casualty list not equaled again on a single day until the attack on the Pearl Harbor navy base on December 7, 1941. It would begin two days exemplifying naval technology in flux. First the ironclad demonstrated the fatal vulnerability of wooden naval ships, and at the same time seemed to demonstrate the importance of ramming using the new steam technology. In less than twenty-four hours, the first turreted warship stymied a broadside-casemate warship, signaling yet more changes to come.

The attack on the blockading fleet began with the *Virginia* aiming directly at the sailing sloop-of-war *Cumberland*, and taking fire from both that ship and the fifty-gun sailing frigate *Congress*. It was immediately obvious that *Virginia*'s casemate was impenetrable: witnesses talked of projectiles bouncing off her like "so many peas," and doing no apparent damage. However, the Union gunners, at close range soon found her weakness: the slowness of the manufacturing process had resulted in *Virginia* coming out with very few of her port shutters in place – leaving gaping gunports as perfect targets. During the fusillade most of the casualties on *Virginia* were at the guns: there were direct hits that blew the muzzles off two guns, wounding several and killing two crewmen.

Offensively, the *Virginia* had a field day, not least because her victims were at anchor or grounded in the shallows. The wooden walls had no watertight compartmentation so the one large aperture punched below the waterline by the *Virginia*'s ram sank the stationary *Cumberland*. Unfortunately, the ram was so deeply imbedded in the victim that *Virginia*'s weak engines had difficulty extracting her. The *Cumberland* came close to taking *Virginia* down with her until the ram finally sheared off. The next in *Virginia*'s sights was *Congress*, which had grounded in the mud. She was mercilessly pounded by a barrage of hot shot from the implacable ironclad. She surrendered and blew up later that night.

Damage to *Virginia* was superficial, though practically everything topside was demolished – her funnel was riddled and boats smashed to splinters. She also had a leak where her ram had been wrenched off. Captain Buchanan had been wounded while firing away with his rifle at Union soldiers on shore, and that night he was invalided onshore. When the day was done, it appeared a certainty that the hip-roofed monster would return at first light and destroy the remaining vessels of the blockading fleet – at least one of which was grounded and helpless – and get away unscathed.

Though the southerners had heard rumors of Ericsson's odd-looking ironclad, her appearance the next morning was still unexpected. All plans for a field day destroying the Union fleet were blunted when *Monitor* steered toward *Virginia* and a three-hour short-range slugfest began, this time with *Virginia* commanded by Thomas Catesby Jones. The only casualty of the day was the *Monitor*'s commanding officer, who was wounded by a shot to the ship's pilothouse. Because of the difficulty in aiming and turning the rotating turret, the *Monitor*'s gunners were not able to target *Virginia*'s gunports again. Also, an order had gone out restricting the powder charge for *Monitor*'s eleven-inch guns to fifteen pounds, when in fact they could have been charged with thirty. As it was, they only managed to dent *Virginia* and no shots penetrated her casemate. On *Virginia*, she had been armed with shells, expecting only to encounter wooden vessels. These did little damage to *Monitor*'s eight-inch thick iron turret sides. When the shooting stopped both vessels were still viable fighting units, leaving a wide field for victory claimants on both sides.

From the Union side, the dramatic appearance of *Monitor* plus some political string-pulling, resulted in a large building program – all of monitor type vessels. From the Confederate perspective, the two days probably enhanced the concept of ramming as a tactic. The epic fight also cemented the *Virginia* as a basic pattern for the configuration of the majority of subsequent Confederate ironclads. The angled casement

The Battle of Hampton Roads, the second day (March 9, 1862). After sinking two first line Union sailing warships the previous day, the way appeared clear for the Virginia to demolish the remainder of the Union blockading fleet – all of which were wooden-hulled and unarmored. The magnificently timed appearance of the Union ironclad Monitor stymied the Confederate plan and there followed an indecisive three-hour engagement, the first in history between ironclad vessels. Both vessels remained essentially intact at its conclusion, leaving both sides to claim victory. Naval Historical Center

became a staple of the genre, as well as the low freeboard ends and screw propulsion. The type also would include a ram.

The major drawbacks to *Virginia* also became an unfortunate pattern. These were her deep draft and weak engines. Her draft effectively prevented her from approaching other targets during the first day of the battle. And, though her engines performed adequately at Hampton Roads, they soon reverted to inadequacy for the rest of her short career. In many instances, "weak engines" also hampered later ironclads, many because they were often taken out of much smaller merchant vessels for use in massively built armored vessels. These two factors, but particularly that of deep draft, continued to plague nearly every Confederate ironclad built throughout the war.

Post-Script: after Hampton Roads

With the *Monitor* still undefeated, pressure was on to keep *Virginia* an active force, with secretary Mallory forcefully suggesting that *Virginia* be sent north to attack major northern ports, specifically New York City.[56] The ironclad immediately went into drydock for repairs.

It appears that the damage to *Virginia* was more extensive than generally thought, and in fact the Confederacy's best interests lay in obfuscating the issue. Buchanan, writing to Mallory on March 19, was particularly insistent that *Virginia* was still "experimental" and that *Monitor* was "her equal." Also, he said she was "by no means invulnerable," noting that, "two or three other heavy beams [and] plating were crushed in by the enemy's shot and shell." Later, in a letter to Josiah Tatnall, the new commander of the vessel, Buchanan, advised him, "not to engage *Monitor* unless the covers are in place." Another report indicated that when her casemate was hit at right angles, not only was the iron broken through but the "wood would also be broken through, but not displaced." It appears that the damage to the bow was more serious than was admitted at the time. The momentum of a 3,200-ton vessel at more than four-knots would certainly have forced more than just the two-foot long ram into the *Cumberland*. This would also explain the difficulty in extricating the *Virginia*'s bow from the sloop-of-war and the fact that the official report said her stem was "twisted" and leaking. The leak was exacerbated the next day when *Virginia* attempted to ram the *Monitor*. A crewmember later wrote that a bale of oakum was stuffed into the break to stop the leak, and it was necessary to return to Norfolk as soon as possible to dock the vessel.[57]

Soon workers at the yard were swarming the ship. A new and larger ram was soon being forged, the damage topside was being rectified and additional plating was being applied. Significantly, a two-inch layer was attached from the edge of the "eaves" down forty-two inches for over 160-feet of her length.

In April she was out of the dock and sent to do battle again, but her engines balked and the expedition was aborted. On May 20, the navy yard was abandoned to Federal troops and the *Virginia* was destroyed to prevent her capture. A plan to send her to safety up the James River was abandoned due to her deep draft. This exemplifies one of the most common challenges of the Confederate ironclads: as more armor was applied to increase protection, the deeper the vessel floated, further limiting the usefulness of the vessels in the shallow southern rivers and ports.

Louisiana

Chronologically, both *Louisiana* and *Mississippi* were begun about the same time. There were other similarities: both were among the largest in size and projected number of guns of all the Confederate ironclads. Both were for the defense of New Orleans and in fact were built at adjoining shipyards. Each also had a unique propulsion system.

On September 18, 1861, a contract was made with E.C. Murray of Kentucky, for an ironclad that would become the *Louisiana*, which he had originally proposed as early as April, but funds had been unavailable. His vessel was to cost $196,000 and be completed by January 25, 1862.[58]

Dimensionally, this would be one of the largest Confederate ironclads: 264-feet long by sixty-two-feet beam, with depth of hold of seven-feet, displacing 2,751-tons. She was designed to

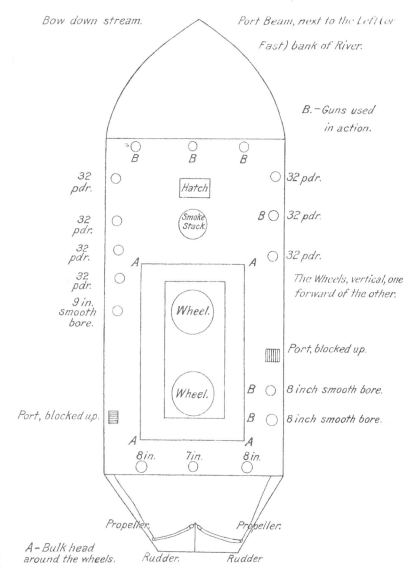

Gun Deck of "Louisiana" (Confederate) April 24, 1862.

Bow down stream.   Port Beam, next to the Left (or Fast) bank of River.

B. – Guns used in action.

32 pdr.   32 pdr.   32 pdr.   32 pdr.

Hatch

Smoke Stack.

9 in. smooth bore.

The Wheels, vertical, one forward of the other.

Wheel.   Wheel.

Port, blocked up.

8 inch smooth bore.

8 inch smooth bore.

Port, blocked up.

8 in.   7 in.   8 in.

Propeller.   Propeller.

A – Bulk head around the wheels.   Rudder.   Rudder.

Wartime diagram of ironclad Louisiana, one of the Confederacy's largest ironclads, based on sketches in the Virginia Historical Society's John K. Mitchell papers. Note the gundeck could mount twenty-two guns. Note the circles indicating location of two nearly full width paddle wheels, operating in tandem. This arrangement proved inefficient. Official Records

draw only six-feet of water, and carry twenty-two guns: sixteen nine-inch, four thirty-two-pounders, and two eleven-inchers, have a crew of 320 and carry fuel for three days steaming.[59]

The design for her casemate was not unusual: the sides slanted at forty-five degrees, and were covered with two layers of railroad t-iron. The inner layer was bolted through the top of the "T" to the wood backing, and the "upper" layer rails were driven in between each lower pair from the end to form a somewhat smooth surface, providing a shield about 3½-inches thick, in total. The wood backing was to be twelve-inch square pine covered by four inches of oak. The plating went only to the waterline. The boat was wide enough to allow three gunports across each end.[60]

Her designer, Joseph Pierce, was determined the vessel would not sink: to ensure this the hull was a warren of cubicles, formed by ten longitudinal members, five of them keelsons, crossed by seventeen athwartship bulkheads. Pierce's specifically called these "watertight" compartments and pipes were run from each cubicle to an auxiliary "doctor engine" which operated a pump to free these from water when needed.[61] This was very advanced thinking for the time, though in practice a wooden hull was extremely difficult to make watertight.

On the other hand Pierce's machinery was not so much advanced as merely strange. Main propulsion was to be not one, but two paddle wheels, each twenty-seven feet in diameter and nineteen feet wide, placed one in front of the other in the after part of the boat. According to the original specifications, these were to be inset about fourteen feet from the stern. However, all illustrative material found thus far point to these fourteen feet being measured from the stern of the casemate rather than the aft of the hull. To assist the vessel's two rudders in maneuvering the vessel, one four-foot diameter propeller was to be mounted on each side at the stern. Power was to come from six thirty-foot long, forty-inch

diameter boilers, and the two paddle wheels were to be turned by two thirty-inch by nine-foot stroke cylinders, which were from the paddle steamer *Ingomar*, built in 1854 and dismantled in New Orleans. A smaller, seventh boiler was to operate the doctor engine.[62] (It is unfortunate that no original plans exist of this vessel: only a sketchy diagram of the gun deck at the Virginia Historical Society survives). It is not clear from existing documents how the two cylinders would be connected to the tandem paddle wheels. Two smaller cylinders were to operate the stern screw propellers, but nothing is known about that mechanism either. The latter would necessarily need separate cylinders to operate independently for steering.[63]

The vessel's keel was laid on October 15, 1861. Construction was hampered by the usual lack of capacity in Southern foundries, particularly to forge the wheel and propeller shafts. In the shipyard itself, the labor force proved troublesome, with local workers balking when outsiders brought in by the government for the work were paid more than they. A strike occurred and Murray, after some delay, agreed to the new terms. Local workers were also subject to militia drills, further impeding progress. The ship was far from finished near the end of January, the contracted deadline for completion. The ship was launched on February 6, 1862, but much was still undone: the machinery was available but not on board and there was no iron on the shield. She was not ready for armament and had no pilothouse in place.[64]

The pace of activity accelerated with spring and the rumors of impending action by the Union navy. Rumor turned to fact on April 18, when Flag Officer Farragut's mortar flotilla opened up on Fort Jackson, below New Orleans. Two days later, *Louisiana*'s captain was ordered to move the still incomplete steamer downriver towards the forts. At this point, the steering engines were not in place, so the ordered "maiden

voyage" was not to be as designer Pierce would have liked it.

Indeed, the hulking ironclad's rudders were useless and she needed two towboats to steer her. The senior engineer wrote: "the after wheel could do no good whatever, and again when the wheels were working they would force the water out under the stern so that it would form an eddy around the rudders so that it would not stear [sic.]… she was unmanageable in the Mississippi River." And her engines would barely stem the current.[65]

When Farragut showed up with his fleet and passed the forts below New Orleans, *Louisiana* was little more than a floating battery. Her guns were in place, numbering sixteen: two seven-inch rifles, three nine-inch shell guns, four eight-inch guns, and seven thirty-two-pounders. The usefulness of the guns was severely limited by her small gunports that allowed a maximum of five degrees elevation and no lateral movement. A senior officer wrote of her situation: "[she was] unfit for offensive operations … but also for defense … her guns all around could only command about forty degrees of the horizon, leaving 320 degrees … on which she could be approached by an enemy without being able to bring a gun to bear."[66]

The ironclad, restrained by hawsers to the shore, received and returned the fire of Farragut's ships, in turn as they passed the forts. At one point, the USS *Iroquois* was caught by the current and "brought up against" the *Louisiana*, which fired into her, causing many casualties on the Union vessel. *Iroquois* returned fire, probably from a pair of eleven-inch Dahlgrens, as well as two nine-inch Dahlgrens, none of which penetrated the casemate. After the engagement the *Louisiana* was still intact, and the work continued on her steering engines. It was to no avail, as both forts Jackson and St. Philip surrendered on April 28. *Louisiana*'s commanding officer did not consider the surrender of the

Ironclad Louisiana under tow. With the approach of Farragut's fleet, this proved to be the only means to move the unwieldy vessel. Her two paddle wheels virtually cancelled each other out and the rudders were insufficient for steering. Battles and Leaders of the Civil War

army's forts to apply to naval forces. Consequently, he set the *Louisiana* adrift and afire. She blew up shortly afterwards.[67]

Mississippi

The second of the large New Orleans defenders was the product of two brothers who were long-time associates of Secretary Mallory: Nelson and Asa Tift. Their relationship went as far back as 1842, when Mallory, at Key West, acted as Asa Tift's attorney. By the Civil War, the Tifts were politically influential in Florida and Georgia, and still had profitable business contacts with northern merchants; though their relations with the Federal government may have soured when their Key West shipyard was seized in 1861.[68]

The Tifts had developed a model for an ironclad and, in August 1861, presented it to Mallory, along with a proposal offering to superintend construction of the vessel "without pecuniary compensation." This generosity was compounded by the fact that the Tifts would be forced to begin from scratch, as they had no shipyard to build the vessel in New Orleans or vicinity. Of course Mallory approved the contract and wrote: "I have concluded to build a large ship at New Orleans on Nelson Tift's plan … I will push it."[69]

Tift's design was simple: the vessel's design was reduced as far as possible to straight lines and pine timber. This would make construction as fast as possible, employing common house carpenters and readily available lumber. It was a nineteenth century precursor of Henry Ford's World War I Eagle boats.

In keeping with this design, the hull had no traditional ship frame – there was no rib structure put in place to be covered with planking. Instead, the hull work was "commenced at the bottom and completed as the work went up." Therefore the hull was flat bottomed, with perpendicular sides. The bottom "was twenty-two inches thick, in solid planks, solidly bolted and calked, and its walls two feet solid in thickness, with numerous thick keelsons to brace it." The depth of this box-hold was fifteen-feet. The overall length was 260-feet, by fifty-eight-feet, and over 4,000-tons. The original design apparently called for a hull 240-feet in length, but the designers deemed it necessary to add more boilers, for a total of sixteen. These were thirty-foot long, forty-two-inch diameter units in two rows across the ship in the hold, to obtain what they expected to be 1,500-horsepower. Thus the width of boilers alone was twenty-eight-feet, to which the designers planned to add five-foot wide coalbunkers on either side, between the boilers and sides of the vessel.[70] Above the hold was the casemate, with sides slanted at thirty degrees, covering a gundeck capable of mounting twenty guns. Three and

¾-inch armor (three layers of 1¼-inch each) was planned for the casemate, using plates seven inches wide and twenty-feet long, laid alternately vertically and horizontally. Approximately twenty-six-inches of wood was to provide backing.[71] Despite the longitudinal members and massive beams, the hull was also given hog braces, to prevent its sagging at the ends.[72]

A three-cylinder engine was built for the vessel, with thirty-six inch diameter cylinders and thirty-inch stroke. Each cylinder operated a single eleven-foot diameter propeller. The propeller shafts were nine-inches in diameter; the center one fifty-feet long; the side shafts, thirty-three feet long. The size and length of the center shaft precluded its local manufacture, and eventually Tredegar works fabricated the item by welding two shorter shafts from a burned-out steamer. The length of the completed shaft necessitated constructing a purpose-built rail car to transport it from Virginia to New Orleans.[73]

Construction was rapid, but only when no external obstacles were met. In November, Tift wrote Mallory: "… today will complete the fourth streak of lumber all around," and, "We fasten, calk paint and finish perfectly as we advance."[74] As with the *Louisiana*, the workers struck and were given raises. Another deficit was the lack of skilled engineers to deal with the unique machinery. The difficulties in forging the propeller

Wartime diagram of the hold of the ironclad Mississippi. Note the twin banks of boilers. Though fourteen are shown, sixteen were eventually installed. Each of the three propellers was powered by a single cylinder. Official Records

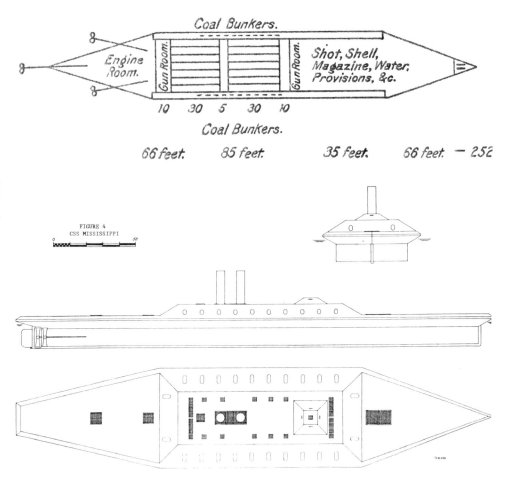

Ironclad Mississippi, plan by Bob Holcombe. The vessel's hold reflects the unusual construction technique. All curves were eliminated and thus the scow-like structure was built from the "ground up" using house-building methods. Bob Holcombe

shafts prolonged the process: the fifty-foot shaft did not reach New Orleans until April 9th and one of the side shafts would not have been ready for another ten days. Though much was yet to be done, the *Mississippi* was launched on April 19th, although even this was not without incident. An early attempt to launch had failed and an inspection revealed (so the story goes) that some saboteur had driven a nail or pin through the bottom into the ways, providing sufficient resistance to prevent her going into the water. There were riots in the streets as rumors of sabotage ran rampant, fed by growing panic at the approach of the Union fleet. The Tift brothers themselves were suspected of Yankee sympathy.[75]

However, the vessel was still at least two weeks from completion when the forts fell. An attempt was made to tow her upstream out of danger. Despite two tugboats, the current prevented *Mississippi* from escaping and she was burned to prevent capture.

The *Mississippi* was an extraordinary vessel, with great potential, both defensively and of-

fensively. In an era when four boilers was relatively standard, this vessel's sixteen would definitely have supported the three cylinders and propellers, and her armor and backing was substantial – more than that on the *Cairo* and her class vessels of the Union navy. The might-have-beens make interesting speculation.

Arkansas

The *Arkansas* was to be the only Confederate casemate ironclad on the Mississippi during the course of the war. The genesis of the vessel was from John T. Shirley, veteran steamboat captain and Memphis businessman. With a sketch of his idea, and advice from local rivermen, Shirley traveled to Richmond and met with John L.

Porter and Syephen Mallory, with the former working on adding specifics to Shirley's sketch work. The Confederate congress, with some prodding by Mallory and the naval committee, voted funds for two ironclad gunboats for the defense of Memphis and the Mississippi River. The next day, Shirley was presented with a contract for $320,000 for the two vessels, to be delivered on December 24, 1861.[76]

The vessels' specifications were surprisingly detailed, as follows: The overall length was to be 165-feet, breadth thirty-five-feet, with a twelve-foot depth of hold, and with a draft when in service of eight feet. At the waterline, the wales were to be six inches thick. A cast-iron ram was specified, weighing "no less than two tons."

The engines and boilers were limited to a space forty-feet long and thirty-two-feet wide. Four boilers were called for, providing steam for two independent steam cylinders, each thirty inches in diameter and with a stroke of twenty-four inches. They were to be direct acting, non-condensing units, mounted horizontally, operating athwartship, with the center of each mounted seven feet from the vessels' centerline. The engines were to power two propellers, each, six-feet nine-inches in diameter, revolving at 75-80 turns per minute, running on steam at 75-90psi. Each propeller shaft was to be sixty-feet long and seven-inches in diameter.

A six-foot-high rail was to run the length of the ship, though its height was reduced twenty-five-feet from the prow and forty-feet from the fantail, to allow a wide field of fire for fore and aft pivot guns. The specifications called for bulkheads of the casemate to be built at a forty-five-degree angle, and be composed of railroad iron and timber. Railroad t-iron was to run vertically on the sides, composed of two interlocking layers, with alternate rails reversed. This iron was to extend eighteen-inches below the waterline.[77] These specifications would not be strictly adhered to as construction proceeded.

Preparation to build the vessels, named *Arkansas* and *Tennessee*, was begun in September 1861, at Fort Pickering, south of Memphis, in the shipyard of Maine-native Primus Emerson, long-time boat builder in the mid-West and upper South. Ways had to be built, cranes fabricated, and workshops constructed before actual construction could begin.

The initial problem was gathering sufficient lumber for the project, and sawmills as far as 100-miles away were scavenged for pine and oak. A more critical element was the iron necessary for the casemate. Railroad iron, or T-iron, was the fastest method of obtaining the massive amounts necessary. Of course, ordering the materials was the simple part: awaiting fulfillment of the orders was the time consuming element. It was toward the end of October that the keels of both vessels were complete.

Finding laborers would be a continuing frustration, with carpenters and mechanics being in short supply. The army would prove to be the most immoveable obstacle, refusing to release soldiers for this work; despite pleas from Mallory himself to the various army commanders. At one point, a senior commander agreed to release the soldier-carpenters, provided each one provide his own substitute to the army. Thus, men with the needed skills were brought in from as far away as Maryland. This manpower shortage was the major reason progress was minimal through the end of 1861. In December, the shortage caused Shirley to concentrate the work onto one vessel – the *Arkansas* – in order to make best use of the manpower available.[78]

As the work progressed upward, the casemate itself was begun. At this point, the decision was made that the casemate sides were to be vertical, rather than angled. They were of oak timbers, ranging from eighteen inches thick to twelve inches, with the latter dimension at the top of the casemate. The slanting fore and aft casemate

bulkheads were of one-foot square oak beams, crossed by six-inch horizontal strips.[79]

The slow pace of construction did not become a critical issue until March of 1862, with the movements of Ulysses S. Grant's army and the taking of Forts Henry and Donelson, and Island No.10. The latter, on the Mississippi River, surrendered on April 7, and suddenly Memphis was vulnerable to the enemy. The *Arkansas* and *Tennessee* would need to be moved to a safe haven. However, an officer reported on April 10, that the latter vessel was basically keel and ribs and would not be ready for launch in less than six weeks. *Arkansas*, he continued, could possibly be in the water in "twenty days."[80]

The launch of the *Arkansas* was sometime later in April, and the vessel was soon towed to the Yazoo River, near Greenwood, Mississippi, along with a workboat and barge carrying parts and supplies. The *Tennessee* remained on the stocks and was later burned to prevent capture. (It was often confused with the other *Tennessee* – the ironclad at Mobile Bay). The little flotilla arrived on May 10, and sometime in the next few weeks the barge sank, carrying with it 400 rails intended for the ironclad's armor.[81]

Late in May, Lt. Isaac N. Brown arrived to take over command of the vessel and get her into service. What he found was discouraging: "The vessel was a mere hull, without armor; the engines were apart; guns without carriages were lying about the deck." The spring rising of the river further hampered operations: the levee broke and soon the *Arkansas* was four-miles from dry land. When the waters receded sufficiently and dry land appeared, Brown set to work with intensity and soon had fourteen forges and 200 carpenters at work, and much of the sunken iron was brought up from the riverbed.[82] From this point on, Brown had his crew working around the clock on the vessel, by the light of lanterns strung about at night. The side became an ad hoc navy yard, with

Cross section of the ironclad Arkansas. Possibly the only Confederate ironclad with vertical casemate sides, the vessel had two cylinders, each powering a propeller. Bob Holcombe

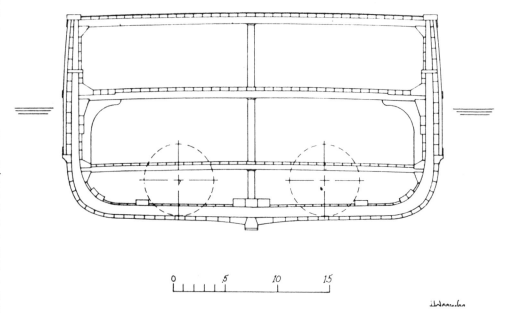

a blacksmith shop, makeshift hospital, and cook tent all erected for the project.

As work moved forward, Brown added two ports to the casemate, allowing for a total of ten guns. The rectangular gunports were protected by two-part shutters and were hinged at the top and bottom of the port openings. Then carriages had to be made locally by carpenters who literally had never seen a naval gun. The resulting carriages were all of the traditional trucked variety. There were four gun types in all: eight-inch Columbiads (two, both forward), nine-inch Dahlgrens (two, one starboard and one port broadside), six-inch rifles (one starboard, one port and two at the stern) and thirty-two-pounders (two, one on each broadside).[83]

Other miscellaneous aspects of the vessel should be noted: she carried iron-work "baskets" around her propellers to ward off river debris and snags, the top of the casemate was ½-inch boiler iron, the tops of her upper decks, forward and aft of the casemate, were wood; she had three foot high, v-shaped "bulwarks" on the forward and aft decks, as well as a two-foot high pilot house formed from one-inch iron bars. A seven-foot diameter funnel was erected for the exhaust from the six boilers. Because original plans do not exist, and in fact may never have existed, many important features are yet uncertain, one of which was the length of the casemate itself. Estimates for the top of the casemate range from eighty-four down to fifty-eight-feet. The longer measurement, plus the additional footage due to the angled bulkheads, would seem most likely, and would come closer

to the original specifications that called for a fore deck of twenty-five feet and aft deck of forty-feet.

There is some disagreement about the armor plating. A contemporary source said the rail t-iron was "interlapped" for a total of six inches thickness. Another source says it was one 4½-inch layer of iron. It was probably similar to that of the *Louisiana*, with a layer of t-rails, alternating their "tops," to give a smooth surface. Additionally, lining the inside of the casemate was some six inches of compressed cotton, covered with another layer of wood to contain it.

The vessel had a ram: specifications called for one of cast iron weighing "no less than" two-tons. It is worth noting that this mention of a ram predates (August 24, 1861) the attachment of a ram to *Virginia* and may be contemporary with the construction of *Manassas* as a ram. (There is no mention of a ram in connection with either

the *Louisiana* or the *Mississippi*.) When *Arkansas* was inspected shortly before her launch, the ram was on her prow and it was described as "cast iron" weighing 1,800-pounds. However, a wishbone or tuning fork shaped piece of wrought iron work found at the shipyard site where the *Tennessee* and *Arkansas* were built was the subject of a sketch by Union naval officer Henry Walke. It was about nine feet long, five feet of this were the "tines" of the fork that would be secured onto the sides of the prow, and four feet would have protruded in front of the stem. It was about three feet in its vertical dimension. This could well be similar to the "1,800lb." ram described above.[84] However, Walke also wrote a description of the *Arkansas* about this time. He described the "enormous beak" ram as "like a wedge into a piece of wood" and weighing 18,000-pounds. The dimensions he gives for the ram, however,

hour, though this may have been with the current; as half of that was expected against the current. The engine malfunctioned later, however, when one cylinder froze at top-dead-center. That is, one of the engine's crankshafts froze, probably with the piston at the end of its stroke. At this point the crank pin, center of the crankshaft, and piston rod are in a straight line and there is not enough momentum to continue the revolution. This stopped the attendant propeller. Only sweaty enginemen wielding crowbars and pry-bars could manually lever the crank up or down from its immobility. Meanwhile, it was found that the rudder could not counteract the single remaining prop, and the vessel would run in circles until the malfunction was corrected. One of her officers wrote that the engines never stopped "of themselves at the same time" and the effect was to turn the vessel around "despite the rudder." Another problem developed in the fireroom, as there was nothing insulating the boiler fronts. The red-hot boilers soon heated the enclosure to 130 degrees, to the detriment of the crewmen assigned there. Short shifts and many reliefs were required to maintain the fires under those conditions.[87]

Despite her ramshackle appearance and improvised condition, *Arkansas* was forced by circumstance into combat.

Arkansas in Action

The *Arkansas* was in four engagements in the course of her three weeks of active service, July

are nearly the same as those for the item found at the shipyard, and it is not possible that three-foot by nine-foot iron bar of that configuration would weigh nine tons. It also should be noted that there were contemporary newspaper accounts that claimed the ram weighed ten tons. The problem with all these wartime descriptions is that the ram was below the waterline, and therefore none of these writers would likely have actually seen the item in question.[85]

By mid-June, *Arkansas* was ready for the shakedown cruise, an event influenced by the approach of the Union navy and army as well as the river stage now declining. She was not an impressive sight. Lt. Brown wrote of the improvisations: "Without waiting for the apparatus to bend the railway iron to the curve of our quarter and stern, and to the angles of the pilot house … we tacked boilerplate iron over it (the stern) and very imperfectly covered the pilot house … with bar iron." Her unkempt appearance was not enhanced by whatever paint was or was not applied over the ironwork, much of which had been at the bottom of the river shortly before becoming part of the casemate. Whether by paint or rust, the ironclad was brown.[86]

The engines were satisfactory, in their initial tests, pushing the ram to eight-miles per

15 through August 6, 1862. First, the Union gunboats *Carondelet*, *Tyler* and *Queen of the West* engaged her in a running fight. *Carondelet*, like the others of that class of Eads "turtles" was not armored at the stern or on the quarters, and the other boats were also lightly plated. The *Arkansas* pursued the three, effectively using her two forward Columbiads, but the enemy avoided her attempts to ram. The fight was unequal as *Carondelet* only mounted two thirty-two-pounders at her stern. Eventually *Carondelet*'s weak casemate allowed a shot to sever her rudder chains and she went aground. The shallow water prevented pursuit by the Confederate ship, which continued after the *Tyler*. There were four killed and six wounded on *Carondelet*; one killed and another wounded on *Arkansas*.

This encounter led directly to the second, most famous exploit of the *Arkansas*. *Tyler* led her directly to Farragut's fleet, thirty-three vessels, all lined and moored on the river. The ram was not expected at six-fifty in the morning and only one vessel, the lightly armored ram *Lancaster*, actually got under way to attack. The *Arkansas* put a shot into her machinery, disabling the vessel and killing two crewmen. In the previous engagement a shot had damaged *Arkansas*'s fireroom and uptakes and this decreased her speed significantly, eliminating the possibility of using the ram, but Lt. Brown ranged the length of the fleet, firing at will, at times firing all guns simultaneously into the "target rich" environment. The rebel ironclad was moving at a rate that prevented the Union vessels from getting off more than two broadsides each, and in any event most of the shots bounced off. Though some of the Union vessels pursued, this ended when the ram came under the protection of the guns at Vicksburg. A later newspaper account indicated that the ships of Farragut's fleet had taken seventy-three hits from *Arkansas*, with forty-two killed and sixty-nine wounded.

The ironclad had caught the Union fleet flatfooted (Farragut said he was "mortified"), and revenge was planned.

Arkansas had not been unscathed. She had been hit literally hundreds of times, and two eleven-inch projectiles had done serious work: one smashed the pilothouse the other tore into the already damaged port casemate and decimated a gun crew. Her stack had been riddled and of course her machinery was knocked out of line. There were ten killed and fifteen wounded.

A few days later, the ironclad *Essex* and the *Queen of the West* came out to do battle. First, *Essex* attempted to ram, but this was parried and the *Essex* let off a broadside at fifty yards, piercing the *Arkansas*' armor and killing seven. The *Essex* then grounded temporarily and fell under *Arkansas*'s broadside, then under her stern guns. At that point *Essex* freed herself from the mud and left the scene. *Queen of the West* then attempted to ram, and succeeded, but did no serious damage. After another exchange of fire the latter vessel departed. The *Arkansas* had survived again, this time with a crew numbering only forty-one – with the men literally running from gun to gun. The rest of the crew had been relieved from duty as the vessel was not considered "ready for service."

The end, however, was not long delayed. On August 6, while moving downriver towards Baton Rouge, the ironclad's starboard engine failed. She piled into the bank and was unable to move. Nemesis *Essex* appeared in the offing and there was little to do but abandon and fire the ship.[88]

It can readily be seen that the *Arkansas* was a formidable vessel. The "makeshift" armor had withstood a massive fusillade from the entire fleet, and resisted the fire of five vessels in other actions. Her key weakness was obvious: her engines had never been reliable and had finally placed her in harm's way, with no escape.

Baltic

Baltic was one of many unsung Confederate ironclads. The ex-towboat did survive the war, but participated in no combat. Though stationed at Mobile, by the time of the 1864 battle, *Baltic* had been declared unfit for service (February 1863).[89]

The vessel was purchased as the result of an act by the Alabama legislature on November 9, 1861, which appropriated $150,000 for an "iron-clad gunboat" for the defense of Mobile. The vessel was to carry two sixty-eight-pounder guns, be "coated" with iron, have an iron ram, and draw seven feet of water. About a month later, $40,000 was paid to a M. Blainard for the towboat *Baltic*, complete with machinery, tackle, furniture, etc. Converting the boat began about a week later, as records remain showing payments for the workers' payroll.[90]

The vessel was a side-wheel steamer, 186-feet overall, with a thirty-eight-foot beam and twenty-nine-foot diameter wheels, each eight-feet wide. Construction records indicate she was "coated" with iron bars fifteen-feet long, seven-inches wide and 2½-inches thick "laid edgewise" and attached with bolts having heads and nuts on the inside.[91]

Her machinery consisted of four forty-two-inch diameter, twenty-four-foot long boilers and two steam cylinders. These engines were of the "usual western rivers type and arrangement." They were twenty-two-inch diameter pistons, seven-foot stroke, horizontal, non-condensing, high-pressure cylinders. These "western river" engines were simple in design and operation and their basic configuration had been in place for decades. Each cylinder operated a side-wheel, independently, allowing great maneuverability and short turning radius. Most repairs could be accomplished by a local blacksmith and parts were simple, easily obtained and in many instances, interchangeable between boats. It was not unusual for steam cylinders to be installed in several boats in sequence and, in fact, the engines were the most durable parts of these lightly built boats.[92]

Ironclad Baltic at Mobile. A converted shallow draft sidewheel steamer, the vessel mounted three guns. Admiral Buchanan, in charge of Mobile's defenses, pronounced the vessel "unseaworthy." Naval Historical Center

Such construction records as remain indicate little about how the hull was strengthened, but extra sturdiness was certainly called for given the guns carried and weight of the iron plating attached. This was a "usual" western rivers boat: a classic riverboat with shallow draft and lightly built cabin structure. Her draft was six-feet five-inches forward; five-feet seven-inches aft, meaning the vessel's depth of hold was not much more than the larger of those two numbers. With a 186-foot wooden hull only seven-feet from keel to main deck, there could not be much longitudinal strength. Two of the items purchased for this conversion were hog chains, along with eight hog chain blocks. These chains were actually lengthy iron bars about two-inches in diameter, anchored on the vessel's keelsons, fore and aft, and forming an arch sometimes higher than the cabins, over supporting struts and

masts, literally holding up the ends of the vessel. The chains could be adjusted to maintain the necessary tension. The chains' necessity, as well as effectiveness, is illustrated by contemporary photos of riverboats that had gone aground on hilly terrain. When the water receded the hull literally draped itself to conform to the land on which it lay. And sometimes the vessel would regain its shape when refloated. In any event, shallow-hulled vessels such as this one, as well as many others converted during the Civil War were poor candidates to support the iron plating and guns required of them. Hog chains also became dangerous when severed by shot. And when chains were hit during battle, serious hull structure problems were inevitable.[93]

The *Baltic* went into service at Mobile in mid-May 1862, with a crew of eighty-six and mounting two Dahlgrens and three thirty-two-pounders (also reported as one forty-two-pounder with two thirty-twos).[94] The only known illustration of the vessel shows a pup tent shaped casemate forward with bow gun and three broadside ports, only two of which show guns in place.

She was described as slow and cranky, and sometime in mid-1864, Admiral Buchanan declared her "unseaworthy."[95] So she remained idle while Farragut entered Mobile Bay. A post-war Union report said her upper works were "rather rotten" and the timber engine supports were very much decayed, but the hull was in good condition.[96] She was probably carrying far more weight than her structure warranted and the shocks to her timbers from the recoil of heavy guns may well have done her in.

She was turned over to the victorious Union forces at Hanna Bubba Island at the end of the war and was afterwards sold.

IRONCLADS, 1862, PART 1:

A SYSTEMATIC APPROACH

Where 1861 saw the Confederate navy department engaged in gathering a fleet by any means available: seizure, conversion, purchase, or new construction, the next year was one of consolidation and the beginning of a more systematic approach. Though some ironclad projects were still in the pipeline and were conversions of already existing vessels, the department set out in 1862 to standardize the designs so that "classes" of vessels would result. Thus, single sets of specifications and plans could be disseminated to the many contractors all over the South who would be building the vessels.

The drive to standardize the navy's ironclad construction program may explain why some well-intentioned plans were overlooked. Late in 1861, the Texas legislature authorized proposing the *Sea King*, a Texas designer's concept, to the navy department. This vessel was to be iron clad, was expected to steam at eighteen-knots and to employ a "submarine cannon" in addition to an above-water battery. On the debit side, it was to be powered by a "hot air" engine, a concept long ago attempted by John Ericsson and proved to be useless.[97] There is no record that this idea ever reached the navy department.

Before looking at the new construction, there were two vessel conversions in hand as 1862 began: *Eastport* and *Atlanta*. The riverboat *Eastport* was being converted into a war vessel. The vessel was far from complete when Union forces took

Forts Henry and Donelson, and she was captured by Federal forces in early-February 1862.[98]

The single major conversion from merchant to naval vessel on the east coast was begun in Savannah, with the steamer *Fingal*, on which James Bulloch had returned from Great Britain through the blockade (after negotiating construction of the commerce raiders *Alabama* and *Florida*). The intention was for the *Fingal*, which had been built in Scotland, to evade the blockade again and return to the increasingly profitable sub-rosa trade. However, the Union navy had effectively shut down the port of Savannah and *Fingal* was stuck. She was a nearly new vessel and it was decided she could be cut down and rebuilt as an ironclad. This process began in early-1862, under a contract with the Tift brothers.

Even before the engagement at Hampton Roads, the navy department was sorting out the direction they needed to take with the next generation of ironclad vessels. The *Virginia* was obviously unique: no other large seagoing frigate was going to fall into Confederate hands, and it was also plain that much smaller vessels would be more efficient. *Virginia's* draft, at over twenty-two feet was excessive for the James River and vicinity, as well as most other Southern ports. Henceforth, new construction would be limited to vessels with eight- to fourteen-foot draft, with concomitant reductions in dimensions and tonnage. Reducing dimensions would also facilitate

The river ironclad Eastport, was under conversion by the Confederates when captured by Union forces, then completed. Lack of longitudinal strength caused her to "bend double" from the weight of the eight large guns. The battery was afterward reduced to four weapons. Public Library of Cincinnati and Hamilton County

construction of these vessels in small civilian shipyards across the South.[99]

The upshot of these considerations was an ironclad plan by John L. Porter, which became the basis for the *Richmond* class of vessels: generally agreed to be comprised of: *Richmond*, *Chicora*, *Palmetto State*, *Raleigh*, *Savannah*, and *North Carolina*. All were laid down by late-spring 1862. Vicissitudes of conditions, materials available, etc., meant their commission dates ranged from July 1862 to April 1864. Porter's plan of course retained the *Virginia*'s sloping casemate, but replaced the curving ends with flat angles. The hull had ship's lines and rounded bilges.[100]

Eastport

Eastport was built in New Albany, Indiana, in 1852, and was one of the larger side-wheel river packets, at 280 feet by forty-three feet by a 5.5-foot depth of hold. The two cylinders were twenty-six-inch diameter and a nine-foot stroke, and were of the standard poppet-valve, western-rivers type. There were five boilers, each forty-two inches in diameter and twenty-eight feet long. When in commercial work, she ran between the Tennessee border and New Orleans.[101]

In January 1862, she was acquired by the Confederate navy and work was immediately begun to convert her into an iron-armored gunboat. This work came to a halt on February 7, when

Union forces captured the vessel. About two weeks later, Union navy Commander S.L. Phelps and Captain A.H. Foote reported her machinery was "first quality" and "complete." The hull itself was sheathed with oak planking and had oak fore, aft, and athwartship bulkheads. The side timbers of the casemate were also complete. "The *Eastport* is beautifully modeled" they reported and recommended completing the vessel, as there was sufficient material available to accomplish the conversion.[102]

Some indication of what had been done to strengthen the hull during the conversion can be deduced by a report made later, after she had grounded and gone for repairs. "The [hull] timbers broken were 10 in number in a space of 32 [ft.] long x 18 [ft.] wide and 14 inches thick, with a spring of 6 inches. There were two stirrups upon each end with screws & nuts by means of which the bottom had been forced to its proper position."[103] If these timbers were athwartship, there was one fourteen-inch timber every 3.2-feet, therefore about twenty-four inches apart.

Despite the substantial strengthening of the vessel's hull, it was soon noted that she could not carry the weight of her original battery. Adm. David D. Porter suggested that her battery be reduced, in the hope that she would not "bend double any more." Subsequently, her six, nine-inch guns and two, 100-pounder rifles were replaced by four guns.[104] The vessel highlighted the challenge of building a heavily armed war steamer on a shallow-hulled riverboat.

Eastport lasted in Union service until April 1864, when she hit a mine and was run aground. Shortly thereafter, she was abandoned and blown up.[105]

Atlanta

The ironclad *Atlanta* began Confederate service as a blockade runner, and indeed had been purchased for that purpose by James D. Bulloch in September 1861. Originally the *Fingal*, the vessel was the first ship purchased by the Confederate agents in Europe.[106]

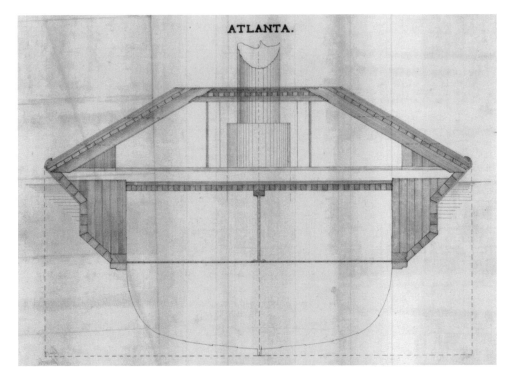

ATLANTA.

Cross section of the Ironclad Atlanta showing masses of wood and iron protection added to sides of the original hull of the blockade runner Fingal. The wood timbering was over four-feet thick and over four-feet below the waterline. National Archives

Bulloch was in search of fast vessels, with sailing rig and steam power, capable of remaining at sea for long periods. The *Fingal* was built at Glasgow, Scotland, and launched in May 1861, as a fast channel steamer, with two-mast rig, square sails on the foremast, and a hoisting screw. The latter would facilitate cruising under sail alone.[107]

Her builders were James and George Thomson and she was iron-hulled, 185.5-feet by 25.4-feet and 12.9-feet depth of hold, measuring 352 registered tons (650-tons carrying capacity). Her machinery consisted of two vertical direct-acting cylinders, thirty-nine inches in diameter and with a thirty-inch stroke, each producing 120 nominal horsepower. A single, double-flue boiler was installed, with two furnaces at each end. She was

reported to run at thirteen-knots, making her fast for her time. Bulloch was looking to send a large shipment of munitions to the South and *Fingal* appeared to be an appropriate choice.[108]

Through an intermediary, Bulloch purchased the ship from owners David and Alexander Hutchinson and David McBrayne for £17,500. She arrived in Savannah in November 1861, with what was said to be largest shipment of munitions ever brought into the Confederacy. After several unsuccessful attempts to run out through the blockade from Savannah with a cargo of cotton, it was decided she was a good candidate for conversion to an ironclad.[109]

The ship was turned over to Asa and Nelson Tift (who had built the *Mississippi* at New Orleans)

for conversion. In early May, the vessel was towed up the Savannah River to Purrysburg, South Carolina, where the builders leased a wharf and began the project.[110] The first step was cutting her down: removing masts, bridge, and upper works. Rather than cutting to the waterline or berth deck, as had been done with *Virginia*, *Fingal* was cut only to the main deck. Then the sides of the hull were built out with timber to a knuckle, adding nearly sixteen feet to the beam of the vessel, most of it below the waterline. In fact, the solid timber extended over seven feet below the waterline, and was over four feet thick at least five feet down. This kind of sub-marine protection was unusual for a typical Confederate casemate ironclad. It is possible that the reason for this can be found in her engines. These were vertical, direct-acting engines, which means the cylinders necessarily were above the line of the propeller shaft, therefore very high in the vessel. (As a merchant vessel, *Fingal* had no need to mount the engines to avoid enemy fire). The need to keep the machinery below the waterline may also explain why the hull was only cut down to the main deck, and the substantial side timbering was also to bring her main deck down to about two feet above the waterline. (It was also noteworthy that the Tifts had built blowers to increase the air supply to the engines in the event the funnel was penetrated, and in this connection had made the funnel detachable when necessary.) A substantial gun deck was constructed of seventeen-inch-thick timbers, supported by

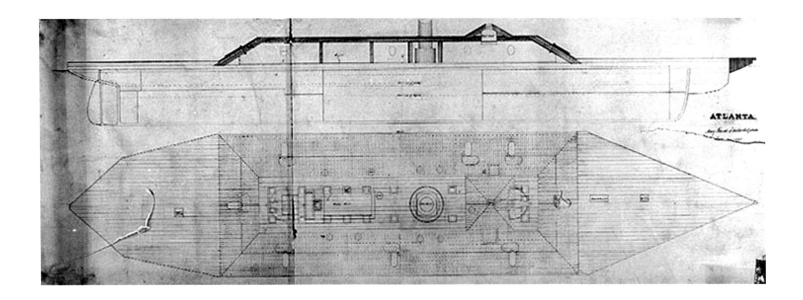

ATLANTA

Ironclad Atlanta. The plans shown here made after her capture in June 1863. There were eight gunports for the four weapons, and chains were used to operate the port shutters. Official Records

ten-inch beams. The wooden backing for the casemate was built up of fifteen inches of pine and three of oak. Two layers of two-inch iron, seven inches wide, encased the wood, laid in vertical and horizontal layers and bolted through the iron and wood. The casemate sides were inclined at about thirty degrees. Bolts 1¼-inches in diameter were countersunk on the outside and secured inside the wood by nuts and washers. The bow was extended some six feet forming a ram, making her a total of 204-feet in length.[111]

The casemate was cut with eight gunports. This provided three ports each for the forward and aft pivot guns, plus one on each side for two additional broadside guns. The broadside ports were not directly opposite each other, but were located – one each – fore and aft of the funnel. Thus the *Atlanta* could theoretically fire a three-gun broadside. There was very little room to train the guns laterally and they had a maximum of seven degrees of elevation. Also forward of the funnel was a pilothouse, a four-sided pyramid whose sides were continuations of the casemate ironwork. The top of the pilothouse was about three feet higher than the casemate and was provided with slits for conning the ship. A ladder was provided for the pilot to climb up onto a steering platform a few feet below the level of the casemate.

The gunport shutters were also of two layers of two-inch iron, riveted together. These were rectangular with a pivot point on one top corner, with a chain running from inside the casemate to the opposite lower corner of the shutter. Pulling or releasing the chain, from the inside, opened the shutter or allowed it to fall by gravity over the aperture.[112]

The *Atlanta* steamed back to Savannah in late-July 1862, completed in a mere three months in hand. The vessel was manned by a crew of 145. Her draft was fifteen-feet nine-inches, which was some three-feet deeper than that of *Fingal*'s before the conversion. On her trial runs she made 5½-knots; then, with the funnel detached and blowers operating she did 3½-knots. She also leaked significantly by way of the sponsons. The pumps were in constant use and managed to keep the leakage under control. Another problem was the lack of ventilation, particularly in the engine room where temperatures reached 150 degrees and transmitted these temperatures to the casemate, to the extreme discomfort of the crew.[113]

After her capture, the Union inspectors remarked on the "roughness of all the work …" and that the comfort and sanitary needs of the crew were "disregarded." Instead of wood bulkheads, canvas hangings were used to partition off the officer's quarters. There was no wardroom

Ironclad Atlanta in drydock after her capture. Note the prominence of her underwater protection as well as the curvature of the original Fingal's hull. Mariners Museum

Atlanta versus Weehawken

Atlanta first faced the enemy near Fort Pulaski, in July 1862, on her trail trip. Her appearance brought considerable perturbation in the North – it was still less than five months after Hampton Roads and shortly after *Arkansas* ran amok through Farragut's fleet. However, Commodore Josiah Tatnall, commanding the ship, was hampered by his vessel's deep draft, the unpredictable currents in the area, and the defensive obstructions that had been placed in the river.[116]

On June 17, 1862, the *Atlanta*, now under Lt. William A. Webb, got under way and encountered the adversary in Wassaw (then Warsaw) Sound. Two monitors, *Nahant* and *Weehawken*, each carrying one eleven-inch and one fifteen-inch gun were available for the action. This was a disadvantageous match for the *Atlanta*: each of the Dahlgren fifteen-inch projectiles weighed 440-pounds; the eleven-inchers, 136-pounds. The seven-inch Brooke fired a 110-pound projectile. Each monitor's turret was composed of eleven inches of iron.

Webb hoped for a short-range fight, to maximize the destructiveness of his rifled guns. As it was the *Atlanta* grounded, but Webb freed her. However, there was insufficient water depth for her helm to answer, and she grounded again, less than 600-yards from the *Weehawken*. The monitor, under Captain John Rodgers, moved in to about 200-yards for a short-range cannonade. The first shot, a fifteen-inch projectile, struck the side of the casemate and, "broke the armor completely through … and left a large hole entirely

and the anchor chains ran through the junior officers' areas in the forward part of the ship. One original crewmember wrote that even in broad daylight, "… in our quarters … oil is the only light we ever see … it is pitch black at all times and is also damp." Lt. Charles H. McBlair, first commanding officer of the vessel, wrote that he felt "more like the captain of a flat boat on the Mississippi" and that it was "dark as pitch" on board.[114] No doubt the rush to build the vessel outweighed including some of the niceties which otherwise might have improved the habitability of the ship.

As completed, the vessel mounted two seven-inch and two 6.4-inch Brooke rifles. The larger guns were on pivot rails fore and aft. Additionally, a torpedo frame extended forward of the ram, with a lever that would allow the explosive device to be lowered into the water when nearing the expected victim.

The addition of the mass of timber and iron had its obvious effects on the handling of the completed ship. She now could barely make six to seven-knots (probably with the current), and steered badly. No doubt the mass of wood "projecting overway" as one writer put it, contributed substantially to her unwieldiness.[115]

through the armor and backing …," sending splinters and debris flying and disabling some thirty men. One report said one of the fifteen-inch projectiles had smashed, "eight to ten feet of wood" backing. A second shot hit a port shutter and broke both layers of this and indented the armor below. Another shot struck and destroyed the top of the pilothouse, wounding the pilots. *Atlanta* fired about eight rounds, all missing their mark. Most of her guns would not bear on the target. Webb had little choice but to surrender his vessel. *Nahant* took no part in the action.[117]

Atlanta was repaired and became a part of the Union blockading fleet. After the war, she was sold to the Haitian navy.

One could argue that the *Atlanta-Weehawken* engagement was a fluke: a short-range fight against a helpless, grounded victim. Certainly the *Atlanta* had no defense against the fifteen-inch gun. However, the deep-draft design of the *Atlanta* placed constraints on the vessel that brought on the disastrous result. It should also be noted that the commanders of the *Atlanta* and the Savannah station had been under significant political pressure to "do something" about the blockading fleet – and, in fact, Tatnall had lost his command because he failed to take on the Union forces. Part of the senior officers' reluctance, of course, was based on the possibility that the tide and currents in the shallows of the Savannah river approaches would turn against them. And they did.

It is also worth noting that the Tifts allowed no naval officers to oversee their work on *Fingal/Atlanta*. In July 1862, Nelson Tift had visited Commodore Tatnall and showed him a letter from secretary Mallory giving the brothers "absolute authority" over the vessel's construction, and Tatnall "abstained from interfering in any shape whatever."[118]

Richmond

The anticipated appearance of the ironclad *Richmond* was the subject of much speculation and some trepidation. After *Virginia* was destroyed in May 1862, *Richmond* was the obstacle most feared in the Virginia theatre of operations. She was variously dubbed *Merrimac No.2* and *Young Merrimac* and hysterical descriptions abounded: she had, they said, sides five feet thick, made of solid oak, and bore six inches of armor.[119] Erroneous also applies to a much-publicized "plan" and an illustration of the vessel showing nine guns, eight in broadside, and a very high freeboard.

It should be noted here that systematic information on the six 150-foot Porter-designed ironclads – *Richmond*, *Raleigh*, *North Carolina*, *Chicora*, *Savannah*, and *Palmetto State* is sparse. One general plan exists, with few details. However, a cross-section and partial longitudinal, inboard plan for the *Savannah* has survived. Dimensions worked out from these plans substantially match a written description of the *Richmond* and, with other scattered documents, provide a reasonably good basis for studying these vessels.

No exact date for the *Richmond*'s keel-laying has been found. Various sources give dates from late-1861 onward. The only established parameter was her launch: May 6. The builders were under severe pressure to get the hull into the water and up the river to escape the Union forces approaching Norfolk, making it likely that the ship was laid down in March 1862.

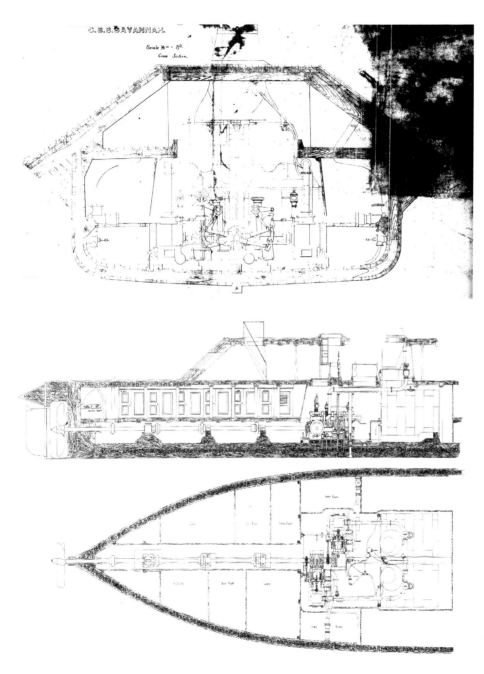

Cross section and stern plan of the ironclad Savannah. These provide the basis for other reconstructions of the Richmond class ironclads: the others being Chicora, Palmetto State, North Carolina, and Raleigh. Generally, the casemates and hulls of the vessels were similar, but their machinery varied considerably. Many were given underpowered engines re-cycled from smaller vessels. Note the pilothouse, or hatch, abaft of the funnel. National Civil War Naval Museum

The earliest descriptions and drawings of the *Richmond* come from an "honest Union or loyal man," who happened to be a "mechanic" at the Norfolk yard, named G.B. Davids, and dated July 22, 1862. The information was essentially repeated later by a John H. Burroughs, who described himself as "Superintendent Government Shipyard," and the information was routed to Union Admiral S.P. Lee.

The Davids description puts the vessel at 160-foot length of keel, and forty-one feet "out and out" (overall) breadth, eleven feet depth of hold, and 12½-foot draft, and the drawings show the waterline eighteen inches higher than the level of the fore and aft decks. The casemate sides are at a thirty-five degree angle, each extending four feet out from the hull. The casemate was composed of two layers of two-inch iron covering wood in three layers: two of three-inch plank and one of eighteen-inch timbers. The pilothouse is at the fore end and made of ten-inch-thick cast iron. The fore and aft decks were covered with two two-inch layers of iron. The battery consisted of four guns: two in broadside and two at the casemate ends.

The Burroughs report, written in November 1862, differs in some details, and adds much on the construction itself. He gives the length as "between perpendiculars" at 150-feet and moulded beam at thirty-two feet and depth of twelve-feet. Note that Davids' forty-one feet includes the eight

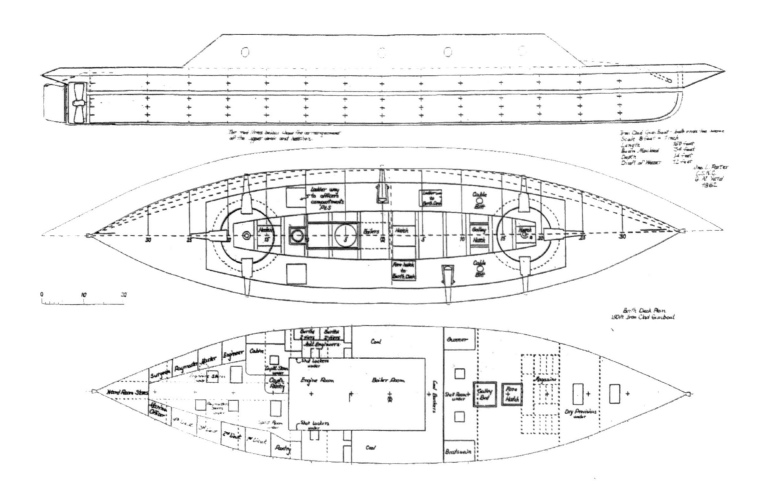

Hull and arrangement of CSS Richmond. This ironclad was 150-feet long with a draft of twelve feet. Typically on the Confederate rams, one gun was mounted on each end, on pivot rails enabling its use on either broadside as well as forward or aft. Bob Holcombe

feet overhang of the armored sides, subtracting that brings the beam of the hull itself down to thirty-three feet. Deducting the thickness of the planking gives a moulded beam of thirty-two feet. Burroughs adds that there was two-foot spacing between the hull frames, with the latter sided eight-inches and moulded ten inches at the keel and 6½-inches at the head. He has the casemate of three wood layers but totaling twenty-one inches, plus the four-inches of iron, equaling twenty-five inches.[120]

These descriptions are surprisingly accurate. The dimensions taken from the cross section of *Savannah* and other Porter drawings are thirty-three feet extreme beam (to outside of planking), and thirty-two feet moulded beam (to the inside of the planking), and 150-feet of length (between perpendiculars) and 174-feet overall. There is a five-foot overhang on each side, making a total of forty-three feet overall breadth. The hull frames are about ten-inches at the keel (sided) and tapering to six-inches at the deck level. The depth of hold (from bottom of deck beams to top of floors) is about eleven-feet. The casemate was about 100-feet long, with its outer planking four-inches; the second layer about five-inches, and the inner course is fourteen-inches for a total of twenty-three inches. Adding in the two two-inch iron layers makes the casemate walls twenty-seven inches thick. The top of the casemate is about ten-inches, composed of one-inch of iron on top of two layers of planking and about ten-inches of oak timber, totaling about sixteen-inches. The hull cross section shows a slight deadrise of about 2 to 4 degrees. The Porter plans also indicate a decided improvement over the *Virginia*. Whereas the *Virginia*'s casemate ended with an overhang ending much like the eaves of a house, Porter's design built a knuckle onto the bottom of the casemate sides, resulting in a ninety-degree angle to reconnect to the hull about four feet below the level of the casemate edge.[121]

Unfortunately, the *Savannah* plans do not show the machinery arrangement for *Richmond*. The eighty-horsepower system had been re-cycled from the old wooden steam brig *Arctic*, which had been built in 1854, and which was about 125-feet long and 125-tons. It appears that this was a single, direct-acting cylinder with two boilers, driving a three-bladed, nine-foot propeller. Confederate Lt. John Taylor Wood wrote of the *Richmond*'s "very weak engine" and expected her to do less than five-knots, and another sailor remarked on her "bad engines." This would be in comparison to the *Savannah*'s machinery which was two cylinders, each about twenty-four inches in diameter and with a twenty-eight inch stroke, probably purpose built at the Columbus, Georgia, naval machine shop facility.[122]

When completed and put into commission, in November 1862, the *Richmond* was armed with four guns: all seven-inch Brooke rifles, as well as a torpedo apparatus. This remained her battery through the war. The gunports were arranged to allow the fore and aft pivot guns to fire through the end gunports, as well as, on either side, and the broadside ports were not directly across from each other.[123] Her crew numbered 150.

Richmond at Trent's Reach

In January 1865, the Confederate squadron, including ironclads *Virginia* 2, *Fredericksburg*, and *Richmond*, made a sortie down the James River intending to attack Grant's supply depot at City Point, making use of the spring freshet and high tide to provide sufficient depth for all the vessels. Unfortunately, they overestimated the depths available. Both *Richmond* and *Virginia* 2 grounded in early morning and they were under fire continuously from shore batteries and snipers. It was 10:30am before the waters rose sufficiently to float both ironclads. This timing was fortunate as the Union twin-turret monitor *Onondaga* had joined the action, firing her two fifteen-inch Dahlgrens and pair of 150-pounder Parrot rifles. For over three hours *Richmond* had come under heavy fire from shore batteries, mostly thirty-pounder and 100-pounder rifled cannon, though it was said that the Union fire was concentrated on the *Virginia* 2. *Richmond*'s commanding officer reported: "The ship was struck so constantly by shot and shell that it was impossible to keep account of the number." The results were slight indentures and knocking off the heads of bolts, plus two gunport shutter chains were severed. Of course, the smoke pipe and stays were hit as well as the ventilators. During the same action, a fifteen-inch projectile stuck *Virginia* 2 and made a "hole through" the casemate armor and wood backing. It is doubtful that any fifteen-

inch projectiles hit *Richmond*. There were no injuries on *Richmond*.[124] When it was obvious that the Union vessels had the range and more firepower, the Confederate vessels terminated their sortie.

Obviously, the weakness of the *Richmond*'s machinery was not a hindrance in this engagement. Her formidable casemate was sufficient to survive a nearly disastrous encounter intact. Had the *Onondaga* arrived earlier in the engagement, however, there may have been a significantly different outcome.

Palmetto State

Early in 1862, the Navy department began construction of other vessels in critical port cities using constructor Porter's 150-foot ironclad plans.[125] In Charleston, the first laid down was *Palmetto State*, probably in February. The second, *Chicora*, financed by the state of South Carolina, was begun in March. Other ironclads built to Porter's plans were begun in Savannah and Wilmington.

The *Palmetto State* was built at Marsh & Sons shipyard. New machinery was not available for the vessel, consequently, older machinery was commandeered. In this case, the engine was originally from the tugboat *Lady Davis*.[126] As with the *Richmond*, use of a tug engine was not the optimum choice, but possibly was the only machinery available at the time.

Construction of the *Palmetto State* was hampered by the usual factors: lack of materials and uncertainty in the transportation of materials to the work site. Oak timber was in short supply and, when the state legislature authorized cutting the timber, they exempted "shade and ornamental trees." These could only be cut when permission from the owners was obtained. When the vessels were ready for "ironing," the Confederate army claimed priority on use of the rail cars needed to

Confederate ram Palmetto State. This vessel, along with the Chicora, temporarily "raised the blockade" at Charleston in January 1863. Naval Historical Center

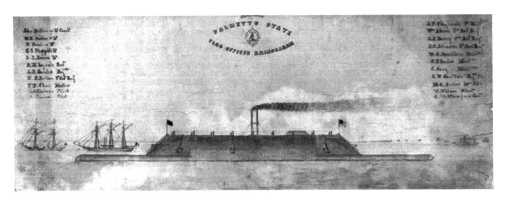

transport the armor from Tredegar to Charleston. Another governmental problem was with the Confederate treasury department, which strained relations with contractors when they failed to make payments on time.[127]

The financing of the *Palmetto State*'s construction was aided by a local ladies' initiative. A check for $30,000 was turned over to the navy at the vessel's christening ceremony, the result of the ladies' "gunboat association" efforts. The funds also earned the group the right to name the ship. Mary Chestnut, the famous diarist suggested, not necessarily with tongue in cheek: "She Devil." As she wrote: "it is the Devil's own work it is built to do."[128]

Launching the ironclad was delayed several times due to lack of sufficient water depth at the end of the ways. After tons of mud were dredged from the river she went into the water sometime in September, and an elaborate christening was held on October 11 at the Marsh wharf, with local dignitaries as well as General P.G.T. Beauregard and a "large number of the fair sex" in attendance on her deck. The climax of the proceedings was the appearance of *Chicora* – which was commissioned in September – steaming up the river with flags flying.[129]

Dimensions of the vessel were as set out for the *Richmond*: length 150-feet between perpendiculars (174-feet overall), breadth (hull) thirty-four-feet, depth of hold twelve-feet, draft fourteen-feet. The casemate iron and wood dimensions also matched those of the *Richmond*. The iron was from railroad track rolled at Tredegar

works into two-inch by seven-inch wide strips, in twenty-foot lengths. The inner layer was laid horizontally, the outer, vertically, bolted through the backing. The pilothouse or hatch was placed abaft the funnel, above the steering wheel and engine room hatch on the gundeck, to facilitate communicating orders from pilot to helmsman and the engine room. The *Savannah* had this arrangement despite the funnel blocking the pilot's direct forward view. It appears that *Chicora* had two pilot hatches.[130]

The *Palmetto State* had four guns in her battery, a seven-inch rifle forward and 6.4-inch aft on pivots, plus two eight-inch shell guns, one on each broadside. In January 1865, she was reported to have had ten guns, all seven-inch, four on each broadside and one on each end. This is difficult to credit, as it would have required a significantly larger casemate and it would be unlikely that her hull could support such weights.[131]

The crew of the vessel was about 120 strong, and she had a torpedo "frame" projecting 15-20 feet ahead of the vessel capable of allowing the torpedo charge to be submerged about six feet beneath the surface.[132]

Both *Palmetto State* and *Chicora* (sometimes mislabeled "Courier") were charged with patrolling around Ft. Sumter and would stand a nightly watch to prevent a Federal attack. Both vessels were most noted for their sortie of January 1863, attacking the blockading fleet. Both ironclads set out around 4:00am and *Palmetto State* steamed straight for the wood hulled U.S. steamer *Mercedita*, ramming and firing the forward gun on impact. The projectile disabled the Union vessel's machinery and her commanding officer surrendered. It was found that the ram had smashed through seven planks and one hull frame timber.[133] Pumps were easily able to stanch the flow, and she later went to Philadelphia for repairs. *Chicora* meanwhile had engaged and chased off the gunboat *Keystone State*, and for a short time the rams held the field, technically "raising the blockade." It is not surprising that *Mercedita* surrendered, as her guns could not be depressed enough to hit the adversary. However, it is remarkable that the ram did not do catastrophic damage to her wooden hull, especially considering the fact that *Mercedita* was a converted merchant ship, not a heavily built naval vessel. Possibly the "weak" engines of *Palmetto State* limited her speed and thus contributed to her lack of "punch" when ramming. For instance, if *Mercedita* had been targeted by the CSS *Virginia,* she would have certainly been sunk.

Ironclad Chicora, stern view at the dock. The light hue of the casemate shows her 'blockade grey' color to good effect. National Archives

attempted to ram *Chicora*, but gunnery from the ram disabled her machinery and *Keystone State* struck her flag. This victory was cancelled when the Union vessel's engineer was able to resurrect her engines. *Keystone State* managed to escape, with her commanding officer blithely ignoring his earlier surrender. The entire engagement cost the Union navy forty-seven killed or wounded; to the Confederates' none.

Both *Chicora* and *Palmetto State* had uneventful subsequent careers and were destroyed when Charleston was evacuated on February 18, 1865.

Savannah

The *Savannah* was the second iron-armored vessel begun at the port of Savannah. She was preceded by the *Georgia*, which was originally and ostensibly to have been an ironclad, but which, because of inadequate machinery became, by default, a floating battery. *Georgia* will be covered in the appropriate chapter. *Savannah* also falls into a large category of Confederate ironclads: those that had little or no significant or obvious impact on the course of the conflict.

Savannah had its origin in early-1862 with a visit by Henry F. Willink, Jr. to Richmond, to discuss construction of ironclads with secretary Mallory. This was not a cold visit: Willink, who owned a shipyard in Savannah, already had in hand a contract to build two wooden gunboats. Mallory showed him Porter's plan and inquired whether such a vessel could be launched in four months. Willink was skeptical, indicating six months would

Chicora

The *Chicora* was financed by the state of South Carolina and built by the firm of James Eason. She was laid down in March 1862. Built to Porter's plans, there was little difference in her hull and casemate than those of the *Palmetto State*. She is the only one of the Richmond class for which a photograph exists. A wartime drawing by Alfred R. Waud indicates *Chicora* may have had two pilot hatches, but the photograph is not sufficiently distinct to confirm or deny this, though it does seem to show a pilothouse aft of the stack. The black and white photo is also notable because it highlights the vessel's light color: light blue-grey or "blockader grey."

Both ironclads were saddled with inadequate machinery, re-cycled from tugboats. *Chicora*'s

was from the *Aid*, and was "single-acting" with a diameter of thirty-inches and stroke of twenty-six inches. This drove an eight-foot, three-bladed propeller. It was said that there was 500-tons of iron armor on her casemate, and it extended five feet below her waterline.[134]

Like her sister ironclad, *Chicora* was severely underpowered. In one instance, the ship was unable to maintain position near Fort Sumter: her engines could not stem the ebb tide and the anchors were dropped … and they dragged. One officer wrote: "… this craft is only fit for a floating battery for harbor defense …[due to] her want of speed."[135]

With the *Palmetto State*, *Chicora* temporarily raised the blockade in January 31, 1863. *Chicora*'s part was a successful attack on the wooden *Keystone State*. Amazingly, the *Keystone State*

be more realistic. Mallory settled for Willink's pledge to do his best and a verbal agreement was made. On March 31, a contract followed.[136]

Even six months was to prove unreachable. The problem was not materials, at least at the outset. Massive stands of oak were available at nearby Ossabaw Island. The war itself impinged on the progress when Union forces converged on Fort Pulaski in early-April, intending to invest and take the fort, which lay at the entrance to the Savannah harbor channel. Bombardment began on April 10 and, to the consternation of the citizenry of the city, the fort surrendered two days later.

In the excitement of the ensuing weeks, obstructions were sunk at the approaches to the city, and workers were pressed into the job. Willink's shipyard personnel were not exempted from the draft and work came to a standstill on the ironclad.[137]

In July, the vessel's frame was complete, and Willink received the first of the government's payments for the ship. At this point, Willink was offered an extra month on his contract if he would "loan" some of his workers to assist the work on converting the *Fingal*. He refused, indignantly, resenting the implication that the *Fingal* conversion was more important than his ironclad. It was not until February 4, 1863 that the *Savannah* finally slid off the ways.[138]

After launching, the ship was still minus her engines, boilers and iron armor. The latter became a more persistent problem when Willink inquired whether the Gate City ironworks, run by Scofield and Markham in Atlanta, would bend the plates to fit the corners of the casemate. He was informed that the firm only cut the iron into lengths, and did not work to drawings or specifications. It was later learned that both proprietors of the firm were in fact Northerners and were unwilling to exceed minimal expectations for their southern clientele. In any event, their lack of cooperation significantly added to the work that was to be done at Willink's yard.[139]

Supplying the engines was a simpler task. Yankee incursions up from Pensacola had stopped work on a gunboat being constructed by F.G. Howard at Milton, on the Florida panhandle. The engines designated for this vessel were shipped to the Columbus, Georgia ironworks to be modified for use in the *Savannah*: two horizontal direct acting cylinders, each approximately twenty-two-inch diameter and with a twenty-eight-inch stroke. They were mounted athwartship, with one cylinder on each side of the shaft, and the port cylinder forward of the starboard cylinder. The *Savannah's* screw shaft was in sections, totaling over fifty-inches in length, driving a ten-foot, three-bladed propeller. The shaft was mounted on bedplates bolted to three pedestals mounted on her keelson. There were two boilers, each approximately thirteen feet long and nine feet in diameter.[140]

Savannah had "raised panel doors and finished woodwork" in her wardroom and officers' cabins.[141] This attention to detail was in stark contrast to the crude work on *Atlanta*.

The *Savannah* made her first trial trip on June 29, 1863. Everything went well with the ship making 6½-mph and drawing 12½-feet of water. A second trial about a month later resulted in a "broken" engine: a stray rivet had lodged in the gap between piston and cylinder. The cylinder, head, piston, and rod had to be returned to Columbus for repair.[142]

After her machinery was repaired the ironclad proved to be quite satisfactory. She mounted four guns: two seven-inch single-banded Brooke rifles and two 6.4-inch double banded Brookes. The former weighed 15,000-pounds each; the latter, 10,000. However, until Sherman's men took the city, the ironclad was simply a menacing presence. She used her guns to little effect when fired upon by Sherman's field artillery in December 1864, and plans were made to steam to Charleston to escape Sherman's onslaught. Obstructions and torpedoes prevented her escape and the *Savannah* was abandoned and fired by her crew on December 21, 1864.[143]

Raleigh

One of two Porter-designed ironclads constructed at Wilmington, North Carolina, the *Raleigh* was built by J.L. Cassidy at the foot of Church Street and laid down in the spring of 1862. While original documents pertaining to the ship are scarce, her submerged remains have been found and were documented in the 1990s.

A sufficient portion of the *Raleigh* survives and there is little evidence that she was in any way significantly different from her sister ships. The casemate sides, for instance, were in three layers of wood and two of iron. Yellow pine vertical timbers about a foot thick formed the inmost layer, followed by five-inches of pine and four-inches of oak, the latter laid vertically. The two layers of two-inch iron matched the 2x8 dimensions of the Tredegar rolled plates. The inner, horizontal layer was laid on with an inch gap between the plates, apparently to allow bolts from the outer layer through to the wood backing. The knuckle was armored and layered in the same way as the casemate itself. The bolt heads were countersunk and there were no gaps in the vertical outer layer.[144]

At the stern were a few significant features. The rudder was iron and 3½-inches thick fore and aft. On the underside of the knuckle was a propeller chamber, a semi-circle made to accommodate the diameter of the propeller. The interior of the chamber was armored like the casemate.[145]

Though early salvage reports suggested the engines had been removed, the modern divers found them essentially complete, except for the crankshaft. The cylinders were two-feet in diameter and three-feet long, and mounted as shown in the CSS *Savannah* plan cited above. The report did not specify whether these dimensions were of the actual bore and stroke or were simply the outside of the cylinder casting itself. The engines were similar to those of the *Savannah*, though the valve arrangement was different for each: the valves were located on the sides of the cylinder on *Raleigh*, on the top for those of the *Savannah*.[146]

Though *Raleigh* and *North Carolina* were begun the same month, in the same city, the former was not commissioned until 1864, the latter in late-1863. Several factors seem to have caused the delays in *Raleigh's* construction. In 1863, Flag Officer William F. Lynch reported there were only sixty men on the navy rolls in the entire state of North Carolina. As each ironclad needed over 150 men, the deficit was crippling. It was not until March of the next year that Secretary of War James Seddon released 1,200 men from the army specifically for naval service. Shortly thereafter, *Raleigh* was commissioned.[147]

Materials were also in short supply. It is possible that in 1863 priority for iron and other materials was for the light-draft ironclads being built in the sounds, specifically the *Albemarle*, to counter Union movements in that area.[148]

Another factor that affected both ironclads was a massive yellow fever epidemic in Wilmington. Reportedly brought in by sailors from the blockade runner *Kate*, the fever raged from August through November, 1862, and hundreds were infected or fled the area.[149]

In any event, though the vessel was later coming into commission, *Raleigh* was conceded to be much superior to the *North Carolina*. The latter was, as will be seen, relegated to floating battery status for most of her service life.

The major factor in *Raleigh's* favor was her engines. Rather than being recycled from a small tug, hers were built new by the Talbot Brothers foundry at Richmond. Instead of a single cylinder installation of uncertain age, the *Raleigh's* machinery was new and probably at least twice the nominal horsepower (a simple calculation based on the bore and stroke of the engines) of

the *North Carolina's*. Once in commission, *Raleigh* was reported to have attained six to seven-knots and to turn "very quickly."[150]

When completed, *Raleigh* had a crew of 197, plus twenty-four marines, and carried four seven-inch rifles. Her draft was around thirteen-feet. Her date of commissioning is uncertain. Secretary Mallory's April 30, 1864 report lists her in commission, but her first sortie down river had occurred on April 19, under the command of J. Pembroke Jones.[151]

The vessel's career was astonishingly short. After meeting with the *North Carolina* on the 19th, *Raleigh* had to be lightened, probably by reducing her stores or coal, to get her over the Cape Fear River bar. Accompanied by two smaller vessels the ironclad crossed the bar at the New River Inlet on the evening of May 6. Fire was exchanged with blockaders *Brittania* and *Nansemond* and there was some contact with the blockaders through the night. The next morning, *Raleigh* engaged the *Howquah*, *Nansemond*, *Mount Vernon* and *Kansas*, but at some distance. The *Raleigh* inflicted a twenty-three-inch hole in the funnel of *Howquah* at an estimated one-and-a-half mile range. *Raleigh* was hit but registered no material damage. The heaviest guns on the Union vessels were a 150-pounder Parrott rifle and several nine-inch Dahlgren smoothbores. Around 6:00am, *Raleigh* attempted to return across the bar and grounded. The ironclad had straddled the bar and as the tide ebbed her ends dropped, breaking her back. One report said: "...[the] weight of the iron on (the Raleigh's) shield just crushed her decks in."[152]

North Carolina

As noted, the *North Carolina* was built to Porter's 150-foot ironclad plans and there is no indication that she varied from them as far as her hull and casemate is concerned. The ironclad was laid down the same month as *Raleigh* and was built by Berry (or Barry, or Beery) Brothers in Wilmington.

The only major difference in the two vessels was in the engines. North Carolina used a single-cylinder powerplant from the tug Uncle Ben. The rush to get ironclads into service on the James River, North Carolina and Charleston may have been the impetus leading to the use of whatever machinery was immediately available, however inadequate. On the James, McClellan's Peninsular campaign provided imminent danger; and it was obvious that the Union navy's priorities pointed towards Charleston rather than Wilmington, building towards an assault on the "seat of the rebellion" in early 1863. There was small immediate danger in Savannah, once the port was closed. Thus four of the six 150-foot ironclads made use of tugboat machinery, and all four (*Richmond*, *Chicora*, *Palmetto State* and *North Carolina*) proved to be exceedingly slow.

The rush to build also resulted in use of green timber in the *North Carolina*. As the wood dried, warpage set in. A contemporary report indicated that the decks became so uneven that the guns were "almost unserviceable"; below the waterline, seams opened and serious leaks resulted.[153]

The ship was launched in late-September 1862, but was still without her armor in February of the next year. Union reports from that month describe the appearance of a suspicious vessel coming down the river. This may have been *North Carolina*, long before her armor was completed. There was also one instance of the ship crossing the bar and grounding. She had a thirteen-foot draft and the water at that point was only eight feet deep. Fortunately the tide got her off.[154]

Most of her career was spent in the shallows of the river, maintaining a twenty-four-hour watch on her pumps. When *Raleigh* rendezvoused with her in April 1864, she was awaiting high water to allow her up the river to deal with the seaworms in her hull. On September 16, 1864, she succumbed to the inevitable and sank at her moorings, near Smithville, North Carolina.[155]

IRONCLADS, 1862, PART 2:

IN DEPTH

John L. Porter's 150-foot ironclad plan was the first systematic approach to defending the Confederacy's ports against the encircling Union "Anaconda" blockade. It ensured that an ironclad of some description was placed in each of the East coast's strategic or threatened areas: the James River, Wilmington, North Carolina, Charleston and Savannah. To give some depth to this initial defensive system, two other groups of ironclads were initiated in 1862. One group maintained the ship-like hull form of the 150-foot class but enlarged to at least 180-feet between perpendiculars. Four of these were laid down in 1862: *Charleston*, *Virginia 2*, *Milledgeville*, and *Tennessee*. Another was laid down at Savannah by the firm of Krenson and Hawkes, but this vessel was never launched.

The second group emphasized shallow draft and concomitant reduced battery. The distinguishing characteristic of these ships was the adoption of the "diamond hull" configuration. This marked a break from the "ship" hull configuration, abandoning the shipbuilder's traditional keel and curved frame timber construction, and replacing it with a flat bottom, angled rather than curved bilges, and angled flat flaring hull sides which met the casemate to form a ninety degree angle knuckle. In part, this design was promulgated to simplify construction techniques and facilitate building by inexperienced carpenters unfamiliar with adze and moldloft shipbuilding. Another factor in the adoption of

this scow-like hull was the need for vessels in shallow inland waterways and harbors where seakeeping qualities were unnecessary.[156]

John L. Porter is credited with the diamond-hull design. He had submitted a "harbor defense" ironclad proposal in the spring of 1861. In cross section the hull showed an angled casemate, and was flat bottomed, with angled, flat-hull sides with the knuckle somewhat below the waterline. When it was decided to convert the former Union frigate *Merrimack*, this design was laid aside. The similarity to the diamond hull is obvious.[157] There might have also been influence from the Union navy's "City Class" ironclads, begun in late-1861. These showed the angular knuckle and flat bottom, though they were wider in beam than the Confederate vessels. In any event, when ironclads were needed for inland and shoal waters, the Porter design was resurrected and modified for the purpose.

The diamond-hull types, begun in 1862, were the *Tuscaloosa*, *Huntsville*, *Fredericksburg*, *Neuse*, *Albemarle* and *Missouri*. Another was begun at Tarboro, North Carolina and two at Oven Bluff, Alabama. These last three were never completed.

The most unusual of the ironclads laid down in 1862 was the *Nashville*. She was very large and driven by side wheels. This vessel was designed by Porter and was a variety of the diamond hull type. Another sidewheel ironclad

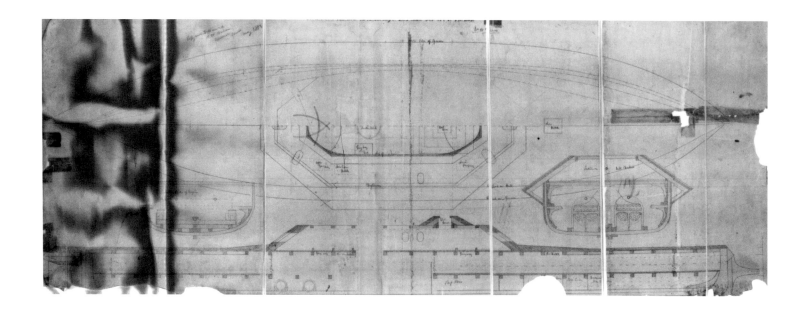

Plan of Graves' 180-foot ironclad, as modified in July 1863. At that time the casemate length was reduced from about 100-feet to about seventy feet. The reduction was to compensate for increased weight of casemate armor, which in turn was made necessary by the Atlanta's vulnerability to the Union's fifteen-inch guns. The shortened version was used for ironclad Virginia 2, while the Charleston retained the long casemate. This plan is in the National Archives and is scheduled for restoration. National Archives

was begun at Oven Bluff, Alabama in mid-1862, but was never finished.

It is noteworthy that, by the end of 1862, the Confederate navy department had about seventeen ironclads in the works in the various states (in addition to those being built in Europe). Some were recent contracts. However, many were on "hold" awaiting such necessities as engines or iron armor.

The year would mark the high water mark of naval construction, with the majority of the service's vessels having been begun during the year.

Virginia 2

The *Virginia 2* was based on a design by William A. Graves, a shipbuilder based in Norfolk. He had begun government work with a contract for one of the small Maury gunboats. He was appointed naval constructor in March and had begun work at the shipyard opposite the Rocketts yard in Richmond. The little gunboat was not complete when it was burned to prevent capture at the Norfolk yard in May 1862.[158]

Graves' ironclad design called for a hull 180-feet between perpendiculars, beam of thirty-four feet, and depth of hold fourteen feet. With armored knuckle, her breadth was forty-four feet. The casemate was about 100-feet long and was to be encased with four-inches of iron and mount

six guns: two fore and aft on pivot rails, able to fire forward as well as on either broadside, and four broadside guns.

The keel of *Virginia 2* was laid the second week of April 1862, to the gratification of the local citizenry, particularly the Ladies Aid and Defense Society, (or more popularly the "Ladies Gunboat Society") which had sprung up earlier in the year to raise funds for the ship. In addition to cash, however, the effort became a scrap drive of sorts, calling for contributions of materials, tools and metals: "Iron railings … old and new, scrap iron about the house, broken plough shares about the farm, and iron in any shape …," ran one solicitation. While materials such as iron were sent to Tredegar for re-cycling into the sinews of war, other commodities and donations were sold at bazaars and the cash turned over to the government.[159]

Apparently the funding for the ship was sufficient. However, the work itself was exceed-

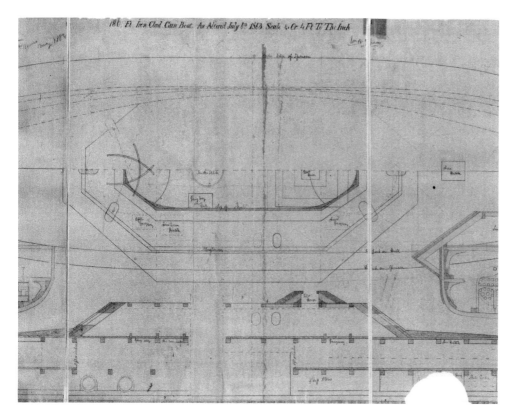

Central section of Graves' plan, enlarged for details. Notes two cylinders mounted transversely and differing locations for starboard and port broadside gunports. Distance between berth and gundeck is five feet ten inches. National Archives

ingly slow: it was not launched until June 29, 1863. Part of the delay can be attributed to the concurrent building of the ironclad *Fredericksburg*, across the river at the Rocketts yard. In the spring of 1863, the director of the Tredegar works reported that iron simply was not available, and apparently it was then decided that the completion of the *Fredericksburg* would take precedence over *Virginia 2*.[160]

The launch of the ship did not mark a sudden surge in her rate of construction, however. In fact, an event in Georgia on June 17, 1863, added still further delays. On that day, the ironclad *Atlanta* succumbed to not more than seven projectiles

from the Union monitor *Weehawken*. The *Atlanta*'s four-inch iron plus backing was no match for the monitor's fifteen-inch Dahlgren smoothbore gun. The consternation this event caused among those responsible for building the newest Confederate ironclads can be easily imagined. In fact, the fifteen-inch Dahlgren was not even tested until October 1862. The first of the Passaic class monitors, each one of which carried a single fifteen-inch Dahlgren, plus an eleven-inch Dahlgren, was not commissioned until November of that year.[161] Thus, this monster gun had not been a factor during the design stage of these Confederate ironclads.

The immediate result for *Virginia 2* was a major redesign: the iron casemate armor would be increased significantly: it would be no less than eight-inches on the forward casemate and six inches on the sides and aft.[162] Even adding only two inches all around would have increased the cladding's weight by one third, with obvious consequences for the draft of the ship. To compensate and bring the overall weight back to something resembling the original displacement, it was decided to shorten the length of the casemate. From about 100-feet, it was reduced to about seventy feet (measured at the base of the structure). Thus, the new casemate was actually shorter than that of the Richmond class ships, therefore, the battery was necessarily reduced from six to four guns.

The steam machinery for the *Virginia 2* was probably similar to that of the *Charleston*, her semi-sister vessel (*Charleston* not having had her casemate shortened). This was a two-cylinder, horizontal engine of about 500hp with thirty-six-inch diameter cylinders, two boilers, and driving an 8½-foot propeller.[163]

The vessel was finally commissioned on May 18, 1864, over two years after the laying of her keel. Her battery was three seven-inch, double-banded, Brooke rifles in broadside and forward, and one ten-inch smoothbore at the stern port. In September 1864, the forward gun was replaced by an eight-inch rifle and the aft ten-incher with an eleven-inch smoothbore.[164]

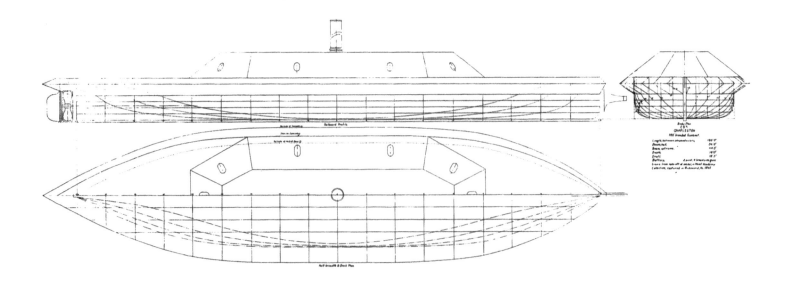

Virginia 2 at Trent's Reach

The ironclad served as flagship of the Confederate James River squadron, and participated in actions at Dutch Gap and Signal Hill. Her final engagement was at Trent's Reach in January 1865. She grounded and came under heavy fire, mostly from army artillery. Flag Officer J.K. Mitchell estimated she was hit over seventy times. The most damage was done by a fifteen-inch projectile from the monitor *Onondaga* fired at over a mile range. This struck the shield "breaking the iron and crushing the woodwork completely in, making a large hole completely through. One man was killed and two wounded by the concussion and splinters," wrote her commanding officer later. A second projectile had "broke [n] the iron and crushed the woodwork …," but it is not clear whether this was a fifteen-inch or 150-pound rifled projectile.

The action at Trent's Reach might have been significantly different had *Onondaga* come into the engagement earlier, while *Virginia 2* was grounded and struggling in shallow water. It appears that the extra two inches of iron on the sides of the casemate mattered little to the 400-pound fifteen-inch, solid shot. Possibly the eight inch armor on the ends might have been effective, but in fact the end casemate faces presented a much smaller target than the sides.

The *Virginia 2* remained on the James for the remainder of the war. She was destroyed on April 4, 1865 when Richmond fell to Union forces.

Charleston

Shipbuilder J.M. Eason completed the ironclad *Chicora* in late 1862 and shortly afterwards (December), laid down a larger ironclad, to be named *Charleston*. In this instance the vessel was built to Graves's 180-foot plan used for *Virginia 2*.[165]

Unlike *Virginia 2*, construction of the *Charleston* was relatively efficient and she was completed in nine months. Her dimensions were 180-feet between perpendiculars and a thirty-four foot beam (forty-four feet extreme beam at knuckle). The vessel's hold was fourteen feet and she drew twelve-feet three-inches in the water.

Unlike *Virginia 2*, *Charleston*'s casemate – which was octagonal – was not shortened nor was her iron armor increased. If she was completed by September 1863, it is likely that, by the time news of the fate of *Atlanta* was received, progress was too far along to admit a major change to the

Charleston harbor, painting by Conrad Wise Chapman and John Gadsby Chapman. On left is the Palmetto State, and on right is probably the Charleston. Earlier identifications had the right hand vessel as Chicora, but the latter ironclad and Palmetto State were nearly the same size. Naval Historical Center

casemate design. Simply adding two inches to the casemate cladding, without decreasing the casemate size, would have added unacceptably to her draft. In any event, she was completed with four inches of iron on the casemate, and mounted six guns. Four of the guns were 6.4- or seven-inch Brooke rifles; two were nine-inch smoothbores.

Her two cylinders were thirty-six inches in diameter, and she had two boilers and a single 8½-foot propeller.[166]

The vessel became the flagship on the Charleston station. She is shown in a famous Charleston harbor scene by artist Conrad Wise Chapman, identified as the "Ladies Gunboat." As with several other Confederate ironclads, funds had been raised from the populace by an active ladies association.[167]

Charleston was described as the "strongest and swiftest" of the Charleston squadron, but her career was uneventful.[168] She was burned to prevent capture when the city was evacuated in February 1865.

Milledgeville

H.F. Willink of Savannah began his second Confederate ironclad in December 1862, eventually naming it *Milledgeville*, for the then-capital of the state. The design, by Porter, was an effort to reduce draft and increase maneuverability in shallow waters. The hull was 175-feet and only twelve-feet in depth of hold, with expectations that she was draw only nine-feet of water. Her machinery powered twin screws.[169]

As with *Virginia 2,* construction of *Milledgeville* was an extended process. Her hull was complete in June 1863, and engines were being installed in November. The timeline of her construction apparently made it possible to incorporate changes to adapt her to the lessons learned from the *Atlanta*. Her casemate was shortened and a total of six-inches of iron was used on the forward face of her casemate.[170]

The vessel was launched just prior to October 19, 1864 but was yet incomplete when Union forces entered Savannah. The vessel was burned to the "water's edge" in December 1864.[171]

Tennessee

Of the Confederate ironclads, three held sway in fame: *Virginia, Arkansas*, and *Tennessee*. All three took on entire squadrons and thus earned their laurels. Interestingly, two of the three were commanded by the same man: Franklin Buchanan. After being wounded at Hampton Roads on the *Virginia*, Buchanan became the Confederacy's first admiral. He was then transferred to Mobile and placed in charge of the defenses of that city. Part of his responsibility was the preparation of a squadron that included several ironclads under construction. One of these was the *Tennessee*.[172]

Buchanan arrived to take up his command in September 1862, to find two floating batteries under construction at Selma. Construction had begun in May, and these would become the *Tuscaloosa* and *Huntsville*. Commander Ebenezer Farrand, detailed in August by the Secretary of the Navy to organize shipbuilding in the Mobile area, had initiated a contract for a side-wheel ironclad to be built at Montgomery, in September 1862. The same month, construction of the *Tennessee* was begun at the Selma Ordnance and Naval Foundry shipyard, a government-owned facility.[173]

Tennessee (or *Tennessee 2* if one considers the never-completed *Arkansas* sister ship), was one of three loosely described as a "class" of vessels, because all were the same basic hull, measuring 189-feet between perpendiculars, and a thirty-four foot breadth of beam, not including

Ironclad Milledgeville, designed by Porter, was given a shallower hold in an attempt to reduce her draft, and twin screws. As with Virginia 2, the casemate was shortened and six inches of armor was to be employed. The vessel was never completed. Drawing by Bob Holcombe

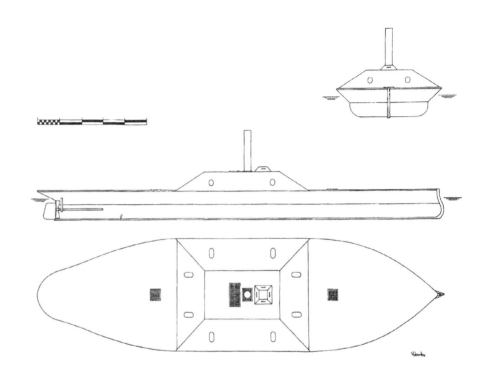

the knuckle. The other two would be the *Columbia* and *Texas*.[174]

Of the three, the *Texas* differed substantially from the others, having twin screws and a very short casemate. Whereas the *Texas* casemate was about sixty-two feet, *Tennessee* and *Columbia* had casemates about eight-eight feet and seventy-eight feet long, respectively. Also the twin-screw propulsion necessitated differing engine arrangements, as well as a completely dissimilar stern. An original plan exists, labeled *Texas* and *Columbia*, signed by Porter, indicating the casemates had been shortened for those two ships. On that original plan, the casemate was about 114-feet in length, a dimension not reflected on any of the completed vessels.[175]

Construction of the *Tennessee* was fraught with difficulties. The supply of iron plating was slow and at times nonexistent. The firm of Schofield and Markham, in Atlanta, was unable to fulfill their plating contract, and another source was found at the Shelby Iron Works in Columbiana, Alabama. Administrative quirks and some inter-service friction also hampered deliveries with one Confederate army major refusing to ship a load of iron without authorization from Richmond. Another chronic malady was shortage of personnel, with the army reluctant to release men to navy service. In a related incident, at one point, the workers at Selma struck for better wages. Buchanan handled this efficiently if not with subtlety: He called in the local conscription officer and reminded the strikers that if they were not doing "essential work for the government" they were eligible for the draft.[176]

In late-February 1863, the *Tennessee* was launched into the Alabama River and was immediately taken in tow to be completed at Mobile. She was still without armor, engines or guns, but her arrival at the port city was a significant public occasion.[177]

After the news of the loss of the *Atlanta*, and its implications for the casemate armor of the vessels under construction, Buchanan wrote Mallory indicating the *Tennessee*'s casemate could be shortened by nineteen feet and thus save over forty tons of iron and wood and yet retain the same battery. The weight saving could be used to add another inch of iron on her sides and two on her forward casemate, plus a layer of oak on the interior. Presumably this was done. However, another

suggestion, that better machinery be provided for the ship, was overruled as too time consuming.[178]

The balance of 1863 was spent working on the armor plating and awaiting the arrival of weapons for the vessel. The former task was made significantly more difficult with the ship already in the water. The underside of the knuckle or sponson was submerged, of course, but still required the heavy layers of iron. The solution was a substantial demonstration of leverage: twelve-inch square timbers, each twelve feet long were run out of her gunports. Tons of pig iron were then placed on the shore end of the beams to bring the opposite side of the ship out of the water and thus allow the work to be done. Even then the workers were waist deep in the

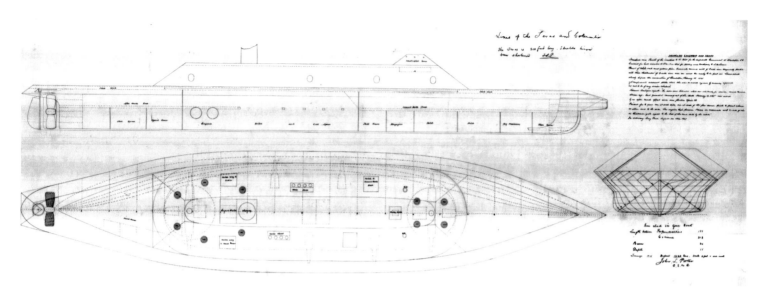

This general plan for ironclads Texas and Columbia was used also for the Tennessee by John L. Porter. All had hulls measuring 189-feet between perpendiculars and a thirty-four foot beam (inside of the knuckle). All three had casemates shortened to compensate for added weight of iron armor. The designed casemate was 114-feet, but that on Tennessee was about ninety feet in length. National Archives

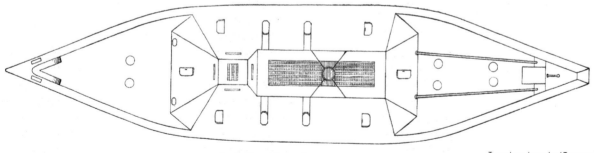

CONFEDERATE STATES RAM TENNESSEE. DECK PLAN.

Top view, ironclad Tennessee. The vessel carried a battery of six guns and some 1,000-tons of armor. Note the exposed rudder chains on the aft deck. Official Records

water, hefting iron plates easily weighing over 900-pounds each.[179]

It was not until February 16, 1864, that the *Tennessee* was put into commission. But there was yet one more – literal- bar to be crossed before the ironclad could defend Mobile Bay and its city. The Dog River bar shoaled at eight feet, effectively blocking the thirteen-foot draft *Tennessee* from entering the lower bay. Two methods could be used to reduce a ship's draft: the first possibility was to remove weight from the vessel, the second was to use "camels": the latter were heavily weighted scows or lighters lashed to both sides of the ship. When the weights were removed from the lighters and they moved upwards, they would lift the ship with them.

Buchanan's attempt with camels reduced *Tennessee's* draft a total of twenty-two inches. Calculations indicated removing all her guns would only gain another four inches. Not deterred, Buchanan employed then-current floating drydock technology to do the job: six rectangular, water-tight iron tanks were built, calculated to contain the weight of water equal to the displacement of the *Tennessee*. These were maneuvered into position on both sides of the ship and pumped full, sinking them. The ship was then secured between the two rows of tanks, and the water was pumped out again. The tanks rose, along with the ironclad, to the required eight-foot threshold, and the entire agglomeration was towed across the bar. On May 18, 1864, after over two months dealing with the process of crossing the bar, the *Tennessee* was finally re-floated on lower Mobile Bay. Interestingly, Buchanan was not as much concerned about the success of his methods, as he was that Admiral Farragut would strike Mobile before the *Tennessee* was available to challenge him.[180]

And Buchanan's vessel was not an empty threat. *Tennessee* was described by A.T. Mahan as, "the most powerful ironclad built, from the keel-up, in the Confederacy."[181] The vessel was described in detail after her capture, as well as by her commanding officer.

The casemate was seventy-eight feet eight-inches long and twenty-eight-feet nine-inches wide on the inside, about eight-feet high, at an angle of thirty-two degrees. It was framed by thirteen-inch yellow pine beams "closed together," covered by a layer of 5½-inch horizontal planking and another of four-inch oak. The latter was placed vertically, the former, horizontally. Another 2½-inches of oak ceiled the inside of the casemate. The iron plating was five inches thick on the sides and aft, two layers of two-inch and one of one-inch plates. The forward end was covered by six-inches of iron. The pilothouse was about eight-feet long and raised three-feet above the remainder of the shield, and was also given six-inches of plating. The plating continued from the knuckle, about two-feet below the waterline at a reverse angle, meeting the hull about seven-feet under the waterline.[182] After her capture, a Union report on the "prize" vessel estimated her iron armature weighed 1,018-tons.[183]

The top deck of the shield was formed by a grating composed of two by six-inch iron bars. These were supported by foot-square wood beams. Four-inch square apertures were left to provide ventilation to the gundeck and there were sections of the grating mounted on hinges to allow access from below. The upper decks fore and aft of the casemate were protected by two inches of plating. A ram was formed by the extensions of the plating and protruded about two feet below the waterline at the prow. There were ten gunports. The ports' wooden backing was cut away on the inside to allow leeway for training the guns. The gunport shutters were of five-inch thick wrought iron, in layers, on pivots operated by pulleys and chains from within the casemate. As with similar shutters on other Confederate ironclads, there was the obvious danger that an enemy projectile could jam them in the closed position. A single central hole was bored through each, to allow the rammer and sponge to be used after the gun had been fired and shutter closed.[184]

The weaponry consisted of six guns: four 6.4-inch Brooke rifles in broadside and two seven-inch Brookes on pivot carriages fore and aft. The latter pair could also be fired through broadside ports. Thus, a six-gun broadside was possible, throwing about 400-pounds of metal at the enemy.

Below decks, the crew and officer accommodations were "large and comfortable for an ironclad vessel." Crew quarters on the berth deck were "roomy" and junior officer cabins were built on both sides. Ventilation was provided through the decks forward and aft of the casemate. The wardroom, however, was above the engine and thus subject to excessive heat.

The least satisfactory aspect of the *Tennessee* was her machinery. This consisted of two cylinders each 26¼-inches in diameter and with a 7½-foot stroke. After her capture it was reported that the engines were from the river packet *Alonzo Child*, a large 236-foot sidewheeler that had been built in 1857. This apparently was incorrect. The riverboat in question was not stripped of her engines until December 1863, and existing correspondence indicates the *Tennessee's* machinery was in place as early as April of that year.[185]

These were standard western river steamer engines, and therefore had to be modified for the single screw-propelled *Tennessee*. The cylinders were mounted longitudinally, probably on either side of the screw shaft. The piston rods, rather than operating the side paddle wheels, turned transversely mounted idler shafts. These, in turn, had beveled gears at their inner ends, meshing with corresponding beveled gears on the propeller shaft. Probably the weakest aspect of this arrangement was the beveled gears that were cast iron with wooden teeth. Both cast iron and wood

Tennessee from the stern quarter, after her capture at Mobile Bay. Naval Historical Center

were brittle and therefore easily broken. A steam engineer later remarked that the engines were "totally unfit" for a war vessel. On a trial trip, these engines, and four twenty-four-foot boilers, drove her at eight-knots, but later, with full load, she made about six.[186]

The steering arrangement was also defective in that the rudder chains ran in open channels across the stern deck, completely exposed to shot.[187]

This was the *Tennessee* as Buchanan prepared to meet Farragut at Mobile Bay in August 1864. In battery, she had fewer guns than *Virginia* or *Arkansas*. Her casemate, however, was stauncher than his first command, though that vessel did not encounter the Union fifteen-inch guns. All three vessels suffered more or less from inadequate and unreliable engines. Fortunately for Buchanan,

his command, while on lower Mobile Bay, would not be endangered by shoal waters.

Tennessee at Mobile Bay, August 1864

Admiral Farragut had been contemplating an attack on Mobile since 1862. The appearance of the *Tennessee* served to add to the delay in carrying out his plan. In May 1864, Farragut had observers surreptitiously looking the ironclad over. They concluded that she was "a formidable thing" and Farragut subsequently determined that having his own ironclads would be a prerequisite to an attack on Mobile Bay. When Farragut finally lined up his fourteen wooden vessels for the assault, there were four monitor-type ironclads to accompany

them. In aggregate, Farragut's fleet mounted about two hundred guns.

Admiral Buchanan had three wooden gunboats in addition to the *Tennessee*, mounting a total of twenty-two guns. The wooden ships did little service before succumbing to the Union guns. In the initial phase of the battle, it became clear that the *Tennessee*'s armor made her impervious to even the largest – eleven-inch Dahlgrens and 150-pounder Parrott rifles – of the wooden ships' ordnance. However, *Tennessee*'s attempt to ram one of Farragut's wooden vessels was thwarted by her slow speed. As the entire Union flotilla concentrated on the *Tennessee*, Farragut directed the monitors to train their guns on the Confederate ironclad and that the larger wooden steam sloops ram her as opportunity arose.

In the ensuing melee, *Tennessee* was rammed no fewer than three times by wooden steam sloops of over 2,000-tons displacement – at least two of which had had iron plating added to their prows for this purpose – resulting in little damage to the Confederate ship, but significant damage to the Union vessels from the shock of the encounters.

Meanwhile the monitors dogged *Tennessee*, with the *Chickasaw* striking her at least fifty times from her eleven-inch guns. One of these did the most significant damage when it severed the *Tennessee*'s exposed steering chains. Another slammed into one of her port shutters, killing two sailors and wounding Admiral Buchanan. In the course of the engagement, three of the port shutters were disabled. Then a fifteen-inch Dahlgren projectile from the *Manhattan* "admitted daylight" though the casemate side. This was the only strike

Starboard side of Tennessee. Naval Historical Center

of the day that actually penetrated the casemate. Incidentally, after the loss of monitor *Tecumseh* to a torpedo, the only two fifteen-inch Dahlgrens in Farragut's lineup were on the *Manhattan*. Literally surrounded by the adversaries and unable to steer or escape, the *Tennessee* and her crew held out for another thirty minutes pounding before they hauled down the flag.

In the damage report afterwards, it was revealed that the ramming had done little but increase *Tennessee*'s normal leakage from three inches per hour to five or six inches per hour. There were "between forty and fifty" indentations and marks of shots on her casemate and exterior. Most of the strikes were on her port side and aft end of the casemate. Again, the only penetration was by the single fifteen-inch projectile. Had the *Tecumseh*'s two fifteen-inch Dahlgrens been available, the fight may have been shorter.[188] As it was, the deadly fifteen-inch gun's major drawback was its slow rate of fire – a serious problem in a continuously moving battle scenario.

Fredericksburg

Nine of the "diamond hull" ironclads were begun in 1862. The *Fredericksburg*, laid down sometime in mid-summer, 1862 at Richmond, was among the first three (with *Tuscaloosa* and *Huntsville*) commissioned. However, the latter two were considered failures, while *Fredericksburg* did significant service through the remainder of the war.

John L. Porter's light-draft, ironclad plan shows a vessel 170-feet long between perpendiculars, and 188-feet overall. The overall breadth was forty-feet three-inches over the knuckles,

and a thirty-four foot moulded beam. The depth of hold was about nine-feet, around three feet less than the *Milledgeville* (the "ship hull" light draft design). As with *Milledgeville*, this ironclad had twin screws.[189]

The casemate was designed for four guns: two in broadside, mounted asymmetrically, and the others on pivot carriages. The latter had broadside and end gunports.

Despite a seven-day workweek at the Rocketts yard, progress on the *Fredericksburg* was slow. The vessel was launched on June 11, 1863, on the second attempt. The vessel had balked at the first try, about a week earlier. As probable in these cases, the angle of the ways may not have been correct for launching.[190]

After launch, the armoring of the casemate began, and with it the lengthy process of awaiting iron from the Tredegar works. As noted above, work on the *Virginia 2* competed with that on the *Fredericksburg*, placing high demands on the iron producer. The decision to concentrate on *Fredericksburg* moved her along to comple-

tion before the Graves' ironclad. The situation was not improved by the elements, however. In the spring of 1864, high waters on the James River inundated the Rocketts yard, threatening to wash away large stocks of timber and putting the wharves under water.[191]

The desultory fitting-out of *Fredericksburg* was such that, by April 1864, she was still without her guns and, in fact, had been ready for her battery since the previous November.[192] She was finally armed by May 1864, with her battery at this time consisting of two 6.4-inch Brooke rifles in broadside, one seven-inch Brooke forward pivot, and one ten-inch smoothbore aft.[193]

There is not a great deal of specific information about this vessel. We assume she had what had become standard on the casemate, about two feet of wood covered by four-inches of iron. Porter's drawing also shows two pilothouses, fore and aft, though an operational report only refers to one pilothouse. On the plan, there is a "breastwork" of thin, hinged iron plates running on both sides, for the length of the deck

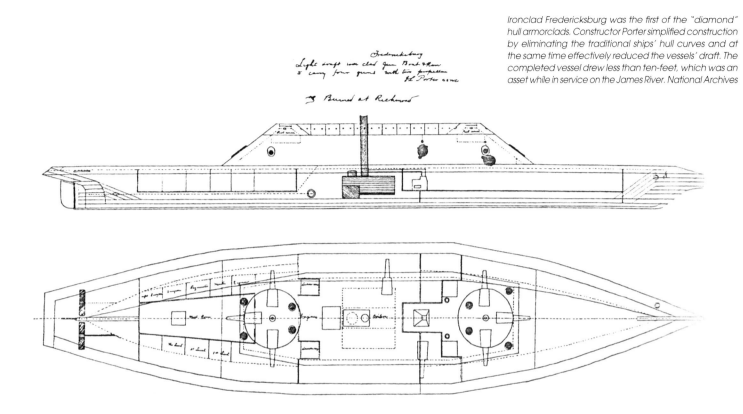

Ironclad Fredericksburg was the first of the "diamond" hull armorclads. Constructor Porter simplified construction by eliminating the traditional ships' hull curves and at the same time effectively reduced the vessels' draft. The completed vessel drew less than ten-feet, which was an asset while in service on the James River. National Archives

atop the casemate. It appears that this was not actually done. The shield's top grating was composed of two-inch thick iron bars, at nine-inch intervals. Her commanding officer later suggested that additional iron bars be put in the center of each interval, to provide better protection to the deck and crew below.[194] The ironclad was referred to as the "lighter ironclad" and was reported to draw only nine-feet six-inches. She had a crew of 150, and her machinery was built by the Tredegar ironworks.[195]

Fredericksburg on the James River, 1864-65

On October 22, 1864, Federal batteries at Signal Hill and Boulware's house on the James River opened on the Confederate James River squadron, first on the gunboats, then the three ironclads, *Virginia 2*, *Richmond*, and *Fredericksburg*.

Fredericksburg came under fire twice, each time for some thirty minutes, mainly from Union field artillery at a high elevation. Her commanding officer wrote, "The ship was struck from twenty to fifty times with shells and bolts, size, I should judge, from 20- to 100-pounder

Parrotts. One shot struck the wooden gratings on the upper deck, fore and aft, the splinters came inside the shield and wounded five men. This shot, I think afterwards struck the pilot house, started a number of the bolts and bolt-heads, and made a considerable indentation in the plate of iron, and from the appearances [I] should say it was a 100-pounder Parrott ... A number of shot and fragments of shells struck the ship, doing but little damage." This engagement prompted the recommendation mentioned above, regarding additional topside iron to defend against plunging fire.[196]

The *Fredericksburg* was involved in a series of engagements on the James in the fall of 1864, then was at the battle of Trent's Reach the following January. In the latter, her light draft enabled her to pass the obstructions that blocked the passage of other two ironclads. Of the three ironclads, *Fredericksburg* seems to have suffered the least damage from shot and shell. Enemy fire, including that from their fifteen-inch guns, seems to have been concentrated on the larger vessels.

Huntsville and Tuscaloosa

These two vessels were built by the contractor Henry W. Bassett at Selma, Alabama. The original contract, dated May 1, 1862, referred to them as floating batteries.[197] However, like the *Georgia* in Savannah, the two were also described as ironclads. They were flat-bottomed, built to a J.L. Porter design. However, the builder was not, "… confine[d] to Porter's plan." Consequently their recorded dimensions differ slightly. *Huntsville* was described as 150-feet in length with a draft of seven-feet; *Tuscaloosa*, 152-feet and with an eight-foot draft. The latter's depth of hold was ten-feet six-inches and breadth, thirty-four feet. Four inches of armor was intended for each, as well as four guns.[198] Both, apparently, had high-pressure, river-steamer machinery. The *Tuscaloosa*'s engines and boilers were from the 162-ton, stern-wheel river packet *Chewala*, built in 1856, and placed in Confederate registry in 1861.[199]

The two vessels were launched on February 7, 1863, and Admiral Buchanan would be disappointed in both. In April, the *Tuscaloosa* made two trial runs. The first was made using wood for fuel, and the vessel barely made headway. Buchanan ordered increased draft to the engines, sealing of boiler leaks and use of coal for the next try. On the second run, with boiler pressure at 150psi, the boat strained to reach 2½-knots. The

Huntsville trials were the following month, and she ran at 3½-knots. Buchanan wrote that the vessel was "not so strong as I supposed" and noted she "trembled" when underway.[200]

Consequently, both vessels reverted to their original designation as floating batteries. *Huntsville* was never completely armored, nor was assigned an entire crew. Her battery was relatively light: four thirty-two-pounders. *Tuscaloosa* mounted three thirty-two-pounders and one 6.4-inch rifle.[201]

The batteries were towed across the Dog River bar into Mobile Bay in May 1864, but did not participate in the decisive battle there. Both escaped up the Spanish River and were scuttled when Mobile was evacuated on April 12, 1865.[202]

The Oven Bluff Vessels

The three vessels begun at Oven Bluff, Alabama, shared the fate of many Confederate ironclad projects: they were never completed and eventually fell into Union hands or were destroyed to prevent their capture. The origin of two of these vessels was a contract dated August 12, 1862, with Sidney D. Porter and I.M. Watson, for two "iron-clad, ram gunboats" to be delivered in ninety days. Their dimensions were to be: 160-feet between perpendiculars, a forty-one-foot breadth at the knuckles, and a 10½-foot depth of hold. The plating and bolts were to be supplied by the government; the engines by the contractor.

The engines were to be two "first class" propeller units, with four boilers for each vessel. They were to have twin screws driven by geared machinery. Total price was to be $270,000. This description indicates they were to be the diamond-hull, Porter-design, light draft vessels.

A third vessel was contracted out, also to Porter and Watson, on August 15, 1862, and this vessel was to be a larger, sidewheel ironclad, measuring 180-feet by thirty-four-feet (moulded beam), with a fourteen-foot depth of hold. The

government was to supply the armor and bolts; the whole to be delivered by January 15, 1863.[203]

All were built at Oven Bluff, about fifty-miles north of Mobile on the Tombigbee River. (The Tombigbee runs almost due north from Mobile while the Alabama River turns eastward towards Selma.) The location itself was to become a substantial hindrance to their completion.

As early as October 1862, the work on the vessels was reportedly delayed by "sickness." The low-lying, swampy country proved to be nearly fatal to the work in progress. The completion deadline was vastly underestimated and as late as November 1863, Buchanan informed Secretary Mallory that the "unhealthiness" of the location had set back the work. By that date, only one of the smaller vessels had been launched (on July 12) and the second was nearly ready to go down the ways. It is almost ironic that Buchanan wrote that "no progress" had been made on the larger vessel due to work being concentrated on the two others.[204]

The two smaller hulls were never completed. They had been towed to Mobile and were there when the city surrendered in April 1865.[205] Apparently, the large sidewheel vessel was never launched.

Nashville

Sidewheel ironclads were exceptions to the rules, both in the Union and Confederate river forces. Their huge paddle boxes blocked out a large section of the sides of the vessels, which otherwise would have housed broadside guns, and the paddle housings were huge, inviting targets. Consequently, a vast proportion of their iron or wood cladding went to protecting these structures. The trade off on the positive side was that side wheel-type engines were standard propulsion on river packets and therefore easily obtained. Furthermore, this type of engine was noted for its simplicity and ease of maintenance. The drive train consisted of the piston rod, which operated the connecting rod

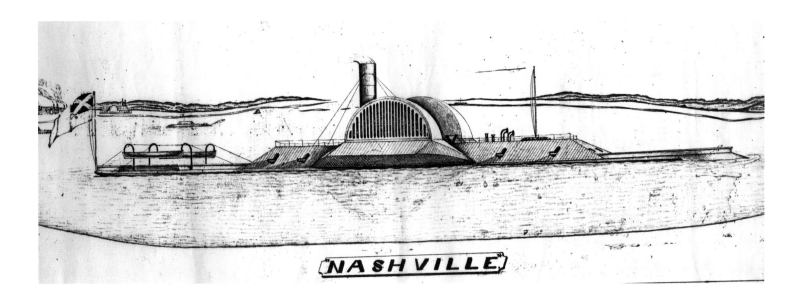

NASHVILLE

Sidewheel ironclad Nashville. Built to a design by John Porter, the vessel was over 270-feet long, but about forty feet on each side was taken up by the paddle wheel housings. The latter had an "angular shield of heavy timbers" for protection. National Archives

(known as the pitman in river parlance). The latter was attached directly to the crank of the paddle wheel. Other than the valve gear and the cylinder itself, most of the installation was wood.

The *Nashville* was built by J.C. Montgomery, of Missouri, and A. Anderson, of Tennessee, at Montgomery, Alabama, via a contract dated September 16, 1862. Completion date was set for May 1863, and a penalty of $200 was to be levied for each day delay past the delivery date. The contract specified – optimistically, of course – that the boat would make 12mph.[206] Admiral Buchanan, was, as commanding officer of the Mobile station, in general charge of her construction.

The vessel's design was likely by John L. Porter; in October of that year, Mallory wrote that Porter had plans for a side wheel ironclad boat "expressly to receive such engines and boilers as may be obtained from river steamers."[207]

The building of the vessel's hull was relatively efficient and she was launched in February 1863. Subsequently, progress was sporadic, for the most part due to the slow supply of iron plating. Though she was reported "ready" for her iron cladding in September 1863, it was still unfinished at the turn of the year. Eventually some of the iron was cannibalized from the decrepit ram *Baltic*. Buchanan wrote that he was having the "front part of the shield" ironed as late as April 1864.[208]

In January 1864, when her guns were being brought on board, a problem arose: the contractors had made the angle of the forward shield twenty-nine degrees, a somewhat sharper angle than that called for in the plans. Consequently, given the thickness of the wood backing (four-feet eleven-inches), plus the six inches of iron, the guns'

muzzles would not clear the outside of the casemate. Two solutions were proposed: one was to cut away the interior wood backing to allow the gun to be moved farther into the embrasure. Another approach was by J.M. Brooke who proposed specially casting two seven-inch tubes, each five inches longer at the muzzle than what was standard. Eventually, the latter course was adopted. At least one of the guns was available in April 1864.[209]

The finished vessel was certainly one of the oddest looking steamers of the war, with her profile dominated by the massive, paddle-wheel housings as well as an "angular shield of heavy timbers" protecting each of them. A post-war description indicates she was 271-feet long, overall, with a 250-foot keel. Including her paddle housings, she was ninety-five-feet six-inches wide; without the boxes her beam was sixty-two-feet six-inches over the knuckles and forty-six feet at the side of the hull itself. The casemate was approximately forty-feet wide, though it is unclear whether this was an interior or exterior

Ironclad Nashville, stern view. With a width, including paddle housings, of over ninety-five feet, the vessel required transverse "hog chains" to prevent the housing from leaning outward. Longitudinal hog chains did not prevent the vessel from sagging at her ends. Alabama Department of Archives and History

dimension, and was armored only on the ends, having three layers of two-inch plates on the forward shield and on her pilot house, and one two-inch layer aft. The shield was 142-feet, extending forward and aft of the paddle boxes. The latter would have been at most forty-feet long, leaving some fifty feet of casemate forward and aft of the boxes. We are not left with a description of the casemate's wood backing, but, at four-feet eleven-inches, it was more than twice the thickness of that of the typical Confederate ironclad. No doubt this was to compensate for the lack of iron plating on her sides. Illustrations show four gunports on each broadside, two forward and two aft of the paddle boxes, and two forward ports. The hull's depth was thirteen-feet and she drew ten-feet nine-inches of water. Her engines were two cylinders, each thirty-inches diameter with a nine-foot stroke. She had seven boilers, each of which was a forty-inch diameter double flue unit. She mounted three seven-inch rifles and one twenty-four-pounder howitzer.[210]

After the close of the war, her hull was hogged – sagging at the ends – indicating her structure was not strong enough to bear the weight of her massive wood and iron casemate armor. Another indication of the weakness of her construction was the presence of hog braces (chains) *across* her wide hull.[211]

Nashville was completed at Mobile, but was not in the battle at Mobile Bay. She first saw action in March 1865 as the federals moved on

Mobile. Her guns were used to good effect on Union army units and she was under fire from field artillery batteries. After the fall of Mobile, *Nashville* and other surviving Confederate vessels went up the Tombigbee River, where they surrendered on May 10, 1865.[212]

Albemarle and the Tar River Ironclad

After the loss of Norfolk navy yard and the gunboats being built there, three contracts were let for ironclads to be built on the upper reaches of the Tar, Roanoke, and Neuse rivers in North Carolina. The Neuse River vessel's contract was with the firm of Howard and Ellis, and the other pair was to be built by Gilbert Elliot and William F. Martin. The contract for the vessel on the Tar River was dated September 17, 1862, and included a clause authorizing construction of "one or more vessels" under its terms. Consequently, when Gilbert Elliot proposed a second ironclad, to be built on the Roanoke River, another contract was not required.[213]

The contract called for a sum of $40,000 to be paid for the first ironclad and Elliot and Martin would provide the completed hull by March 1, 1863. The government (the navy department) was

to supply the engines and iron plating. Payments, as was standard practice, would be parceled out in $5,000 increments. If the work was interrupted by "the enemy," the contractor would be reimbursed for any losses. The second vessel to be built on the Roanoke River was grandfathered into the first contract, with a completion date of the first of April 1863.[214]

In July 1863, construction of the Tar River vessel ended as the result of a major Union raid on Greensboro, Tarboro, and Rocky Mount, North Carolina. The destruction was witnessed by a local plumber who reported that the work had begun in September – but had been suspended a month later, then renewed, apparently in June 1863. There was little to show for the effort: "… about 20 feet of its midship section had been put up …" and "… more of the frame in sections was ready to put up." The writer also indicated the frames were, "… in six parts … (of the bottom four parts, making sides and angle and top)." In other words, these were typical "diamond" hull frames.[215]

Though the agreement to build the second vessel, which would become the *Albemarle,* was dated October 1862, actual construction did not begin until March 1863. In the interim, Elliot had moved from Halifax to Edwards Ferry, just north of Clarksville (now Scotland Neck), on the

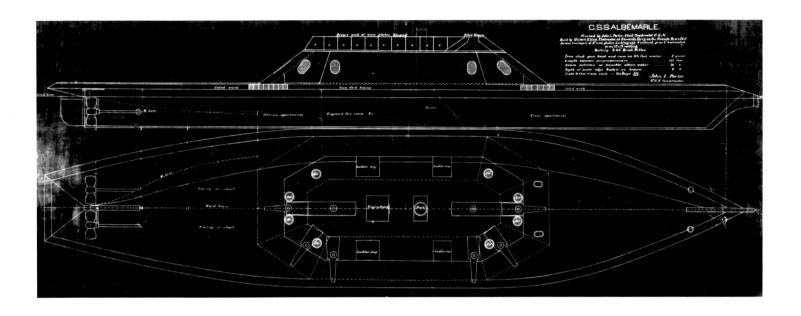

Plan of ironclad Albemarle, by John Porter. The ironclad that created havoc on the North Carolina sounds was relatively small and carried only two guns. Note the folding "shields" atop the casemate. These were not installed. National Archives

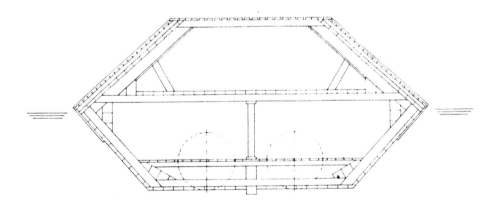

Cross section of Albemarle showing the "diamond" hull configuration and twin screws. Bob Holcombe

Roanoke River. A site in a cornfield was found which would provide an appropriate gradient for the vessel's building stocks. A steam sawmill was set up and there was a forge in the nearby plantation complex. After the necessary infrastructure was in place and materials brought in, construction began. The keel was laid sometime before April 6, 1863.

A post-war article described the hull building process states: "… construction was commenced by bolting down across the center a piece of frame timber, which was of yellow pine eight by ten inches. Another frame of the same size was then dovetailed into this, extending outwardly at an angle of 45 degrees, forming the side, at the outer end of this the frame for the shield was also dovetailed, the angle being 35 degrees, and then the top deck was added, and so on around to the other end of the bottom beam. Other beams were then bolted down to the keel, and to the first one fastened, and so on, working fore and aft, the main deck beams being interposed from stem to stern. The shield was 60 feet in length and octagonal in form."[216]

As can be seen from this description, as well as from the existing plans, this process was far from complicated. At the midship fifty feet or so of the hull, the sides were straight, and all the frames in that section would have been identical. The frames may well have been built individually, then erected as units. The description continued, saying: "… she was a solid boat built of pine frames, and if calked, would have floated in that condition." In other words, there was no frame spacing. However, four-inch planking was added, as well as calking of tar-soaked cotton. (Oakum was scarce while cotton was not.)[217]

The casemate itself was the typical three-layer structure, under the iron plating. The inner vertical frames were twelve- by thirteen-inch members covered by five-inch thick pine laid horizontally, then another layer of four-inch thick oak, the latter laid vertically. The iron itself was in two, two-inch thicknesses. The main deck was formed by one-foot square, pine beams, and the six gunports were twenty-two-inches wide and thirty-inches high. A ram was built at the prow, solidly bolted to the center keelson. It was solid oak, with two-inch thick iron plating.[218]

Anticipating the completion of the casemate, Elliot looked for an efficient method of drilling the two-inch iron plates. Sometime in June a drilling machine was procured from equipment taken from the Norfolk navy yard, but the machine proved to be old and worn out. Each 1½-inch diameter hole required around twenty minutes to drill. Elliot was contemplating significant cost overruns if a more efficient method was not found.[219]

The protracted drilling process no doubt surfaced when the armor plating was begun on the underside of the knuckle, an area that obviously had to be completed before the vessel was launched. And launching was becoming increasingly important: the Union raid which destroyed the Tar River ironclad in July 1863 emphasized the need to move the yet-incomplete vessel to a more protected location.

The launching ways were built on a slight bluff over the river. Therefore the event could not occur until the river rose substantially. In the event, when she went into the water on October 6th, the river had not reached the optimum level. In consequence, when the vessel's stern cleared the ways there was a significant drop before she hit the water, and the hull actually "hogged" – literally bent downward over five inches. Despite this, the vessel remained watertight.[220]

Shortly after the launch, the ship was towed to the navy facility at Halifax, about twenty-miles up the river. For a few weeks after the move, nothing was done of significance, though in the interim one of the local blacksmiths had fashioned a "twist drill" which reduced the time required for a single hole from twenty minutes to about four.[221]

Two major aspects of the vessel were yet undone: armor and machinery. The engines and boilers arrived sometime in October via barge. Some specifics are known about this machinery, though its exact arrangement is not. One writer said they were from a sawmill, another claimed they were built of "odds and ends." In fact, they were from Tredegar iron works and were eighteen-inch (or twenty-inch) diameter cylinders, with a nineteen-inch stroke, mounted horizontally, side-by-side. Four bevelled gears, measuring about three-feet in diameter, transmitted the power to the two prop shafts. They were non-condensing, high-pressure units operating from two boilers, producing, about 200-horsepower each. There were no blowers for the engines. The two propellers were about seven-feet in diameter with three blades.[222]

As to the iron plating, this process would continue, though not at a steady pace, past the ship's commissioning date (April 17, 1864), and in fact until the day before the ironclad's first combat. Blacksmiths and their forges were on board as late as April 18, 1864. The major impediment to the armoring process had been the, "difficulty of getting iron armour for them over the railroads," wrote Secretary Mallory, in a letter to an army officer, in an effort to expedite the proceedings.[223]

The completed ironclad was not a very large vessel. At 158-feet overall length (152-feet between perpendiculars), she was shorter than the smallest of the monitors (Ericsson's original was 175-feet), and about the length of the Union navy's smallest purpose built gunboats (the "ninety-day" Unadilla and class). Her extreme beam was thirty-four-feet and depth of hold, nine-feet. Her armoring, in addition to the two layers on the casemate sides and ends, consisted of two layers of one-inch plates from the deck downward two feet on the knuckle. Forward and aft of the casemate, the decks were covered with one one-inch layer of

Albemarle after its sinking by a Union spar torpedo picket boat under the command of Lt. William Cushing. Note the two broadside gunports and shutters, as well as a forward port barely discernable at right. Comparing this photo with those taken after her salvage, note that her armor is in place in this view. Naval Historical Center

iron. There were six gun ports, one each fore and aft and two on each broadside. Thus each of the two guns (6.4-inch Brooke rifles) could be run out on either side as well as fore or aft, respectively.

Albemarle at Plymouth, 1864

The *Albemarle* joined the ranks of the Confederate ironclads which took on entire Union flotillas. There were two major encounters. In both instances, the adversaries were all unarmored, conventional steamers. On April 19, 1864, she attacked the Union blockaders near Plymouth, North Carolina, as part of a Confederate movement to retake that city. Ignoring the Union naval commander's plan to trap her between the vessels *Southfield* and *Miami*, the *Albemarle*, under James W. Cooke, swiftly slammed the ironclad into the *Southfield* – the ram embedding itself so deeply that there was danger of taking the ironclad down with her. While entangled with the *Southfield*, *Miami* continued sending broadsides into the *Albemarle*, to little effect. When *Albemarle* broke free, leaving *Southfield* in a sinking condition, *Miami* raced for safety. Subsequently, the town of Plymouth surrendered to Confederate forces. *Albemarle* was relatively undamaged. The largest guns on the Union vessels had been firing no more than eighty-pound projectiles, many of which simply shattered on the ironclad's casemate.

On May 5, the ram engaged a Union flotilla of nine vessels, two of which were double-ender gunboats, armed with 100-pounder Parrot rifles.

In the ensuing engagement, *Sassacus* smashed into the side of *Albemarle*, attempting to sink her with a bolted-on ram. The two vessels were enmeshed until a Confederate projectile pierced one of the Union vessel's boilers, decimating the attending crew. *Albemarle* pulled away, pursued at a respectful distance by the Federal vessels. The *Albemarle* had been under fire for at least five hours. The damage was not serious: seven damaged plates, a gun muzzle blown off, and the smokestack riddled.

As conventional means had done nothing to seriously damage or destroy the *Albemarle*, in the next few months the Union resorted to extraordinary methods. Two torpedoes were hand-carried to the river and put into the water, to be guided to the target by five volunteer swimmers. The men were seen in the water, approaching the ironclad, and the attempt failed. Finally, the ironclad was the target of Lt. William B. Cushing, thirteen men, and a spar-torpedo-equipped steam launch. On October 27, 1864, Cushing attacked and sank the ship at her moorings, though losing most of his men in the process. The *Albemarle* had been effective both in combat and in her effect – simply by existing – on the Union forces in the Carolina sounds.

Neuse

The third ironclad, begun on the North Carolina rivers in 1862, was built by contract with the firm of Thomas S. Howard and Elijah W. Ellis of New Bern, North Carolina. The construction site was the hamlet of White Hall, now Seven Springs, about 100-miles south of the North Carolina-Virginia border and fifty-miles west of New Bern.[224]

The contract was dated October 17, 1862, and the vessel was to be to the same design as the *Albemarle*. Construction was begun immediately, utilizing large stands of pine timber at the building site. As with the majority of the Confederate navy's ironclad projects, there would be many factors delaying the proceedings. In this instance, the Union army provided an early obstruction. Forces under Union general John G. Foster raided the area and, on December 11, 1862, attempted to burn the beginnings of the hull. When this failed, it was the target of his field artillery. The extent of the damage is unknown. Nevertheless, the hull was launched in mid-March 1863, and was floated to Kinston, North Carolina, for completion.[225]

The machinery for the ship arrived in January 1864. It was said that it was shipped from Virginia;

Albemarle at Norfolk Navy Yard after the war. The vessel is sitting high in the water and the outer iron armor has been removed. Naval Historical Center

Stern wheel ironclad Missouri model at the National Civil War Naval Museum in Columbus, Georgia. The paddle wheel was recessed into the vessel's stern, and the hull was of the diamond configuration, designed by John Porter. Though the ironclad drew less than nine-feet of water, falling river levels prevented her from active service during the conflict. Model by O.L. Raines. National Civil War Naval Museum. Photo by Author

but it was also said to have been recycled from the Pugh Mill, a factory in New Bern. Possibly, the cylinders were from Tredegar and the boilers from the mill. The boilers were lowered into the hold in February, under the supervision of navy commander Robert Minor, who had been detailed to the yard to expedite the work.[226]

Then in March, there was a pay dispute with the workmen, and a continuing concern about the levels of the river. The ironclad was expected to draw six to seven feet, while the stream was at five feet at the time. Consequently, work was begun on camels to be used, if needed, to get the vessel down river. However, the iron plating was the major source of delays. B.P. Loyall, the ship's commander, supervising the work, wrote on April 7th: "At one time *twenty-one* days passed without my receiving a piece – the fault was on the W.&W.R.R. [Wilmington and Weldon Rail Road]. Every time I telegraph to [Commander W.F.] Lynch he replies: 'Army monopolizes the cars.'"

On April 22, 1864 the *Neuse* set out on the river, though still in an incomplete state. Less than one-half mile from her starting point, she grounded and remained there until May.[227]

As completed, the vessel was 152-feet long and thirty-four-feet in beam and carried two 6.4-inch Brooke rifles. But there was some question as to the expected effectiveness of the ship. Her commanding officer wrote: "The vessel will draw nearly 8ft. [of] water when complete. Mark what I say. When a boat built of green pine & covered with four inches of iron gets under the fire of heavy ordnance, she will prove anything but bomb proof. This vessel is not fastened & strengthened more than a 200 ton schooner. Her upper deck is 2ins. Pine, with light beams & is expected to hold a pilothouse. I should not be surprised if said pilothouse is knocked off. There is very little to hold it on."[228]

In any event, the *Neuse* remained inactive for the rest of the war. On March 12, 1865 the vessel was burnt when Kinston, North Carolina was evacuated.

The remains of the *Neuse* exist today. After several moves necessitated by poor facilities and Hurricane Floyd, the bottom of her hull is currently at a site on Queen Street in Kinston. Plans are in hand to preserve the remains in a climate-controlled facility.

Missouri

The *Missouri*, by default, became a class unto itself. John L. Porter concocted a design combining the diamond hull configuration with stern-wheel propulsion or, to be more precise, a vessel with a paddle wheel recessed into the stern of the vessel. Two of these ironclads were begun, the *Missouri* and the *Jackson* (the latter originally named *Muscogee*). The latter was modified mid-construction and given screw propellers, while *Missouri* retained its designed stern wheel. *Missouri* therefore was the closest Confederate ironclad in design to the *Cairo* class Union steamers.

On riverboats of this era, the sternwheelers, as opposed to sidewheelers, could have narrower beams and lighter draft. On the other hand, side-wheel vessels were significantly easier to steer.

Riverboat captains Thomas Moore and John Smoker, of St. Tammany Parish, Louisiana, received the contract for the *Missouri*'s construction, though neither had experience in shipbuilding. The contract was dated November 1, 1862 and required that the vessel be completed in six months and capable of 10mph, at a cost of $336,500. The contractors proceeded to obtain riverfront property in Shreveport suitable for a shipyard.[229]

Lt. Jonathan H. Carter was appointed to supervise and facilitate the construction of the vessel. This included dealing with the persistent lack of iron suitable for the boat's casemate. This iron was standard railroad t-iron, and in some instances this iron was seized from the area's railways. Carter wrote to the director of the Vicksburg, Shreveport and Texas Railroad: "It is my wish to obtain the iron *with* your consent, but if that is refused, I shall certainly use the iron, if needed, although such a course will be repugnant to my feelings."[230]

Carter also ran interference with the army in obtaining the steam machinery. Army general Pemberton was intent on sinking a riverboat as an obstruction on the Big Black River when Carter requested that this operation be delayed until the machinery could be removed for use on the *Missouri*. Similarly, Carter prevailed upon army authorities to provide workers, particularly caulkers, for the project.[231]

Construction of the hull progressed rapidly and most of the frame was up by February 1863. Planking was then begun and drilling the railroad iron. The vessel was launched on April 14, 1863, and machinery installation began.

Two months later, the *Missouri* made her first trial trip. Lt. Carter had predicted that she would not produce the speed required by the contract, and this proved correct. The vessel made six-knots upstream. Some modifications were then made at the stern in an attempt to increase her speed, but to little effect.

The *Missouri* was turned over to Confederate naval authorities on September 12, 1863, though she, as yet, had no guns. Her three guns were mounted sometime between November 1863 and March 1864, when she was reported ready to take on the Union forces in the Red River campaign.[232]

The *Missouri* was the subject of a reasonably complete post-war description at the time of her capture. The vessel was 183-feet long, overall, with a casemate measuring 130-feet six-inches at the base and 105-feet at the top deck. Her extreme beam was fifty-three-feet eight-inches, which was the width of the base of the casemate, tapering to twenty-nine-feet wide at the top. The depth of hold to the main deck was ten-feet three-inches and height of the casemate from water's edge was eleven-feet six-inches. The boat drew a reported eight-feet six-inches of water.

T-rail formed the armor, with two tiers being laid "with the crowns placed alternately in and out, and locked into each other, and spiked with common five-eighth-inch spikes, one in the center and one at each end of each alternate rail." On the casemate sides the rails were laid on diagonally; on the fore and aft faces, the layers were vertical. The total thickness of the two-rail armor was $4\frac{1}{2}$-inches, and was backed by twenty-three-inches of pine. The iron extended below the waterline about six-feet. On top of the forward part of the casemate was a pilothouse, which added about nineteen-inches to the height of the structure. Steering was by three rudders operated by a steering wheel positioned on the gundeck directly under the pilothouse.

There were two gunports on the forward casemate face, and three on each broadside. She carried only three guns: one an eleven-inch Dahlgren. This gun was said to have come from either the U.S. ironclad *Indianola* or the captured ex-Revenue Cutter *Harriet Lane*. However, the latter vessel never carried an eleven-inch gun, while the ironclad mounted two of them. Pivot rails were let into the deck to enable it to fire through one of the forward ports, or through a starboard gunport. Likewise, an "old-fashioned" thirty-two-pounder siege gun was mounted to fire forward or through the port broadside gunport. The third gun was a nine-inch Dahlgren (which may have come from either the *Indianola* or the *Harriet Lane*). Pivot rails enabled its use through the farthest aft gunports on either broadside. No guns were mounted to use the center broadside gunports.

The recessed stern paddle-wheel was twenty-two-feet six-inches in diameter, with buckets (blades) seventeen-feet long and each with a twenty-two-inch face. The description indicates that eight-feet four-inches of the top of the wheel was exposed above the casemate.

Within, the woodwork was "generally sound," though with rather poor living arrangements. Officers' cabins were aft in the casemate, with junior officers' on the orlop deck beside the engines and wheel. Shell rooms and magazines were abreast the boilers.

The powerplant consisted of two cylinders, each twenty-four-inches in diameter with a seven-foot stroke, operating at right angles to the paddle wheel shaft. Steam was provided by four boilers, each forty-inches in diameter, and twenty-six-feet long. Another boiler was for the auxiliary "donkey" engine that supplied water to the boilers. It also operated the capstan, the blower for the engines, and a small pump. There was a single funnel.[233]

The *Missouri* never saw combat, mainly due to her draft. The same falling water levels that nearly destroyed Admiral Porter's Union fleet in the Red River campaign thwarted any attempts to bring her into action. She was surrendered to Union forces on June 3, 1865.[234]

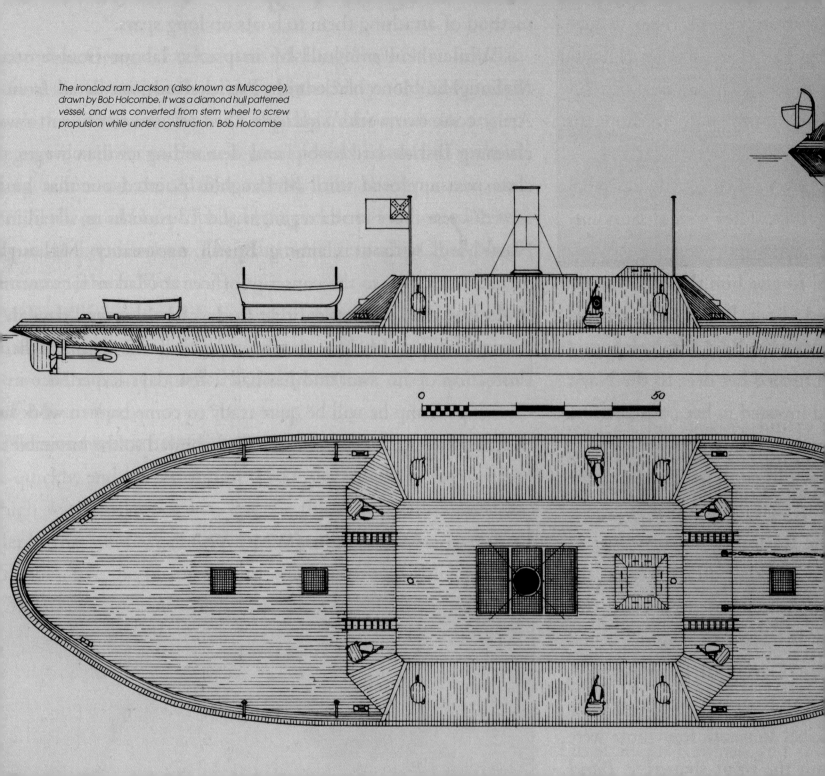

The ironclad ram Jackson (also known as Muscogee), drawn by Bob Holcombe. It was a diamond hull patterned vessel, and was converted from stern wheel to screw propulsion while under construction. Bob Holcombe

0   50

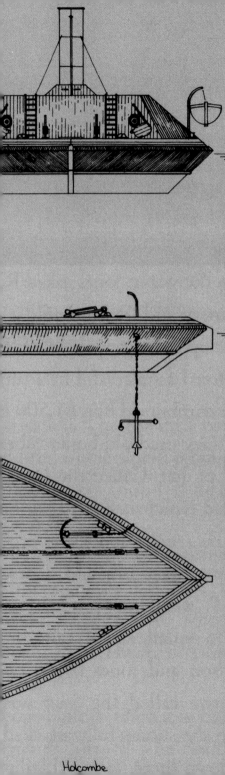

IRONCLADS AT LAST: 1863-65

The majority of the Confederate Navy's domestically built ironclads were begun in 1862, but many factors prevented a significant number of these from entering service until 1864 or 1865, and, some remained unfinished at the end of the conflict. Thus, there were relatively few laid down from 1863 onwards. The three major vessels in this category will be described here.

Additionally, there were several concepts or projects that never reached fruition. They remain fascinating as 'might-have-beens' only. In some cases, actual work may have begun, but the scarcity of official or unofficial records leaves even this in doubt.

Jackson

The last of the "diamond hull" ironclads to be laid down was built at the Confederate navy's facility at Columbus, Georgia, on the Chattahoochee River. Originally to be named *Muscogee*, its design was based on that of *Missouri*, John L. Porter's recessed stern paddle wheel vessel.[235]

Construction of the vessel was under the direction of Lt. Augustus McLaughlin, who had been instrumental in creating the Confederate navy yard and ironworks at Columbus. McLaughlin had begun work on the wooden steam gunboat *Chattahoochee* at that site, and the ironworks was heavily engaged in providing ironwork and machinery for various ironclads at every stage of construction, mostly in the Deep South.

McLaughlin began gathering materials for the project late in 1862 and it appears that actual construction began early in 1863. As with the *Missouri*, the Columbus vessel was comparatively wide, to accommodate the recessed paddle wheel (*Missouri* was fifty-three-feet extreme beam; *Jackson*, fifty-nine-feet.) *Missouri* was 183-feet overall, but there is uncertainty about the designed length of *Jackson*: it may have also been 183-feet, but a mid-construction re-design clouds the issue. The draft of the ship was not to exceed six-feet.[236]

Work on the hull moved ahead steadily and McLaughlin reported on December 26 that he was only awaiting the rise of the river to send her into the water. Unfortunately the rise was precipitous – one report said it rose ten feet on the last night of the year – and there was no time to knock out her supports and allow the hull to be free. The freshet actually raised her stern, but did not dislodge the heavy vessel. Within twenty-four hours McLaughlin had engaged a riverboat to tow her off, but to no avail. The next day the river began to recede, and conditions did not improve through January.[237]

The failure to launch attracted attention from higher up: Constructor Porter visited late in the month and recommended against launching at all, if the vessel was likely to exceed the requisite six feet draft. The sudden rise had wetted her stern to five-feet nine-inches, and that without armor, guns, engines, coal, etc. It was obvious that some major design change would be necessary if the ironclad was to meet the navy's requirements.[238]

Holcombe

Launch of the Jackson, December 22, 1864. Construction took some two years, with significant delays resulting from the major design changes. The vessel was never in service and portions of her hull are preserved today at the National Civil War Naval Museum in Columbus, Georgia. Naval Historical Center

Porter's recommendation reached Secretary Mallory, and shortly thereafter McLaughlin himself arrived at Richmond to discuss the situation. McLaughlin's solution to reduce the draft of the vessel was not a simple one. He proposed to "carry out the floor to the sternpost, lengthen the vessel thirty feet and substitute two eight-foot propellers instead of the center wheel." The changes, he said, would keep the vessel on the stocks "for several months." Porter, McLaughlin wrote, had agreed to these ideas with the additional requirement that the casemate be shortened by fifty-four-feet (Though, of course, a part of this fifty-four feet would have been removed in any event, when the casemate sides adjacent to the wheel's recess were eliminated.). The arduous task of removing a portion of the solidly built casemate began in mid-March 1864.[239]

Work on the vessel would drag on for another year, accompanied by public criticism. A local newspaper article derided the "slantin dicular" hull still "propped up on legs" on the banks of the Chattahoochee and called it a "great failure."[240] Indeed, it was obvious that there was little except the central section of the hull and casemate that was not affected by the changes.

The change from stern wheel to screw propulsion also necessitated moving the machinery. Originally the cylinders were to be above deck level, in line with the paddle wheel axis. As modified, the cylinders were necessarily below the deck, on a level with the two propeller shafts.

However, since the original engines had not yet been installed when the new design was formulated, it was not necessary to remove the machinery and re-locate it. The engines were being installed late in April 1864.[241]

McLaughlin reported that the newly reconfigured shield was completed and being planked in late July. The work, however, was being delayed somewhat by Union General Sherman's Atlanta campaign, as well as local activities against the Union blockaders on the Appalachicola River. Both of these situations resulted in workers being pulled from the construction site.[242]

Once the new casemate was framed and planked, the iron armoring began, at which point

the perennial shortage of iron seriously slowed the work. Lt. George W. Gift wrote that, "to maintain 6½ ft. draft we decided to only plate [the] forward shield and probably on the sides in the wake of the broadside guns and let her go at that." One can detect a level of frustration in that final phrase. The "make do" attitude continued as Gift requested that the guns be shipped, noting that if the 6.4-inch rifles were not available, "I will mount the 9-in. from the Chattahoochee & pivot it side to side."[243]

The *Jackson* was successfully launched on December 22, 1864. Her draft forward was 5.4-feet and aft, 4.4-feet. McLaughlin then moved her bunkers, magazine, and shell rooms farther aft "to

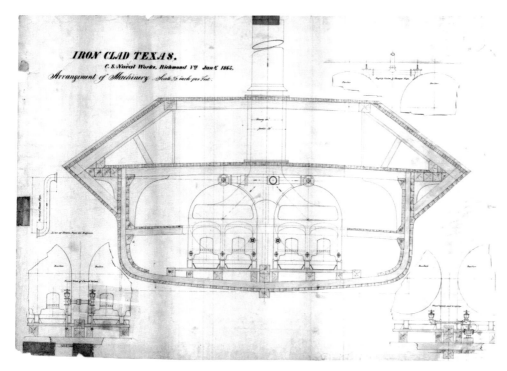

even her out." The local paper noted that she was, "one of the snuggest and most compact, and securely built craft yet afloat upon our waters."[244]

The ironclad at this point had no guns aboard. She had been designed for six: five of them 6.4-inch rifles and one seven-inch rifle. The latter was to be mounted forward and four of the others in broadside. As late as December 22, McLaughlin was unsure whether she could carry them and maintain the required draft. [245]

Work would continue on the vessel until nearly the day the city of Columbus fell into Union hands, and correspondence indicates some of her guns had been shipped from Selma and had arrived. As part of a report, a Union cavalry officer surveyed the Columbus navy yard facility

and described the captured *Jackson*. First, after noting that he was not a navy officer, the writer noted the vessel's length to be 250-feet, breadth, forty-five feet, draft, 6½- to seven-feet. A solid oak ram extended fifteen-feet at her bow. The engine was two thirty-six-inch by thirty-six-inch cylinders and four boilers, with two 7½-foot propellers. The "gunroom" measured twenty by forty feet, with nine feet of headroom, and had ten gunports. The armor plating curved over the knuckle and extended below the waterline. He did not elaborate on the extent of the armor plating or thickness of the wooden backing. Furthermore, the general accuracy of this description is doubtful. His "gunroom" was vastly undersized with modern reconstruction indicating

the gundeck was about eighty-feet long at its base and about sixty feet at the top. The actual width may have been somewhat over forty feet, if one factors in the thickness of the casemate sides. In any event apparently four of her guns were in place when she was captured. Both the cavalryman's overall length and breadth figures are not accurate either, and may have been simple estimates. Whether the engine dimensions were based on actual measurements or estimates is also not known. Contemporary confirmation of this description was shortly afterwards rendered impossible, when the navy yard and its contents were burned by the Union forces, including the ram *Jackson*.[246]

However, the burning hulk drifted down river and eventually sank thirty-miles south of the city. The ironclad's remains, consisting of her bottom and portions of her bilges, were raised in 1961 and have been preserved at the National Civil War Naval Museum at Columbus.[247]

Columbia

The fourth ironclad constructed in Charleston, South Carolina, was built by F.M. Jones, with iron armor by Eason, also of Charleston. The contract was dated October 16, 1862, but the hull was not laid down until January 1863. Her plan was by Porter and the basic hull was 189-feet between perpendiculars and a thirty-four-foot

Ironclad steamer Columbia plan made by her captors. The vessel never saw service but was considered one of the most powerful Confederate ironclads. Note that this plan shows significant deadrise and slack bilges – visibly very different from the hull form shown in the Texas and Columbia cross sections. It is possible that this plan was made while the vessel was afloat, as opposed to a definitive plan made in the dock with her lines taken off. National Archives

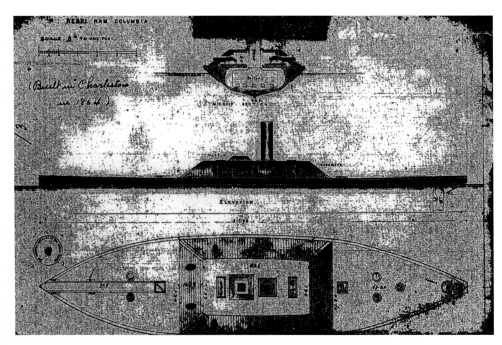

beam (moulded). The ironclads *Texas* and *Tennessee* also were built to this general hull configuration.[248]

Progress on the vessel was such that the navy sent a steam engineer to assist in the construction as early as April 1863. Then, in mid-June, boilers were shipped to the site, and instructions were sent from the Confederate ironworks at Columbus on the configuration of the smokestack passage through the top of the casemate. These indications appear to reflect substantive progress, but again, the most damaging delays would come in procuring the iron armor. Consequently, the vessel was not launched until May 10, 1864.[249]

The *Columbia*'s casemate and hull design reflected a modified version of the knuckle seen on the earlier Confederate ironclads. On those vessels, the side of the hull, the main deck and the casemate side met at a single junction point, ending the deck at the "traditional" side of the ship. On the *Columbia,* the side edge of the deck extended beyond the hull side by at least three feet and there met the lower edge of the casemate. This configuration added much needed transverse deck space, with obvious benefits for managing large weapons. The ironclads *Milledgeville* and *Texas* also exhibited this design feature.[250]

As with most of the later ironclads, *Columbia*'s casemate was shortened significantly in comparison to Porter's original plans (and was annotated as

such on the building plan). The 110-foot-plus "citadel" was shortened to less than seventy-five-feet. The weight saved was applied to increasing her armor to a full six inches thick using three two-inch layers. More importantly, though, the old and the new casemate designs each had ten gunports and each mounted six cannon, the wider gundeck allowed two forward and two aft-facing guns. There was now a gun at each corner, each firing through a side and an end port; plus two guns firing through the center broadside ports. The new knuckle configuration was apparently developed some time after Porter drew his original plans, as the "old" plan scales out to about a forty-five-foot breadth, whereas the dimension reported after the war was 51½-feet.[251]

The ship was powered by two non-condensing, high-pressure cylinders, with thirty-six-inch

diameter cylinders and a twenty-four-inch stroke, driving a single ten-foot eight-inch, three-bladed propeller, and built by the navy ironworks at Columbus, Georgia. There were five boilers, each twenty-feet long with five flues each. The vessel was 216-feet overall and had a depth of hold measuring thirteen-feet; her draft, loaded, was thirteen-feet six-inches.[252]

She was described as the most powerful ironclad ram built by the Confederacy, arguably second only to the *Tennessee*. Though both had six guns mounted, the *Columbia*'s six-inch armor was not limited to the end of the casemate, as was that of the *Tennessee*. It also appears that the Charleston ironclad was powered by much better engines.

For the South, *Columbia* was too little and too late and her career was stillborn. She struck

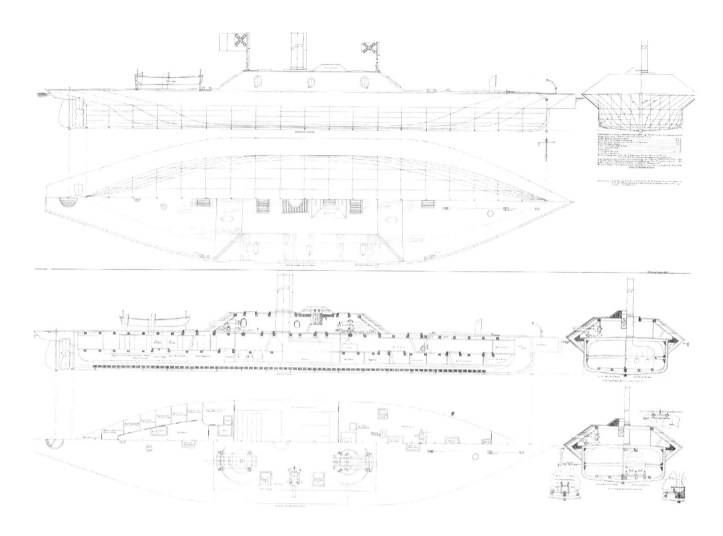

Modern plans of Columbia and Texas, showing cross sections of each, reflecting both single and twin-screw propulsion. The plan does not show the shorter Texas casemate. Smithsonian Institution

a sunken wreck near Fort Moultrie and grounded fast. Her guns and some of her armor were removed in attempts to re-float her, but she remained immobile. The vessel was found in place after the city was evacuated. The U.S. Navy refloated the ironclad and she steamed under her own power to Norfolk. She was sold for scrap in 1867.[253]

Texas

When Richmond fell in April 1865, there was one named, incomplete ironclad in the water at the Rocketts yard. This was the *Texas*, which had been laid down sometime in early-1863 and launched late in 1864. Porter's 189-foot plan was her starting point, making her a sister to the

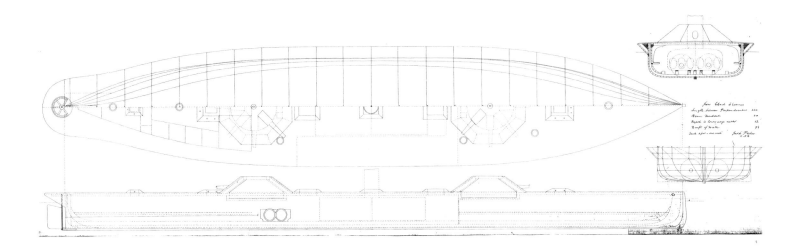

Unbuilt ironclad at Wilmington. The two turrets, or "citadels," were non-rotating casemates with the guns mounted on pivot rails and firing through fixed gunports. Note the twin-screw propulsion. At 225-feet in length, the vessel would have been similar in size to the Union twin-turret Onondaga. This vessel was never completed. National Archives via Maryland Silver Co.

Columbia and a near sister to the *Tennessee*.[254] Most of the information on the incomplete ironclad is from Union reports after the capture of the yard.

The hull was 217-feet overall and forty-eight-feet six-inches wide; depth of hold, thirty-feet. The casemate was of the improved knuckle design and was even shorter than that of the *Columbia*, at about sixty feet on the gundeck, designed to mount four guns. Six-inches of plating was planned as well as twin-screw propulsion (*Columbia* had a single screw).[255]

The incomplete state of the vessel is reflected in the fact that her engines and boilers were found, uninstalled, at the yard by the Federal forces. These were described as horizontal, direct acting, condensing cylinders, measuring twenty-six-inches in diameter by twenty-inch stroke, with steam supplied by two return flue boilers. These were unusual engines, first because they were condensing engines that were more common to oceangoing vessels than river steamers. Furthermore, there were four cylinders, with a pair operating each propeller. It was said that these engines were taken from the twin-screw blockade runner *Kate* that had run aground in 1863, and whose machinery had been removed.[256]

Though the ironclad was described as "one of the best and most valuable" hulls built by the Confederate navy, the *Texas* was never operated as a U.S. Navy vessel. After being towed to Norfolk, she was drydocked and her bottom sheathed. After a total of some $12,000 was spent on her – probably not enough to install her machinery and complete the vessel – she

was sold for scrap in October 1867, never having left Norfolk.[257]

Unbuilt Proposed Ironclads

In the North, the turreted ironclad was nearly the rule, and most of the coastal monitors were also iron-hulled. Unlike the states in rebellion, there was no shortage of iron or of the technology to apply it to naval uses. As has been seen, the Confederacy's most critical lack in ironclad construction was the iron itself. Another factor in ironclad design was the preponderance of operations on the southern rivers, where the capability of end-on fire was at a premium in narrow waters, hence the rotating turret was an asset in this environment. Towards the end of the conflict there appeared three Confederate ironclad designs all of which were significant departures from the "standard" Confederate casemate configuration.

In the fall of 1864, Secretary Mallory reported that there was "on the stocks" at Richmond, an ironclad with a short citadel and mounting only one gun. The vessel's dimensions were 220-feet by twenty-seven-feet with an eleven-foot six-inch depth of hold. This long, narrow vessel was of very light draft and was intended for river operations. Its most unusual feature was the vessel's ends "being both alike." She was powered by four engines and four propellers, two per end. With two identical rams, she could ram in "either direction." This may in actuality have been the vessel recommended earlier in the year by a congressionally mandated board, instituted to report on "harbor defense vessels." The board had presented a design for such a double-ended ironclad but with two octagonal casemates ("citadels") each with a single gun. In September, Mallory wrote James D. Bulloch, in Europe, directing him to have engines built for two of these vessels, and, when completed, shipped to the Confederacy via blockade runners. This idea may have been inspired by the Union navy's paddle wheel "double-enders" which were exceedingly useful in river operations. A key

difference would have been in paddle wheel versus screw propulsion: the side-paddle wheels could simply reverse directions without detriment to speed or maneuverability. On a screw vessel, the two propellers not in use would create immense drag through the water. The single gun per casemate configuration would also have been awkward. Without the use of a turret, the guns' field of fire would be limited by the number of gunports in the casemate.[258] Two of these vessels were supposedly begun at Wilmington and Richmond. The former may have been a more conventional (single ended) vessel with two citadels (see below). A third was authorized for Charleston but not begun. None were completed.[259]

A plan exists for an ironclad that was "burned at Wilmington." It is a Porter design, with two octagonal "citadels," each pierced to allow a single gun to fire through seven gunports: forward, on the quarters, and on each broadside. The dimensions were 224-feet between perpendiculars, thirty-four-foot moulded beam, and twelve-foot depth of hold. Its extreme breadth was over forty-

two-feet across the main deck. It was designed to draw 9½-feet and be capable of "going in and out of the harbor" at all times, and had two-cylinder machinery, four boilers, and two eight-foot screws. The machinery was said to have been built at the Columbus, Georgia, works and ready to be placed in the vessel, but it is unclear how much progress had been made on this ironclad when the city fell to Union forces in February 1865.

The only known Confederate navy assay on a rotating turret vessel was a proposal by Chief Engineer James H. Warner in early 1865. He posited a light draft (six-feet) vessel 175-feet in length by a forty-five-foot beam, and nine-foot depth of hold. The "tower" was to be twenty-one-feet in diameter and mount two eleven-inch guns. The turret would have 11½-inches of plating plus fourteen-inches of wood protection. Warner indicated it could be built in ten months. It is worth noting that in major dimensions as well as armament, this would have been very nearly the same as Ericsson's original *Monitor*. At this stage of the war, this was a wildly impossible project, and nothing came of it.[260]

THE COMMERCE RAIDERS AND CRUISERS

The four aspects of the Confederate Navy's Civil War operations that caught the public imagination, for good or ill, both north and south, were the ironclads, the blockade runners, the submarines and torpedo boats, and the commerce raiders. All were the avenues of resistance the Confederacy selected as substitutes for a conventional battlefleet that they did not have the time or resources to build.

The concept of striking against Union maritime commerce surfaced as early as April 17, 1861, in the form of privateering, as authorized by President Jefferson Davis on that date. Of course, privateering involved no commitment of government funds or resources, and represented no organized effort by the Confederate navy department. However, on the same day, Raphael Semmes received his orders directing him to proceed to New Orleans to command the first of the commerce raiders, the steamer *Sumter*.[261] This vessel was obtained sometime in April by a committee detailed to purchase or build suitable vessels for the navy in New Orleans. Two days later, President Lincoln declared the blockade of the Southern coast.

The blockade was considered an attack on Southern commerce and resulted in a flurry of activity on the part of Secretary Mallory, who had been disappointed to learn how few suitable hulls were available domestically. By May 9, 1861, he had already dispatched James D.

Bulloch to England with authorization to "purchase six steam propellers," each provisioned for six months at sea.[262] These vessels, as well as the *Sumter*, were intended to drive the North's merchant marine from the sea, strike a blow at Northern industry, and thus decrease political support for the war, and divert Union naval forces from the blockade. Mallory may well have harkened back to the massive impact the American navy had on the British during the War of 1812, as inspiration for this strategy.

In any event, James D. Bulloch arrived in Liverpool in early-June and immediately set out to create the first of the foreign-built Confederate raiders.

In the end, the Confederate commerce raiders numbered eleven: *Alabama*, *Shenandoah*, *Florida*, *Tallahassee*, *Georgia*, *Chickamauga*, *Nashville*, *Retribution*, *Sumter*, *Sallie* and *Boston*. These vessels were named in the post-war "Alabama Claims" proceedings and were responsible for $17,900,633 in claims for ships and cargoes. All but $4-million of this was accumulated by *Alabama* and *Shenandoah*.[263] These depredations had a massive impact on the American merchant marine, by the actual losses in vessels and cargoes, but, more importantly in the long term, the movement of American sea commerce to foreign vessels.

However, it is obvious that Mallory's strategy had no significant impact on the war itself. Merchant shippers merely moved their cargoes

CSS cruiser Sumter was the first Confederate naval command of Raphael Semmes. The former merchant steamer Habana was converted at New Orleans by adding crew accommodations and five guns. Though slow and inefficient under sail, the cruiser was responsible for eighteen captures of Union merchant vessels. Naval Historical Center

to foreign vessels and trade continued, nearly unabated. Furthermore, the number of Union naval vessels re-directed to pursue the commerce raiders was not significant enough to hamper the major operations of the navy against the Confederacy. The only time a major effort was made to snare Confederate cruisers was in late-1864, when both the *Tallahassee* and *Chickamauga* appeared off the U.S. coast. In this instance, many of the hastily prepared pursuit flotilla were local vessels, including tugs, hired for the occasion.

Sumter

In March, 1861, the Confederate navy department formed a committee to purchase or build naval vessels at New Orleans. Commander Lawrence Rousseau, Commander Eben Farrand and Lt. Robert Chapman proceeded to survey the waterfront for any vessels they considered adaptable to naval service, preferably without incurring major expenses for conversion. The committee's report, forwarded to Secretary Mallory, was discouraging. All the vessels were found to have significant defects. However, Mallory passed the list on to Raphael Semmes, whose attention was drawn to a "small propeller steamer" which he suggested might be a good candidate for an ocean-going commerce raider. Mallory acceded to the suggestion and telegraphed the committee with instructions to obtain the vessel.[264]

The vessel in question was the merchant passenger steamer *Habana,* belonging James B. McConnell's steamship line operating between New Orleans and Havana. The vessel was a wooden hulled screw steamer built in Philadelphia by Byerly & Lynn and launched on May 18, 1859, with machinery by Reaney, Neafie & Company. *Habana* typically ran the New Orleans to Havana route in fifty-five hours.[265]

She was a relatively small steamer, 152.6-feet long and 27.7-feet broad, and 12.5-feet depth of hold, with a draft of ten-feet, and 499 54/95 registered tons. The iron and copper-fastened oak hull had one deck, a round stern, and scroll head. One of her steam engineers suggested she was "light of frame." Her original registration indicates there were two masts, but all existing illustrations show her with three. Illustrations also show her with a barque rig, whereas the only photo of her shows a square yard on the foremast only. The latter picture is thought to be later in

the war when she was being converted to the blockade runner *Gibraltar.*[266] A less substantial barquentine rig would have been appropriate for blockade running.

The vessel's engine was a single cylinder, fifty-inches in diameter with a thirty-three-inch stroke. This was a condensing, direct acting installation, arranged vertically, with the cylinder mounted directly over the propeller shaft. There were two boilers, a single funnel that could be lowered, and a ten-foot diameter bronze screw that could be uncoupled from the engine but not hoisted from the water. On trials the vessel made 14mph.[267]

The vessel had been rejected by the naval committee for two reasons: she carried only sufficient fuel for five days steaming and she had insufficient room to berth a naval crew. When Semmes arrived in New Orleans on April 22nd,

Sumter after being sold out of Confederate naval service, and in the process of conversion to the blockade runner Gibraltar. Henry E. Huntington Library and Art Gallery

he immediately began to rectify these defects and convert her for the service intended.

To begin with she was, "full of upper cabins, and other top-hamper, furniture and crockery." But Semmes was pleased with her, "general appearance. Her lines were easy and graceful, and she had a sort of saucy air about her." In the next six weeks the ship would be transformed into a vessel of war, with Semmes the general contractor, doing the work that, under other circumstances, would have been done at a navy yard. Here, everything had to be improvised, all the plans and drawings made to suit, and local skilled workers located and hired for the occasion.

And the work to be done was substantial. After the superfluous top hamper and passenger accommodations were removed, the main deck was strengthened with heavy beams to support the weight and recoil shock of naval guns. Second, below the main deck, a berth deck was built for the crew. Given her twelve-foot depth in her hold, there would have been adequate room to build a deck with sufficient headroom for the men,

probably in the fore part of the hull. Third, Semmes dealt with the vulnerability of the vertical engine configuration that placed the cylinder very high in the hull, some of it above the waterline. Semmes had a wood and iron-bar protective "system" built around these un-protected but vital engine parts. The final hull work consisted of installing water tanks for a three month's supply, and rearranging the cabin area to house the ship's officers, and presumably, building an ammunition and shell room. Her hull was painted black.

Topside, the main work was to give her sufficient sail power for long cruises at sea – as opposed to the merchant role of relatively short passages between fixed points. Thus the two-mast configuration was scrapped in favor of three masts, with square sails on the fore and main.

Finally, Semmes provided the necessities for the crew and operations: hammocks, bedding, a new suit of sails, ship's boats and, of course, the guns. There were five: four light thirty-two-pounder smoothbores and one eight-inch, sixty-eight-pounder shell gun. The latter was placed

amidships with pivot rails inset on the deck to enable use of the gun on either broadside. This weapon weighed over three tons and required a gun crew of seventeen men. Each broadside gun was, according to regulations, manned by seven men. The total number in the crew was ninety-two men – including twenty marines – and twenty-one officers.[268]

Semmes placed the ship, now named *Sumter*, in commission on June 3, 1861. In the ensuing two weeks, Semmes tried the ship on the river and exposed some of her defects. Her lack of speed was notable: she could do little more than nine-knots. And, under sail alone she was hampered by the drag of her propeller, which had no mechanism for hoisting. Finally, no more than eight days' supply of coal could be stored in her bunkers. Hence, the propeller drag would be an evil that would harm her on extended cruises.[269]

The career of the *Sumter* was brief, from June 30, 1861 to January 18, 1862. Under Semmes' command the *Sumter* captured eighteen vessels and burned seven of them, setting the stage for the more dangerous cruisers, *Florida*, *Alabama* and *Shenandoah* – the second of which would also be under Semmes' command.

Semmes' own autobiography makes a good source from which the vessel's effectiveness can be judged. The first significant event was the escape of the little cruiser through the blockade at New Orleans. At first, the scene looked hopeless, the steam sloop *Brooklyn* was less than eight-miles away and coming fast and she was reputed to be a swift ship. Worse, the sudden call for steam resulted in *Sumter*'s boilers foaming, inhibiting the buildup of steam. Semmes at this point ordered his confidential papers readied to be thrown overboard in the event of capture. However, the foaming soon ceased and a few more turns were gotten out of her, probably to just over 9½-knots, sufficient to outdistance *Brooklyn*, which in any event had an overrated reputation for speed.

The end of *Sumter*'s first week at sea brought home her major problem: she had less than a day's fuel remaining. Semmes realized whatever strategy he would adopt for this cruise would be one where he would not be forced to make a weekly stop for coaling. He would also have to take into consideration her performance under sail alone. He then found that when he relied on sail, *Sumter* moved with "more grace than speed" at a sedate four-knots.

In mid-August, Semmes was able to make an attempt to alleviate part of this problem: he had two of the larger water tanks removed from the hull and rearranged the appropriate bulkheads to enlarge the coalbunkers. *Sumter* now could steam for twelve days in succession. Improvement though this was, Semmes wrote: "Still the *Sumter* remains fundamentally defective as a cruiser, in her inability to lift her screw."

Semmes had sailed *Sumter* southward with the intention to work south of Cape St. Roque, the easternmost point of South America. However, the ship's inadequacies resulted in a different plan. Strong tradewinds south of the cape would most likely make any attempted capture into a chase scenario, which *Sumter* would probably lose by dint of her lack of speed or, in the long run, her lack of coal. Semmes, instead opted to cross the Atlantic in the belt of calm at about five degrees north latitude. Here he could rely on sail. In such weather, he wrote: "I could lie in wait for my prey, under sail, and if surprise and stratagem did not effect my purposes. I could … get up steam … and capture without the expenditure of much fuel."

Semmes shortly thereafter made one capture, then moved northward, eventually to Martinique. From there he set out eastward, making the comment that he hoped, in Europe, to "exchange the *Sumter* for a better ship."

On the crossing *Sumter* met heavy weather, which did not increase Semmes' respect for the vessel: "I had no confidence in her strength. Her upper works, in particular, were very defective. Her "bends, above the main deck were composed of light pine stanchions and inch plank." Indeed one heavy sea stove in the starboard bow port.

Adding to the misery was a substantial leak which, by the time they approached the European coast, had the pumps operating continuously. The *Sumter* put in at Cadiz "in a crippled condition." In the dock it was found that the propeller sleeve, where the propeller shaft passed through the sternpost, had worn through. A temporary fix was made, but her boilers were also in poor condition by this time. Semmes laid up the ship at Gibraltar on January 18, 1862.

Semmes had a few final thoughts on the *Sumter*. On the positive side, she was, "buoyant, active and dry as a duck." On the other hand, she was an inefficient ship, "always anchored, as it were … by her propeller." He felt that, "a fast ship, propelled entirely by sail power, would have been better."[270]

The Confederacy was not finished with the ship, however. Though the vessel was sold, she was later re-acquired and renamed *Gibraltar*. Under this guise the ship ran the blockade into the South at least twice.

Florida

In May, 1861, after President Lincoln declared the blockade of the Southern coast, Secretary Mallory reluctantly acknowledged that there were few ships available domestically for conversion to naval uses. In direct consequence, the Secretary dispatched James D. Bulloch to England to obtain what could not be had at home. Bulloch, a Georgian, former U.S. naval officer, and merchant vessel captain, arrived at Liverpool on June 4, 1861 and immediately set out to contract with British shipbuilders for oceangoing, steam vessels capable of preying on Union merchant shipping.[271]

Bulloch's first item on his agenda was to contact Charles K. Prioleau, Liverpool agent for the firm of Fraser, Trenholm & Co., the unofficial Confederate financial agency in Europe. There he learned that funds for his proposed purchases had yet to arrive, but that the firm would take interim responsibility for any expenses he accrued. Next, Bulloch entrained to London to consult with the Confederate commissioners William Yancey and Dudley Mann and inform them of his intentions.[272]

Bulloch then returned to Liverpool, one of the hubs of the British shipbuilding industry, to select builders for the proposed vessels. It appears, from this brief timeline, that the choice of builders may have been already in place by some previous arrangement. That is, Bulloch visited, discussed, and planned the vessel which became the *Florida*, and agreed to a contract with William C. Miller & Sons of Liverpool, sometime between returning to that city around the middle of June and the end of that month, when actual construction began.[273]

Bulloch had precise ideas for the ships he had in mind: the *Florida* first as well as the follow-on cruisers throughout the war. Extended cruising on the open ocean would be the norm. This would maximize the impact the cruisers would have on enemy commerce, and, by the same token, reduce to a minimum stops for re-fueling and re-victualing. Furthermore, infrequent port calls were imposed by stringent "Admiralty rules," which specifically restricted belligerents from visiting the ports of any neutral nation or its colonies more than once every ninety days. This limitation was even more onerous in that the Confederate cruisers would not have the luxury of calling at the seaports on the Southern coast – or at least could not do so without risking total loss at the hands of the Union blockading squadrons.

Extended sea cruising imposed very specific characteristics on the proposed vessels. First, Bulloch insisted on wooden hulls. Though iron was quickly replacing wood in shipbuilding, and in fact was the cheaper material, wooden hulls were more easily repaired than iron. Such work could be accomplished in ports where there were minimal shipfitting and building facilities.

More obvious criteria included a hull strong enough for the open ocean and a considerable capacity for coal, ordnance stores, and victuals. Added to this was the need for a substantial sailing rig capable of propelling the vessel in any circumstance which weather and steam power, or lack of it, imposed.

Finally, Bulloch expected a turn of speed, whether under sail or steam, or both. This necessitated a screw propeller that could be hoisted out of the water to eliminate its drag when sail power was in use.[274] Semmes' experience with the non-hoisting screw of the *Sumter* demonstrated the point perfectly.

At William C. Miller and company, Bulloch found what he required. The firm had a long-standing reputation and its senior member had been a Royal Navy constructor. Thus, they were acquainted with building vessels with large crews and with decks designed to support naval ordnance. Most recently they had built two Philomel-class gun vessels for the Royal Navy. These were *Penguin* and *Steady*, launched in 1860. These were 145-feet long on the gundeck by a twenty-five foot beam, each mounting a single, sixty-eight-pounder, pivot gun and four smaller broadside guns. They were wooden-hulled, barque-rigged, and driven by a single screw.[275]

Bulloch, in his book on his wartime operations in Europe, written in 1883, described the design process as follows: "Mr. W.C. Miller had a scale drawing of one of her Majesty's gunboats, which we adopted as a base to start from." Modifications to this design included lengthening the hull at the mid-ship section and flattening the floors; these to increase her capacity and add to her speed. To enable sailing efficiently when close-hauled or with the wind on the beam, the rig was substantially enlarged.[276]

The product of this collaboration would become the cruiser *Florida*, but in the interim, before coming under the Confederate flag, she was named *Oreto*, ostensibly being built for Italian owners to be sold to the Italian government. Of course, this was a fiction – one among many – employed by Bulloch to avoid scrutiny by British authorities. A second stratagem was to avoid any outward evidence that the vessel was to be a war vessel: gun ports were not provided, pivot rails were not built into the decks, and munitions were not placed aboard. Any evidence of warlike intent would have been sufficient pretext for seizure by British authorities as a violation of neutrality conventions.[277]

It is interesting to note that James D. Bulloch, a private citizen and foreign national was able to contract for a major ocean going vessel, and see its construction begin within the space of three weeks – all with no actual funds changing hands. The Fraser, Trenholm firm had no doubt paved the way for the transaction long before hand.

The ship itself, laid down at Toxteth dock, was to be a steam sloop of about 700 displacement tons (or 410 Gross Registered Tons), with a coppered, wooden hull. Her length was 191-feet overall (184-feet six-inches between perpendiculars), twenty-seven-foot two-inch beam, and fourteen-foot depth of hold to the bottom of the gundeck, with an expected draft of twelve feet. Her barque rig was proportioned for sailing close to the wind, with particularly tall lower masts, giving her large fore and aft sails on all three sticks. Her standing rigging was wire.

Her engines were two horizontal cylinders built by the firm of Fawcett, Preston, & Co., also of Liverpool. These were forty-two-inch stroke, by twenty-four-inch diameter units operating directly on the screw shaft, and producing 200hp. The screw itself was two-bladed, with a mechanism to hoist it out of the water into a recessed opening at the stern. The crew provided the power to raise the screw, using heavy line and a pulley arrangement. There were two elliptical boilers and two funnels. The latter were telescopic and could be lowered to rail level if necessary to give clearance for the main sail, or give the appearance of a sailing ship. Her battery was to be two seven-inch rifled guns on pivot rails and six six-inch rifles on broadside carriages. Rather than traditional gun ports, she would have hinged double ports, opening rather like gates. The battery was not mounted, nor were the gunports cut into the bulwarks until the vessel departed from British waters.[278]

Though Bulloch did not specify the name or class of the scale drawing of the gunboat used as the basis for the *Florida* design, there are a couple possibilities. If the plan had been of the Philomel-class ships built earlier by Miller, then it is obvious that the plan was lengthened by around forty-feet (145-feet to 184-feet) and widened by two-feet, and the depth increased from thirteen to fourteen-feet. The armament would have been enlarged from a single pivot gun and four broadside guns to two pivots and six in broadside.[279] These were major alterations and the entire hull would have to been re-designed. Because of the added breadth, very few of the original design's frames could have been utilized.

Another intriguing possibility for the origin of the *Florida*'s design is possibly in the Royal Navy's Cormorant-class gunboats, of this same era. These were barque-rigged, 185-feet on the gundeck and twenty-eight-feet four-inches wide, with a fourteen-foot hold, mounting two large

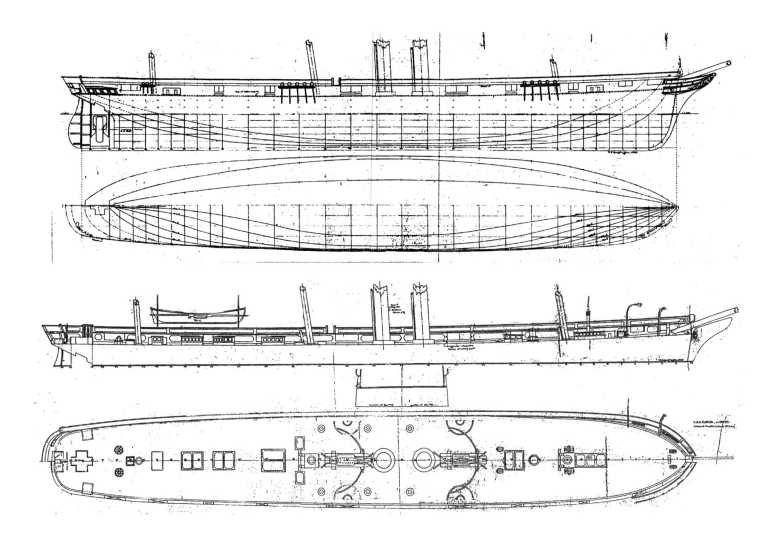

Hull lines, inboard, and deck plan of the CSS Florida, James D. Bulloch's first British built commerce raider. Note the sharp forward lines, predicting a fast hull. Not shown are the pivot rails for a gun aft of the mizzenmast. "Documentation of CSS Florida and USS Cumberland"

pivot guns and two rifles in broadside. Many of these vessels had two funnels and similar sized 200hp machinery.[280] The similarity in dimensions as well as general arrangements to those of the *Florida* is striking, but raises questions about Bulloch's narration of the modifications made to the original Miller plan.

Construction of the vessel was uneventful, with the hull being launched in January 1862, but the atmosphere of intrigue was not. Though Bulloch was exceedingly scrupulous about adhering to the letter of the British neutrality statutes, Union consular and diplomatic officials were highly suspicious. Their agents eventually investigated her "Italian" identity, soon learning that no such vessel was being built for that nation. Pressure was building to have her seized as being in violation of the officially neutral stance of the British government. However, before this could be implemented, *Oreto* was at sea on an ostensible "trial trip," departing on March 22, 1862. This fiction was supported by the presence of several visitors, including ladies, on board. When all save one of the passengers later returned to shore via small boats and the pilot vessel, the ruse was revealed and *Oreto* was well en route to Nassau. The final "passenger" was in fact Bulloch's agent tasked with taking delivery of the ship for the Confederate Navy.[281]

The passage to Nassau is notable for the report made by Bulloch's "passenger" who was Master John Low, who was slated to turn the vessel over to Commander John Newland Maffitt while at sea. The vessel, he wrote, did an average of 9½-knots, steaming, and under sail, "with the wind abeam or quarterly, so that the fore and aft canvas will draw, 12-knots." More importantly, Low wrote what he had seen her do, specifically: "Under steam … 10½-knots." With a quartering breeze so they could carry maintop gallant, studding sail, 13½-knots. He deemed her a strong vessel, "when pitching, you could not see her work in the least."[282]

The career of the *Florida* is well known, but generally is in the shadow of the *Alabama*. The latter captured sixty-four vessels – *Florida*, thirty-eight – not including those taken by *Florida*'s "protégés" *Clarence* and *Tacony*. Much of the difference in numbers of vessels taken was due to the lengthy periods *Florida* was out of commission. The following summary emphasizes events that reflect the effectiveness of the vessel, rather than a blow-by-blow narrative of captures and voyages.

Though the *Florida* departed from England in March 1862, the vessel did not make its first capture until January 1863. In the interim, she was first at Nassau, where a significant number of her crew, on learning the true nature of the ship and her mission,

took permanent leave. Then yellow fever struck the remaining crew, including Commander Maffitt. Further hindrances came in the form of three seizures by British colonial and naval authorities. Again, her unarmed condition was the factor that allowed her release. Her guns were finally off loaded from the chartered schooner *Prince Albert* in August, at Green Cay, in the Bahamas. On August 17, 1862, *Oreto* was finally commissioned as a Confederate vessel and her name was officially changed to *Florida*.

Having her guns on board was not, however, equivalent to being a viable warship. Through some oversight, the equipment necessary to work the guns had not been available from the *Prince Albert*. These were rammers, sponges, sights, et cetera, so *Florida* was still essentially defenseless. And yellow fever continued to decimate the crew. At the time the guns were loaded, there were a total of about thirty men, including officers, on board. Her total complement was to be 146.

Maffitt steamed to Cardenas, then Havana, Cuba, intent on finding more crew, as well as obtaining the needed ordnance equipment. At Cardenas, six of his men died, and many of the sick were taken to the local hospital, but about twelve new recruits signed on. Spanish colonial authorities also refused permission to purchase the ordnance supplies locally.

On the first of September, Maffitt opted to run into a Confederate port, in this instance, Mobile, Alabama.

Maffitt calculated the risk, knowing the number of blockaders in the vicinity. He rejected a night approach due to lack of navigational aids. With no operational weapons and a skeleton crew – probably fewer than three dozen, including officers – he decided that bluff and speed would have to suffice.

Knowing his ship was nearly identical to Royal Navy gunboats, Maffitt banked on Union reluctance to fire on her until the identification was sure. He further clouded the issue by flying the British flag and steaming directly for the nearest blockader, as if to request permission to pass

through. Captain George H. Preble, on the steam sloop *Oneida*, fell for it, allowing the Confederate within eighty yards of his vessel before yawing to avoid collision and firing warning shots. Maffitt did not slow as *Oneida* let off a broadside, including eleven-inch projectiles. These went high, and did no damage. The smaller and slower blockaders *Winona* and *Rachel Seaman* joined the chase and barrage, but Maffitt had taken the advantage from the start. The chase was entirely under steam. When Maffitt ordered sail put on, Union fire sliced through the rigging and prevented sheeting it home, and Maffitt ordered his men below. Maffitt apparently did not expect to come away unscathed, and indeed there were five casualties, one of them dead. The ship's standing rigging, hammock rails and boats were mangled, and a shot had penetrated the coalbunker and berth deck. The action had lasted about twenty minutes, ending when the blockaders approached shallow waters, and *Florida* anchored under the guns of Fort Morgan.[283]

When the news of this debacle reached Washington, Captain Preble was immediately dismissed from the service. He protested and gained a hearing. His defense was that the *Florida* was "built exactly like a British warship," plus the element of surprise and her speed. The chase, however, was clearly one-sided. *Oneida* was operating on one boiler, due to problems with the other. Under the best circumstances, she would make 10½-knots; under these conditions it was said she did little more than six.[284]

Florida's arrival at Mobile, in a damaged condition, led to the next period of enforced idleness. The yellow fever was still present and the men and vessel were under quarantine until the end of September. When repairs began, the delays were attributed to supply problems, in some instances items not available through normal channels had to be fabricated on site. Wire rigging, most of which had been damaged by Union gunnery, was relatively rare in this era and may well have been difficult to find. Transportation

of supplies and parts also proved to be a problem: her draft prevented her docking at Mobile itself, and she remained down the bay, over twenty-five-miles from the town. Lastly, inclement weather hindered progress, particularly of re-rigging the ship.

It was during this period that Buchanan suggested that the vessel be re-painted "lead color" to pass through the blockade. This color was mixed on board, a combination of lampblack and whitewash. Lampblack, in turn was made with litharge (lead oxide) and soot. Being hand-mixed the exact shade would be difficult to document.[285]

The delay in readying *Florida* for sea was irritating to all concerned and led to Mallory's sudden decision to sack Maffitt. Admiral Franklin Buchanan, overall commander at Mobile, intervened and conveyed an independent confirmation of the difficulties of supply and logistical situation, and Maffitt was reinstated.

Maffitt was ready to take the *Florida* to sea on January 10, 1863, for the first time with a complete crew as well as operable guns. Weather conditions and running aground in Mobile Bay further delayed the event, and Maffitt finally took her out in a light mist early on January 17. It had been nearly ten months since *Florida* had first gone to sea.[286]

Maffitt's first task was to avoid the blockaders, particularly the *R.R. Cuyler*, which was reputedly one of the fastest ships in the Union navy. He eluded two of the Union vessels and was pursued for a short time by a third. When the *R.R. Cuyler* came on the scene, Maffitt at first avoided her notice by taking in *Florida*'s sails, shutting down the engines, lowering funnels, and lying low in the heavy swells. Once out of immediate danger, Maffitt put on all steam. But by daylight, *R.R. Cuyler* had her in sight, some five-miles ahead. The chase lasted all day in gale conditions and heavy quartering seas. George F. Emmons, the commander of the pursuer, wrote of "resorting to every expedient" to increase his speed, travelling at 11½- to 12½-knots, sometimes gaining on his quarry. The seas were such that his propeller was at times clean out of the water, and in one instance, came uncoupled from the shaft. Later the Union vessel lost her topsail yard and sail. Emmons later wrote, wryly: "From fancying myself near promotion in the morning, I gradually dwindled down to a court of enquiry at dark." Later Emmons supposed in different conditions and with a cleaner hull and boilers, the outcome would have been different. The vessel was reportedly capable of 14.8-knots. As for the *Florida*, on this first day of her first operational cruise, with a relatively clean bottom, and newly refurbished engines and rig, she ran an exhilarating 14½-knots under steam and sail – the fastest of her career.[287]

This began the *Florida*'s first cruise, which would last until she went into port in France for repairs and refit. This cruise was by far the most profitable for the ship and Maffitt, with twenty-five (of a total of thirty-eight) captures in some seven months at large on the Atlantic.

A few highlights of the cruise stand out, including a second high-speed chase. On February 1, 1863, the Union paddlewheel gunboat *Sonoma* sighted her and hared after, with a full head of steam. The pursuit ran two days, with the Union commander insisting that he had *Florida* "almost under our guns" three times. An engine malfunction slowed *Sonoma* in one of these instances. However, when the winds freshened, *Florida* drew sharply away. This was not surprising. The *Sonoma* was built for river duty and had a minimal rig, and was rated at about 11-knots under steam alone.[288]

On February 12, 1862, after coaling, *Florida* captured the ship *Jacob Bell*. En route from China, the vessel carried 1,380-tons of tea and 10,000 boxes of firecrackers with an estimated value of $1.5-2-million. This was the most valuable prize taken by any Confederate cruiser through the entire war.[289]

It was during this first cruise that Maffitt was able to send out three additional ships to cruise against the enemy. First was the barque *Lapwing*, then the *Clarence* and finally the *Tacony*. The first was equipped with a twelve-pounder howitzer and directed to cruise a short distance from *Florida*, to expand her horizons in search of prizes, and be available with her supply of coal. The *Lapwing* proved to be too slow for this duty and was eventually abandoned.[290]

The brig *Clarence* was captured in May and twenty-three-year old Lieutenant Charles W. Read was detailed as her commander. Read proposed raiding Hampton Roads, but then opted to move northward, capturing six vessels en route. At last he captured the barque *Tacony* and transferred his command to that vessel. While in command of *Tacony* Read captured sixteen vessels. The last of these was the fishing schooner *Archer*, taken off the coast of Maine. Discarding the *Tacony*, Read took the *Archer* directly into Portland harbor at midnight, and boarded and seized the U.S. Revenue Cutter *Caleb Cushing*. The topsail schooner was supposedly well armed, but in actuality carried only one thirty-two-pounder smoothbore and one light twelve-pounder. In the morning, when the Yankee sailors came out in a flotilla to reclaim the revenue cutter, Read found himself with only five projectiles for defense. Expending these, Read fired the *Caleb Cushing*, then surrendered. The revenue cutter then blew up. Thus the first cruise of the *Florida* indirectly netted an additional twenty-two merchant captures, plus one U.S. Revenue Cutter.[291]

Maffitt cruised *Florida* northward and closed in on the U.S. coast, eventually to encounter the U.S. steam ship *Ericsson*, which had been among those chartered to hunt down Confederate raiders. In one of the Confederate cruisers' few offensive actions, Maffitt cleared his decks and made ready to take on the *Ericsson*. The latter would have been easy prey: she was armed with a single twenty-pounder Parrott rifle and two twelve-pounders. After Maffitt's first broadside, the Union vessel's crew panicked and hid behind the bulwarks. A second volley would probably have taken the ship, but a patch of fog intervened. When next seen, *Ericsson* was well on the way back to New York. In ordinary circumstances, Maffitt probably would have given chase, but *Florida*'s most recently acquired coal was exceedingly poor, dampening her speed considerably. An additional damper was the news that the Union navy had sent out several ships in search of *Florida*. Furthermore, the Confederate cruiser was uncomfortably close to New York City. In fact, *Ericsson*'s position when sighted by *Florida* was about 125-miles east of Montauk Point, Long Island.

After taking additional prizes, Maffitt set a course for Bermuda, away from the expected swarm of Union pursuers. *Florida* was now in need of coal as well as repairs. Maffitt hoped to obtain permission to use a government dockyard for the latter, but was refused. However, the colonial government there did afford *Florida* a gun-for-gun salute. This may have been the only instance this honor was given to a Confederate warship.[292]

Admiralty rules prevented Maffitt from taking his ship into another British port for ninety days after leaving Bermuda, so he opted for Brest, France, hoping for a positive reception and use of the naval dockyard. The ship arrived at the port on August 23, 1863, and went into the drydock about two weeks later. Her hull coppering needed attention and the machinery was due for overhaul. Running engines at high speed quickly wore down bearings and resulted in excessive pressure in the boilers, and Maffitt had done his share of fast moving since leaving Mobile. The vessel was in the dock for five weeks then continued the repairs in harbor. It was not until late-January 1864 that she made a trial trip, and even then additional repairs were required. She finally departed from France on February 10, 1864.

Again, *Florida* had an enforced down time. A letter written by one of her engineers the day she went into dock indicates some of the work that was necessary. The engines "thumped" from the shaft being out of line or the "derangement in the outer bearing near the propeller," but their general condition was fair. Any major problems could be taken care of by obtaining parts from Liverpool. The hull was "much strained" and she worked continually in a seaway, spewing out oakum regardless of how well she was caulked. On the hull two sheets of copper were missing and those under her counter were "crumpled." He felt her decks were too light and they continually leaked water below. Her coalbunkers had settled and would need to be re-stayed to maintain their integrity.

The writer's main concern was with the weight of the guns on the deck. Apparently on the *Florida*, the after pivot gun was not mounted immediately behind the aft funnel, as was the usual practice, but was between the mizzen-mast and the propeller hoisting mechanism. This was poor weight distribution and made her "sink too much in a head sea." He suggested moving the pivot gun to the waist, but thought the deck was too weak to allow this. (Later it was suggested that the pivot guns be mounted side by side, amidships, and worked by one crew, but apparently this was also not done, also for the same reason.) Finally, the writer noted that the spars were "tolerably good" and the rigging was serviceable "but not neat."[293]

The work on her hull below the waterline would have been relatively straightforward. This

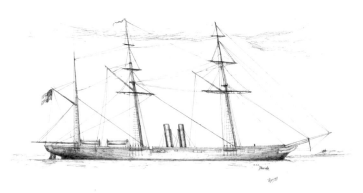

CSS Florida, author's drawing, based on photos, contemporary illustrations and plans. Author

THE LATE OUTRAGE ON THE NEUTRALITY OF BRAZIL.

The cruiser Florida at Bahia harbor, with the Union sloop of war Wachusett in the background at far left. Note the position of the Brazilian warship between the two adversaries. This did not prevent Union commander Napoleon Collins from colliding "accidentally" with the Confederate steamer, and ending the vessel's commerce raiding. Illustrated London News

was done in the first five weeks. Engine and boiler work was more specialized and accounted for some of the remaining time. Part of the work was installing a blower system: forced draft for the furnaces, improving the oxygen flow and efficiency of the burning. Most of the time-consuming work was on the engines. The French mechanics were not familiar with the English machinery and when repairs failed, replacing parts became necessary. The latter resulted in down time while they were shipped from Liverpool.[294]

Another factor in the delay was obtaining a crew. When Maffitt docked the vessel, he discharged fifty-nine of the men to economize expenses during the downtime. Then there was a considerable delay in paying off the discharged sailors, and a very public complaint and petition went around, encouraged by the American consul at Liverpool who also did whatever he could to discourage new recruits for the Confederate vessel. The newly enrolled crew was one of mixed nationalities, and, of course, most of them were unfamiliar with the ship and its machinery. There were also two new commanding officers in the interim: Maffitt left for medical reasons and was replaced by J.N. Barney. Then Barney was determined to be unfit for a long cruise and was in turn replaced by Charles M. Morris.[295]

Morris took the *Florida* on its trial trips in January and was sorely disappointed. The blower system had indeed made it possible to get a few more turns out of the engines. However, the cost was in creating "dangerous vibration," to the extent that high speed was to be used only in emergencies. Overall, the ship was now only capable of eight-knots under steam alone – two-knots slower now than on her first cruise.[296]

Florida's second cruise would run from February to October 1864. She captured thirteen vessels, all but one of which were sailing ships.

The *Electric Spark*, taken on July 10, was a screw steamer. She was one of four vessels taken on the same day, all within thirty-five-miles of Maryland's eastern shore.

Subsequently, Morris turned east, then south. For six weeks they cruised without making a capture, as much of the commerce in the area was under foreign (non-U.S.) flags. The *Southern Rights* was seized and bonded on August 22, and the *Mandamis* on September 26, 1864. The long period of idleness for the crew contributed to significant unrest and nearly a mutiny, with eight men brought up on charges, and three convicted. At this point, Morris determined to make for a nearby port and allow liberty for the crew.[297]

Florida arrived at Bahia, Brazil on October 4, 1864. Unfortunately, the U.S. steam sloop *Wachusett* had arrived a week before, and was still in the harbor. Brazilian authorities were aware of the latent danger in the situation and attempted to prevent any confrontation in their waters. However, Union navy Commander Napoleon Collins, abetted by the local U.S. consul, "accidentally" rammed his vessel into the *Florida*, forced her surrender and towed her out to sea. Brazilian shore batteries lodged an ineffectual protest. The *Florida* was then taken to U.S. waters and sank under somewhat murky circumstances at Hampton Roads. Eventually, the United States apologized to Brazil for the violation of her neutrality. Collins was court martialed and convicted, however, a few months later the conviction was overturned by Secretary of the Navy Gideon Welles. Had the *Florida* still been afloat, it was likely that the vessel would have been required to return to Brazilian waters – an unwanted public relations debacle for the Lincoln administration.

It is rather difficult to evaluate the *Florida* in her role as a commerce destroyer. Certainly, from the standpoint of the ship itself, she was outstanding: fast, well armed, and a good sea boat. Though her speed obviously decreased after her Brest refit, this did not necessarily reduce her capabilities under sail. It is worth noting that most of the Union naval vessels that were equal to or faster than *Florida* under steam were converted merchant ships: *Vanderbilt* and *R.R. Cuyler*, for instance. However, none of these were built for speed under sail and, as converted merchant ships had batteries significantly inferior to that of *Florida*. By the same token, the double-ender gunboats such as *Sonoma* were fast under steam but had minimal sailing rig and relatively shallow draft. The latter had potent batteries, however, and, had they been able to catch the Confederate cruiser would have been strong adversaries in a gunfight. Few of the similarly sized Union steam sloops, such as *Kearsarge* and *Wachusett*, were very fast under steam and certainly were slower than *Florida* under sail. But their batteries were equal to or better than

Florida's – as would be proven by the *Alabama-Kearsarge* fight.

Other factors figured prominently in her level of success, most notably the extended down times, particularly at Mobile. At this point early in the war, Union merchant vessels were still abundant on the sea lanes and the transition to foreign flags had not become prevalent, meaning that taking prizes was simply a matter of being available at sea. The down time at Brest was less significant in that by that time Union merchant shippers were herding over to foreign registration to avoid just such vessels as *Florida*.

One historian also noted the difference in *Florida*'s commanding officers.[298] Certainly Maffitt was significantly more aggressive than Morris, and another commander with Maffitt's audacity may well have taken more risks during the second cruise, with possibly more rewards.

As to the *Florida*, it is obvious that James D. Bulloch succeeded admirably in his first acquisition of a commerce raider for the Confederate navy. His second would confirm the wisdom of his selection as agent for the navy in this matter.

Alabama

While the Miller firm was working up a proposal for what would become the *Florida*, James D. Bulloch made a visit to a second British shipbuilder. In this instance, it was to John Laird Sons and Company and their ironworks at Birkenhead, across the Mersey River from Liverpool. The Lairds were a leader in naval construction and had been pioneers in building iron vessels.[299]

Bulloch proceeded to make his proposal and rehearse his criteria to Lairds and by this time had access to Confederate funds. On August 1, 1861, a contract was signed to build the *Alabama*, or, for the purposes of anonymity, simply "290," Laird's construction sequence hull number. While construction was under way the vessel would

also be known to the outside world as *Barcelona* or *Enrica*.[300]

When Bulloch later wrote of his dealings with Lairds he used the term "dispatch vessels" for the starting point in the discussion of his requirements for this vessel. This term leads to some confusion. The Crimean War showed the need for handy, shallow-draft vessels for inshore work, and these vessels were initially termed dispatch vessels. These ranged from 106-feet up to 200-feet in length and the term "dispatch vessel" was soon dropped in favor of the more accurate "gun vessel." Bulloch may have used the term "dispatch vessel," but he obviously was not in the market for a shallow draft vessel for inshore work. Lairds had indeed built several of the smaller vessels (106-feet in length), but these certainly could not have been the basis for the vessel Bulloch needed.[301]

The contract for the ship was between the firm and Bulloch himself, as a private individual. The contract and specifications reveal a substantially built ship and one that explicitly includes warship characteristics.

The greater part of the hull was to be of English oak. The exceptions were the keel that was to be partially English elm, and the keelson was to be teak or greenheart. It called for some Danzig fir for deck beams, and mahogany for the plank sheer and channels. All was to be copper bolted; that is, the timbers were to be drilled with holes slightly smaller than the diameter of the bolt, and the bolt driven through and clinched.

Iron was used for deck knees. Further, there were to be iron diagonal riders or strapping, measuring four-inches by 5/8-inches, attached to the inside of each frame with copper or iron bolts. These strips ran from the upper deck to the keelson and formed a "basket" strengthening the hull. English oak truss pieces also formed diagonals, again fastened to the frames and crossing the iron riders.

The scantlings were appropriately large. The keel measurements were fourteen-inches wide ("sided" dimension) at midship, narrowing to eleven-inches towards the fore and aft of the ship. The vertical ("moulded") dimension was sixteen-inches for its entire length. The keelson was similar except only fifteen inches high. The first futtocks (the lowest part of each frame) were eight inches square where they met the keel, tapering slightly upward. The beams of the main deck were nine- by ten-inches.

Warship-standard construction was specifically called for in several places in the contract. The upper deck beams were to be Danzig fir or mahogany, except under the pivot guns and masts, where English oak or teak was required. Oak was also specified for the deck planking under the guns. Also, shot racks were specified as well as a magazine and shell rooms. The latter were to be as "usual in H.M. Service." The screw propeller's lifting frame was also to be as "adopted in H.M. Service." However, neither the contract nor the builder's specifications mentioned guns or circular deck rails for the pivot guns.[302]

The vessel was to be completed by the first day of June 1862. The total cost was 47,500 pounds, paid in five increments, the first at the execution of the contract; the second when the frame was up and the last when she was tried and delivered "uninjured" on the Mersey River.[303]

Construction of the vessel was unmarred by delays and she was launched under the name *Enrica* on May 14, 1862. At the launching, there was a short lapse after the shores were removed and she remained static on the ways. Then the foreman had the men on the forecastle "dance." This vibration was sufficient to get her in the water. Bulloch's fiction to mislead the British authorities in this instance was that she was built as a steam frigate for the Spanish government, hence the name and obvious naval aspects of her construction and contract.

The ship's first trial trip was on June 12, and she went back to the dock to complete fitting out. In the interim, Bulloch had been diligent both in recruiting a crew and setting in motion preparations to ship the guns and equipment to the *Alabama*, after she departed from British waters. The bark *Agrippina* and steamer *Bahama* were acquired, loaded, and dispatched southward, to rendezvous with the cruiser. Expecting imminent seizure by British authorities, and concerned about reports of the Union steam sloop *Tuscarora* arriving at Southampton, Bulloch arranged another "trial" trip on July 29th, with guests aboard. The latter were returned to British soil by the accompanying tender, while the errant "Spanish steam frigate" steamed to rendezvous with Bulloch and forty new recruits off the coast of Wales. From there, the cruiser steamed towards the Azores to meet her supply ships, as well as her Confederate commanding officer, Raphael Semmes, formerly of the *Sumter*. After transferring the ordnance and equipment onto the new vessel, Semmes commissioned her on August 24, 1862.[304]

As completed, the *Alabama* was a slightly larger version of *Florida*, with the obvious visual distinction of having a single funnel. Both vessels had characteristically long lower masts, barque rig, and two large pivot guns on rails, capable of firing on either broadside, plus broadside carriage guns.

The *Alabama* as completed was 213-feet eight-inches long between perpendiculars and 201-feet eight-inches on the load waterline; thirty-two-foot extreme beam and thirty-one-feet two-inch moulded beam. Her depth of hold was eighteen-feet from limber strake to top of the upper deck beam, and was 1,044 24/94 builder's displacement tonnage. The vessel drew fifteen-feet of water, forward and aft.[305]

The vessel carried some 14,500 square feet of plain canvas, not including studding sails. She had topsails, topgallants, and royals on fore and main, but no main sail. Her standing rigging was wire rope and masts were of yellow pine. Studding sails were carried on foresail, topsail, and topgallant yards, and main topsail and topgallant. Early illustrations show her carrying only topsails and topgallants, but later ones show the royal yards. Semmes wrote that on entering Cherbourg in 1864, he rigged a cross-jack yard as well as topsail and topgallant yards on the mizzen, giving her the appearance of a full-rigged ship.[306] The ship's lower masts were designed to optimize the fore and aft sails and were particularly tall. It was said that her distinctive masts, "came to be recognized as a sign of danger to American skippers in all seas."[307]

The steam power for the ship was a condensing two-cylinder horizontal installation with cylinders operating athwartship. Though it has been described as direct acting, the plans indicate it was a back-acting engine. That is, there were two piston rods per cylinder that operated across the crankshaft (one above and one below the crankshaft), and were connected to crossheads. The crossheads operated the connecting rods that turned the crankshaft. (In a direct-acting engine, the piston rod operated directly on the crankshaft). The pistons were fifty-six-inches in diameter and with a twenty-seven-inch stroke. The condenser enabled re-use of boiler water at sea, obviating the need to use corrosive salt water in the boilers. The engine was rated at 300hp and had four boilers, each with three furnaces. The coalbunkers carried 350-tons of fuel, and it was estimated she used sixteen-tons per day, and thus could steam twenty days on engines alone. The funnel could be telescoped down as far as the rail, and a brass-lifting frame enabled the screw to be hoisted from the water. The screw itself was fourteen-feet in diameter with two blades and pitch of thirty-five degrees. In Andrew Bowcock's book on the vessel, he notes that the propeller most likely could not be raised entirely clear of the water because of its diameter: the upper end of the blade would

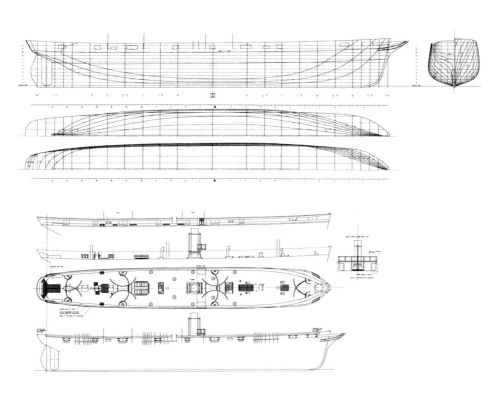

Hull lines, deck plan and sail plan of CSS Alabama. Built by the respected Lairds shipyard at Birkenhead, the vessel's specifications clearly called for naval-grade structural elements, though no pivot rails or gunports were on the plans. James D. Bulloch's cover story was that the vessel was intended for the Spanish navy. Plans by Andrew Bowcock, used with permission

Sail plan of the *Alabama* redrawn from that in the Merseyside Maritime Museum. (scale = 1:384)

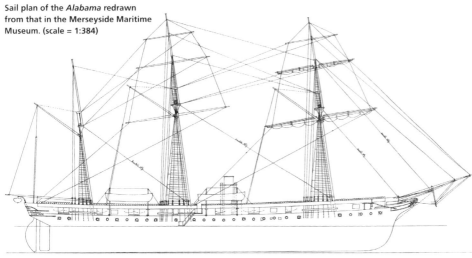

have been higher than the ship's rail, interfering with the spanker boom.[308]

Her lower deck housed accommodations for a crew of 120, plus twenty-four officers. At the stern, the commanding officer's cabin was a roughly triangular room just aft of the wardroom. The latter was lit by a skylight and had a "handsome suite of staterooms" for the officers on either side. Forward of the wardroom and officer cabins were the midshipmen and engineers quarters. Appropriately, the engine control room was directly forward of the engineers' quarters and of course immediately above the machinery. A coalbunker ran the width of the ship and occupied about ninety feet forward of the machinery spaces. In the middle of this bunker was a walkway, divided off by iron bulkheads, leading forward to the stoke holds and the mechanism for hoisting the funnel. Forward of the bunker were the crew accommodations, which measured about fifty-feet longitudinally and were as wide as the ship. The galley stove was in this area and a "seat" ran around the perimeter of the room. This was apparently a bench type affair that doubled as storage for the mens' sea bags. Hooks in the deck above were provided to hang their hammocks.[309]

Below the lower deck were the usual storage areas, engines, shaft tunnel, boilers, bunkers, and magazines. There was also a large iron water tank. This was filled weekly by a condensing apparatus operating from the boilers.[310]

The upper deck was dominated by the boats, funnel, the bridge structure that spanned the deck, four ventilators, various hatches and skylights, and the battery. A pair of boats was amidship, another two on the quarters, and a dinghy aft, all on davits. Hammock rails ran atop the bulwarks amidships, and were covered by canvas. The ship's deck plans show four sets of pivot rails (sweeps): one forward of the funnel, one between the main and mizzen-mast, another forward of the foremast and the fourth aft of the mizzen mast. The seven-inch, 100-pounder Blakely rifle was on the rails forward of the funnel; the eight-inch, sixty-eight-pounder smoothbore was on the other midship sweep. The extreme forward and aft sweeps were not used. The six thirty-two-pounders were on standard, four-wheel, truck carriages and were moved about as needed. At one point Semmes mentioned moving all but one weapon to one side, making a seven-gun broadside. Due to the height of the gun barrels, the hammock rails over the pivot gunports were to be unshipped when the guns were used. There originally was a plan to add another pair of thirty-two-pounders to the battery, but this was never done.

Externally, there was carved work aft and on the knee of the head. The former was in the form of a faux, gilded stern gallery: a row of false windows with carving above and below. These were pure decoration as there was no cabin in that part of the stern. Forward, the head was given a carved shield and anchor, the former painted red, the attendant carving, gilt.[311]

The *Alabama*'s qualities were later described by Semmes. Her speed, he wrote, was, "always greatly overrated by the enemy. She was ordinarily a ten-knot ship. She was said to have made eleven-knots and a half, on her trial trip, but we never afterward got it out of her. Under steam

and sail both, we logged on one occasion, thirteen-knots and a quarter, which was her utmost speed."

Semmes also commented on her battery, particularly the 100-pounder rifled Blakely gun. The weapon was, "so deficient in metal, compared with the weight of the shot it threw, that after the first few discharges, when it became a little heated, it was of comparatively small use to us, to such an extent were we obligated to reduce the charge of powder, on account of the recoil."

Semmes was particularly pleased with the hoisting propeller that could be disconnected and lifted clear in about fifteen-minutes. Lowering the screw was less time consuming.[312]

Semmes took advantage of the seasonal whaling activities for *Alabama*'s first seizures. The Massachusetts whaler *Ocmulgee* was his first prize, on September 5, 1862 – eleven days after *Alabama*'s commissioning. Surprise was complete: Semmes approached under the U.S. flag and the whaler's captain assumed *Alabama* was a U.S. naval vessel sent to protect the whaling fleet. Semmes remained in the area and took eight more vessels before September 8, when he made passage towards the Grand Banks.[313]

Six more prizes came his way before October 16, when *Alabama* encountered a "cyclone." The raider took the worst of it: two hours before and after the eye passed, she endured the "sledgehammer" blows that nearly knocked her down. Before it was all over the ship had lost the mainyard and one boat was demolished. She was finally down to a single small staysail, riding it out. Semmes noted the barometer reading at 28.64, which equates approximately to 100mph winds. Semmes noted that, "she behaved nobly."[314]

Despite the worsening weather, *Alabama* headed toward the North Atlantic in October, Semmes had made some seventeen captures in seven weeks since commissioning. He then turned the *Alabama* south and made for Martinique

where she put into port for the first time since leaving Britain. By this date Semmes had taken twenty-two ships.[315]

There was potential disaster at Martinique, with the arrival of the U.S. steam sloop *San Jacinto*, armed with eleven guns: ten nine-inch Dahlgrens and one eleven-inch Dahlgren smoothbore. Semmes cared little for these odds, though *Alabama* was certainly the faster vessel, and quietly moved out one rainy night.[316]

From Martinique Semmes opted to steam westward, intending to harass a rumored Union army and naval expedition on Galveston. There was some delay however, occasioned by an engine breakdown. A broken valve chest casting was taken in hand at sea, with much hammering and bellows work. This was one of the few instances where machinery malfunctions hampered *Alabama*'s operations. She was immobilized for three days.[317]

Semmes arrived off Galveston on January 11, 1863, and found five Union vessels shelling the city. The largest, the steam sloop *Brooklyn* was under repair and the steamer *Hatteras* was sent to confront the stranger. Semmes allowed *Hatteras* to "chase" *Alabama* farther from possible assistance then wheeled to face the Union sidewheeler. It was, as Semmes expected, an unfair fight: the Union vessel was a converted iron excursion boat mounting four thirty-two-pounders and two rifles (twenty and thirty-pounders). In thirteen minutes of continuous cannonading at point blank range – from 100-yards down to thirty – *Hatteras* was in a sinking condition, having her cylinder pierced and the engine's overhead walking beam demolished. Whole sheets of iron were torn off her sides and few of her shots had told on the Confederate cruiser. Without engine power or operating pumps, the *Hatteras* surrendered. Casualties were light, however, with two killed and five wounded on the Union ship and only one crewman hurt on the *Alabama*. Damage to the *Alabama* was negligible. This engagement marked

THE CONFEDERATE PRIVATEER STEAMER "ALABAMA" ("290"), CAPTAIN RAPHAEL SEMMES.— FROM A PHOTOGRAPH TAKEN AT LIVERPOOL, BEFORE SHE WAS RIGGED.

The Alabama at sea. Bulloch specified very long lower masts for large fore and aft sails for long distance cruising without the large crew compliment required for the square sails of a ship rig. It was said that mariners learned to recognize this characteristic rig and prepare themselves for the Alabama's arrival. Naval Historical Center

machinery, hull and rigging, and of course, re-caulking and painting. Her water condensing apparatus had also broken down and Semmes was able to replenish from a nearby schooner.[322]

To this point, *Alabama* had captured over fifty Union vessels, and had been in commission about a year. Her stay in South Africa was marred by the usual complaints from pro-Union citizens, machinations of Union agents, a great number of desertions, as well as a dearth of prizes: one sixteen-day cruise along the coast netted no victims at all. When the speedy Union side-wheeler *Vanderbilt* came into the area there were two occasions where the two barely missed each other – and her skipper had let it be known that he intended to sink *Alabama* by ramming. Thus, there were sufficient reasons for Semmes to move elsewhere.

Semmes pointed *Alabama* eastward "in compliance with the suggestion of Mr. Secretary Mallory," crossing the Indian Ocean towards the Straits of Sunda and Singapore. Moving east along the fortieth parallel, Semmes proceeded exclusively under sail: twenty-four days, covering over 4,400-miles, averaging 178-miles per day. He was in Singapore late in December and found a discouraging sight: twenty-two laid up American merchant ships and he learned similar stories of American ships at anchor at Bangkok, Canton, Shanghai, and Japan. The fear of the *Alabama* had preceded him and consequently there were few Union merchant prizes to be had.[323]

the only instance when a Confederate vessel sank a Union naval ship at sea.[318]

Semmes then made for Port Royal to land prisoners and make repairs. After less than a week he moved south, intending to attack the traffic in the sealanes off the east coast of South America. The *Alabama* crossed the Equator in March and cruised in Brazilian waters through June and early July, seizing twenty-six vessels.[319]

One of his prizes was the "tidy little bark" *Conrad* taken on June 20. Semmes renamed her *Tuscaloosa* and mounted two twelve-pounders on her deck. With a crew of fourteen, she was dispatched to prey on Union shipping, and then to meet *Alabama* later at the next destination:

South Africa. The little bark took two prizes, both of which proved to have neutral cargo, and which were released on bond.[320]

Semmes had now determined to move on to other cruising grounds. This decision and timing was based on his estimate of the interval it would take for news of *Alabama*'s presence in South Africa to reach the U.S. and for a Union warship to steam down in pursuit.[321] Thus, *Alabama* arrived in South African waters at the end of July.

Semmes and his crew were virtually lionized at Cape Town and they remained in those waters for two months. A year's worth of cruising had taken its toll on the cruiser and she was leaking in her bends. Semmes ordered an overhaul of

The Alabama at Singapore, before returning to Cape Town in early-1864. Semmes' next port of call would be France. Tennessee State Library and Archives

Alabama (foreground) and the U.S. steam sloop Kearsarge in combat off Cherbourg, June 1864. Semmes would later admit that his guncrews were unskilled and undertrained and that his ship was "limping" from extended months at sea. Kearsarge's two eleven-inch Dahlgren smoothbores and deliberate gunnery outmatched the Alabama, ending the feared cruiser's havoc on the high seas. Naval Historical Center

A return to the Western hemisphere was Semmes next decision and *Alabama* was back at Cape Town on March 20, 1864, six months after leaving the place. She crossed the Equator in May. Later, Semmes wrote of his ship: "The old *Alabama* was not now what she had been then. She was like the wearied fox-hound, limping back after a long chase." Earlier he had written that she needed maintenance, her speed was diminished and her bottom copper was dropping off in sheets.[324] By this time, Semmes declared he was determined to return to England or France and put the ship in dock for extensive overhaul. En route to European waters, *Alabama* made her last capture, the bark *Tycoon*, and she steamed into Cherbourg, France on June 11, 1864.

Three days later, the U.S. steam sloop *Kearsarge*, with Captain John H. Winslow commanding, came into the same harbor. Despite his ship's condition, Semmes immediately communicated with the Union skipper, agreeing to come out as soon as he coaled. It was said that Semmes wanted to make quick work of *Kearsarge* before other Union ships arrived and blockaded *Alabama* in the port. Semmes did not want to repeat his earlier experience with *Sumter*. *Kearsarge* had been one of the three vessels that had trapped that steamer at Gibraltar, two years before.

A blow-by-blow account of this, possibly the last one-on-one ship duel of the transitioning age of sail, is not necessary here. It was a test of gunnery, not speed. The vessels simply circled

about seven times and maintained nearly the same range. Confederate gunners fired fast, high and inaccurately; Union men were slow and deliberate. *Kearsarge*'s eleven-inch Dahlgren shells outweighed that of both *Alabama*'s pivot guns, and soon their toll accumulated. *Alabama* sank, stern first, with Semmes escaping on an English yacht. Later, Semmes cried foul claiming he was hoodwinked by Winslow, who had the temerity to drape bights of anchor chains on the ship's sides over the engine spaces – and had neatly boxed them in. The use of this chain armor had become common practice in the Union navy since Farragut had used them on his wooden vessels at New Orleans in April 1862. In fact, Semmes' point was moot: of over 350 projectiles reportedly fired by *Alabama*, a dozen even struck her hull and only two Confederate shells struck the "armored" area.[325]

The career of the "pirate" – as the Union press and pundits called her – *Alabama* was over. The cruiser had been almost continuously at sea for over twenty-one months and had taken sixty-eight prizes, most of which she had burned. More importantly, she had created havoc with Union shipping interests – particularly insurers – and panic on the high seas. It was not very long before Yankee cargoes were being shipped in hulls which did not carry the stars and stripes, and it can truly be said that this was the beginning of the sharp decline of the American shipping industry – an industry which, before the Civil War, had challenged that of Great Britain.

One historian characterized *Alabama* as the "most perfect cruiser" and with much justification. She was perfectly adapted to the role, particularly when under the command of a judicious, but wary commanding officer. She had sufficient speed to catch almost any merchant vessel and was built to keep the seas under sail as long as her stores would allow.

The role *Alabama* was not designed for was the one that sealed her fate. Semmes decision to fight *Kearsarge* was unnecessary and outside of the role for which the ship was built. Furthermore, Semmes had admitted his ship was "limping" and worn down, and that the crew had had little gunnery practice. Semmes later wrote that, "though the enemy was superior both in size, stanchness of construction and armament … they were of force nearly equal." Surely, an inaccurate assessment of the two vessels.[326]

Shenandoah

Chronologically, the *Shenandoah* is one of the last of the Confederate commerce raiders. However, the vessel ranks among the most recognizable of the group, partly because of her far-flung expedition and partly due to the unusual end to her story – long after the official surrender of all the Confederate armed forces.

The *Shenandoah* has the distinction of being the only Confederate cruiser acquired for a specific mission and objective. Secretary Mallory wrote Bulloch in August 1864 of the importance of operations against the American whaling trade. He indicated that "his opinions" on it were shared by both Commander Brooke and Lt. R.R. Carter. Mallory, inspired no doubt by the example of the *Essex* in the War of 1812, had suggested obtaining a ship specifically to send against that peculiarly New England trade which thrived in the Arctic and North Pacific waters. Mallory hoped that the resulting financial repercussions of this raid would reduce political support for the war in New England.

Mallory at first was of the opinion that only a sailing vessel would be appropriate for cruising at such long distances, far from friendly ports. J.M. Brooke responded that a "fast vessel with auxiliary steam power" would be capable of such a mission. Lt. Carter confirmed this and had information on a specific class of such vessels which had been constructed for the China trade, but which would meet the navy's requirements. One of these was the ship *Sea King*.[327]

Brooke described the following itinerary for the proposed ship: Leave Cape of Good Hope on the first of January for Australia, depart from the latter in March, then move up through the Sea of Japan, Okhotsk and to the North Pacific, and be in, "position about the 15th of September, north of the island of Oahu, distant from 60-100-miles, to intercept the North Pacific whaling fleet bound to Oahu with the products of the summer cruise."[328]

It is interesting that this expedition would not be in accordance to the mission of the commerce raiders: the whaling industry was somewhat ancillary to the maritime merchant commerce that was the usual target of the cruisers. Second, given the distances involved, it was unlikely that any Union naval vessels would be drawn away from the blockade to deal with the situation. The only Union Navy vessels in striking distance to the whaling waters were in the Pacific and obviously not involved in the blockade of the South. However, the expedition did have one positive aspect: the whaling fleet was concentrated in one area and was not expecting such an attack; they would be easy pickings for any armed adversary.

Late in September 1864, Bulloch wrote Mallory concerning the purchase of the *Sea King*, "a fine composite ship, built for the Bombay trade, and just returned from her first voyage." The vessel measured 1,160-tons builder's measure, had been built at Glasgow by the firm Alexander Stephen and Sons to a design by noted naval architect William Rennie, and launched August 17, 1863. Her contract specifications called for a length of 216-feet between perpendiculars, which was later lengthened by four feet. Her breadth was thirty-two-feet (extreme) and later made thirty-two-feet six-inches, and depth of hold, twenty-feet six-inches. Her hull structure was composite iron and wood. Iron was used for her frames and deck beams, and it was claimed that she was the first composite hull screw steamer. She was sheathed from the keel up with East India teak, coppered to the eighteen-foot line; her decks were yellow pine planks, 5½- by four-inches on the upper deck, three-inches on the lower deck. Her 'tween deck stanchions were to be of teak or oak, and there was a poop structure some fifty-feet long as well as a house which contained the wheel and the manually-operated propeller-hoisting mechanism. A house on the forward deck provided quarters for engineers and some of the crew and the remainder berthed under the topgallant forecastle. Between decks measured seven-feet six-inches and she had been originally configured for transporting troops to the Far East.

Hull and sail plans of the CSS Shenandoah. Designed by William Rennie, of clipper-ship fame, the Shenandoah had clipper-like hull lines and proved to be very fast. Plans by David Macgregor

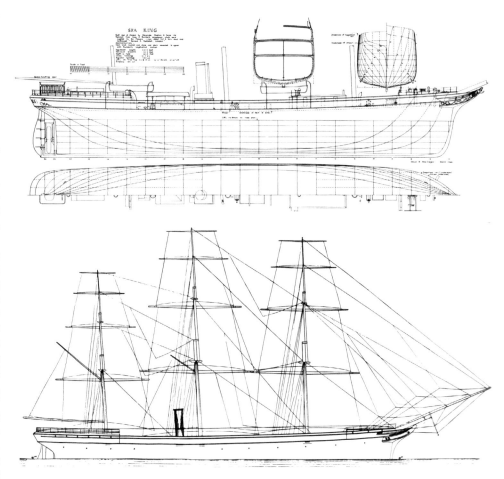

The vessel was ship-rigged, with iron lower masts and lower and topsail yards and bowsprit. One source indicates that the upper masts and yards were steel, whereas the Denny specifications called for pitch pine or spruce. Bulloch stated that she had "rolling" topsails, which corresponds to the contract's "patent" reefing apparatus. "Cunningham's Patent Self Reefing Topsails" were reefed by a mechanism that lowered the topsail yard. The yard rotated as it descended, wrapping the sail around the yard. The evolution was accomplished by three men working lines on the deck. This eliminated the hazards inherent in sending men aloft in bad weather to accomplish the same task. Her commander wrote later that the iron topsail yards were so heavy that he doubted the crew could have handled them efficiently, making the "rolling" system particularly necessary.[329]

The vessel's machinery consisted of two cylinders, built by A. & J. Inglis, each forty-seven-inches in diameter and with a thirty-two-inch stroke. Since she was built as a merchant vessel, there was no need to employ an engine low in the hull, therefore the steam cylinders were vertical and direct acting. Her commander later wrote that her cylinders were five feet above the water line and the boilers, eighteen inches over that line. Bulloch wrote that the engines produced 220 nominal horsepower, or 850 indicated horsepower. The two boilers had "ample grate and heating surface." The vessel had an apparatus for lifting the screw out of the water, another for lowering the funnel to the level of the rail, and an apparatus capable of condensing sea water at a rate of 500-gallons a day.

Bulloch also noted she was a fast ship under sail. Her log showed one twenty-four-hour run of 330-miles – a remarkable 13½-knots. She made the return passage from Shanghai to Deal in seventy-one days, which included five days stopped for coaling. Under steam, she ran at nine-knots and her commander wrote she was only capable of ten-knots under steam alone. That the vessel had quite a turn of speed is no surprise: William Rennie designed noted clipper ships in

the 1860s, including *Fiery Cross*, and, later, *Norman Court*. The *Sea King*'s hull form was described as differing "little from a pure sailing ship." Bulloch's broker called her a "capital ship" and noted that she had been classed as A-1 by Lloyds of London for fourteen years.[330]

Once the purchase was completed, in September 1864, Bulloch worked his strategies to get the vessel to sea without interference from British officialdom. Fortunately, mere purchase

Shenandoah in an Australian drydock, early-1865. Note her composite hull: wood planking over iron frames. She was said to be the first composite hull screw steamer. Under James Waddell the vessel decimated the Union Arctic whaling fleet and fired the last gun of the Confederacy, in June 1865. Naval Historical Center

until nearly the end of October that the first captured vessel became the source of rope suitable for the gun tackle. [333]

Waddell proceeded south, capturing six vessels in the South Atlantic, and rounded the Cape of Good Hope. The cruiser arrived in Australia in January 1865 and was docked to repair the propeller bearing. From thence the cruiser sailed to Ascension Island and vicinity, in search of Yankee whalers. In April 1865, while the Confederate armies were surrendering to Union forces in Virginia and North Carolina, Waddell was seizing four whalers.

At this point Waddell and his crew were ignorant of the fate of the Confederacy and continued onward. They passed through the Sea of Okhotsk and reached the Bering Sea on June 16, 1865. The whalers in the vicinity were unaware a Confederate cruiser was amongst them and, when accosted, put up no defense. Waddell seized twenty-four ships from June 22nd through 28th, burning all but four.

During the third week in June, Waddell was informed that Lee had surrendered, but that the Confederate government had removed to Danville, Virginia, and President Davis had vowed to continue the fight. *Shenandoah* continued her depredations through the first of August, capturing at least nineteen additional vessels. On August 2, 1865, she encountered a British vessel carrying recent newspapers with confirmation of the war's end. At that point Waddell determined to de-militarize his vessel and return to England. Most of the return voyage

of a vessel was considerably easier to accomplish for the Confederacy than superintending a vessel's construction from keel to completion. The vessel, commanded by a British skipper, left London, unarmed, on October 8th, and made passage to Madeira. There the ship was met by the tender *Laurel*, which supplied the guns, provisions, and coal. By October 19th, the trans-shipment was complete. Renamed *Shenandoah* by her new Confederate Navy commanding officer, Lt. James I. Waddell, the vessel now had six guns: four eight-inch smoothbores and two rifled Whitworth thirty-two-pounders. [331]

Waddell's first problem was obtaining an adequate crew. A large number who came out in her as a so-called merchant ship refused to sign on to a Confederate warship, particularly in view of the recent sinking of the *Alabama*. This left Waddell with nearly the same number of enlisted men as officers. Eventually, men were acquired from captured ships bringing the total number of sailors to fifty-one, with twenty-two officers. [332]

A second quandary immediately appeared: the *Laurel* had not brought tackle for the guns, leaving the cruiser essentially unarmed except for a couple of brass twelve-pounders. It was not

was under sail, with Waddell reluctant to put in to any port where Union warships might seize the ship. They arrived at Liverpool on November 5, 1865, and all went ashore five days later.

In thirteen months, Waddell and his crew had sailed his ship around the world – the only Confederate vessel to accomplish this. They had covered some 58,000-miles and visited all the Earth's oceans except the Antarctic. *Shenandoah* had taken thirty-eight prizes and burned thirty-two of them. The last gun defending the Confederacy had been fired from the *Shenandoah* on June 22, 1865, in the Arctic Ocean.[334]

The *Shenandoah,* under Wadell, had accomplished the goal for which she was acquired. The Yankee whaling fleet was decimated and *Shenandoah* had performed as expected: in rough figures she had sailed over 140-miles *a day* for thirteen months, and had gone eight months without dropping anchor. Though the vessel was fast, generally Waddell had been a conservative sailor, rarely pushing the vessel under sail to avoid incidents which would have injured her canvas in mid-ocean. She had gone for several days in the westerlies making around fifteen-knots. One of her best days was 262-miles, under plain sail, averaging 10½-knots.[335]

The *Shenandoah* was turned over to United States authorities at Liverpool and then auctioned off. She was still a staunch vessel, however, and was later purchased by the Sultan of Zanzibar, ending her days on a reef in the Indian Ocean in 1879.[336]

Tallahassee

The *Tallahassee* did not meet the design criteria for a deep-sea, ocean-going commerce raider, but nevertheless created greater havoc in a short time than any other Confederate raider, capturing or destroying some thirty-four vessels in less than two weeks in August 1864. Adding further insult

to this "outrage," most were taken within eighty-miles of Sandy Hook, New Jersey – therefore in the immediate path of all shipping to and from the largest Union port: New York City.

Atalanta – the Greek virgin huntress – was the first of several names for this vessel, the others in Confederate service being *Tallahassee*, *Olustee* and *Chameleon*, resulting in confusion for the researcher as well as for the vessel's contemporaries. Adding to the confusion – then and now – was in misspelling it "Atlanta."

The ship was built at the John and William Dudgeon shipyard at Millwall on the Thames, London, and launched in 1863. She was designed by T.E. Symonds, a naval architect who was an early advocate of twin-screw propulsion, and, in particular, independent screws, these making it possible for the vessel to turn in a very short distance by idling one propeller and powering the other. (The U.S. Navy had built the steam sloop *Pawnee* in 1860 with two screws, but these were geared to operate only in concert.)[337]

By the time *Atalanta* was built, Dudgeon had become noted for exceedingly fast iron vessels. *Flora*, also with twin screws, built in 1862, had been hailed as the "fastest screw steamship afloat" attaining fourteen-knots, and had been swiftly taken into the lucrative blockade running trade. Dudgeon also built *Edith* about the same time as *Atalanta*. This vessel became the Confederate *Chickamauga* (see below).[338]

The *Atalanta* was 220-feet long and twenty-four-feet in beam, and a fourteen-foot depth of hold. No original plans of the ship are available, making these dimensions only approximations, but it is clear that the ship's length to breadth ratio was about 9:1. In an era when most vessels rarely exceeded a 6:1 ratio, it is obvious that the *Atalanta* was to be very fast.

The two screws were powered by four cylinders, arranged in pairs, with each pair operating one propeller shaft. These were horizontal cylinders,

thirty-four-inches in diameter and twenty-one-inch stroke, operating at twenty-nine pounds steam pressure, and delivering 200-horsepower and 120 revolutions of the shafts per minute.

Though news reports, when she was first built, claimed she was for cross-channel service and was ostensibly built for the London, Chatham and Dover Railway, she was purchased by Edgar Stringer and Edward Pembroke for their Mercantile Trading Company, for blockade running. Furthermore, in a post-war article, the Dudgeons said the ship was "designed as a blockade runner." As a publicity stunt or a speed test, there was staged a "race" with a channel steamer (named either *Empress* or *Queen*) in April 1864. The Dudgeon vessel quickly left the competition in the lurch, doing the Calais to Dover run in seventy-seven minutes, compared to a dawdling 107 minutes for the other ship. If the Calais to Dover distance is about twenty-five-miles, the older vessel was moving at over fourteen-knots; while the *Atalanta* made in excess of nineteen-knots.[339]

As a blockade runner, the ship made three round trips to Wilmington, via Bermuda, in 1864. After arriving in Wilmington in July, the vessel was purchased by the Confederate government and converted for commerce raiding, this involving mounting guns on her deck and installing a munitions magazine. Some additional berthing areas were probably added, as her crew would number about 120. The guns were a single eighty-four-pounder, two twenty-four-pounders, and two thirty-two-pounders. Later, two of the guns were removed.[340]

Under the command of John Taylor Wood, *Tallahassee* sailed out of Wilmington on August 6, 1864. The vessel easily outdistanced five blockaders the first day and another contingent the next, and Wood steamed northward. Five days later, some eighty-miles off Sandy Hook, Wood took his first prize, the schooner *Sarah A. Boyce*. Seven prizes were taken on August 11; six on the

Confederate States Steamer 'Tallahassee.'

Confederate cruiser Tallahassee, formerly the blockade runner Atalanta, as she appeared at Halifax, Nova Scotia in late-1864. A twin-screw steamer with a reputation for speeds in excess of eighteen-knots, the vessel created panic off the New England coast, capturing thirteen Union vessels in one week. Note that the steamer's main mast is broken off near the rail, the result of a collision with one of her prizes. Naval Historical Center

Plan, of the CSS Tallahassee, modern reconstruction by F.A. Les'Ard. F.A. Les'Ard

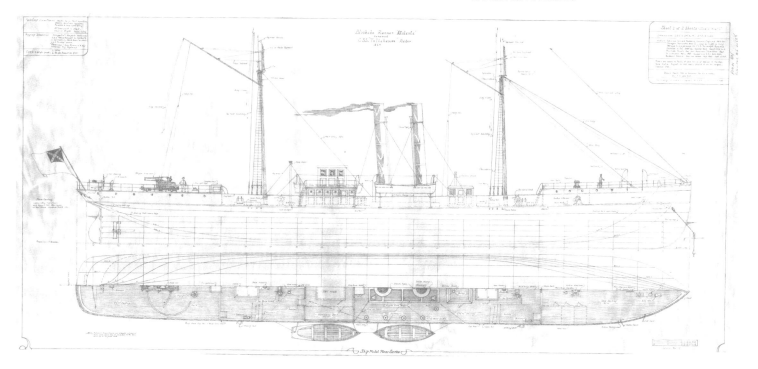

12th, and Wood was contemplating a raid on New York when news came that a half-dozen Union naval or chartered vessels were in pursuit. He then moved northward and called at Halifax for coal. *Tallahassee* had bagged thirty Union ships in less than a week. Wood found no welcome in Nova Scotia, and departed some forty hours after coming in. He ran the ship in through the blockade at Wilmington on August 26, at one point pursued by the *Quaker City*, which tailed her for over two hours, maintaining over twelve-knots in the effort, to no avail.[341]

The only known photograph of the ship, taken at Halifax, and eyewitness descriptions give some idea of her appearance. One officer wrote that coal dust was everywhere and "officers have very small quarters and plenty of dirt."[342] Thus the original white or light grey paint was darkened and streaked. The photo also confirms that her mainmast was broken off, near the rail, the result of an accidental collision with one of the prize vessels.

The steamer's second cruise began October 29th, this time under the name *Olustee*, named after a Confederate victory in Florida earlier in the year. She returned to Wilmington on November 6, after taking six additional prizes. Off Cape Henry, she caught the attention of the Union double-ended gunboat *Sassacus* and a two-day chase ensued. At first, in high winds, the pursuer was able to carry more sail and was gaining on the Confederate ship. On the second day, the winds failed and *Sassacus* was on steam only, maintaining at least twelve-knots, all day. The Union vessel's commanding officer later insisted that his inexperienced firemen could not keep the necessary steam pressure and, besides, his ship was running deep with newly acquired stores: coal and ammunition.[343]

Another pursuer at this time was the *Lillian*, a fast, steel-hulled, captured blockade runner re-constituted as a blockader. This vessel chased her for over three hours, keeping the sea at over

11½-knots. At one point her engineer suggested that "a few half barrels of pork" would enable him to raise steam pressure another ten pounds to snag the Confederate cruiser. In any event, the Confederate steamer again gained the safety of the port of Wilmington.[344]

At this point John Wilkinson, former commanding officer of the ex-blockade runner, cum raider *Chickamauga*, expressed the opinion that the "makeshift gunboats" such as *Chickamauga* and *Olustee* were detrimental in that their existence resulted in considerable stiffening of the Union blockade, impeding the inflow of necessities to the South. Consequently, *Olustee* was re-converted to an unarmed blockade runner, this time appropriately named *Chameleon*.[345]

Chameleon, under the command of Wilkinson, in December 1864, again ran the blockade, calling at Bermuda to take on supplies for the Confederate army. By the time the blockade runner returned to the Southern coast, there was no un-captured port, and *Chameleon* returned to England. British authorities seized her on April 9, 1865, the date of Lee's surrender at Appomattox, and she was eventually awarded to the United States and sold.

In sum, the Dudgeon-built vessel proved only to be an efficient short-range raider, but with great speed and maneuverability. Wilkinson later wrote that on attempting to cross the bar into Wilmington, he suddenly was faced with two blockaders and "Nothing saved us from capture but the twin screws, which enabled our steamer to turn as upon a pivot in the narrow channel."[346]

However, the ship's minimal rig prevented speed under sail, forcing reliance on her engines. Hence, her short range was a direct result of her coal-hungry machinery.

Wilkinson also questioned the entire policy reflected in the commissioning of blockade runners as raiders, in that the objective was to attack the small and family-owned vessels of the "coasting trade and fisheries of the North" as opposed to

the fleets of the "capitalists" that supported the Federal government politically.[347]

Georgia

The Confederate cruiser *Georgia* seems to have been an ill-starred ship from the beginning. She was purchased in Scotland in March 1863. The purchaser on behalf of the Confederate government was Matthew Fontaine Maury, famed early oceanographer dispatched to Great Britain and empowered and funded by Secretary Mallory. That Maury's mission seemed to duplicate that of Bulloch's seems not to have been taken into the Secretary's consideration.

Maury had an agent who spotted a vessel nearing completion at the Denny shipyard in Dumbarton, named *Japan* and intended for merchant service in the Far East. At her launch on January 10, 1863 the vessel's name was changed to *Virginian*, then, when purchased in the name of Maury's cousin for £27,500, changed again to *Georgia*.[348]

The ship was an iron-hulled steamer, 212-feet long and twenty-seven-feet in breadth and thirteen-feet nine-inches depth of hold. (Another source indicates she was 219-feet from the "fore part of the stem under the bowsprit to aft side of the head of the stern post" by twenty-seven-feet five-inches to the outside of the planking. The registered tonnage was 427.25 and gross tonnage 600. There is no indication that the screw propeller was equipped with a hoisting mechanism, but it probably could be disconnected when necessary to reduce drag when under sail.[349] There is some indication that the hull had watertight compartments.[350]

She was brig rigged, with a full poop. One source indicates she had a fiddle head; another, a "demi-woman." Her machinery was a two-cylinder steeple engine geared to the propeller shaft. A large gear with lignum vitae teeth operated a smaller, iron-toothed gear on the propeller shaft

Deck plan, CSS Georgia. After being purchased by Matthew Fontaine Maury, the Denny-built merchant vessel was brought back to the builder and altered. Note the locations for two guns forward of the poop cabin and another in front of the funnel. National Archives

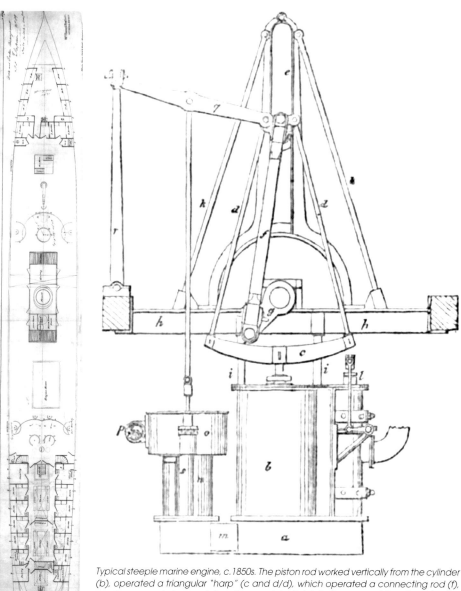

enabling a relatively slow turning engine to drive a faster-turning propeller. Lignum vitae is a South American hardwood noted for its density and resin content. The latter characteristic renders it self-lubricating. It is used for propeller shaft bearings, and in early steam engines, was utilized for gear teeth. The engines' cylinders were forty-four-inches in diameter and a forty-eight-inch stroke, and were rated at 200hp. Unlike the standard vertical engine, where the piston was above the propeller shaft and the piston rod operated downward, directly on the shaft, in the steeple engine the piston rod operated upward to move a crosshead up and down. The cross head, in turn, moved rods which reached downward below the piston and rotated the crankshaft, or in this case, turned the large gear. Steam was generated by four, two-furnace main boilers and one auxiliary boiler.[351]

Once the vessel was purchased, she was taken back to Denny's yard for conversion from merchant to commerce raiding warship. This involved strengthening her deck to support heavy guns as well as building a secure ammunition storage room. The main deck plan shows that it was expected that she would carry three guns on pivots. Deck pivot rails were to be installed between the funnel and the foremast for a fifty-pounder Blakely rifle. Additionally, there were to be two twenty-pounder Blakely guns just forward of the poop cabin. The latter were to be stowed parallel to the vessel's centerline.

While the ship was under conversion, a crew was hired and given to believe that the ship was

Typical steeple marine engine, c.1850s. The piston rod worked vertically from the cylinder (b), operated a triangular "harp" (c and d/d), which operated a connecting rod (f), moving up and down rotating the crankshaft (g). In the case of the Georgia, the crankshaft rotated a large gear, which in turn actuated a smaller gear on the propeller shaft. The large gear had wooden teeth, which at times fractured and became dangerous projectiles, injuring the enginemen. Wikimedia Commons

The Georgia fitting out. She proved to be inefficient under sail, with her brig rig simply not sufficient for her size. From April to October 1863, the vessel captured eight Union merchant vessels. The vessel had a short career as a cruiser and was eventually captured by Union steam frigate Niagara. Illustrated London News

The former Confederate cruiser Georgia after the Civil War. This photo emphasizes the diminutive proportions of her masts, though apparently in this photo the vessel has been reduced from a brig to a schooner for merchant service. She was a merchant vessel in Canadian waters until 1870. Heyl Collection, Bowling Green University

to sail to the Far East. When it appeared that steps were being taken by the British to seize her, the vessel sailed from the Clyde, with carpenters still at work on board. After these men were taken off by a local tug, the *Georgia* made for Plymouth, then for Ushant. At the latter place there was a rendezvous with the tender *Alar*, which carried the guns of her battery as well as the Confederate naval officers for the vessel. Her commanding officer was Commander William L. Maury, cousin of Matthew F. Maury, who commissioned her on April 9, 1863.[352]

Transshipping the guns from the *Alar* was at first uneventful, due to a relatively smooth sea. The two twenty-four-pounders and two ten-pounder Whitworth rifles were safely transferred first in the waters off Ushant. However, a rising sea prevented the movement of the large thirty-two-pounder Blakely gun. This was loaded off the mainland near Brest. One of the vessel's officers later wrote of the "little" ten-pounder rifles, indicating they were mounted on the quarterdeck and used as stern chasers.[353] Thus, it appears that the two twenty-fours were probably mounted on the pivot rails just forward of the poop cabin and the thirty-two-pounder on the rails forward of the funnel. Note that the guns planned for, as noted above, differed somewhat from those actually mounted.

Once at sea and in commission, Maury made his first capture on April 25, 1863, the merchant ship *Dictator*. Six more vessels were taken en route to the Cape of Good Hope by way of Trinidad and Bahia, Brazil. This part of the cruise was marked by an incident in which the machinery's wooden "cog" teeth fractured and spewed wood splinters about, injuring several sailors.[354]

By the time the cruiser reached South Africa, she had masses of foul growth on her underwater hull, measuring eight to twelve inches deep and severely impeding her speed. One writer indicated she had dropped from a nominal nine-knots to about five. Only two more prizes were taken after departing from the Cape. The final vessel, *Bold Hunter* collided with *Georgia*. The prow of the *Bold Hunter* sliced the "fragile plates" of *Georgia*'s quarter like "cheese," wrote one of her officers.[355]

Returning northward, she put into Cherbourg in October 1863 to have her bottom cleaned and machinery overhauled. The vessel remained there until February 1864, by which time it was determined that she was unfit for further service as a commerce raider. Consequently, a rendezvous was planned with the recently acquired Confederate steamer *Rappahannock*. They were to meet off the coast of Morocco and transfer *Georgia*'s guns, stores and some crewmembers to the newer vessel. French authorities, however, blocked the departure of the *Rappahannock* and the meet never occurred.

At Mogador, in North Africa, the crew was allowed shore leave and there followed a fracas with an armed group of Moors, resulting in a hurried chase back to the ship – where the guns were run out and a few rounds let off to frighten away the crowd. This was later somewhat facetiously referred to as the Confederacy's only "foreign war."[356]

Georgia then returned to France, but was ordered by the authorities to depart from Bordeaux in twenty-four hours. She then evaded two Union navy vessels and sailed to Liverpool where she was decommissioned on May 10, 1864.

Though the ship was sold and converted to merchant service, the U.S. consul declared that the transfer would not be recognized by the U.S. government and that she was liable to seizure if found by a U.S. naval vessel. She was, in consequence, captured by the U.S. steam frigate *Niagara* in August 1864, and was subsequently condemned in a U.S. prize court. She later became a merchant steamer in Canadian waters.

In retrospect, it seems obvious that the *Georgia* would not have been an efficient commerce raider on the high seas. Her two main drawbacks were her iron hull and brig rig. The former was subject to fouling in a short time in salt water – requiring docking to clean off the hull. The fouling severely reduced her speed, which apparently was never very high, in any event.

The brig rig was simply inadequate. One of her officers wrote that her "sail power was insufficient owing to her length" and that it was almost impossible to put her about under sail. Note that the *Florida* and *Kearsarge*, both nearly

the same length as *Georgia*, were barque rigged. This inefficiency under sail resulted in much reliance on her engines and consequent frequency of coaling.[357]

Her engines were another drawback. As has been mentioned, the combination of iron and wood gear teeth was literally hazardous. There were at least two incidents when the wooden gear teeth fractured and sent fragments flying, injuring anyone in range. Another theoretical disadvantage on this quasi-warship was the placement of her engines and boilers. All were located high in the hull – a distinct problem in any combat situation.[358]

In summary, one of her officers later described the *Georgia* as a "poor miserable tin kettle." Despite her drawbacks, in about four months of active cruising the *Georgia* captured nine vessels with a value of about $406,000.[359]

Chickamauga

As mentioned previously, *Chickamauga* was similar to *Tallahassee* in several key aspects. Both vessels were built by Dudgeon, at Millwall, London and were twin-screw, iron steamers. She was launched under the name *Edith,* in March 1864, and was essentially a smaller version of *Tallahassee* with a straight stem, closely spaced twin funnels, and light fore and aft rig. Where *Tallahassee* (*Atalanta*) was 220- by twenty-four-feet with a fourteen-foot' depth; *Edith* was 175- by twenty-five feet with a fifteen-foot depth of hold. Both ships drove twin screws with quadruple cylinders, thirty-four- by twenty-one-inches in capacity. *Edith* measured 531-tons (510 displacement), and ran at 13.4-knots on her sea trials.

Alexander Collie purchased the vessel in April 1864, and she ran into the South ten times through

The commerce raider Chickamauga, was formerly the blockade runner Edith. Built by the same firm that produced the Tallahassee, this vessel also had twin screws and operated against Union commerce off the East Coast of the U.S. in 1864 – at nearly the same time as the Tallahassee. Neither vessel could remain at sea longer than their coal supply lasted, reducing their potential as commerce raiders. Mariners' Museum

the blockade – about twice monthly.[360] In September 1864, she was purchased by the Confederate government for use as a coastal commerce raider.

John Wilkinson, her commanding officer in Confederate service, was not impressed with the vessel as a cruiser, referring to her as a "so-called man of war" – despite the fact that the vessel mounted three pivot guns on her deck: a twelve-pounder forward, a sixty-four-pounder amidships, and a thirty-two-pounder rifle at the stern.[361]

"She was more substantially built than most of the blockade-runners, and was very swift, but was altogether unfit for a cruiser," he wrote. He explained, "She could only keep the sea while her supply of coal lasted." Her progress under sail was materially hampered by the inability to disconnect her twin propellers. Under her light suit of canvas and short masts, sail was only efficient to steady her in a seaway. "Under all sail and off the wind, without steam, she could not make more than three-knots in a stiff breeze; by the wind under the same circumstances, she had not even steerage way."[362]

With guns in place and now named *Chicka-mauga*, Wilkinson ran the vessel out of Wilmington on October 28, 1864, outrunning one blockader which fired on her to no effect. Wilkinson steamed northward and took his first prize on October 30, the *M.L. Potter*, a barque out of Bangor, Maine. By November 2, Wilkinson had taken six additional vessels, all in the waters around New York, including the entrance to Long Island Sound. It should be noted that these captures were nearly simultaneous with those of the *Tal-lahassee*, that was operating off the Delaware capes the first three days of November.

Wilkinson, finding his ship in need of coal, then took the *Chickamauga* to Bermuda, arriving there November 8, 1864. The authorities at St. George limited the amount of coal Wilkinson could load to that which would carry the vessel to the nearest Southern port. This meant that the vessel could only make a direct return to Wilmington and eliminated any chance of further cruising. The *Chickamauga* entered Wilmington on November 19, again chased by several of the Union blockaders.

Wilkinson had hoped to take the ship on a second cruise, this time with quarters provided for officers and crew, as well as "proper spars" and a means of disconnecting the screws. This plan died with the Union attacks on Fort Fisher, and the ship was later taken up the Cape Fear River and burned to prevent capture.[363]

Rappahannock

The *Rappahannock* was another "Maury Cruiser," referring to Matthew Fontaine Maury's vessel purchases in Great Britain, the first having been the *Georgia*. In November 1863, Maury was searching for a vessel to replace the unsatisfactory *Georgia* and located an ex-Royal Navy gunboat or gun vessel, HMS *Victor*. The wooden-hulled steamer was for sale at Sheerness dockyard, with the official reason for her sale being "numerous mechanical defects."

The ship had been launched in November 1855, and was commissioned in January 1856, one of many warships resulting from the Crimean War building programs. She was one of six of the *Intrepid* class, measuring 200- by thirty-feet four-inches with a fourteen-foot six-inch depth of hold. They were 868-tons (builder's measure) and *Victor* was built by Money, Wigram & Son,

Confederate cruiser Rappahannock, formerly the British navy's gunboat HMS Victor. Built in 1855-56, the vessel was deemed mechanically unsound and sold to Confederate agents in Britain. Naval Historical Center

Plans of the Rappahannock, a slightly larger version of the Florida and smaller than the Alabama. Her commanding officer found the vessel to be "unseaworthy" and refused to take her to sea. She remained a Confederate "White Elephant," sitting at a pier for the remainder of the war. Smithsonian Institution

at Millwall. The engines were by Miller, Ravenhill & Co. These were two horizontal cylinders developing 1,166hp driving a single screw and capable of driving the ship at 11½-knots.

The *Victor* had twin funnels, a barque rig, and was to have a complement of 100. Originally, her battery consisted of five guns: four thirty-two-pounders and one sixty-eight-pounder rifle, the latter on pivot mount. As a class, the ships were apparently less than stellar. All were broken up or sold out of the service by 1866.

The *Victor* was sold to Gordon Coleman & Company, renamed *Scylla*, and then re-sold to an agent of the Confederate government. At the time of her sale, she was not rigged. On

November 24, 1863, she was towed from the dockyard and across the Channel to Calais, to complete her repairs.

In mid-channel, with workmen still aboard, she was commissioned as a Confederate naval vessel, now named *Rappahannock*, and taken over by Lt. William F. Campbell. Campbell's intention was to rendezvous with the *Georgia* at Cherbourg and receive the latter's armament. However, Campbell quickly learned his vessel's defects: apparently her hull was rotten and boilers equally unsound. The problems were so manifest that immediately on arriving at Calais he wired Bulloch that the ship was "unseaworthy." Campbell then refused to take her to sea, thus defeating the plan to meet the *Georgia*. She lay inert for five days at Calais and this was sufficient to bring her to the unwelcome notice of the French authorities, who were incited by the American consul's claim that she was intended for war purposes.

The *Rappahannock* was refused permission to depart from Calais and therefore remained there as a depot ship. The vessel's manifest defects gained her the nickname "the Confederate White

Elephant" and her crew and officers were detached in March 1865. She was sold four months later.[364]

Alexandra

Another of the Confederate navy's still-born cruisers, *Alexandra* began as a project of Fraser, Trenholm and Company, and was intended to be a gift to the Confederacy. She was built by the Miller Company at Liverpool, with engines by Fawcett, Preston. This was the same arrangement that had produced the *Florida*.

Of course, the vessel came under the scrutiny of the U.S. consul and Union agents and numerous reports resulted. On February 28, 1863, the American consul Thomas H. Dudley reported to Secretary of State Seward that the ship was nearly ready to launch. She was reported, according to Dudley's sources, to be 145-feet long, overall, and with a moulded beam of twenty-six-feet and depth of hold of seventeen-feet, to draw 9 to 10-feet of water. The informant continued: "Her speed will be from 15- to 16-knots," driven by, "engines about 90-horsepower capable of working to some 200. She is built of wood very strong

THE ENGLISH PIRATE "ALEXANDRA," SEIZED BY THE BRITISH GOVERNMENT AT LIVERPOOL.—[See Page 567.]

Potential Confederate cruiser Alexandra, built as a gift for the Confederacy by financiers Fraser, Trenholm and Company. The small vessel (165-feet in length) was seized by British authorities less than a month after her launch, in April 1863. Naval Historical Center

Designed to be a large version of the Alabama, the Texas was to have seven guns and an iron protective belt around the machinery. When British authorities suspected a Confederate connection for the vessel, they moored a gunboat beside her and had her steering mechanism removed. Post-war, the vessel was sold to Chile then became the Spanish gunboat Tornado. The ship captured the filibustering vessel Virginius in 1873. www.csa-dixie.com

oak and teak with iron deck beams over engine and boilers … Her screw works in a copper slide weighing five tons and is so arranged as to be lifted out of the water. Her rig topsail schooner."[365]

Of course, the informants' reports were not necessarily accurate. Illustrations of the vessel show a barque rig, for instance, and expectations of speed were almost invariably high, also a seventeen-foot depth of hold would have been unlikely on a vessel of this small size.

The vessel was launched on March 7, 1863, and was later reported to be "faster" than the *Florida*. She was still incomplete, with workers on board when she was seized by British authorities on April 5th, citing her structure and design were of a warlike nature.

Legal actions served to keep the vessel out of Confederate hands for months afterwards. Eventually a "narrow" interpretation of the statutes involved was reached and she was released in April 1864, on condition that the vessel would be converted back to a merchant steamer. The vessel, now renamed *Mary*, reached Nassau in November 1864 and was seized again. The war was over before she was re-released in May 1865.[366]

Texas

In mid-1862, Secretary Mallory sent yet another emissary to Britain with instructions to have a steam cruiser built, along the lines of the *Alabama*.

Lt. George T. Sinclair was to coordinate with Bulloch in the matter, though Bulloch did not have funds for the project. Sinclair found another source of funds, in this instance via "cotton certificates," amounting to over £50,000.

A contract was made with the J. & G. Thomson firm in Glasgow, in August 1862, for a composite hull vessel that was somewhat larger than *Alabama*. Various sources indicate the hull was iron-framed and teak planked and either 220- or 230-feet long, with a thirty-two-foot beam. The depth of hold was nineteen-feet eight inches and she was barque rigged, with iron fore and main masts and patent reefing topsails. There was a four-inch iron belt protecting the engines and boilers. Propulsion was a two-cylinder, back-acting installation, with cylinder diameter of fifty-six-inches and a thirty-inch stroke, developing a nominal 330-horsepower with four boilers. The screw was to have a hoisting mechanism and the funnel was to lower to the level of the rail. The ship's battery was to be three eight-inch rifles, on pivot mountings, plus at least four broadside guns.[367]

As construction proceeded, under the cover name *Canton*, Union agents and the U.S. Consul monitored the progress, scrutinizing the vessel for evidence of warlike intent, in particular the cutting of gun ports and placement of ringbolts on her decks for gun training tackle. At one point a newspaper article noted that there had been ringbolts and gunports, but the ports had been covered in and bolts removed. On the other hand, Confederate navy Captain John Maffitt was reported to have visited the yard, and had been seen "supervising the fitting of watercocks." These would, according to the report, allow flooding of parts of the hull, thus lowering the ship's profile in battle. In addition, berthing and lockers for 150 men was being built. Finally, her head was to be decorated with the Goddess of Liberty perched on a bed of palmetto leaves – the latter of course the symbol of South Carolina. (The accuracy of these assertions can be questioned, however, as some of the Union informants were of less than sterling character, and some were paid informants.)[368]

In any event, the ship was launched October 29, 1863, and her sea trials were to begin in late-November, when British authorities acted. She was detained and a Royal Navy gunboat moored alongside her on November 20. In response to rumors that the Confederates were planning to snatch the ship surreptitiously, the local collector of customs had her steering mechanism removed and taken ashore. The ship now lay in limbo until the courts weighed in. On May 5, 1864, it was agreed that the vessel would be released only on condition that she would not be sold for two years. Despite another story, that the ship would be seized by Confederate hirelings, the ship was towed to Dumbarton and remained there for the balance of the Civil War.[369]

The ship's post-war career was more interesting. She was sold to Chile, in 1866, and sailed under the name *Pampero*, until captured by the Spanish off Madeira in 1870. She was rated a screw corvette in the Spanish navy and armed with three guns. Now named *Tornado*, the ship brushed with fame in 1873 when she seized the filibustering ship *Virginius* in Cuban waters. The "Virginius Affair" led to a major crisis in U.S.-Spanish relations when Spain executed the vessel's crew, including a number of Americans.

The vessel was later used as a torpedo-training vessel, then as a dormitory for children of injured sailors. She was sunk by Spanish Nationalist aircraft in 1938 then broken up the next year.[370]

The French-built Corvettes

In 1863, James D. Bulloch ordered six vessels to be built in shipyards in France. Two were ironclad rams, which will be covered in the following chapter. Four were to be steam sloops, termed corvettes in Europe. Bulloch later wrote about the missions he proposed for this flotilla: "The two Bordeaux ironclads and the four corvettes would have been a formidable attacking squadron … upon the Northern seaboard."[371]

Bulloch signed an agreement with shipbuilder Lucien Arman, on April 15, 1863, for the four sloops, after learning that Napoleon III himself had suggested that the Confederacy ought to build warships in France. Later, when Napoleon's minister of marine backed away from the Emperor's assertion, there had been a period of uncertainty on Bulloch's part. However, it became apparent that the French attitude would be positive, as long as another cover story was adhered to: that the vessels would be for service on the China seas, where piracy was rampant and a substantial battery would be an asset. This rationale would enable the vessels to be completed and armed and sail under the French flag. In June, when the Minister of Marine gave Bulloch written authorization for arming the vessels, a document which included the number of guns to be mounted, the way seemed clear for their completion for the Confederate Navy.[372]

Bulloch's contract called for building four, "clipper corvettes of about 1,500-tons and 400-horsepower, to be armed with twelve or fourteen six-inch rifled guns." The guns were to be of the standard French naval pattern, which would facilitate having them built in France. Two of the sloops were to be built at Bordeaux in the Arman yard, a third at the Jollet et Babin yard in Nantes, and the fourth at the Dubigeon facility also at Nantes.[373]

Construction of the ships "progressed rapidly," but by the end of 1863 the American ambassador had begun to protest to the French authorities concerning the possible connection between the Confederacy and these ships. Furthermore, it was rumored that the Minister of Marine had stated that the ships would not be permitted to leave France. Unfortunately, for Bulloch's plans, a clerk in one of the shipbuilders' offices stole documents confirming the true identity and eventual owner of the ships and this information became public. A further incentive for the French to squelch the Confederates' plan was the need to prevent anything from interfering with Archduke Maximilian's imminent move into Mexico. By February 1864, Bulloch wrote Mallory that the Minister of Marine had ordered that the two ironclads not be permitted to sail. As for the corvettes, they were not to be armed in France, but must be sold to, "some foreign merchant and dispatched as ordinary trading vessels." Thus there was nothing Bulloch could do to forestall or prevent French authorities from embargoing the ships. Thus, all four corvettes were completed but none went into Confederate service: two went to the Prussian navy; two to Peru.[374]

French-built corvette Georgia, one of four "clipper built" vessels contracted by James D. Bulloch to form a squadron with the Confederate ironclads also being built in European shipyards. Despite early assurances that the French government would not interfere with their completion, in the end, they were sold to Peru and Prussia. Re-named America in the Peruvian navy, the vessel was driven ashore by a tsunami in 1868. Naval Historical Center

As completed, the ships were rather large for their mounted battery, but were otherwise unremarkable, wooden-hulled, steam sloops. They were fully rigged ships with iron spars, 243-feet long by thirty-five-feet six-inches breadth, and an eighteen-foot (draft?). They reportedly had large poop cabins and topgallant forecastles. Their 1,300 indicated horsepower engines were single expansion with four boilers and rated at 13½-knots. The engines were built by the French Mazeline company.

The two in Prussian service were *Louisiana*, renamed *Victoria,* and *Mississippi*, called *Augusta*. They were armed with eight twenty-four-pounders and six twelve-pounders and had a complement of 230 men. *Texas* was named *Union* in Peruvian service, and *Georgia* was commissioned as *America*. Three of the four met untimely ends. *Augusta* was lost in a hurricane in 1885; *America* was washed ashore at Arica, Peru (now Chile) in a tsunami in 1868 – the same cataclysm that ended the career of the U.S. Navy steamer *Wateree* at that place. *Union* was scuttled to prevent capture by Chile in 1881. *Victoria* was broken up in 1892.[375] Bulloch's vision of a Confederate squadron essentially ended when the two ironclads were

prevented from going to the Confederacy. The corvettes were far too well armed and manned to merely be commerce raiders, so their usefulness to the Confederacy was fatally compromised.

Ajax and *Hercules*

These two specialized ships, as will be seen, might be considered cruisers, or gunboats, or towboats, or blockade runners. In mid-1864, they were ordered by James D. Bulloch for the waters about Wilmington. Bulloch wrote: "They have been designed as tow boats, to deceive the Federal spies, but will require insignificant alterations to convert them into serviceable gunboats for local work." The ships could provide cover for blockade runners in the approaches to the Cape Fear River, as well as tow off stranded runners, if necessary.

The vessels were 170-feet in length by twenty-five-feet breadth, and 12½-feet of depth of hold, to draw no more than seven-feet six-inches. They were iron hulled with twin screws and double horizontal, twenty-eight-inch cylinders for each propeller. The boilers were to produce

30psi and have separate steam chests to produce superheated steam as necessary.

After the ships had departed from British waters, the decks were to have extra stanchions installed beneath the "permanent" location for the guns. Two weapons were planned, both on traversing carriages: one eight-inch rifle "to penetrate the enemy's Monitors" and one nine-inch rifle.[376]

The vessels were built at the Denny shipyard at Dumbarton and launched on December 15 (*Ajax*) and December 29 (*Hercules*), 1864. Throughout their construction they had been the object of much speculation and Union spying, but in the end British authorities could find no specific evidence the ships were for warlike purposes.

Ajax sailed in January 1865, and Bulloch wrote John Low, her eventual skipper: "Although the *Ajax* is designed for conversion into a gunboat for harbor defense ... she may nevertheless be profitably employed in bringing out cotton." In any event, regardless of their intended missions, the war ended and neither vessel saw service for the Confederacy.[377]

Adventure and *Enterprise*

Simultaneously, with the ordering of the above two vessels, Bulloch ordered construction of two larger ships. These, Bulloch wrote, "were designed for the purpose of making more extensive cruises, from Wilmington, along the enemy's

Proposed Confederate towboat/blockade runner/gunboat Hercules. Bulloch intended this vessel, and its sister Ajax, to patrol the North Carolina sounds, attack Union commerce and run the blockade as needed. Their decks were strengthened for naval guns and had large winches for towing. Both were completed too late for Confederate service. Henry E. Huntington Library and Art Gallery

Adventure and Enterprise were to be twin-screw multi-purpose vessels designed to carry heavy guns and keep the seas on extensive cruises. They were sold to South American governments and never saw Confederate service. Shown here is a model of the ex-Adventure as Argentine navy's Amazonas (later the General Brown). www. histamar.com

coast." Therefore they were to have engines and boilers below the waterline and compartments above them, "to be filled with cotton for additional protection." Bulloch was instructed earlier by Mallory that these would be "blockade runners," which could "cruise against enemy commerce" and make "dashes" at said commerce as well as run the blockade "at pleasure." To accomplish these aims, Mallory suggested a carrying capacity of 200-250-tons, a single screw or two if they could be disconnected for sailing, decks which would support three heavy guns with clear sweeps for the fore and aft pivots, the ability to minimize smoke, and have berth decks and magazines.[378]

The two were named *Adventure* and *Enterprise* and called "tug steamers." They were built by Denny at Glasgow and were 250-feet in length

and thirty-feet in breadth, with sixteen-feet depth of hold. Except for a mid-ship house and possible topgallant forecastle, they were to be flush decked. There were to be two large cargo holds and cabins for ten officers. Also on deck were two steam winches supported by heavy deck beams.

The hull frames were of ½- and ⁷⁄₁₆-inch iron, 4½- by 3½-inches, on twenty-one-inch centers. The latter were strengthened by reverse frames and the whole was on a 4½-inch angle iron keel. The main deck beams were nine-inches deep and four watertight bulkheads were installed, made of ⁵⁄₁₆-inch plates strengthened by angle iron. The hull plating ranged from ⅝-inch at the garboard strakes to ⅜-inch at the rails.

Two pairs of horizontal cylinders, measuring forty-two-inches, provided 300 nominal horsepower and had "larger than usual" condensers

for operation in "warm climate." Superheating steam chests were to be provided. The cast-iron propellers were to have three or four blades and the propeller shafts were to run on brass bushings and lignum vitae bearings. An arrangement was built-in to allow exhaust steam to be vented below the waterline, rather than out via the funnel. The latter would reduce the vessel's noise signature when attempting to evade the blockaders.

Topside, there was to be a barque rig, similar to that of *Alabama*, in having long lower masts and short topmasts. The rigging was galvanized iron. The contracted speed to be met was to be fourteen-knots and the delivery dates for the two ships were April 6 and June 6, 1865.[379]

With the end of the war, both ships were sold off to other buyers. *Adventure* became the Argentine *Amazonas*; the *Enterprise* went to Brazil as *Brasil*.[380]

FOREIGN-BUILT IRONCLADS

Secretary Mallory's early decision to employ the newest naval technology to meet and nullify the Union navy was the pivot on which most of the Confederacy's naval efforts were based throughout the war. The need for ironclad vessels was preeminent in Mallory's thinking, and in May 1861, he proposed acquisition of such ships from European sources. These vessels, unlike the domestically built ironclads, which would be unsuitable for the open seas, would "traverse the entire coast of the United States … and encounter with a fair prospect of success," the Union navy.[381]

The Confederate Congress quickly authorized the "purchase or construction" of such vessels, and Mallory immediately dispatched Lt. James A. North to Europe, and specifically to England and France on this mission.

As of May 1861, there was only one oceangoing ironclad in existence, the French navy's *Gloire*, which had been completed in August 1860. The Royal Navy's *Warrior* would not go into service until October 1861. There were two additional ironclads under construction in Britain and thirteen being built in France.[382] Hence, Mallory's directive to purchase such a vessel was, in theory, not an unreasonable concept.

Whether purchased or built, any ironclad the Confederacy acquired in Europe would of necessity be an oceangoing vessel: by virtue of the fact that its delivery to the South would require a trans-Atlantic voyage. It is worth noting here that, throughout the war, none of the domestically built Southern and very few of the Union ironclads were capable of going to sea without significant danger of capsizing in heavy weather. The Union's *New Ironsides* was the only one with obvious ocean-going capabilities, including a full sailing rig, sufficient freeboard to withstand high seas, and gunports high enough to allow working of the battery in a seaway.

If the Confederacy could have an ironclad built in Europe, it would necessarily be some variation on the *Gloire* or other ironclads then under construction. The *Gloire* was essentially an iron-armored steam frigate, 255-feet long and fifty-six-feet in beam, with about a twenty-seven-foot draft, carrying thirty-six guns. Her wooden hull provided about two feet of wood as backing for over four inches of iron armor on her sides and under her upper deck. Her engine and eight boilers produced 2,500-horsepower and drove her at twelve-knots. She had a barque rig, and later a complete ship rig.[383] In this era of inefficient steam engines, the sailing rig continued to be a necessity for long-distance cruising. Note also that all these European ironclads mounted their guns in broadside ports; none employed guns in revolving turrets.

As Mallory suggested, the appearance of a Confederate version of *Gloire* or even a smaller cognate, on the U.S. coast would immediately imperil any existing Union oceangoing naval vessel; all were wood, none were armored.

After the Confederate emissaries learned that neither France nor England was disposed to sell any of their ironclads, North as well as Bulloch

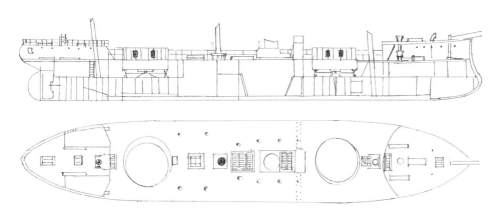

General arrangement and deck of the "Laird Rams." James D. Bulloch oversaw their design, which included the first use of Coles-type rotating turrets, as well as watertight compartmentation and double-bottoms. Coles also suggested the "eccentric" turret mountings, to balance the weights of the guns when run out. Approximate scale: 1 inch = 22 feet. Drawing by author based on plans from National Maritime Museum, Greenwich

set out to have them built. In all, five oceangoing ironclads were completed on order for the Confederacy, three in Britain and two in France. All were formidable vessels but none ever went into action in service to the Confederate states. In fact, only one was commissioned in the Confederate navy and actually encountered a hostile Union naval vessel.

The Laird Rams

The ubiquitous James D. Bulloch was responsible for the construction of two of the armored vessels built in England. Bulloch, after arranging for the construction of *Florida* and *Alabama*, had run the blockade in *Fingal* (later to become the ironclad *Atlanta*) and visited Richmond. By the time he returned to Great Britain, on March 10, 1862, the *Virginia/Merrimack* and *Monitor* battle had been fought and ironclads were the cynosure of all naval minds on both sides of the Mason-Dixon line – with Union technology based on Ericsson's turret and southern ironclads on less-technologically advanced broadside casemate armorclads.

On January 14, 1862, Secretary Mallory had emphasized the mission he now had for Bulloch. He directed Bulloch to the subject of

building, "iron- or steel-clad ships in France or England." He suggested an, "armored steam sloop of moderate size, say of about 2,000-tons, and to carry eight or ten heavy guns." He enclosed a plan drawn by Constructor Porter and Chief Engineer Williamson to be used as a starting point. Once Bulloch found a builder and had developed a practical plan, Mallory said, funds would be immediately available.[384]

When Bulloch arrived in England, he found that Lt. James North had preceded him and had Mallory's instructions to build or purchase an ironclad. North was awaiting funds for a vessel "for which he had made arrangements to contract" and this ship would eventually be built as "No.61," a very large, deep draft ship.[385] Indeed, the ship would prove to be too large for efficient use on the Southern coast and would never be completed for the Confederacy (see below).

Bulloch, on the other hand, opted for a relatively shallow draft design, in consultation with the Laird firm at Birkenhead – the builders of the *Alabama*. The ships he proposed would be capable of "acting efficiently either in the attack or defense of our coast, and its estuaries." A contract was signed in July 1862 with Lairds, for two of such ships, numbered 294 and 295, in the Laird

yard. Bulloch wrote Mallory a fairly specific description of the proposed work on July 21st. In order to achieve the "minimum draft compatible with seaworthiness and invulnerability," it was decided that turrets should be used rather than a broadside battery. In this way, "the sides would be relieved of much strain and the heavy weights be thrown near the center." In this original plan, there were three turrets. These would not revolve, however, but merely be circular casemates within which the guns would be set up on turntables. That Bulloch was not ignorant of the latest technology is evident in the last page of this letter to Mallory: "I am fully aware of the superior advantages of the revolving turrets, but the admiralty have bought Captain Coles' patent and have not yet decided whether private builders will be allowed to use it. I have all the plans and drawings, however, and it will not be too late to make the change three months hence."

The resulting ships would be 220-feet long, extreme breadth forty-two feet and draft with crew and stores for three months, fifteen feet. They would be barque rigged and the engines would be 350-horsepower, nominal, and achieve 10½-knots. Tonnage would be about 1,800.[386]

Other characteristics of the ships were detailed in this letter. The sides of the hull were to be plated from over three feet below the waterline up to the waterways of the upper deck. The central 120-feet of the hull was to have plating 4½-inches thick, covering the magazine, engines and boilers, and the thickness of this armor would decrease as it neared the ends. Twelve inches of teak was to back the iron armor, tapering to six inches towards the ends. The turrets would be protected by iron 5½-inches thick backed by a foot of teak.

For increased survivability, Bulloch had a series of watertight bulkheads in the plan. Fore and aft of the central armored area, the hull was to be broken up into a series of compartments. In the midship section, two longitudinal bulkheads were planned, which would be riveted to two athwartship bulkheads, forming "an inner ship." Further compartments were to be constructed between the longitudinals and the sides of the "ship proper." He calculated that if they were penetrated by shot, shell or ramming, "filling the whole of them on one side would only list the ship a few inches."

Above the main deck, the bulwarks were to be hinged at the bottom to allow firing the turret guns and Bulloch was considering a steam-powered mechanism to operate the gunport shutters. The lower masts were to be iron and hollow, set up to allow the slimmer, wood topmasts to telescope down inside the lower masts. When going into battle, the yards were to be lowered and "tripped" vertically, then lashed to the lower masts. The bowsprit was to be hinged in order to stow it out of the way when the ram was in use. Finally, there was to be a double bottom, about 2½-feet above the actual bottom. The space between the two would be a tank or compartment to be filled "at pleasure" to bring the ship down if necessary to, "preserve proper immersion of the armor plating when the ship is light from the consumption of fuel."

Bulloch expected the first of the ships to be ready in March and the second in May 1863. The cost of each was £93,750, without battery and magazine fittings.[387]

Bulloch's quick adoption of the revolving turret at this early date was a considerable leap of faith. On the British side of the Atlantic, the Admiralty had finally begun construction of the *Prince Albert*, their first Coles-turret ironclad, in February 1862, and the entire subject of turret-versus-broadside was hotly debated at this time, with Coles and his supporters critical of the broadside-battery *Warrior,* which had been completed late in 1861.[388]

How much Bulloch knew about Ericsson's *Monitor* and its turret is unknown. The vessel was launched on January 30, 1862 to much public interest and sometimes derision. It is not known whether Bulloch learned of this before he left the east coast through the blockade. The fight at Hampton Roads, however, had play in the London newspapers as early as March 29th. Bullock did note, in September 1862, that he was considering a "compromise" between Coles and Ericsson's patents, thus implying a working knowledge of both systems. (The main difference in the two systems was that Ericsson's turret rotated on a central spindle while Coles' turret operated on rollers under its perimeter.)[389]

Bulloch wrote in September 1862, that he had made the decision to use rotating turrets. Then, after specifics of the guns and their weight and character were accumulated, he determined that there would only be two turrets, each mounting two nine-inch guns, each gun weighing eleven tons, and firing 240-pound projectiles. The decision to use turrets was critical to the future of the project and Bulloch was quite aware of this, writing that their use would "run the risk of being interfered with." Turrets were definitely war-like structures and would not stand the scrutiny of British officialdom, so Bulloch resorted to another stratagem: having the vessels ostensibly being built for the Viceroy of Egypt, and named *El Tousson* and *El Mounassir*.[390]

Once the rotating turret principle was incorporated, Bulloch applied for and received a "treaty" for authority to use the Coles system turret. He wrote: "… our dimensions were almost precisely those adopted by Captain Coles for the Royal Sovereign, and the size and weight of guns, as well as the method of mounting them, are so nearly identical that one would suppose there had been previous consultation, which was not the case." Coles did, however, suggest that the turrets be "eccentric, so that when the guns were run out, the weight would be balanced and the training more easily effected."[391] Each turret was a, "polygon, composed of as many sides as the number of plates necessary to form it. Practically the figure may be considered circular, and we have avoided the necessity of bending any of the plates, a process which has been found … to injure … the cohesiveness of the iron." Bulloch wrote that the plates were vertical rather than horizontal, eliminating the need to bend them, and that their edges were, "accurately planed so as to make close fits at the butts." Additionally, Bulloch said that triple hammock rails and nettings were mounted around the perimeter of the turrets, with the intention of creating "rifle pits" therein. The turrets, each of which weighed 150-tons without their guns, were supported by a series of stanchions that were in turn supported by a circular "keelson built upon the main keelson and floors." The turret's wheels on which they rotated moved on a circular race and pivot from the center. The *Royal Sovereign*, mentioned by Bulloch, was the Admiralty's "test bed" vessel for the Coles turret, authorized in April 1862. It was a massive conversion of a wooden steam ship of the line that was cut down and on which were four turrets, one mounting two guns, the others, single guns. It was designed only for coast defense and had minimal rig.[392]

Bulloch also described the poop and forecastle cabins. These were added in mid-construction and were of light materials and not "permanently connected to the hull proper." They could be "shot away" or "entirely removed" without injury to the hull or armor.[393]

British authorities closely monitored the vessels' construction and seized both within three months of their launch. At left is the North Carolina, code named El Tousson, with RN warship Majestic on guard, just astern. Behind Majestic is Mississippi (El Mounassir) not yet rigged. Illustrated London News

HMS Wivern near Plymouth, England in RN service. Note the folding bulwarks and "rings" of hammock rails around the turrets, forming "rifle pits." The vessels' low freeboard and heavy roll made their sea-combat usefulness limited and both were out of main-line service by 1870. Naval Historical Center

Construction of both the Laird ships was relatively uneventful, and protection from inclement weather was provided by gas-lighted shiphouses. The first launched was named *North Carolina* and the second, *Mississippi*. The former went into the water July 4, the latter on August 23, 1863.

Bulloch's fears that the vessels would not see Confederate service were accurate. Both ships were seized in October 15, 1863, and commissioned in the Royal Navy in 1865. *North Carolina* (No.294) became HMS *Scorpion* and *Mississippi* (No.295), HMS *Wivern*.

The completed ships were much as Bulloch had described them earlier, as quoted above, in addition to a ram projecting some seven feet forward, below the waterline. Some indication of the iron hull components was provided by one of the Union agents that had interviewed workmen and been at the shipyard. He reported that there were two twenty-two-foot diameter rings for the turrets ("towers"). The deck beams were ten-inches deep which broadened to about two-feet at their ends where they were riveted to the frames. The

beams were of plate or "Bull iron" with two angle irons back to back forming their top. The frames were of "angle iron 5x3½ fore and aft."[394]

The ships in RN service were 224-feet six-inches between perpendiculars, forty-two-feet four-inches beam, and drew fourteen-feet forward and sixteen-feet aft, displacing 2,751-tons. The armor belt was 4½-inches with up to ten-inches backing; five-inches with ten-inch backing in the turrets. The guns were four nine-inch, muzzle-loading rifles. The propulsion was two fifty-six-inch diameter, thirty-six-inch stroke, direct acting, horizontal cylinders, and four boilers. These produced 350-horsepower and eleven-knots.[395]

One major change made in British service was modification to reduce the standing rigging, which interfered with the turret guns' fields of fire. Struts were installed, running from the main and fore tops angling down to the sides of the deck. This was the first use of tripod masts, a feature which was prominent on the later, ill-fated HMS *Captain* (which also had two of Coles' turrets).

Later, use of the ships in Royal Navy service indicated that they had limited capabilities. One authority reported that they were, "good seaboats but with a deep roll and low freeboard, their fighting efficiency in a seaway was doubtful." Both ships had short, active, service lives and had been relegated to secondary roles by 1870. *Scorpion* became a guard ship at Bermuda in 1869; *Wivern* was a coast guard vessel as of 1870, then a guard ship at Hong Kong in 1880.[396]

Bulloch had high expectations for these two decidedly formidable vessels, writing: "I respectfully propose, then that the ships…should be ordered to … Wilmington, North Carolina. One could fall in with the land at New Inlet, and the other … at the mouth of the Cape Fear river … By steaming in at early daylight they might entirely destroy the blockading vessels." In Bulloch's scenario, they would then range the coast either north or southwards, destroying the blockaders and possibly even "render Washington itself untenable."[397]

Some idea of their armor's strength can be estimated by an 1866 experiment on the similar

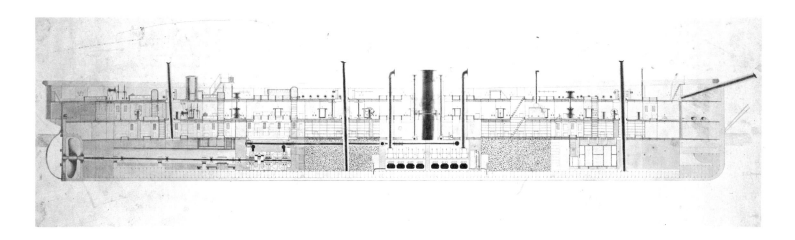

Longitudinal section of "North's Ironclad," also known as "No.61" and Santa Maria. Similar in size to the French Gloire, the vessel was to carry twenty Whitworth rifles on the gundeck and would have had the largest crew of any Confederate naval vessel. Henry E. Huntington Museum and Art Gallery

after turret of the *Royal Sovereign*. Three rounds were fired at the ship's turret, from a nine-inch gun at a mere 200-yards – point blank range. "None … interrupted the working of the turret but the one that hit the back disturbed a plate."[398]

One can speculate on possible match-ups between either of these ships and Union ironclads, such as *New Ironsides*, mounting sixteen eleven-inch guns with 130-pound projectiles and four-inches of side armor, or the twin turret monitor *Monadnock*, mounting four ten-inch rifles. In any event, the appearance of either of these ships in American waters would have meant much grief for any wooden ship in the United States Navy and a significant challenge to the ironclads of that navy.

North's Ironclad: "No.61"

Lt. James H. North was the first of Mallory's agents to arrive in Europe with instructions to purchase or build an ironclad vessel. Though he reached Britain in May 1861, shortly before Commander Bulloch, North was unable to make headway in the project until May 1862, when he reached an agreement and contract with the J. & G. Thomson firm of Glasgow, which had built the cruiser *Florida,* for an ironclad frigate. It is worth noting that when Bulloch met with Mallory in Richmond in late 1861 to discuss the need for ironclads, the Secretary said he had not had communication with North since the lieutenant had departed for England. Furthermore, there apparently had been little or no consultation between North and Bulloch when the latter had been in Britain, placing the orders for *Florida* and *Alabama*.

Lt. North's directive to purchase an existing ironclad – like the famous *Gloire* – presumably led him to believe that building a vessel of a similar size and character would be appropriate in the event a purchase was not feasible. This germ of thought resulted in the vessel variously known as "North's Ironclad," "No.61," "Santa

Maria," "Glasgow," or the less complimentary "Scottish Sea Monster." However, when North showed Bulloch his plan for the proposed ship, Bulloch objected, contending that a smaller, lighter draft vessel would be more useful for the South. North stood firm, however, saying his orders were "specific and preemptory." Here Bulloch left the situation, and North proceeded with the ship's construction.[399]

North signed a memorandum of agreement on May 21, 1862 with the Thomson firm on the Clyde River, to build an "armor-plated screw steamer," for a total of £182,000, to be delivered in June 1863. The contract specifications for the vessel show the level of sophistication in design incorporated in the vessel.

The hull was iron, 270-feet on the load line, by a fifty-foot beam. The depth of hold to the main deck was twenty-feet and displacement tonnage was 3,200 (builders measure). North's vessel was longer than *Gloire* but broader in beam.

Significant portions of the hull were wrought iron. The keel was fourteen-inches deep and five-inches thick, "hammered scrap iron." The stem was forged onto the keel; the frame for the screw was "forged in one piece." The after-stern post

"No.61" fitting out at the pier. The vessel was far too large to use along the Southern coast and the contract was cancelled in late-1863. Naval Historical Center

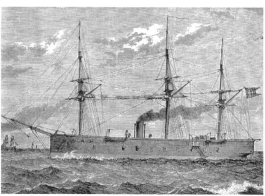

Danmark under sail in Danish naval service. The vessel served until 1907. Wikimedia Commons

was twelve- by six-inches; the inner post, twelve-by seven-inches; the lower portion, connecting the two, was twelve- by eight-inches and was to have "6- to 8-feet of keel forged to it." The hull frames were six- by 3½-inches and spaced eighteen-inches center to center. Angle iron edged the frames from the floors up to the "place where they are cut for recess for iron plating." The angle iron was doubled on the frames by the engines and boiler spaces.

The floors – the lowest part of the hull framing – were thirty-inches deep at the centerline and tapered, becoming narrower towards the sides of the hull and met the frames at the five-foot waterline. There was a center keelson, side keelsons, and bilge keelsons. The first was thirty-eight-inches deep and five-inches thick; the rest were thirty-two-inches deep. The forepeak – about the first nineteen-feet from stem to the forward watertight bulkhead was strengthened to "resist shock of collision," by reinforcing iron, plate-breast hooks spaced "three feet apart."

The deck beams were "bulb iron" and were ten-inches deep for the main (gun) deck, eight-inches for the upper deck, and nine-inches for the lower deck. The deck beams were mounted on alternate hull frames and were "turned down" on the ends so that each joint of the beam to the frame was twice as wide as the beam itself. Iron stringers (longitudinal members fastened on top of and connecting the deck beams) were forty-two-inches wide on the upper deck and thirty-six-inches on the lower two decks.

Watertight bulkheads were to have doubled frames at the hull sides and were to have vertical stiffeners thirty-inches apart running up to the main deck. Specifications mention at least two, watertight, bulkheads: one at the forepeak and one right aft. There were most likely others fore and aft of the engine and boiler spaces. Additionally, there were compartments in the center of the coalbunkers that were designed to carry water ballast. An appropriate steam pump and piping was installed for this purpose.

The iron armor was extensive, running from the fourteen-foot waterline upward to the gunwale, from bow to stern. It was to be four-inches thick, except at the extreme ends where it was one inch less. It was to be bolted to the ship's side through teak backing eighteen-inches thick and was inset into the hull frames so as to form a smooth outer hull.

The hull was to have twenty gunports, each two-feet wide and three-feet high. A later alteration indicated the gunport covers were to be double: an armor-plated outer cover and a watertight "blind" on the inside. The latter was to be worked by block and tackle, the former by exterior chains. (However, the date of this alteration is uncertain and may have been after the vessel's sale to the Danish navy.)

The decks were to be pitch pine and the masts either wood or iron. The specifications left it open as to whether the vessel should be barque or ship-rigged.[400]

The ram was to be conical in shape and located six or seven feet below the waterline, and six feet long. This location was selected because at that level the ram would impact the adversary below the armored belt. The conical shape would allow the ship to easily be backed free from the victim. The specially strengthened watertight fore peak was expected to maintain the integrity of the hull even if the "prow [was] carried away."[401]

The machinery for the ship was two direct-acting cylinders, horizontally mounted. The cylinder diameter was seventy-five-inches; the stroke, thirty-six-inches, producing 500 nominal horsepower. Four tubular boilers produced the steam and the coalbunkers were to hold 1,000-tons. The funnel was to telescope below the level of the rail.[402]

One important item had been omitted from the specifications: a lifting screw. North later "explained" this omission by saying he "knew little about engines." By the time this problem was noticed it was too late to rectify, and the builder substituted a clutch mechanism by which the three bladed iron screw could be disconnected.[403]

Work on the ship moved steadily through early-1863, and there was some attempt to disguise the vessel's intended end user, hence the cover name *Santa Maria*, but the negative aspects of the vessel, as well as a hardening of the British attitude towards the Confederacy soon led to the rejection of the project. One of the major shocks to North's superiors occurred when North began looking for a crew: the ship would need 500 men plus twenty-nine officers. This would give No.61 the largest crew in the Confederate Navy – with the expenses to match. When the British authorities seized Bulloch's Laird rams in the fall of 1863, it was obvious that the equally warlike Clyde River ironclad would not be allowed to join the Confederate Navy. North, therefore, terminated the Thomson contract on December 21, 1863.[404]

The ironclad was launched in January 1864, and sold to Denmark later that year. She was then armed with twenty sixty-pounder rifles and eight eighteen-pounders. In Danish service, named *Danmark,* she drew nineteen-feet six-inches and was rated at 8½-knots. She was broken up in 1907.[405]

This ironclad probably had great potential in any theoretical encounter with Union navy ironclad vessels. The *New Ironsides* was closest in type and design, carrying guns in broadside

and having four inches of iron over about seventeen inches of oak, on an oceangoing platform. (Oak and teak, used on No.61, are similar in density.) Had North's ironclad been armed exclusively with twenty seven-inch Whitworth rifles, her broadside would have been 1,100-pounds; the Union vessel's was nearly the same (seven eleven-inch Dahlgrens, one 150-pounder rifle, and one fifty-pounder rifle). *New Ironsides'* non-compartmentalized wooden hull would have been its true drawback, as well as its preponderance of smoothbore guns, though in some situations its significantly shallower draft may have been an advantage. In smooth waters, a Union twin turret monitor mounting four 150-pounder rifles might have put up a good fight if it could maintain a rapid rate of fire. However, had No.61 been armed with breech loading rifles, her rate of fire would far outmatch any Union naval vessel.

Stonewall

Bulloch travelled to France in mid-1863, and visited the Lucien Arman yard at Bordeaux where he looked in on the progress of the wooden corvettes he had ordered and were then under construction at that place. He also inspected two ironclads being built there for the French navy. In June of that year, he had learned that the Confederate congress had voted two million dollars for construction of ironclad vessels to be built in Southern Europe. With funding supposedly assured, Bulloch, on July 16, 1863, signed a contract with the Arman firm for two ironclad rams to cost one hundred thousand pounds each.

The design for the two vessels was based partially on the premise that they should be of lighter draft than the Laird Rams. Bulloch wrote that vessels for service in the Mississippi River should be of light draft and "comparatively short; they must have great steam power, to contend with the rapid current, and they must be handy, with capability to turn in short space." Furthermore,

their armor must be capable of withstanding fire from eleven- and fifteen-inch guns. Finally, they would necessarily have to make a 5,000-mile sea voyage to reach their fighting ground.[406]

The move to acquire vessels in France was done with the supposed knowledge and consent of high officials in the Imperial government of Napoleon III; indeed Bulloch wrote that he had a letter from M. Chasseloup Laubat, the Minister of Marine, granting authority to build the rams. Thus the construction of the ships proceeded without interruption or undue political pressure, under the code names *Sphinx* and *Cheops*.[407]

The two vessels were 157-feet six-inches between perpendiculars, 165-feet nine-inches on the waterline by thirty-two-feet six-inches, with a draft of fourteen-feet three-inches. As such they were shorter than most Union iron or wood ships – the ninety-day gunboats, for instance were 158-feet in length. Further increasing their maneuverability was the provision of twin four-bladed screws, each independent of the other, as well as a rudder and sternpost for each screw. Bulloch wrote that this arrangement would allow the vessel to turn "as on a pivot."[408]

The two horizontal, direct-acting engines were 300 total horsepower and operated independently. The coalbunker capacity was 280-tons. The hull was of composite wood and iron construction, with iron beams, keelsons, ceilings, and sheathed with red copper. The armor itself measured 4½-inches (twelve-centimeters) at midships and tapered to 3½-inches (nine-centimeters) at the extremes; about fifteen-inches of teak backed the armor.

The battery consisted of three guns, all founded by Armstrong in England. Forward was a 300-pounder rifle weighing twelve-tons. This was mounted in a stationary "turret." While the vessel was under construction, Bulloch wrote that there was only a single, forward firing gunport, but later he indicated there were three ports, allowing fire directly forward and on either bow. Photos of the ship appear to show side ports also. Astern was a single, circular turret structure, again stationary, housing two seventy-pounder rifles, with each given two side gunports.

The ironclads had exaggerated ram bows, extending over fifteen feet forward of the waterline and measuring over seven feet vertically and twelve feet across where the structure met the hull proper. The ram actually extended farther forward than the bowsprit. With the ram bow and skegs for the twin screws, the vessel's hull form was decidedly unusual. The vessel was brig-rigged and was to have a complement of 135 officers and men.

Bulloch wrote that these ships, with their great maneuverability and forward firepower could, "fight head on to their adversaries, thus being in a favorable position to glance shot and to make use of their formidable beaks."[409]

Though actual construction of the vessels was uninterrupted and both were launched in June 1864, the situation on the diplomatic front had thoroughly deteriorated for the Confederacy, reflecting, among other things, the struggling nation's battlefield reverses as well as growing sentiment against slavery. Additionally, the U.S. Ambassador to France, William A. Dayton, received credible documentation that the vessels were being built for the Confederate states. He quickly confronted the French authorities, demanding that action be taken to prevent their possession by the Confederate navy and that they be sold to neutral parties. Apparently, Bulloch's earlier confidence that the French authorities were complaisant with his plans was misplaced. Consequently, by May 1864, both Arman ships were slated for sale, *Cheops* to Prussia and *Sphinx* to Denmark.

The sale was delayed significantly, however, by the war between Prussia and Denmark, leaving the two ironclads idle at Bordeaux. Ironically, the end of this short war was the factor that allowed the Confederacy to finally acquire the *Sphinx*. The vessel was now in Danish waters but the Danes no longer needed the vessel and were looking for a reason to avoid paying for them. With the French out of the picture, a legal transfer was now possible. Bulloch made the arrangements that involved significant extra expenses to satisfy all parties, and the sale to the Confederacy was completed in December 1864.[410]

Once the transaction was complete, Bulloch made haste to see that the ship went to sea before

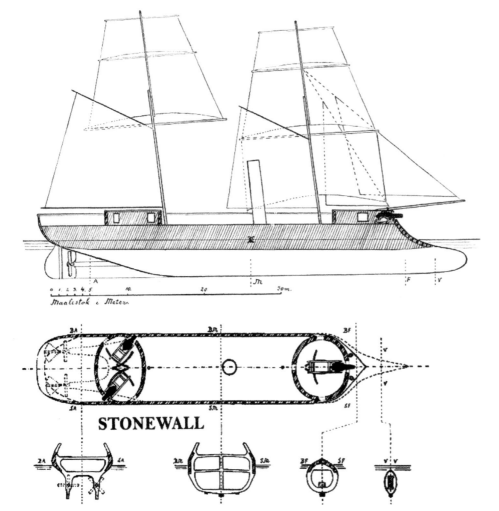

Conjectural plan of French built ironclad, either Stonewall or Prinz Adelbert; the latter was sold to Prussia. Note the twin screws and rudders, as well as the outsized ram. The vessel was designed for use in southern rivers and estuaries, where close-in maneuverability would be at a premium. Wikimedia Commons

Post-war image of the ironclad ram Stonewall at the Washington Naval Yard. Note circular two-gun "turret" aft of mainmast. Each weapon had two side gunports revealed when bulwarks were folded down. Naval Historical Center

any further complications arose. The steamer departed from Copenhagen on January 7, 1865, under the command of a Danish skipper, only to be forced into port at Elsinore by heavy weather. Out to sea again, the ironclad met with a Confederate-chartered vessel on which were her stores, ammunition and crewmen. She finally left the French coast on January 28, 1865.[411]

Now under the command of Lt. Thomas J. Page, Confederate Navy, the vessel was christened *Stonewall*. Unfortunately the ship's progress was immediately impeded by a violent gale appropriate to the January season. Page wrote of the ship's behavior in the storm. The ram's peculiar hull configuration, "did not permit her to ride gracefully over the waves. She defied them by cutting through them with her long and formidable spur." As the waves receded rising from, "her almost submerged condition, she would shake the torrent from her decks and again walk the water like a thing of life." He reiterated: "she exhibited her 'power of diving' and coming up again as if for the amusement of those on board." The waves came over her bows "and [she gave] them free exit through her quarter ports." Despite the weather, the little ship managed nine-knots through the ordeal.

The vessel was not unscathed, however. A serious leak was found at the stern where the caps of the two rudder heads had become detached. A temporary fix was made and they then put in to Ferrol to make permanent repairs.[412] Subsequently the *Stonewall* continued across the Bay of Biscay into Spanish and Portuguese waters en route to the rapidly declining Confederate States of America.

The *Stonewall*'s single encounter with the Union navy occurred off Coruna, Spain, in March 1865. The steam frigate *Niagara* and steam sloop *Sacramento* – both wooden hulled – were positioned to waylay the ironclad as she made for the open Atlantic. The frigate mounted a dozen 150-pounder Parrott rifles; the *Sacramento*, three 100-pounder Parrott rifles, six eight-inch smooth-bore shell guns, and one fifty-pounder rifle.[413]

The commanding officer of the *Niagara* deemed the state of the sea and winds was unfavorable and let the *Stonewall* pass. Though the number and size of guns available to the Union officer was significantly larger than those on the ironclad, other factors would have favored the Confederate vessel. *Niagara* was literally twice the size – about 350-feet in length – of the *Stonewall* and consequently was very awkward, taking fifteen minutes to turn around at sea, and of course neither Union vessel was armored. In any event, the Union commander was later court martialed for his inaction, but exonerated.[414]

Stonewall ended the war at Havana and never again met a Union adversary. She was turned over to the United States and was later sold to Japan, where she was named *Kotetsu* and, later *Adzuma*. She was the flagship of the Imperial squadron and participated in the war between the imperial forces and those of the shogunate. She remained afloat until broken up in 1908.

The second of the pair was taken into the Prussian navy and named *Prinz Adalbert*. Though she was completed and armed, she had a short service life. Her light draft made her a poor sea boat and her composite hull quickly fell to rot. She was placed in reserve in 1871 and broken up in 1878.[415]

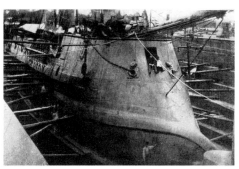

Stonewall in drydock showing gunports for the forward 300-pounder rifle: one directly forward and one on each bow. The large ram was meant to be the vessel's primary weapon, its use facilitated by the ironclad's small turning radius. Both images, Naval Historical Center

BLOCKADE RUNNERS

The naval history of the American Civil War cannot be understood in its entirety without significant attention being given to the U.S. Navy's blockade of the Southern coast. And, by extension, the Union blockade cannot be evaluated or studied without looking at the Navy's adversaries that continuously tested that cordon which was tasked with slicing off the South's maritime lifelines.

Therefore, though the blockade runners were certainly not naval vessels in the strict sense, many of them were certainly not merely merchant ships either. This became more and more obvious as the war continued and necessity caused construction of increasingly specialized ships designed to outrun and evade the Union flotillas prowling the Confederate coasts. Therefore, blockade runners are a necessary part of this book.

However, this will not be a comprehensive catalog or description of all these ships. First, they were far too numerous: Stephen Wise lists about 350 runners in his book *Lifeline of the Confederacy*, and these were only the steam-powered vessels.[416] Sailing vessels formed a large portion of the runners and these were significant numbers, though of course they were generally smaller vessels.

Second, a definitive list of these ships would be difficult to compile. The majority were operated by private firms or even individuals who were not necessarily bound to be truthful about their activities or even the identities of their vessels, destinations or cargoes. It was obviously to the blockade runners' advantage to allow (or sow) confusion with the blockaders. Furthermore, post-war accounts must be taken with great amounts of salt as the narrators were not averse to exaggerating their prowess in evading the Yankee blockaders.

Third, the character of many of these ships makes their inclusion unnecessary. At the outset of the war, the runners were simply merchant vessels making passage through dangerous waters – successfully or not. When the Union blockade became more thorough and dangerous, the "casual" blockade runner became the exception rather than the rule.

Once the casual runners were winnowed out, however, the participants in the trade were vessels specially selected, then, later, built specifically for the task. These ships became significant sometimes because of their success rates. But many times they were examples of the application of the latest maritime technology in their quest to bring cargoes into, as well as out of, the Confederacy. High profile and slow ships soon went by the board, leaving those with sufficient speed to make a successful run even if pursued by an increasingly adept foe. It also became obvious that long-range ships were unnecessary: all that was needed was sufficient fuel to make the distance between various Southern ports and the closer-in islands: the West Indies, the Bahamas, or Bermuda became the popular origins and destinations. Another important factor which effected the design of these ships was profitability: as the war continued the profit levels became enormous and it became

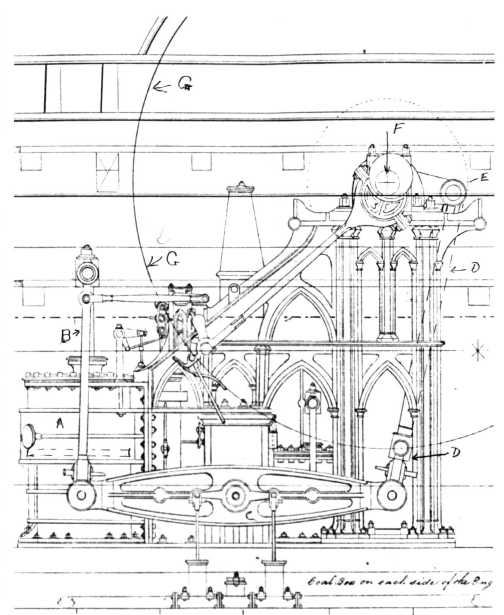

Side-lever marine engine: side view. Cylinder and piston is at left (A and dotted lines), moves vertically, operating connecting rod (B), which rocks the side-lever (C); opposite end of side-lever moves rod (D/D); which turns crank (E) on the paddle wheel shaft (F), turning paddle wheel (G). The cylinder on the Nashville was eighty-six inches in diameter with a stroke of ninety-six inches (eight feet), operating thirty-two-foot diameter paddle wheels. The side lever design was developed to keep a large portion of the engine's weight low in the ship's hull. National Archives

less and less necessary for a ship to bring in large cargoes in order to make the trip worth the money earned.

The vessels included here are intended to be a sampling of historically important vessels as well as those exhibiting significant new maritime technology. The various types are represented, from the re-cycled American coastal or oceangoing merchant vessel, such as the *Bermuda,* to the "imported" steamers fresh from Irish Sea or English Channel service. There are wooden hulls, composite hulls, iron hulls, and steel hulls – the latter were some of the first steel ships ever built. There are sidewheel vessels and single- and twin-screw ships. Some were officially commissioned in the Confederate Navy, a few were owned by other Confederate government entities, specifically the army's ordnance department and the state of North Carolina. Note that two twin-screw blockade runners, which became commerce raiders *Tallahassee* and *Chickamauga,* were covered in the previous chapter.

The vessels covered will give the reader a good overview of the types of vessels that were used, as well as outline a narrative of how the vessels changed through the course of the war, with particular emphasis on how evolving maritime technology was applied to these ships.

Side view of the Nashville at London. The passenger steamer was not appropriate for conversion to a warship and was typical of early vessels pressed temporarily into service as blockade runners. Illustrated London News

As to sailing blockade runners, the numbers of these were enormous, probably in the hundreds. Most were small schooners or sloops, with limited capacity and small crews. The most significant of the sailing blockade runners was the schooner yacht *America* of America's Cup fame. The vessel was for a short time the blockade runner *Camilla*.[417] In any event, these vessels are beyond the scope of this book.

It should be noted here that four vessels – *Ajax*, *Hercules*, *Adventure* and *Enterprise* – sometimes considered blockade runners, have been included in Chapter 6 as cruisers.

Nashville

The merchant steamer *Nashville* has been categorized as a cruiser, a blockade runner, and a privateer. Her two captures of Union merchant ships could put her into the cruiser category. However, she also made several runs through the blockade.

The vessel was a wooden-hulled, side wheel ship designed for passenger service and built by Thomas Collyer of New York in 1853. The design was patterned after the steamer *Union*, built by William H. Webb two years earlier, but with reduced rig and by replacing a two-cylinder engine with a single-cylinder unit. Her hull measured 215-feet six-inches by thirty-four-feet six-inches with a twenty-one-foot nine-inch depth of hold – with each of these dimensions within a foot of those of the earlier vessel. The *Union* was 1,200-tons; the *Nashville*, 1,220.[418]

The single-cylinder, side-lever engine was built at Novelty Iron works in New York and the cylinder was eighty-six-inches in diameter with an eight-foot stroke. The side-lever configuration was in a way an inverted version of the vertical walking beam engine: instead of an overhead beam rocking on a fulcrum and transmitting power from the cylinder and piston rod on one end of the beam to the paddle wheel shaft at the opposite end of the beam, the side-lever engine had two rocking beams mounted beside and below the cylinders. One end of these beams was operated by rods moving up and down with the piston rod. When the side-lever beams rocked downwards on the piston end of the engine, the opposite ends rocked up, pushing rods which cranked the paddle wheel shaft. The paddle wheel shaft was usually located at about the level of the ship's main deck. The main advantage of the side-lever system was that it eliminated the high center of gravity inherent in the walking (or "working") beam. Keeping the center of gravity low was particularly important in a sea-going vessel. The engine in the *Nashville* was quite large and could be compared to the engine of the *Union* mentioned earlier, which had two cylinders sixty-inches in diameter and a seven-foot stroke.[419]

Steam was produced by two, twenty-four-foot long, return-flue boilers, each about twelve-feet wide with five furnaces. A blower system provided ventilation for the boiler rooms and the system could provide 28psi and about nineteen revolutions of the paddle wheel per minute. The paddle wheels were thirty-two-feet in diameter and the twenty-eight floats on each wheel were ten-feet long by twenty-inches wide. Her coal-bunkers carried 185-tons of anthracite and she carried an insubstantial fore topsail schooner rig.

Nashville in Britain, from the stern, elevated view. Note the length of deck cabin. Attempts to convert and arm the vessel were stymied by British authorities. Naval Historical Center

The "Dauntless."   The "Meshuan."   The "Nashville" in Dock.   The "Tuscarora."

THE "NASHVILLE" AND "TUSCARORA" AT SOUTHAMPTON, ENGLAND.—[SEE PAGE 107.]

The hull was substantially made with floor timbers – those lowest on the frames and which secured the keel to the frames – 14½-inches square. The room and space (center to center) of the frames was twenty-nine-inches. There was a topgallant forecastle and a large deckhouse running the width of the ship and from the taffrail forward nearly to the foremast. This structure, if it followed the pattern of the earlier *Union,* had officers' cabins forward, passenger saloons and staterooms aft. Other accommodations were on the deck below. One source indicated the stem had a billet head and trailboards, sailing ship style, but period illustrations show a much plainer head.[420]

Nashville was owned by the Spofford, Tileston firm and was on their New York to Charleston run in 1854, but was then chartered for the trans-Atlantic route, regularly making the passage to Liverpool in twelve days; the return to New York in fourteen to sixteen. This compared to the larger liners that made the Atlantic run in as few as nine days. She was half the size of the large Collins and Cunard liners – and it was necessary to reduce the number of passengers for the west to east run in order to have sufficient space for the necessary coal.[421]

Back on the coastal routes she made the New York to Charleston run in forty-five hours – at about fourteen-knots. In April 1861, she was immediately seized by the Confederate government.

The navy intended to convert the ship into a naval vessel, but found that her decks were not strong enough to support naval ordnance. It was then decided to send her to England to be fitted-out as a warship, and a token armament of two twelve-pounders was placed on her deck.

Nashville ran out through the blockade on October 26, 1861. She called at Bermuda then ran into severe weather that damaged her bulwarks, paddlewheel housings, and deck. The damage was not enough to prevent her from capturing the clipper ship *Harvey Birch* in the English Channel, which she burned.

Strict enforcement of England's neutrality laws prevented arming the vessel in England. Therefore, after minimal repairs were made, she sailed out, evading the U.S. steam sloop *Tuscarora*. En route to the southeastern coast, she captured the schooner *Robert Gilfillan*. Then she ran up the U.S. flag and speedily ran through the blockade into Morehead City, North Carolina. Next, she was at Georgetown, South Carolina where she was sold to the Fraser, Trenholm company and renamed *Thomas L. Wragg*.

In four months the ship made about four runs through the blockade and on the fifth ran into Savannah with a cargo of weapons. By this time, July 1862, Fort Pulaski had fallen to Union forces and Savannah was tightly watched by the Union squadron. The ship was immobile for about eight months.

An optimistic sea captain then purchased the ship, intending to turn her into a privateer. Renamed *Rattlesnake*, she was still unable to escape to sea, but remained near the mouth of the Ogeechee River, south of Savannah, under the guns of Fort McAllister. On the night of February 27, her commander attempted to take her out to sea. Instead, he ran the ship hard aground, where, the next morning, she became a stationary target for the U.S. monitor *Montauk*. There was no hope for the ex-*Nashville* and eight rounds from the monitor's eleven-inch and fifteen-inch guns set her afire. Shortly thereafter she blew up.[422] As of this writing, the remains of the *Nashville* still lie at the bottom of the Great Ogeechee River at Seven Mile Bend, and are being studied by underwater archaeologists for future research.

Nashville falls into the category of vessels acquired "in bulk" by the Confederacy early in the war. Many were very good ships in their civilian or merchant roles, but were never particularly successful for naval purposes or for blockade running.

Bermuda

The iron steamer *Bermuda* is considered the first blockade runner. After President Lincoln instituted the blockade in April 1861, there was a period of uncertainty and a natural reluctance on the part of shipping companies to break through this international legal barrier. However, as goods destined for Southern ports piled up in British ports, pressure built up and something had to be done. In July, the firm of Fraser, Trenholm & Company loaded the newly built *Bermuda* with private goods as well as munitions – including field guns and Enfield rifles – and sent her to challenge the Union cordon. She sailed directly from West Hartlepool, Britain to Savannah, making the passage in four weeks. To compound her initial success, she turned around and successfully took 2,000 bales of cotton to Liverpool. In both directions she made a handsome profit.[423] However, direct transoceanic blockade runners would quickly become scarce as the Union acquired more vessels to strengthen its coastal squadrons.

Blockade runner Bermuda. Considered the first successful runner, it made direct passage from Britain to Savannah. As Union squadrons grew in effectiveness it became necessary to transship cargoes from large ocean going vessels to faster, smaller and lighter draft ships to enter southern harbors. From F. Bradlee's, "Blockade Running During the Civil War"

The *Bermuda* was considered an auxiliary sailing ship. She had one screw and a brig rig. Her steam machinery had been built by Frossick and Hackwirth and was composed of two vertical, direct-acting cylinders, with forty-four-inch cylinders and a thirty-inch stroke. The vertical, direct-acting engine could be described as a locomotive cylinder turned on its end, with the piston rod operating a connecting rod, and the latter turning the propeller shaft (the locomotive driving wheels in the analogy). There were two boilers and the engine produced about 135 nominal horsepower. Her highest speed was said to be "barely eight-knots."[424]

The vessel's iron hull was built by Pearse & Lockwood, of Stockton-on-Tees, and measured 215-feet in length, 29.2-feet breadth, with a hold about twenty-feet in depth. She was flush decked and had a single-deck structure forward of the funnel, used as a charthouse. She had high freeboard and measured 1,228-tons.[425]

Bermuda had a short life span as a blockade runner. On her second trip from Britain she called at Bermuda, then sailed for the Bahamas, her intended destination, only to be stopped by the Union navy's *Mercedita*. On searching the vessel's papers, the Union officers found that the cargo was ultimately intended for Southern ports, and the ship was seized. Taken to a prize court and condemned, the ship was purchased into the Union navy, became USS *Bermuda*, and had three guns mounted on her: one nine-inch smoothbore and two thirty-pounder rifles.[426]

The ship was credited with five captures as a Union blockader and was sold out after the war. She went into merchant service and was renamed *General Meade*, then *Bahamas*, and was lost in 1882.[427]

Robert E. Lee

One of the most famous runners of the war, *Robert E. Lee,* was a nearly new, paddle-wheel, Clyde River passenger steamer, built by the Thomson firm in Glasgow in 1860. She ran for two years, under the name *Giraffe*, between Glasgow and Belfast, and was then sold to Alexander Collie of Glasgow, who in turn sold her to the Confederates.

Her acquisition was unusual in that she was purchased by an agent of the Confederate treasury department dispatched to England for the purpose.

The vessel was to carry treasury and war department supplies in through the blockade.

Some alterations were accomplished to fit her for running cargo instead of passengers. "Her beautiful saloon and cabins were dismantled and bulkheads constructed to separate the quarters for officers and men from the space to be used for stowage of cargo."[428]

She originally had two oscillating engines, sixty-two-inches diameter by a sixty-six-inch stroke, but under Collie's ownership, these were replaced by a pair measuring fifty-six- by thirty-six inches, developing 960 nominal horsepower, running on six boilers, at forty-pounds pressure. Oscillating cylinders were mounted to pivot on trunnions through a 30- to 40-degree arc. As the cylinder moved, the piston rod extended and returned imparting motion to a rod that operated

Blockade runner Robert E. Lee in a Scottish drydock. Originally the Glasgow, Belfast ferry Giraffe, her bow was described as "sharp as a knife." She was capable of over thirteen knots and broke through the blockade twenty-one times, according to her first skipper. Naval Historical Center

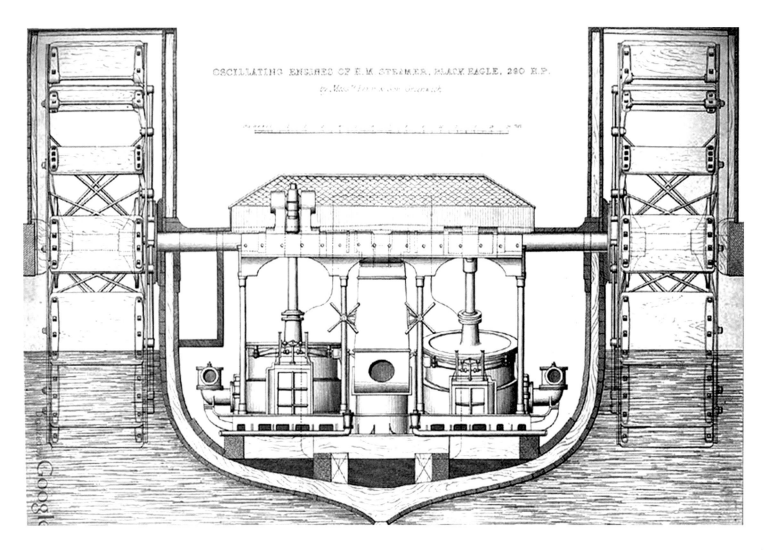

OSCILLATING ENGINES OF H.M. STEAMER, BLACK EAGLE, 280 H.P.

Typical oscillating marine engines, in hull cross section. The cylinders pivoted thirty to forty degrees on trunnions, with the piston rods directly connected to the cranks on the paddle wheel shaft. These were simple and efficient engines and were often found on blockade runners such as the Robert E. Lee. Wikimedia Commons

the crankshaft. The whole motion is somewhat analogous to a knee and leg operating a bicycle pedal. With twenty-six-feet six-inch paddlewheels, the *Giraffe* was said by her Confederate commanding officer, John Wilkinson, to have never exceeded 13½-knots, and this was apparently after she had the smaller cylinder engines.[429]

Her hull was iron, 268-feet long and twenty-six-feet broad (not including width of the wheels or boxes), with a thirteen-foot depth of hold and a draft of eleven-feet. Her hull was described as "a beautiful specimen of naval architecture, low and long and rakish, with a beautiful molded stern and a bow as clean and sharp as a knife." Certainly

USS *Fort Donelson*, the former blockade runner *Robert E. Lee*. The vessel exhibits general characteristics of the type: long, low, rakish hull, minimal rig with raked masts and funnels, side paddle wheels, as well as light grey hull to reduce her visual signature. Her career as a runner lasted just over a year. *Naval Historical Center*

she had an extreme length-to-beam ratio, all in a rather shallow hull. Wilkinson also commented that in a gale of wind the vessel showed "her superb qualities as a sea boat."[430]

With alterations completed, the ship made her first run in late-December 1862, to Wilmington by way of Nassau. Her cargo consisted of munitions and lithography presses and equipment, as well as twenty-six newly hired treasury department lithographers. Forced by Union patrols to wait until dark, her commanding officer, John Wilkinson, ran her in to Wilmington quickly, but she fetched up on a knoll just outside the bar – and uncomfortably close to a hovering blockader. Wilkinson immediately sent the printers ashore. He then attached a hawser and kedge anchor to her stern, and, by working the paddle wheels in reverse, freed the vessel. Once safely at Wilmington the steamer was taken over by the Confederate army's ordnance department, which ran several of their own runners through most of the war.

The *Robert E. Lee* ran through the blockade twenty-one times, according to Wilkinson, who commanded her for most of her career. She had another narrow encounter with the blockaders in August 1863 when steaming out to Nassau. She was sighted by the steam sloop *Iroquois* and the chase began around 10:00am. Wilkinson began by throwing overboard her deck load of cotton – a later report by the *Iroquois*'s commanding officer said they counted 114 bales and five bags floating by – to lighten her load. Then the runner's supply of clean-burning Welsh coal ran out and

she was left with soft North Carolina bituminous. However, this burned poorly and produced masses of black smoke. To increase steam pressure, the engineers burned cotton soaked in turpentine. This, according to Wilkinson, bumped her speed up from nine to thirteen-knots and gave them some respite. However, the cotton soon clogged the boiler flues and the pressure began to drop. By this time, darkness was coming on and Wilkinson ordered the engineer to make as much smoke as possible. Then Wilkinson simultaneously had the dampers closed – shutting off the smoke – and ordered a starboard, ninety-degree turn. They arrived safely at Bermuda two days later. The commander of the *Iroquois* complained that his bad boilers as well as poor coal prevented the capture of the blockade runner – indeed about two weeks later *Iroquois* was sent home for repairs.[431]

The ship also was involved in the Confederate plot to seize the U.S. steamer *Michigan* and free the rebel prisoners held on Johnson's Island on

Lake Erie. The runner transported the Confederate naval leaders of the expedition to Halifax, along with a mass of gold and cotton to finance the operation. Her luck ran out in November 1863, when the Union blockader *James B. Adger* caught her, as one of the officers on board put it, "jammed up in a bay" and could not escape. (By this time, the ship was no longer under the command of John Wilkinson, and he later criticized her new skipper for mismanaging the ship and causing her capture.) She had taken over 7,000 bales of cotton out and had brought significant cargoes of precious munitions into the South during her career.

She was taken into the Union navy in June 1864 and renamed *Fort Donelson*, becoming a part of the North Atlantic blockading squadron for the remainder of the war. As a blockader she captured the steamer *Dacotah* in August 1864. She was sold out of the navy in late-1865 and was in merchant service until purchased for the Chilean navy in 1869. In that service she was named *Conception*.[432]

Blockade runner A.D. Vance (or Advance) high in the water after her capture. Note the feathering paddle wheels. These contrivances enabled the paddle "buckets" to enter and leave the water at right angles, improving their efficiency. Formerly the Lord Clyde, the vessel was owned by the state of North Carolina and ran through the blockade some fifteen times. Naval Historical Center

USS Frolic, formerly the Advance, at Naples after the war. The steamer served in the USN until 1877. Naval Historical Center

Advance

This vessel is an example of a converted English Channel packet, originally built by Caird & Company of Greenock, Scotland. The firm began building ships in 1840 and was associated with John Scott Russell, the eminent naval architect of the era. The ship was originally named *Lord Clyde* and was one of about a dozen Caird vessels that ran the blockade.[433]

The acquisition of the steamer for the South originated with Governor Zebulon Vance, of North Carolina, who thought the state ought to insure that her troops were the best supplied in the Confederate army…and therefore he did not trust the "nation's" army ordnance system to adequately do this. In late-1862, Vance dispatched an agent to Great Britain to purchase a vessel that would carry the state's cargo through the blockade.[434]

The *Lord Clyde* had been launched July 2, 1862, and been owned by the Dublin & Glasgow Sailing and Steam Packet Company. She made her trial runs in October and ran the Dublin-Glasgow route for six months. In May 1863, the steamer was sold to Scotsman John Key, who in turn sold her to Vance's agent. Her first run through the blockade was in June 1863.[435]

There is some interest in the exact name of this ship. It is generally called *Advance* and is listed as such in port registers, but it is consistently referred to in the "Official Records" as "A.D.

Vance." It was said the name was in homage to the governor's wife Adelaide and was in this instance "Ad-Vance."[436]

The ship was an iron-hulled paddle steamer with two side-lever engines, with sixty-three-inch cylinders and a seventy-eight-inch stroke. The vessel's registered dimensions were 237.5-feet, and 26.1-feet wide, and fourteen-feet depth of hold. She drew eleven-feet five-inches forward and twelve-feet aft, registering 808-tons and was schooner-rigged with two funnels and clipper bow. One wartime photo of her shows she had feathering paddle wheels. These had a mechanical contrivance which kept the paddle floats in a vertical position as they entered and came out of the water, making them more efficient than the ordinary non-feathering versions.[437]

Advance was the first of several blockade runners operated by the state of North Carolina, with Governor Vance having a half-interest in four other runners as well. This situation was one of many sources of contention between Vance and the national government, and was part of a generally held North Carolinian view that Virginia's interests were given special consideration by the Confederate government, to the detriment of the Tar Heel state.

The vessel was said to be capable of seventeen-knots, and ran the blockade seventeen times from June 1863 to September 1864. Her capture occurred while running out of Wilmington at night. The vessel was quickly detected by the blockader *Britannia,* which then set off rockets and gave chase. The runner was handicapped by poor North Carolina bituminous coal and she could barely made eight-knots, but this was sufficient to outrun the Union ship. Next morning, however, the steamer encountered the *Santiago de Cuba*, probably the fastest Union blockader, and a long-distance chase began, ending around eight o'clock, when the pursuer ranged close enough to get a shot across her bow. The *Advance* was soon a prize and it was generally agreed that poor coal had been the *Advance*'s undoing.[438]

Governor Vance weighed in on the vessel's loss, again beating the anti-Tar Heel conspiracy drum. He contended that the quality anthracite coal that should have gone to his state's vessel had been allocated instead to the Confederacy's *Tallahassee*.[439]

The Union navy quickly realized the value of the vessel and promptly converted her to a blockader, named *Frolic*, and mounted five guns on her. She was retained in the post-war navy and was sold in September 1883.[440]

Banshee

As the war progressed and profits were increasingly to be had in the "trade," it became apparent that vessels could be purpose-built for the task and still remain profitable. Though British neutrality statutes made construction of warships for the Confederacy illegal, the regulations said nothing about "merchant ships," regardless of what nation they were destined to serve or whether said nation was at war with the United States. Consequently, literally hundreds of blockade runners were constructed in England and Scotland, chiefly between 1862-65.

The three most prolific blockade-runner builders were the Denny company of Glasgow; Jones, Quiggin of Liverpool; and the Dudgeon

Blockade runner Banshee, the first steel hulled ship to cross the Atlantic. Built by Jones, Quiggin at Liverpool, the vessel had a length to breadth ratio of about 10:1 and a depth of hold of about ten feet. The builders overestimated the tensile strength of her steel and on her first Atlantic crossing heavy seas buckled her plating, forcing her to abort the passage. After structural strengthening she became a successful runner. Naval Historical Center

firm based in London. These three launched over fifty vessels for the trade. Jones, Quiggin produced about eighteen blockade runners, though not all were completed before the end of the conflict. One of the most notable of their vessels was the *Banshee*, which was the first ship built from keel up from steel. Additionally she was the first steel ship to cross the Atlantic.

Before the Bessemer patent process, steel had been extremely expensive to manufacture and had never been used for shipbuilding. In 1858, two years after the Bessemer patent, David Livingstone carried a knocked-down steel, steam launch with him on his Zambezi expedition, then erected it on site for the journey. This had been the only steel predecessor to *Banshee*.

The advantages of steel over iron were lightness and strength, compared to iron. However, this early attempt by Jones, Quiggin proved to be somewhat optimistic about the structural strength of steel, as applied to a sea going vessel.

The *Banshee* was 214-feet long and twenty-feet wide, with a ten-foot depth of hold, about an eight-foot draft, and 431 86/94 builders tons. (Note the over ten to one length to breadth ratio). The hull was subdivided into watertight sections. A collision bulkhead was forward, the engines and boiler spaces were in a single compartment, and a bulkhead was placed about thirty feet from the stern. The ship's stowage capacity was for 200-tons of cargo and 100-tons of coal.

The hull framing was both iron and steel. Iron was used for the keel, stem and sternpost. The keel was in three lengths, scarfed together, measuring 4½- by 1¼-inches; the stem was 4½- by one-inch; and the sternpost, six- by two-inches. The hull frames, floors, and deck beams were steel. The frames were $^3/_{16}$-inch thick, three- by 2½-inches, and were spaced eighteen-inches center to center, in the engine and boiler spaces, and with twenty-one-inches spacing fore and aft of these spaces. Reverse frames were added to each frame in the machinery spaces, and on alternate frames fore and aft. The reverse frames were also of $^3/_{16}$-inch thickness, 2¾- by 1½-inches in the midship section and 1¾- by 1¼-inches at the ends of the hull. The floors were nine inches deep except under the engines and boilers where it was one foot deep. The upper deck beams were four- by 2¼-inches thick, placed on alternate frames. These deck beams were $^3/_{16}$-inches thick at the ends of the hull, while the lower deck beams were placed on every fourth frame. The watertight bulkheads were 1/8-inch thick plates and the outer hull plates were $^1/_8$- to $^3/_{16}$-inches thick.

The machinery arrangement centered around two oscillating cylinders, each fifty-two-inches with a forty-eight-inch stroke developing 120 nominal or 350 indicated horsepower, built by the Lairds. These were placed directly under the paddle wheel shaft and the two boilers were on either end of the engine space. When driven at full steam, the engines burned thirty-tons of coal a day, giving the ship about three and a half days range under steam alone. As her sailing rig consisted of two slender masts with minimal stays and no yards – barely sufficient sail power to steady her in seaway – the ship was definitely not built for long-distance cruising.

Topside, the ship had a bridge structure connecting the paddlewheel housings and an after cabin. The latter housed the officers' quarters and galley. Protecting the fore deck was a turtleback covering, extending about forty feet from the stem, almost to the fore mast. The turtleback feature became common in these fast runners, which frequently dipped their bows into head seas and needed a structure to shed off the water before it inundated the main deck and forced the ship's skipper to slow her down.[441]

Banshee was launched November 22, 1862, and attempted her first run across the Atlantic in March of the next year. The attempt was terminated prematurely because of excessive buckling of her steel plates and consequent leakage. After putting in at Queenstown (Cobh), repairs were made as well as some strengthening of her structure. On her second attempt, she arrived at Nassau in April 1863, becoming the first of many steel ships to cross the Atlantic.

The vessel was never as fast as she was expected to be, ranging around nine-knots under steam. It was reported that her engines were too powerful for her frame and that their vibration apparently limited the number of rpms possible before her frames began to buckle and rivets start to give way.[442]

The strengthened vessel became a successful runner, making fourteen runs in the following months, and apparently running in and out of Wilmington on a weekly basis. Her end came in November 1863, when she was sighted by the U.S. army transport steamer *Fulton* and a chase ensued. Six hours into the pursuit, *Fulton* had closed the gap sufficiently to bring the Federal guns to bear and *Banshee* took two hits. Then a second Union blockader joined the pursuit and there was no longer any hope of escape. The *Fulton* was a formidable opponent, and some estimate of her speed can be deduced from one of her speedier days on the Trans-Atlantic run: 288-miles in twenty-four hours, or an average of twelve-knots.[443]

Banshee was taken into the Union navy and made part of the North Atlantic Blockading Squadron. At the close of the war, she was sold and later became the merchant ship *J.I. Smallwood*.[444]

Phantom

The William C. Miller firm on the Mersey River built a second steel blockade runner about the same time as *Banshee* was under construction. Unlike the paddle steamer *Banshee*, the Miller ship was propelled by a single screw, and was named *Phantom*.

Phantom was 192.9-feet in length and twenty-two-feet in breadth, with 12.4-feet depth of hold. Her registered tonnage was 266. This was about a nine-to-one length to breadth ratio and she had exceedingly fine lines fore and aft, inciting a visiting German naval architect to include her plans in a study of clipper ships. She had a single deckhouse aft and two side houses amidships on either side of her single funnel.[445]

A government inspector was appalled by her thin steel structure, calling it of the "most fragile character that can be conceived for a sea-going vessel, her steel plates being but a quarter of an inch thick, her iron frame of the same proportions."[446]

The ship's owners, Fraser, Trenholm and company, had not been satisfied with the ship even before she was launched. Their representative, Charles K. Prioleau, was much distressed by the lengthy building time for the "little vessel" – over ten months.[447] The company sent her through the blockade in July 1863, but was not satisfied with her speed either. She was described as "unsatisfactory from first to last" and consequently the vessel was sold to the Confederate government.[448]

Under the ownership of the Army's ordnance department, she made three additional runs through the blockade. On September 23, 1863, *Phantom* was steaming out of Wilmington at dawn and was spotted by the fast, side-wheel blockader USS *Connecticut*. A four-hour chase ensued with the blockader slowly closing the distance as they skirted northward along the coast. *Connecticut* fired at the steamer to no effect due to the rough seas, but when it was evident that the chase was unequal, the runner's skipper ran her aground at Rich Inlet, North Carolina. The crew set her afire and "scampered" on shore. The Union vessel sent a crew that attempted to douse the fire and re-float the vessel, but they were unsuccessful.[449]

Owl Class

The success of *Banshee* led Jones, Quiggin company to enlarge the dimensions of that vessel and apply them to a set of sister ships, also with steel hulls and side wheels. These were *Owl*, *Bat*, *Stag* and *Deer*. These four were part of a group of runners which were to be owned outright by the Confederate War Department and numbered fourteen ships, ranging from 210- to 270-feet in length and 771- to 1,391-tons. All were ordered in 1864 for Fraser,

Steel blockade runner Bat. One of a class of four built by Jones, Quiggin, it represented an enlargement of the Banshee's dimensions. They were capable of thirteen knots, but only one went un-captured before the end of the war. For a short time the Bat was in Union service. Naval Historical Center

The "Bat"
325 tons. Bound from Liverpool to Nassau, N.P. Put into Cork from stress of weather September 8th and sailed September 13th 1864.

Trenholm company, and those not built by Jones, Quiggin were by Lairds (though two, *Stag* and *Deer* were in turn subcontracted out by Jones, Quiggin.)[450]

The *Owl* and sisters were 230-feet long and twenty-six-feet in breadth and designed with a depth of hold of ten-feet nine-inches to carry 800 bales of cotton while maintaining a seven-foot six-inch draft. Their machinery consisted of two oscillating cylinders, fifty-two-inches in diameter and a fifty-four-inch stroke, with two boilers and 180 nominal horsepower. Bulloch wrote that they were to have sufficient coal bunkerage to make the run from Wilmington to Nassau. They were capable of thirteen-knots, and visually were lengthened versions of *Banshee*, having similar paddle wheel housings, a turtle back over the fore deck, and two funnels located fore and aft of the paddle boxes.[451]

In corresponding with the Army's agent, General C.J. McRae, Prioleau complained of the high price the builders were asking for the ships. But to another correspondent, Prioleau wrote that he expected them to be the "best yet" of the purpose-built blockade runners.[452]

Owl made four successful runs through the blockade and earned sufficient cotton "money"

to pay off the Fraser, Trenholm company and be turned over to the Confederate government in December 1864. The vessel survived the war, and arrived in England in July 1865.[453]

The other three vessels of this group were captured while running the blockade. *Bat* made only one attempt to run the blockade and was captured. For a short time she was the USS *Bat*, then went into merchant service, not being broken up until 1902. *Deer* was sold to Argentina in 1869 and *Stag* became, with much modification, the merchant vessel *Zenobia* that operated on the Atlantic and Maritime Provinces.[454]

Will of the Wisp

As the war progressed, the rush to cash-in on the profits resulted in construction of vessels where good workmanship and substantial materials gave way to speed of construction and inferior materials. The pair of blockade runners *Will of the Wisp* and *Julia* are examples of the latter.

Both ships were built by William Simons and Company of Renfrew, Scotland, and completed in late-1863. They were 210-feet in length and twenty-three-feet in breadth, with a ten-foot depth

of hold. The *Will of the Wisp's* engines were capable of propelling her at seventeen-knots.

On her first Atlantic crossing, *Will of the Wisp* arrived at Bermuda in December 1863, leaking badly. Sent to Halifax for repairs, it was found that there was little that could be done to rectify the original poor ironwork. With minimal repairs in place, her skipper, P. Capper, took her to Nassau. On arrival, she was again leaking copiously, so much so that the commanding officer put her on the beach rather than leave her to sink. It was February 1864 before she was ready for sea again and made her first actual run through the blockade.

Arriving at Wilmington, off New Inlet, Capper had the choice of facing oncoming bad weather in a – as always – leaking ship, or brazening through the blockade. He chose the latter and took at least two hits from the blockaders' guns, before gaining safety under the guns of Ft. Fisher. Moving up river, she was leaking even more – probably due to the strains placed on her by the high revving engines – then the vessel managed to hit a sand bar, further aggravating her leakage. More repairs were made before the sieve-like vessel was ready to break out to sea again. The steamer barely reached the midst of the blockaders when the engineer reported water gathering in the engine room. Despite this, Capper did escape to sea. Her overtaxed pumps were keeping the water at bay – and in fact four of her eight furnaces were soaked, giving her at best five-knots. The crew sent the deck-load of cotton

Merchant steamer Zenobia, formerly the blockade runner Stag, sister ship to Bat. Conversion to merchant service obviously included the addition of another deck as well as pilot house and other deck structures. Peabody Essex Museum

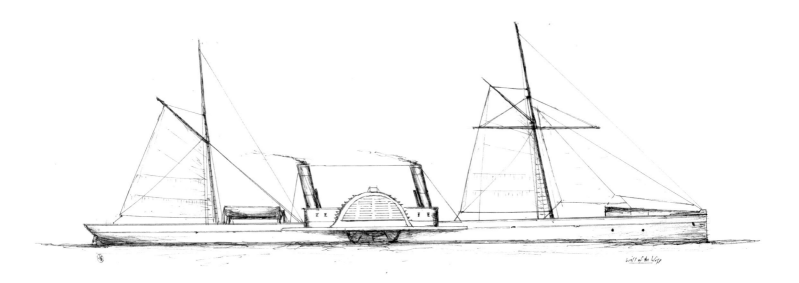

Blockade runner Will of the Wisp. Though capable of seventeen knots, she was poorly constructed and leaked copiously throughout her career. She ran aground in February 1864 off Galveston. Drawing by author, based on plans at University of Glasgow

by the board and this gained enough freeboard to start the other furnaces, and get her out of immediate danger of sinking. They spent three days pumping and bailing en route to Nassau. Less than a half hour after anchoring, she was sitting on the bottom. She was subsequently pumped out, refloated, repaired, and resumed her career above water.

Apparently, the most important part of this vessel was her pumps: despite continual leakage, the ship eventually made a dozen runs through the blockade, the last one in February 1864. The latter was an attempt to run in to Galveston. She

came under fire from the blockading gunboats, which forced her ashore where the Confederates stripped her of her important engine parts before escaping. The Union boat party sent to destroy her decided there was no further need to molest what was left of the broken-hulled iron steamer.[455]

The sister vessel, *Julia,* made one run into the South, in December 1864. She was caught in foul weather off South Carolina and ran aground, where she was later captured by a Union boat expedition. After the war, she was sold to private interests, but only lasted until 1867, when she was abandoned.[456]

Hope and *Colonel Lamb*

These two blockade runners were described by the Union consul Dudley as "larger and superior to most that have been recently built" and one current authority rates them as the war's "best blockade runners." Their dimensions were 281-feet six-inches, between perpendiculars, by

thirty-five- and fifteen-feet depth of hold, measuring 1,132 gross tons. Their hulls were longer than any oceangoing Union warship except the steam frigate *Niagara* and one of the large ironclad monitors, and each could carry a much as three times the cargo of most of the earlier runners.

The hull was iron and steel, with the former comprising the twenty-inch deep keel, stem and sternposts. The frames were steel and placed twenty-one inches, center to center, with reverse frames running up to the bilges, and on alternate frames from the bilges up to the gunwale. There were five watertight bulkheads, in addition to steel coalbunker bulkheads fore and aft of the boilers and at the sides of the hull.[457]

Jones, Quiggin built their hulls and James Jack of Birkenhead their machinery. Each had a two-cylinder, oscillating engine with cylinders measuring seventy-two-inches with a sixty-six-inch stroke, producing 350 nominal horsepower. The four boilers, two fore and two aft of the engines, enabled a boiler pressure of 25psi, the

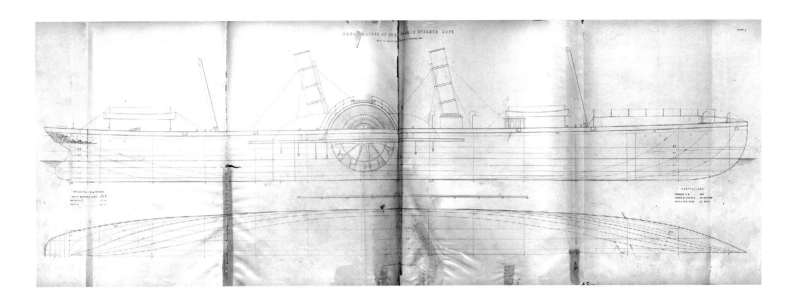

whole driving twenty-six-foot diameter feathering paddle wheels.[458]

Hope was completed first and there are obvious differences between the two. In April 1864, Prioleau wrote that Captain Lockwood, one of the most intrepid of the blockade runner skippers, was in Liverpool. Prioleau hoped that he could, "fit him out with a better boat than the *Hope*." The latter vessel was to be finished in May.[459]

The significant differences between the ships, at least above the main deck, are seen in period illustrations. *Hope* had a turtleback over the fore deck and a bridge connecting the paddle wheel boxes. Beneath the center of the bridge was a house over the engines and above that was the pilothouse with steering apparatus. The *Colonel Lamb* (named for the distinguished commander of Confederate forces at Fort Fisher, North Carolina) dispensed with the turtle back and had a very long deck house extending from about

fifteen feet aft of the foremast nearly to the main mast. It was stated that the changes brought the cost of the new boat to 50,000-pounds, over 12,000 more than that of the *Hope*.[460]

Hope made her first run to Wilmington in July 1864, carrying two 150-pounder Armstrong guns and two Whitworth guns for the Confederate army. When the runner made her escape for the sea, she led the USS *Eolus* for a sixty-five mile chase before a burst steam pipe ended the pursuit and resulted in her capture. After the war, she was sold and became the merchant steamer *Savannah*. She became the frigate *Churruca* of the Spanish navy in 1866 and was stricken off the books in 1880.

Colonel Lamb, under Captain Lockwood, went through the blockade in November 1864. The following year, Lockwood attempted to get her through to Galveston, but was unsuccessful. She returned to England and was later in merchant service as the Greek *Bomboulina*.[461]

Steel and iron hulled blockade runner Hope, built by Jones, Quiggin at Liverpool, was one of the largest runners built for the trade, at 281-feet in length, with watertight bulkheads. Note the turtleback over the foredeck, designed prevent head seas from inundating the deck. The vessel made one run into Wilmington and was captured. Mariners' Museum

This painting of the Battle of Mobile Bay, by J.O. Davidson, shows Confederate gunboats astern of ironclad Tennessee. Steamer in the near foreground is either the Morgan or Gaines, which were similar vessels. Note the prominent pilothouse. Naval Historical Center

GUNBOATS

The term gunboat is generic enough to include many types of vessels used by the Confederate Navy during the Civil War. Many were rigged, but some were not. The majority were wooden hulled and were not purpose built as naval vessels. Their armament ranged from one gun to ten, but since most were converted from civil uses, rarely did they carry more than four. A great number of these were vessels only temporarily in navy service and therefore there is little specific information on them in terms of their construction and design, at least from a naval standpoint. My selection here begins with the vessels of the navy's gunboat construction programs, and even these were not documented thoroughly at the time. Beyond "program" gunboats, the selection I have made is on the basis of historical significance as well as an effort to present examples of different types of merchant vessels and how they were altered for naval use. Because many times these alterations were as simple as installing eyebolts for the gun tackle and cutting gunports into the gunwales, I am not presenting a complete catalog or list of these vessels. Such lists are available elsewhere. If the reader is interested in the details of individual converted vessels not included here, it would be more informative to study the various merchant vessels of the era and interpolate from other sources how they were made ready for naval service.

I should note here that the gunboats in this chapter are those that are not of the classic Western Rivers type vessels converted for war use. These will be included with the Mississippi River defense force in Chapter 10 devoted to converted riverboats, both side- and stern-wheel steamers.

The Gunboat Programs

Despite Secretary Mallory's stated intentions to outmatch the Union navy by employing the latest naval technology in the form of ironclad warships, he ordered the construction of several classes of conventional, wooden hulled, steam vessels. These were intended for use in the harbors, rivers, and estuaries and thus were relatively small gunboats, most of which were to be screw propelled.

There were three groups of these ships ordered in the first year of the war. One group of four were sidewheel steamers, each about 196-feet in length. A second group was a dozen or so light draft, screw propelled boats ranging from 110-150-feet in length with up to six guns. The large vessels of this group were to designs by John L. Porter, and the two smallest boats – *Hampton* and *Nansemond* – may also have been to his design. Though the latter pair are often classified as Maury gunboats (see below), I am setting them apart for three reasons: their construction began before the Maury vessels were authorized; they were built by the navy at Gosport yard, rather than by contract, which was the standard for the Maury boats; and there were design differences between the Maury and Porter vessels. The Maury boats composed by far the largest group of vessels authorized

Diagram of the Battle of Mobile Bay by a participant. Gaines is shown twice, once in line of battle, and once beached near Fort Morgan. This version of the two vessels shows them without pilothouses. Note that both the painting and diagram show the vessels with low freeboard and broad beams. Naval Historical Center

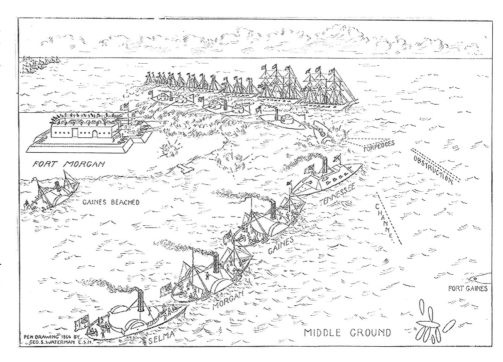

by the Confederate Congress: there were to have been one hundred of these light draft, steam gunboats designed by Matthew Fontaine Maury, each carrying two guns.

Because of the vicissitudes of the war and the sudden emphasis on ironclads precipitated by the *Monitor-Virginia* battle, a large proportion of these vessels were never completed. The South would build only a handful of wooden gunboats throughout the remainder of the war.

Morgan and Gaines

In July 1861, Secretary Mallory ordered two gunboats each to be built at New Orleans and Mobile. Of these four, *Morgan* and *Gaines* at Mobile and *Bienville* and *Carondelet* at New Orleans, we have specific dimensions and construction information only on the *Morgan*. It is assumed that all four were to the same design and only differed in their machinery.[462] The engines were, as in most of the Confederate vessels, recycled from available merchant river steamers.

The *Gaines* was built by contractor William Otis; *Morgan* by Henry Bassett. Both vessels were laid down in September 1861 and the government spread payments out in $10,000 monthly increments to each builder. The *Morgan's* engines were cast-off "standard" Western rivers cylinders of unknown origin; those of *Gaines* were likewise taken from the steamer *P. Dalman*, which had been purchased complete – hull,

machinery and "every article on board," in November, for $7,000. After the machinery was removed the vessel's hull was used as a receiving ship at Mobile.

Progress on the vessels was rapid with receipts for the work indicating the engines for both were in place in January 1862, and the "20 arm" paddle wheels also had been completed for the *Gaines*. January 1862 also saw the delivery of several thirty-two-pounder guns to both ships.[463]

Both were completed in the spring of 1862 and participated in the battle of Mobile Bay in August 1864. *Gaines* was reported to have had eight guns in February 1863: six eight-inchers in broadside and two six-inch rifles on pivot mountings, fore and aft. Two of the broadside guns were later removed. *Morgan* had one seven-

inch and one six-inch on pivots as well as four thirty-two-pounders. The complement of *Gaines* was 120 men.[464]

The *Morgan* was described by one of her officers as "a perfect little beauty," but her captain was more critical: "Her engines … are high pressure and not sufficiently powerful to drive so large a hull with the requisite speed. Her steam pipes are entirely above the waterline, and her boilers and magazines partly above it. So we have the comfortable appearance of being blown up or scalded by any chance shot that may not take off our heads."[465]

The *Gaines* was sunk during the battle of Mobile Bay, but *Morgan* was damaged and escaped. At the end of the war, it was said the vessel was burned to prevent her capture. Though

some battle damage, dry rot, a split stem, and other defects. Their recommendation was that the ship be put up for public sale.[467]

Bienville and Carondelet

These two wooden side-wheelers were for the defense of New Orleans and were contracted out by the navy department in September, 1861. On September 14, John Hughes and Company contracted for the *Bienville* and on the sixteenth of the month, Sydney J. Porter, naval constructor, began the *Carondelet*. Both were built on Bayou St. John, which at that time connected the south side of Lake Pontchartrain to the city, but did not flow into the Mississippi River.

Hughes's contract called for a "gunboat … for the lake" complete with "two good second-hand high-pressure engines with boilers." The hull was to be entirely of yellow pine except for the keel, stem and sternposts, deadwood and knuckle timbers, which were to be of "white oak and oak roots." The cost was to be $76,000 and it was to be built to the specifications set forth by constructor Porter and completed in the "same length of time as the vessel being built by the constructor, and of the same dimensions."[468] (This vessel is not to be confused with the towboat hull Hughes had on the stocks in July 1861 and which was completed as a gunboat named *Livingston* – see below.)

Hughes' vessel was named *Bienville* and was launched in February 1862, then accepted by the

the vessel was damaged, apparently the attempt to burn the vessel was unsuccessful, and Union officers made a survey report of the ship from which much of the information we have about these ships originated.

The hull of the ship was 196-feet long from the after side of the stem to the forward side of the sternpost, and 202-feet overall. The beam was thirty-eight-feet and depth of hold, thirteen-feet, with a draft of seven-feet two-inches. There was a berth deck and spar deck, six-foot six-inches apart.

With exception of the first (lower) futtocks, which were of white oak, and the "swamp cedar" upper deck beam knees, the hull was built of yellow pine. The frames were eleven-inches thick, by fourteen-inches deep, composed of two layers of flitch, on twenty-four-inch centers. The hull was "well keelsoned" but not thoroughly fastened.

The engine was the Western rivers high pressure, non-condensing type, with two twenty-three-inch cylinders and a stroke of seven-feet, driving twenty-six-feet four-inch side wheels.

Four twenty-nine foot six-inch boilers provided steam, each being forty-one-inches in diameter and having two fifteen-inch flues. There were bunkers capable of holding ninety-three-tons of bituminous coal or the equivalent quantity of wood. The two engines were not connected which meant that each side wheel could operate independently. This would obviate one hazard of connected wheels where, in rough seas, one wheel could be buried in the water while the other might be windmilling and racing clear out of the water.

Early on, both *Gaines* and *Morgan* had been partially armored. The rolled iron on *Morgan* was calculated by her captors as weighing some 148,176 pounds – seventy-four-tons. On *Gaines,* the armor had been two-inches thick, and presumably, on both vessels, had been employed to form a ram as well as to protect engines and boilers.[466]

The ship's battery at the end of the war consisted of one six-inch Brooke rifle, one seven-inch Brooke, and four thirty-two-pounders two of which were rifled. The inspecting officers noted

navy on April 5, 1862. The steamer was armed with six guns but still had no crew as of April 20, 1862, five days before the city of New Orleans fell to Farragut's forces. About the same time, on the lake, *Bienville* was destroyed by her crew to prevent capture.[469]

Engines for the *Carondelet* were ordered as early as September 19, 1861, along with boilers, a steam pump and wheel shafts and cranks. Over 97,000 feet of timber for planking was used for building the vessel and she was launched in January 1862. Her dimensions, as well as those of *Bienville*, were 196-feet long by a thirty-eight-foot beam, not including paddle-wheel boxes. Later, the vessel was described as "substantially built" and pierced for eight or nine guns. *Carondelet* was commissioned March 16, 1862 and armed with five forty-two-pounder smoothbores, one thirty-two-pounder rifle, and one smaller rifled gun. The five, forty-two-pounder guns were supplied by the Confederate army forces in the area.[470]

The *Carondelet* was commissioned on March 16, 1862, under the command of Lt. Washington Gwathmey. Early the next month, the steamer was in combat, along with Confederate naval vessels *Pamlico* and *Oregon* off Pass Christian, Mississippi, east of Lake Pontchartrain. They set upon Union naval ships *J.P. Jackson*, *New London*, and *Hatteras*, in an attempt to prevent landing of a Union army force at that place. The attempt was unsuccessful and the Confederate camp that was the target was taken. *Carondelet* returned to Lake Pontchartrain and was destroyed by her crew there on April 21st, to prevent her capture by Union forces.[471]

Chattahoochee

Of the light draft, screw vessels designed by Constructor John L. Porter, there were two contracts for 130-foot vessels. One was to be built in North Carolina by W.F. Martin and Gilbert Elliot, who were also building the ironclad *Albemarle*. This gunboat was destroyed by Union forces before completion, but the second vessel, built by Daniel S. Johnston of Saffold, Early County, Georgia, was completed and named *Chattahoochee*.

The contract for the ship was dated October 14, 1861 and was negotiated by Lt. Augustus McLaughlin of the Confederate Navy. The document called for a twin-screw vessel, 130-feet long and thirty-feet wide, with a ten-foot depth of hold, propelled by two engines with boilers having 800-square feet of fire surface. The total cost was to be $47,500 and completion was scheduled within 120-days. The contractor's shipyard was on the Chattahoochee River, 175-miles south of Columbus, Georgia, and 140-miles north of Appalachicola, Florida.[472] (The Chattahoochee River is a tributary of the Appalachicola River, which debouches into the Gulf of Mexico.)

The 120-day deadline was exceedingly optimistic and indeed, in March 1862, the vessel was not yet planked up or in the water. In part, delays were attributed to exceedingly high waters during the winter months, leaving the uncompleted hull under water for days in a row. Furthermore, the shortage of labor hindered efficient work in the shipyard, and poor workmanship on the machinery parts resulted in many being returned to the ironworks for alterations.[473]

By June 1862, the navy department was "very much annoyed" at the lack of progress on the ship, and of the opinion that the builders had "no disposition … to complete the work." Further delays were incurred when sickness felled a large percentage of the crew in September. Late in the month, it was reported that there were twenty-two in the hospital, having been sent there "because they would have died here." October saw no improvement: it was reported that there were only two men of thirty-eight capable of working.[474]

The vessel was finally launched, probably in August 1862. Her engines were two horizontal, direct-acting cylinders, measuring twenty-eight-inches in diameter by twenty-inch stroke, driving two ninety-inch, three-bladed propellers. The origin of the engines is the subject of some speculation. The Confederate ironworks in Columbus provided the machinery, but the cylinders may have come from a grounded blockade runner or have been part of the cargo of a runner.[475]

After much disagreement about whether the vessel should be rigged as a barque or schooner, the *Chattahoochee* was commissioned on January 1, 1863. She was a three-masted schooner and had a battery of four thirty-two-pounder smoothbores on broadside mounts, plus a thirty-two-pounder rifle and a nine-inch Dahlgren smoothbore shell gun, each on pivot rails. The latter was forward and the former was aft of the mainmast.[476]

In January 1863, the vessel was ordered down the river. This effort proved too much for the new machinery: the boilers leaked and a problem developed with the air pump. The only way the steamer could reach its destination was by employing a tow vessel. Even then, she hit an obstruction that smashed the rudder and sprung the sternpost. The latter resulted in a major leak in the hull. In consequence, the ship did not again move under steam until the repairs were complete. In April, the vessel went downriver as far as the defensive obstructions would permit.[477]

On May 26, the ship attempted to cross the Appalachicola River bar at Blountstown, Florida, but low water forced postponement that night. Next morning, with high tide, steam was ordered up, resulting in a disagreement among the engineers as to the water level in the boilers. The argument was apparently ended when the boilers exploded, sinking the ship and killing eighteen crewmen of a complement of 120. It was later said that the water gauge itself was defective. After being refloated and repaired, the *Chattahoochee* made one more unsuccessful attempt to take on the blockading fleet, then returned to dock at Columbus.

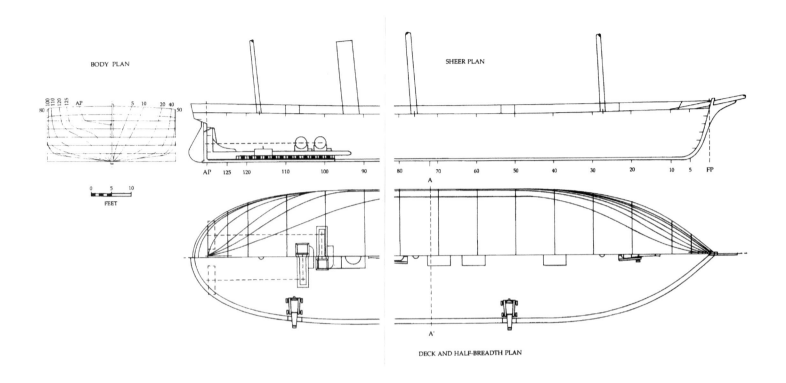

BODY PLAN

SHEER PLAN

DECK AND HALF-BREADTH PLAN

She was finally destroyed to prevent capture in December 1864.[478]

The remains of *Chattahoochee*, including the lower portion of the hull and the two propellers, are displayed in the National Civil War Naval Museum at Columbus, Georgia. The museum also has, in storage, many parts of the steamer's engines, including the two cylinders and bedplates. The sunken vessel was the subject of an archeological survey by East Carolina University, which resulted in a set of plans of the hull as well as the engines.

The archeological report reveals much significant information about both the hull and engines of the *Chattahoochee*. One surprising find was that the breadth of the ship was not thirty-feet as called for in the contract, but was thirty-two-feet. The remains of the hull indicate also that the ship had about a twelve-degree deadrise amidships, a short run aft, and had rather full lines forward. Generally, this light-draft, nearly flat-bottomed hull would not have been appropriate for seagoing service.[479]

The structure of the hull was, according to the report, more appropriate for a commercial merchant vessel than for a warship. The frames were on twenty-four-inch centers (room and space), and measured seven- by 8½-inches at the keel. The keel itself measured ten- by twelve-inches. The planking was three-inch thick pine and the ceiling, 1½-inches thick. Fastenings were spikes and treenails, rather than through bolts,

Lines and deck plan of Confederate gunboat Chattahoochee, based on archeological data gleaned from the vessel's wreck site. Note the side and top view of the two cylinder engines mounted transversely, each one turning a propeller. "Investigation of the Remains of Chattahoochee," East Carolina University

which was navy practice. The structure was not appropriate for withstanding the shocks inherent in movement and firing of heavy ordnance.[480]

The cylinders and bedplates were recovered, and it was noted that the engine bedplates were mounted on wooden timbers. The whole was

Starboard engine of the Chattahoochee showing the iron bedplate and part of the lower hull cross section. The piston is on the left side of the plan view and cross section view. The engine is shown in damaged condition resulting from the Confederate destruction of the vessel before setting it afire. "Investigation of the Remains of Chattahoochee, East Carolina University"

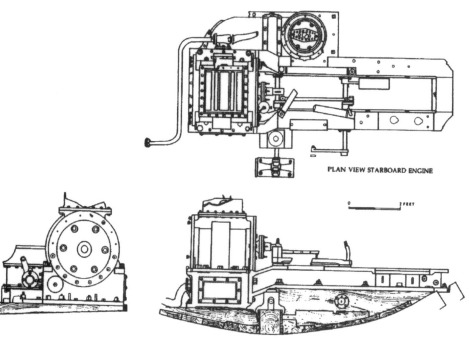

PLAN VIEW STARBOARD ENGINE

END VIEW STARBOARD ENGINE   STARBOARD ENGINE LOOKING FORWARD

secured to the hull using through bolts, running from outside the hull, through the timbers, to the plates. The bolt heads were countersunk into the outside of the hull and wooden blocks filled the gaps around the bolt heads. The cylinders were mounted athwartship, with the cylinder driving the starboard prop placed farther aft than the cylinder driving the port propeller. The cylinders operated independently and each piston rod pushed a crosshead moving on a guide mounted on the bedplate. The connecting rods were attached by pins at the circumference of discs that served as cranks as well as flywheels. These provided momentum and helped avoid the engine stopping at dead center. The discs also were pierced along their circumference with a series of one-inch holes that could be used when it was necessary to manually coax the engines off dead center.

The two iron propellers were canted slightly inward towards the ship's midline, to provide for more bite for the rudder. Each of the 5½- to six-inch diameter propeller shafts was supported by three bearings: one on the bedplate, one where it passed through the hull, and a third at the bracket just forward of the propeller.[481]

In the process of scuttling the vessel before the arrival of Union troops, much damage was done to the engines and some parts were missing. As to the hull, very little was left above the water line, leaving questions unanswered. For instance, the amount of tumblehome, if any, is not known.

Photograph of the Chattahoochee's engines as they are now, in storage at the National Civil War Naval Museum. The bedplate is shown as well as the twenty-eight-inch diameter cylinder. Photo by author

This model of the gunboat Chattahoochee, at the National Civil War Naval Museum, is based on archeological findings and original documents. Model by O.L. Raines. Photo by author

The CSS Macon, a twin screw gunboat stationed at Savannah. A similar vessel was begun in South Carolina waters but was never completed. Drawing by Bob Holcombe

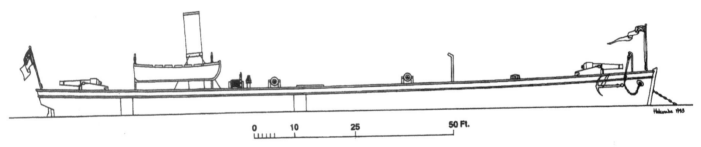

Therefore, the hull plans developed from this study cannot be considered definitive.

Macon and *Pee Dee*

The largest of Porter's gunboat designs was 150-feet in length, of which two vessels were completed. H.F. Willink in Savannah contracted to build two of these vessels on November 11, 1861 and one of which, the *Macon*, went into service. The Confederate navy built another, the *Pee Dee*, on the Pee Dee River in South Carolina.

Willink's contract called for the builder to construct the hulls and provide rigging at a total cost of $36,000 each. Work proved to be exceedingly slow on these vessels, with the *Macon* (originally named *Ogeechee*) going into the water in July 1863. However, as late as October 14, 1864, the steamer was still incomplete and no decision had been made as to adding iron plating to the vessel.[482]

As with the 130-foot vessels, *Macon* had a ten-foot depth of hold, but was twenty-five-feet in breadth. The vessel was to draw no more than eight feet and the screws were seven feet in diameter. The machinery for both ships was contracted out to the A. & N. Miller firm of Savannah. The ship mounted six guns when in service.[483]

Macon was active when the Union army came to Savannah in December 1864, then retreated to Augusta where she remained for the rest of the conflict. In a January 1865 survey, she was found to be in poor condition: Her hull was thoroughly rotten: one could pull out "chunks of wood" with one's bare hands. Furthermore, she was "hogged by the simple action of her machinery about 18 inches" and one of her propeller shafts was bent. The steamer surrendered to Union forces in May 1865.[484]

The South Carolina vessel seems to have been laid down considerably later than the Savannah steamer. Sometime late in 1862, the department sent Lt. A. Barbot to begin a naval depot and boatyard on the "interior waters" of the state. A site was found at the Society Hill Landing (or Mars Bluff) on the Pee Dee River where the stream was at least eight feet deep all the way to Georgetown on the Atlantic. Lt. Van Rensselaer Morgan was directed to establish the facility and build a gunboat.

Morgan arrived and soon had a naval constructor, a surgeon, a commissary, and a hundred carpenters, shipwrights and other workmen on the site. The needed timber was cut locally or rafted down the river to the hurriedly built shipyard. In December 1862, payment was made for part of the vessel's construction, but actual progress was slow, for the most part because of the isolated location of the facility and consequent difficulty in obtaining supplies.[485]

The completed vessel mounted three guns: one nine-inch smoothbore, one 6.4-inch rifle, and one seven-inch rifle and her dimensions were 150- by twenty-six-feet with a ten-foot depth of hold. Her career was terminated prematurely when she was burned to prevent capture near Georgetown, South Carolina, in February 1865.[486] One remaining artifact from this vessel is a rusted propeller, on display at a museum in Florence, South Carolina.[487]

Hampton and *Nansemond*

In September 1861, these two vessels were ordered by Secretary Mallory to be built at the former Union navy yard at Portsmouth. Their construction was concurrent with that of the conversion of the *Merrimack* into the ironclad *Virginia* at the same yard. Though these vessels are sometimes classified as Maury gunboats, their construction began three months before the Confederate Congress authorized the Maury program. Little is known about these vessels, with one source giving a length of 116-feet and breadth of eighteen-feet. They were single-screw vessels with small, steam engines: the engineer of *Hampton* complained that it was a "regular old saw mill affair. In fact it is a miserable affair." He later added "common" and "plain and simple" to his description of the engine. The "sawmill engine" was about the simplest steam engine in terms of moving parts and versatility. It was a horizontal cylinder that resembled a small version of the Western river paddle wheel engine but mounted athwartship with non-adjustable valve gear.[488]

Each gunboat mounted two guns on pivot carriages fore and aft. *Nansemond* had a rifled, banded, thirty-two-pounder, fifty-seven-cwt. on the bow and an eight-inch shell gun aft. *Hampton* had a similar battery.[489]

The only known period depiction of one of these vessels is of the *Nansemond*, and is a sketch done in 1865 by a crewmember. It shows the two guns and protective shields along the sides as well as a pilothouse. A contemporary letter indicates there was an "iron casing" for the pilot structure. The drawing places the steamer's funnel well forward, just behind the pilothouse. This differs from the Maury design, which placed the engines and funnel well aft.[490] Both vessels were completed before the Gosport yard was recaptured by Union forces in May 1862.

Hampton was commanded by Lt. J.S. Maury, the son of the famous oceanographer, and participated in the battle at Dutch Gap in August, and Chaffin's Bluff, in October 1864. The vessel was burned to prevent capture at Richmond in April 1865.

Nansemond remained part of the James River squadron throughout the remainder of the war. The vessel was in combat at Howlett's, Dutch Gap, and Fort Harrison in late 1864 and was burned to prevent capture in April 1865.[491]

The Maury Gunboats

Matthew Fontaine Maury was an internationally known oceanographer by the beginning of the Civil War and his prestige gained him notice at the highest levels of the Confederate navy department and in the Confederate Congress. Maury contended that the seceded states had not the resources or time to build major naval vessels – conventional or armor-clad – and that a cheap, rapidly built alternative was needed. On October 22, 1861, Maury wrote Secretary Mallory proposing a "mosquito fleet" of steam vessels with a single deck and without cabins, galley, or other accommodations on board. These were to be little more than "steam launches" with a twenty-foot beam, and five- to six-foot draft, and "floating just high enough to keep the water out." Each was to mount two guns – "big guns and little ships" was Maury's phrase – and they were to be built and operated in large numbers to overwhelm the Union blockading vessels. Their low profile would make them difficult targets, particularly when close in with the adversary.[492]

Maury suggested that one hundred of these boats be built at about $10,000 each. Their

relatively small size would permit them to be built in small facilities virtually any place in the south where there was access to rivers and inlets, and their simplicity of construction would not require the skills of professional shipwrights. Another advantage, and an immediate one, according to Maury, was that they could be built in less than 120 days – provided the construction could be started while the weather was good.[493]

Maury's ideas were submitted to the Virginia legislature and made their way to the Confederate Congress, and the latter approved the concept on December 23, 1861. $2-million was authorized for the program of "not more than" one hundred of these boats.

Maury, in a letter dated October 8, originally proposed vessels with a twenty-one-foot beam and length of 112-feet, with a six-foot draft. In December, when it was apparent that the Congress would approve the program, a group of senior navy men, including Maury, met and agreed on a length of 106-feet and beam of twenty-feet. Each would be driven by a screw propeller and mount two guns: one nine-inch Dahlgren and a 6.4-inch rifle.[494]

Contracts for at least twelve of these small vessels were let in January 1862 and about fifteen were actually begun. Only two, possibly three, were completed. *Isondiga* was built in Savannah by the firm of Krenson and Hawkes, and *Torch*, built in Charleston, was completed as a torpedo vessel. The gunboat *Yadkin*, built in Wilmington in 1864, may also have been to the Maury design.[495]

Isondiga

The firm of Krenson and Hawkes in Savannah obtained a contract for three "Maury gunboats," to be built at a cost of $16,000 each. The department supplied "Specifications" in printed form for the direction of the builders. This called for a hull of 116-feet extreme length, twenty-one-feet extreme beam and an eight-foot depth of hold and a single deck. The spring of the deck beams was to be three-inches and the draft of the completed vessel no more than six-feet when "loaded for sea."

The keel was a ten-inch moulded dimension (measured from bottom to top of the timber) and a twelve-inch sided dimension (measured across the timber). On top of this was the white oak keelson, also ten-inches wide, and nine-inches deep. The stem and sternposts were to side ten-inches but the latter would "swell" four inches at the propeller shaft line. The frames were to be white oak or yellow pine tapering from 8½-inches at the keel to 5½-inches at the plank sheer. The straighter futtocks could be pine or oak, but the "crooked" futtocks for the bilge were to be white or live oak. Amidships, between the pivot guns, atop the plank sheer was to be an iron hammock netting twelve-inches deep.

The bottom planking was white oak, measuring 2½-inches thick; if pine was used, it was to be three-inches thick. Two 6⅛-inch iron spikes and two treenails attached each plank at each frame. The latter were to be driven through and wedged on the inside. At the ends of the planks they were to have ¾-inch iron butt bolts, driven through and "riveted on rings." The planking at the wales was similarly fastened, but with slightly thinner oak.

Deck planks were to be three-inch yellow pine, held by two six-inch spikes to each beam. The latter were to be nine-inches in width (side dimension) by six-inches on the ends and seven-inches at the centerline. Hanging knees on each beam were to be bolted through from the sides.

The completed vessel was to have two sixteen-foot boats on iron davits, two anchors (one 500lbs; one 700lbs.), and the usual deck equipment: windlass, "two good pumps," "hauser pipes," cat heads, etc. As to the steam machinery, if the word "except" was crossed out in the applicable paragraph and replaced by "with," the contractor was to provide the motive power.[496]

For comparison sake, it is noteworthy that the scantling dimensions described here were similar to those found on the excavated hull of the *Chattahoochee* – as described above – a vessel significantly larger than the Maury boat. Furthermore, the small vessel was also much more solidly fastened, with significant use of through bolts in addition to treenails, where the *Chattahoochee* was for the most part spiked together.

Though the *Isondiga*'s launch date is unknown, and a few unspecified alterations to the boat were directed by constructor Porter, the final payment for the vessel was made on January 17, 1863 and the vessel's trial trip was in September 1863. On this initial run, her commander reported that with a full complement and stores, the propeller was "little over half in the water," reducing her speed from six to four-knots. He stated that the ship

steered "admirably." However, when backing the rudder had "no perceptible effect."[497]

As completed, *Isondiga* was un-rigged and mounted two guns, one 6.4-inch rifle forward and a nine-inch smoothbore aft. She served in Savannah waters until December 1864, when she was burned to prevent capture by the Union forces under William T. Sherman.

The *Isondiga* was apparently the only Maury gunboat completed as designed. The entire gunboat program ground to a halt in March 1862 when the implications of the ironclad fight at Hampton Roads set in. The Confederate Congress squelched the funding for all but the few that were actually under construction. There was some talk of altering some of these boats to ironclads, but this was impractical, and what moneys were yet unspent on the Maury craft were re-directed to the ironclad program.[498]

• • •

Calhoun

The side wheel steamer *Calhoun* could be included in this book as a blockade runner or a privateer and the actual distinction between the privateer and the Confederate gunboat is somewhat murky. It began Confederate service as a privateer, with a letter of marque dated May 15, 1861, and captured at least six merchant vessels. However, by October 1861, the steamer was part of Confederate Commander Hollins' flotilla at the Head of the Passes of the Mississippi. In December of that year, the vessel became a blockade runner, making a single successful run through the Union gauntlet. On January 23, 1862, the vessel was off the Head of the Passes offloading a cargo from Havana, when she was surprised and captured by Union blockaders, ending her Confederate service in any capacity.[499]

The vessel had been, in civilian life, a coastal steamer, built by Lawrence & Sneeden of New

York in 1851. She was a wooden hulled relatively high-freeboard vessel 174-feet four-inches long and twenty-seven-feet six-inches in beam, registering 508-tons. Her powerplant was a single vertical cylinder measuring forty-four-inches and with a ten-foot stroke, operating an overhead walking beam, which in turn actuated twenty-six-foot sidewheels.

In merchant service, she was depicted in a broadside view painting by the famous Bard brothers. She had a light, two-masted rig and was distinguished by prominent hog frames some seventy-five-feet long and about twelve-feet high on either side of her superstructure, strengthening her longitudinally. She had cabin structures on the main deck fore and aft of the wheel boxes, as well as accommodations on the deck below. She carried passengers on routes from Charleston south and west to New Orleans, and was based in New Orleans at the onset of the war.[500]

At the beginning of her war service, she was converted to a gunboat and eventually carried a single eighteen-pounder as well as three smaller guns. The major change for naval use apparently was cutting down her forward bulwarks to give a field of fire for the eighteen-pounder gun. The standard broadside view usually identified as this vessel in Confederate service shows her main aft cabin structure drastically cut back, leaving a large open deck for a stern gun. Also, the illustration shows the hog braces extending to nearly twenty-five feet from either end of the main deck, and beyond the ends of the superstructure. However, there are three wartime illustrations, dated 1863 and 1864 (one of which is included here) of the ship in Union service, which clearly show the weather deck extending to the stern. Also, the vessel's hog frames do not extend beyond the cabin structure.[501]

The USS *Calhoun* was of much more value to the Union navy, serving in combat as a gunboat from early 1862 through June 1864. In April 1863,

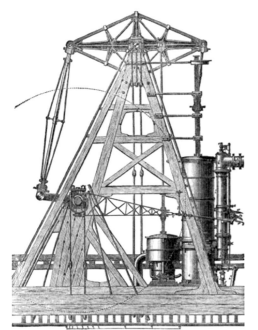

Walking beam marine steam engine of the type in the steamer Calhoun. Cylinder (A) is on the right, and operated the piston rod (B). Transfer of power to the paddle wheel shaft (E) was through the walking (sometimes called the 'working beam') beam and connecting rod (D). Circumference of the side paddle wheel is shown as F. Calhoun's cylinder measured forty-four-inches and the cylinder's stroke was ten feet. These engines were common on river and merchant steamers. However, when used on war vessels, their high profile made them vulnerable to enemy projectiles. Wikimedia Commons (Annotations by author)

Steamer Calhoun, lower right, while in Union naval service in 1864. Note the upper and lower decks that extended to the stern. Naval Historical Center

a thirty-pounder Parrott percussion shell from the *Calhoun* caused the fire which led to the explosion that destroyed the feared Confederate ram *Queen of the West*.[502] After June 1864, she was part of the U.S. Army's Quartermaster Corps fleet, and then became a towboat in the post-war years.[503]

Thomas Jefferson (Jamestown)

A wooden coastal passenger steamer, the *Jamestown* was built by the Jacob Westervelt firm of New York. Westervelt had a long history in the shipbuilding business and had built both clipper ships and steamships – including the Union steam sloop *Brooklyn*. *Jamestown* was 240-feet three-inches by thirty-three-feet six-inches and with a twenty-three-feet five-inches depth of hold – a very substantial vessel for open seas and coastal operations. Her powerplant consisted of two forty-two-inch vertical cylinders with a ten-foot stroke, operating twin overhead walking beams, driving thirty-foot diameter side wheels. She had a minimal brigantine rig with square sails on the foremast only.

She was completed in 1852, and operated for the New York and Virginia Steam Ship Company for five years, then was sold to the Pennsylvania and Virginia Steam Ship Company. The vessel was on the Philadelphia-Norfolk run when the Civil War began and was seized by the Confederate government in March 1861.

Converting the ship for naval use involved adding iron plating and mounting guns. Her battery consisted of two thirty-two-pounder guns. Some sources indicate a battery of ten guns, but her crew numbered around sixty, which would be appropriate for a smaller battery. The iron plating would have been around her engine and boiler spaces. The vertical cylinders would have been high in the hull and vulnerable. Little could be done to protect the walking beam apparatus itself.

BOMBARDMENT OF FORT POWELL BY ADMIRAL FARRAGUT'S FLEET, ON FEBRUARY 24, 1864.—Sketched during the Engagement.

She was renamed *Thomas Jefferson* in Confederate service, but the name was inconsistently used. Her most prominent service was as an escort to the ironclad *Virginia* at the battle of Hampton Roads in March 1862, where her guns were effective against the Union steam frigate *Minnesota*. The vessel's career ended in August 1862 when she was scuttled in the James River. Ironically, the only known photograph of the ship is one of her paddle boxes only, showing where she last came to rest.

Yorktown (Patrick Henry)

The *Yorktown* was a coastal passenger steamer similar in general layout to *Jamestown*, built in 1853 by the William H. Webb company, also of New York.

Her hull was 250-feet on deck by thirty-four-feet (hull only, without paddle wheel housings) with a nine-foot six-inch depth of hold (and seventeen-feet to the spar deck). Her lines, published in Webb's famous book, show a very sharp entrance and run at the stern, but with almost no deadrise. She drew about thirteen-feet – four feet less than *Jamestown*.

Her hull was strongly built with floor timbers measuring fifteen-inches square at the keel. Her frames were on thirty-inch centers and strengthened externally by "double laid" iron straps 4½-inches wide and ¾-inch thick. If these were like those on typical naval vessels of the era, they formed a veritable basket around the frames as far up as the bulwarks.

Like *Jamestown*, her propulsion was provided by two walking beam engines, with cylinders fifty-inches in diameter with a ten-foot stroke. The machinery and two boilers were by the Morgan works in New York, producing steam at about 25psi, driving the thirty-foot side wheels at 20rpm. The paddle wheels were nine-feet wide with twenty eighteen-inch paddles.

The engine and boiler spaces took up seventy-eight-feet of the hold and the boilers were thirty-four-feet long and fifty-inches in diameter. Her coal consumption per day was twenty-six-tons, with exhaust trailing out of a funnel thirty-nine-feet above the boilers.[504]

The vessel went into service with the New York and Virginia Steam Ship Company, running from New York to Norfolk. At war's outbreak, she was seized by the state of Virginia, which later turned her over to the Confederacy. Early on, her executive officer, William Powell, suggested iron armor would be needed for her protection. Mallory approved, and "one-inch iron plates were put abreast of her boilers, extending a foot, perhaps two, below the waterline, and ran a few feet forward and abaft her engine and boilers." Along with the side plating, iron "shields in the form of a V, on the spar deck forward and abaft her engines" were built, which, "when fighting head or stern on, afforded good protection from raking shots, as well as afforded some protection to the walking beam."[505]

These shields were described as thirty-eight-feet long and eight-feet six-inches high, and 3¾-inches thick, each weighing 48,760-pounds. The side sheathings were fifty-feet long, seven-feet six-inches high, and two-inches thick, each weighing 26,750-pounds. It appears that the armor cladding was composed of layers of one-inch plates. Thus, the iron protection on the vessel weighed about seventy-four-tons.[506] It is noteworthy that all this iron armoring was completed about the same time as work *began* on the iron cladding of the steam frigate *Merrimack*.

The steamship Yorktown in merchant service prior to the war. Powered by two walking beam engines, the vessel was 250-feet long and plied the New York to Norfolk run before the war. Naval Historical Center

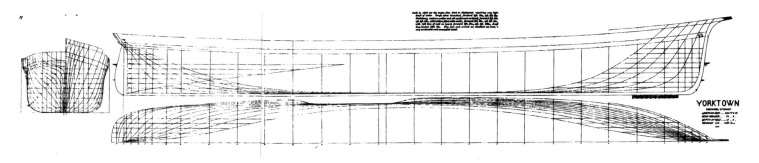

Hull lines of the Yorktown. This vessel was built in New York by noted naval architect William H. Webb. From reprint of "Webb's Book"

Yorktown as converted to school ship Patrick Henry. The vessel served as a dormitory and practice ship for naval midshipmen. Naval Historical Center

In addition to the ironwork, conversion, which was done at the Rocketts yard at Richmond, included mounting a battery. Twelve guns were installed on decks strengthened for the purpose. Ten medium, thirty-two-pounders were mounted on broadside carriages, plus a ten-inch shell gun on a forward pivot and a eight-inch smoothbore on the after deck.[507]

The vessel, renamed *Patrick Henry,* was one of ironclad *Virginia*'s escorts at the Battle of Hampton Roads, suffering a disastrous shot to one of her boilers, killing four men and putting the boiler out of service. Repairs were made and the vessel returned to the action. The day of the *Monitor-Virginia* fight, the vessel fired one long-range shot at the *Monitor,* but did not otherwise participate.

After the loss of Norfolk in May 1862, the James River Squadron retired up the river and the *Patrick Henry* was converted to a school ship for Confederate States Navy midshipmen. This required significant re-vamping of her interior hull spaces to make accommodations for the young sailors, who numbered fifty-two per class. She was burned to prevent capture in April 1865.

Webb (William H. Webb)

William H. Webb was a noted naval architect of the era, famous both for his ships and his scientific

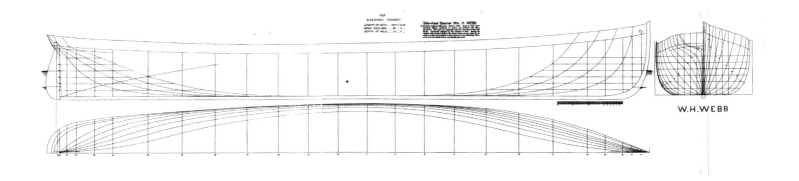

Hull lines of the towboat William H. Webb, which was converted to naval use late in the war, making a wild dash from the Red River to the Gulf to attack Union blockaders. From reprint of "Webb's Book"

approach to shipbuilding. This vessel was built in Webb's shipyard in 1856 as a tugboat for New York harbor, to handle the largest of ocean going vessels. Therefore she was significantly larger than the typical tug and had engines as powerful as many transatlantic steamers.

The wooden hull was 190-feet in length and thirty-feet two-inches in beam (not including paddle housings) and had a twelve-foot depth of hold. She was powered by two "extra heavy" boilers, thirty-feet long and nine-feet in diameter, and two walking beam engines with forty-four-inch cylinders and ten-foot stroke. She was the "largest tug available" in late-1857 when she was called on to aid the huge Collins liner *Adriatic* to sea against both tide and winds. After the two vessels collided in the struggle, it still required a mile fight upstream before the *Webb* was able to bring the steamship about and headed towards the Atlantic.[508]

Subsequently the *Webb* went to New Orleans to perform the same duties, as property of the Southern Steam Ship Company. Though it was said that she had a privateer's letter of marque early in the war, apparently the vessel was not used for this purpose, but continued her utilitarian chores in the harbor.

In January 1862, Major General Lovell was ordered by Secretary of the Army Judah Benjamin to seize a number of vessels at New Orleans and evaluate them for possible military and naval use. About fourteen ships were taken in, among them the *Webb*.[509]

Once taken into Confederate service, the ship was armed and converted into a ram. Accordingly, she was given four twelve-pounders early in the war, then, later, had a single banded thirty-two-pounder rifle. Her bow was strengthened by adding heavy timbers running about thirty feet back and thoroughly bolted together. The latter, in conjunction with her great speed – it was claimed she could do twenty-miles per hour – made her a dangerous bow-on adversary, but little was done to protect her defensively. Lovell wrote in 1863, that she was, "by no means properly protected: the boilers about thirty-feet long and four-feet above the water line had no protection whatever, sav-

ing the side of the vessel which could easily be penetrated by a Minie ball."[510]

The vessel remained so for most of her service, and participated in the taking of the *Indianola* in 1863, then as part of an Army flotilla. In this night action, *Webb* and the *Queen of the West* had a running engagement with the *Indianola*, in which the Union vessel was rammed some seven times. The Union commander reported that, "the sharp bow of the *Webb* penetrated as if it were going to pass entirely through the ship." The only respite came when the Union commander ran the boat ashore to prevent her from sinking.[511]

Webb's last service came at the end of the war. She had been transferred to the Navy and was ordered to cruise against enemy shipping. Charles W. "Savez" Read became her commander and found her "totally unprepared" for such service, not having any guns, crew, or fuel. Read brought 190 bales of cotton onto the vessel, which he backed with twelve-inches of pine, all of which protected her engines. He then mounted a thirty-pounder Parrott rifle as a bow pivot, in addition to two small twelve-pounders.[512]

To find Union commerce against which to cruise, Read had to take the *Webb* from Shreveport on the Red River to the Gulf – past block-

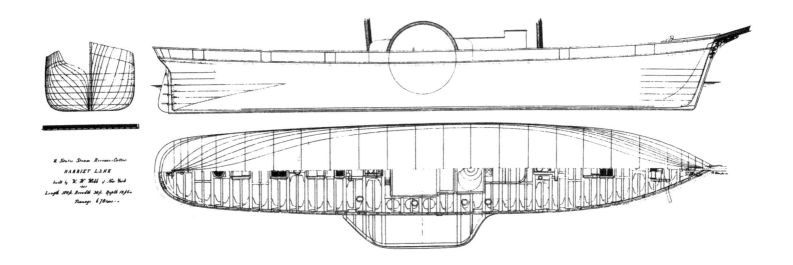

Plans of the U.S. Revenue Steamer Harriet Lane, the Revenue Service's only steam vessel at the beginning of the Civil War. The vessel had been a VIP barge for the Treasury Department and hosted the Prince of Wales during his American tour in 1860. From reprint of "Webb's Book"

aders at the mouth of the Red River as well as the forts Jackson and St. Phillip beyond New Orleans. The intrepid Read nearly made it – running the *Webb* at a reported twenty-five-miles per hour past the city – with the whole city turning out to watch the action. Rumors flew that Read was escaping with the Confederate treasury and John Wilkes Booth was at the helm. Read was finally blocked by the Union steam sloop *Richmond*, twenty-five-miles below the city, and forced to run his vessel ashore and fire her. Read and his crew later gave themselves up to Union naval forces.[513]

Miscellaneous Gunboats

Most of the Confederate small gunboats were of little historical significance, but some gained notoriety in combat and there were several that are of interest because of special circumstances. Two of these were captured Union naval vessels, another had a unique role in the Confederate navy, another was converted to a gunboat while on the stocks near New Orleans, and two others were seized merchant steamers, one of which participated gallantly at the forts below New Orleans and the other at Mobile Bay.

Named for the niece of President Buchanan, who served as White House hostess for the bachelor president, the *Harriet Lane* was built for the Treasury Department in 1857, and was the only steam vessel in the U.S. Revenue Marine (later called the Revenue Cutter Service) from that time to the Civil War.

Built by William H. Webb in New York, the sidewheeler was noted for its exceptional finish and quality of construction and became a favorite VIP barge during this era. She was 180-feet long

and a thirty-foot beam and drew ten-feet of water. Her engine was an inclined cylinder, forty-two-inches in diameter by a seven-foot stroke and the vessel could maintain twelve-knots.[514]

In September 1861, she was taken over by the U.S. Navy and was armed with an eight-inch rifled gun. In February 1862, she mounted three nine-inch smoothbores, one thirty-pounder rifle, and a twelve-pounder rifle.

The *Harriet Lane* fell into Confederate hands on January 1, 1863 when they attacked and re-took Galveston from Union hands. The ex-revenue cutter was rammed by the Confederate steamer *Bayou City* and boarded. Her commander and executive officer were killed, her crew was driven below decks, and the ship was surrendered.

The steamer was taken over by the Confederate Navy in Texas, and was then turned over to the army at the end of March 1863. In 1864, the army planned to have her run the blockade carrying cotton to Havana, to be exchanged for munitions. However, the ship was sold to T.W. House company, renamed *Lavinia*, and evaded the blockading fleet

The Harriet Lane was captured by Confederate forces at Galveston on January 1, 1863, and ran the blockade to Havana, where she remained for the duration of the war. U.S. Coast Guard Historian's Office, drawing by John Tilley

in April, 1864. The steamer reached Havana but was deemed too deep for Texas waters (they had lightened her significantly to run out of Galveston) so she remained in Cuba for the duration of the war.[515] The Revenue Service recovered her after the war, but she was eventually sold and had her machinery removed. She went in to merchant service and was lost off Pernambuco in 1884.[516]

A second Union warship was captured by Confederate forces in June 1864. This was the wooden hulled sidewheel steamer *Water Witch* that had been built at the Washington navy yard in 1852, to replace an iron-hulled vessel of the same name. This ship was 150-feet long and a twenty-two-foot beam, drawing seven-feet ten-inches at 450-tons. Her engine was a single, inclined, 37½-inch cylinder with a six-foot stroke and two boilers. She was the first navy steamer to employ feathering paddle wheels.[517]

The vessel was employed in a survey role in Paraguay in 1855 and was fired upon, resulting in a punitive expedition against that nation. She was part of the South Atlantic Blockading Squadron during the Civil War, and was armed with one thirty-pounder rifled gun as well as three twelve-pounders. After months of inactivity, much of it at anchor off Ossabaw Sound, Georgia, she was captured by a Confederate boat expedition on the night of June 3, 1864. The seven boat loads of Confederates, numbering around 100 men, came within thirty yards of the ship before being noticed. In the free-for-all that ensued, two Union sailors were killed, fourteen wounded and sixty-one captured. Confederate losses were six killed and seventeen wounded.[518]

The *Water Witch* remained in Savannah waters and there were plans to use her for special operations. However, she was still in the area until December 19, 1864, when, with the approach of Sherman's army, she was burned to prevent her re-capture by Federal forces. In 2007, the remains of the steamer were located by the Georgia Department of Natural Resources. An above ground, full-scale replica of the vessel was built at the National Civil War Naval Museum in Columbus, Georgia.

(A third Union naval vessel was also captured by Confederates at the outset of the war: the steamer *Fulton*, originally built in 1837, was being rebuilt at Pensacola navy yard at the time. The Confederates made plans to complete the vessel, but these never came to fruition and she was destroyed on the ways in May 1862.)[519]

Utility vessels of all sorts were commonplace in every port, and many were taken into Confederate service, most to remain tugs or freight haulers for the duration. One, however, was re-cycled for a role never seen before in warfare. This was the little tug *Teaser*, which became a support vessel for the Confederate balloon corps. (It should be noted that the Union's balloon operational support vessel was the unpowered barge *George Washington Parke Custis*). The tug had been built as the *York River* in Philadelphia and was eighty-feet long and eighteen-feet in beam, powered by a thirty-two-inch diameter cylinder with a twenty-inch stroke, one boiler, and single-screw propeller.[520]

The vessel was purchased at Richmond by the Virginia navy at the beginning of the war, and was then turned over to the Confederate navy. She was armed with a thirty-two-pounder rifle at the stern and a twelve-pounder on the forward deck.

The vessel participated in the Battle of Hampton Roads in March 1862, and was then assigned to the Confederate Naval Submarine Battery Service to plant torpedoes (floating mines) in Virginia waters. She also carried balloons to be launched to spy out Union army positions in

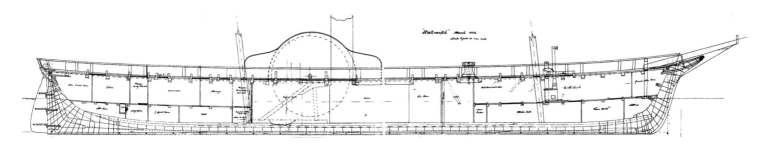

Longitudinal plan of steamer Water Witch. Note the inclined bedplate for the vessel's engine, which operated directly on the paddle wheel shaft. National Archives

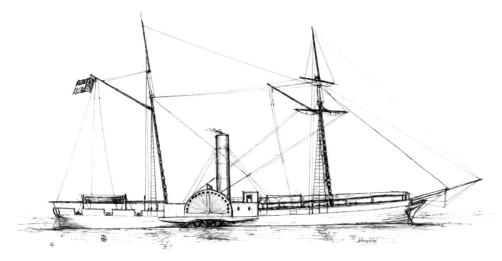

Water Witch drawing based on plans and original photo. This image shows the vessel in blockader grey with awning in place over the foredeck. The vessel was captured by a Confederate boat expedition in 1864, and was later sunk to prevent recapture. A full-scale replica of the ship was built at the National Civil War Naval Museum in Columbus, Georgia. Drawing by author

the vicinity of City Point and Harrison's Landing, during McClellan's Peninsula Campaign. (This was in response to Union balloon operations under Thaddeus Lowe).

On July 4, 1862, while laying torpedoes at Haxall's on the James River and carrying a balloon, she came under fire from the Union double-ender gunboat *Maratanza*, which carried two large pivot guns plus four thirty-two-pounders in broadside. Unfortunately the tug was aground and immobile. Hunter Davidson, commanding officer of the *Teaser*, put up a fight, placing a round into the Union vessel's pilothouse. The latter's return fire exploded *Teaser*'s boiler, ending the one-sided engagement. Davidson and crew escaped. The loss of the vessel itself was a minor event, but when Davidson had evacuated he left important ultra-secret documents on board, revealing much about Confederate torpedoes and operations. Union captors also found the uninflated balloon on board, made of "old silk frocks."[521]

Teaser was repaired and served through the war in the Union navy, still armed with two guns. She was sold in June 1865.[522]

The *McRae* was formerly the *Marquis de la Habana* in service to Miguel Miramon, during the Mexican civil war of the late-1850s. In March 1860, the vessel was captured by the USS *Saratoga* off Vera Cruz as a pirate. The seizure was later invalidated by the courts. (*Saratoga* captured this vessel as well as the steamer *Miramon* at the same time, leading to some confusion as to the identity of this ship.)[523]

The vessel was purchased for the Confederacy in New Orleans in March 1861. Built by William Cramp of Philadelphia in 1852, she was a screw steamer, 180-feet on deck and thirty-feet wide, with an eight-foot depth of hold. Reany & Neafie provided her two steam cylinders, which measured forty-inches in diameter and thirty-six-inch stroke, driving a four-blade, eight-foot diameter propeller by way of 1:2½ ratio gearing. She was fitted out

The gunboat McRae was built by Cramp of Philadelphia and was involved in Mexican Civil War in the 1850s. Seized by the Confederates at New Orleans, the ship saw severe combat during the Union passage of the forts below the city in 1862. Naval Historical Center

with a nine-inch smoothbore mounted on pivot rails amidships and six thirty-two-pounders on her broadsides. Protection was provided by "putting up wrought iron breastwork" around her engine spaces as well as iron on her bows.[524]

The bark-rigged ship participated in the battle at the Head of the Passes in 1861, the actions at Island No.10, and then was severely battered in the fight at the forts below New Orleans in April 1862. At one point she engaged four Union warships and at the end was much cut up. The following day she was used to carry the Confederate wounded to New Orleans under a flag of truce. She then sank at the city wharf.[525]

A second converted merchant steamer was the *Selma*, which fought Farragut's fleet at Mobile Bay in 1864. The vessel had been the coastal packet *Florida*, constructed at Mobile in 1856. Built for the Mobile Mail Line, the vessel was large but of shallow draft, measuring 252- by thirty-feet with a six-foot draft. Her side wheels no doubt added around fifteen-feet to her breadth, and were driven by an inclined, direct acting, non-condensing engine, possibly a variation on the standard Western rivers steamboat engine.

The *Florida* was purchased and converted, with the result that the vessel barely resembled the original. The local newspaper reported she was, "changed from her former gay, first-class hotel appearance, having been relieved of her upper works and painted as black as the inside of her smokestack." It was also said her hog frames were strengthened and 3/8-inch iron was

built around her boilers, "with a considerable inclination inboard on both sides and forward." The result was a steamer with little superstructure other than her paddlewheel housings and a pilothouse. She was armed with four guns: two nine-inch smoothbores, an eight-inch smoothbore, and a 6.4-inch rifle.[526] Two guns were on centerline pivots on each end of the vessel, and the other two were mounted, one on each side, one forward and one aft of the paddle housings.

Most of the *Selma*'s career was spent blockaded at Mobile, but she made her mark early on during a foray escorting a merchant vessel out. She came under fire from the Union blockader *Massachusetts*, then let go a projectile from her rifled gun, which entered aft of the Union ship's engine and, "cut entirely through 18 planks of the main deck ... and exploded in the stateroom ... stripping the bulkheads of four rooms and setting fire to the vessel." A few months later, the

steamer outfaced the blockader *Montgomery*, forcing the latter to flee for safety.[527]

At the battle of Mobile Bay, the vessel harassed Farragut's *Hartford*, and, after the Union fleet passed the forts, was pursued by the *Metacomet*, a fast gunboat mounting eight guns. The Union vessel overtook the *Selma* and was positioning itself to rake her when the Confederate commander surrendered. The ship was later repaired and used by the Union navy until sold after the end of the war.

One of the more unusual vessels acquired by the Confederate navy early in the war was a steamer still under construction at the Bayou St. John shipyard of John Hughes & Company. It was intended to be a tug or ferry boat but, in June 1861, Hughes proposed that the vessel be modified and completed as a gunboat for the Confederacy. Flag Officer Lawrence Rousseau, charged with accumulating a fleet to defend New Orleans,

accepted this plan on June 28, at a price of $42,000, and designated it *Livingston*.

Hughes' plan was for a 180-feet long vessel, with a forty-two-foot beam, apparently not including the paddle housings, and having a depth of hold measuring 9½-feet. The hull was to be of cypress, white oak and yellow pine, with the frames filled in "perfectly solid" from the knuckle up, all around on both sides, as well as where the engines and boilers were placed. The planking was to be 3½-inches at the keel up to six-inches at the bends. He proposed leaving seventy-feet of open deck at each end to allow mounting four pivot guns each, fore and aft, plus six broadside guns, totaling ten for this very beamy vessel. For crew accommodations, he would add a berth deck, and for maneuverability, a rudder at each end.[528]

Finishing this construction required at least 250,000-feet of lumber but the vessel was in the water by January 1862. She was as yet incomplete, however, and was fitting out even as she was en route to join the seventeen-vessel Confederate flotilla under General Lovell at Columbus, Kentucky. After participating in the actions around Island No.10, and against the Union river squadron under Flag Officer Foote, the vessel was sent up the Yazoo River. She was burned to prevent capture there on June 26, 1862.[529]

Though much was expected of this vessel, particularly because of her ability to carry a substantial battery – she was given four shell guns and two thirty-pounders – she proved to be very slow. A midshipman wrote that he suspected that the "wonderful contraption" was designed by a locomotive roundhouse architect, because of her "almost circular shape," and ability to carry three guns on each end. He further added a swipe at her slowness: "her crew facetiously complained that when she was going downstream at full speed they could not sleep on account of the drift logs catching up with her and bumping against the stern."[530]

Stern wheel riverboat under construction. The photo emphasizes the shallow draft of these vessels, and the need for the "hog chain" longitudinal support system. The diagonal hog "braces" on which the chains were mounted can clearly be seen: two forward of the midship section, angling forward, and two in the aft section, angling backward, plus another right aft, angling forward to help support the weight of engines and paddle wheel. University of Wisconsin at Lacrosse, Murphy Library Steamboat Collection

RIVERBOATS OF WAR
AND THE MISSISSIPPI RIVER DEFENSE FORCE

The Civil War on the Western rivers was for the most part not fought by ocean going naval vessels, but by river steamers converted for naval use or newly constructed vessels sharing the riverboats' key characteristics. Therefore, a description of the typical western river merchant steamboat is in order as well as look at how they were converted for naval use.

By the beginning of the war there were literally hundreds of steamboats on the rivers, with one authority putting the number at about 2,000, and what would become the "classic" riverboat design had evolved.[531] The rivers imposed their own criteria: to deal with great variations in the depth of the streams, light draft was necessary. Because the river steamer would not face the oceans' storms or waves, very little freeboard was needed. Generally, only structural considerations limited the length and breadth, and height, of these boats. Availability of fresh water and almost unlimited fuel – both wood and coal – allowed the use of uneconomical, non-condensing high-pressure engines.

The product of these factors was the classic riverboat, essentially a light draft hull with overhanging main deck and a cabin structure above, sometimes reaching three levels or stories. As much of the structure as was possible was of wood, and, to save weight, it was as lightly built as possible. Longitudinal strength was severely lacking if for no other reason than the typical

larger riverboat was around 250-feet in length with a hull depth of hold around six- to seven-feet. Though longitudinal bulkheads were provided in the hull, as well as a keel, these were insufficient in themselves to prevent hogging or sagging at the ends or amidships.

To maintain longitudinal stability, a truss system called "hog chains" came into use, consisting of metal rods running from fore deck to the stern and running over a series of braces mounted more or less vertically on the hull, with the whole resembling an open fan, the hog chains forming a semi-circle connecting the ends of the hull. The steamboat operator could adjust the length of each section of the chains, using turnbuckles to tighten or loosen them as needed to deal with differing cargo loads or river conditions. The practicality of this system can be easily seen in photographs of these vessels which had gone aground: the hull assumed the shape of the ground on which they laid, and all the hog chains simply hung slack. It was not unusual for a vessel in this condition to "straighten herself out" and return to service when the water rose again and the chains were re-tensioned. Of course, the severity of the bending would determine the enormity of the resulting hull leaks.

As for the engines of these boats, simplicity was the rule, in terms of structure, repair, and maintenance. The most common engine in riverboat service, generally referred to as the Western rivers

Western rivers steam engine, shown in stern wheel application. The top view shows the cylinder at left (C) and valve gear: the piston rod operates the "pitman" (L) (shown in dotted lines), which turns the crank (M) that operates the paddle wheel. The lower view shows the engine with piston (B). On top of the cylinder are the steam inlet and outlet poppet valves (F) that are activated by the horizontal bar-like valve levers that in turn are moved up and down by the rocking of the cam (K). A typical cylinder was from twenty-two-inches in diameter upwards. While the wooden steamboat hulls were comparatively frail, the engines were rugged and it was not unusual for the cylinders and apparatus to be re-used in successive riverboats over many years. "Lessons and Practical Notes on Steam," by W.W. King, Van Nostrand Co., 1864

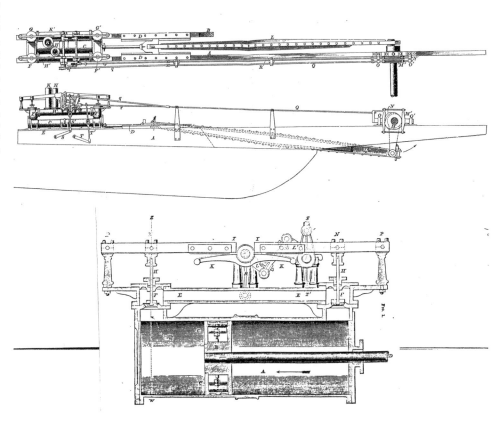

engine, and which was also widely used in towboats of the era, had been developed in the 1830s and, incredibly, would continue essentially unchanged past the turn of the twentieth century. This was a horizontal, non-condensing, high-pressure cylinder operating a long connecting rod (generally called a Pittman rod) that in turn turned the paddle wheel. Generally there were two cylinders, in one application operating twin side wheels, in the other, both ends of a stern-mounted paddle wheel.[532]

The valve arrangement, allowing steam into either end of the cylinder and permitting exhaust steam escape, was based on a rod that moved back-and-forth off a cam that worked off the paddle wheel shaft. The rod lifted and lowered levers on which were attached the engine's valves, opening and closing them with the movements of the levers. These were poppet valves, in design the same principle as those used in modern automobile engines: flat and circular with a valve stem pointing upward and connecting to the valve lever. Thus, the cylinder, cam rod, lifter, valve levers, and valves composed the essentials of this engine. And, in general, the cylinder diameter measured from twenty-two inches upward to forty-inches, and stroke from seven to ten feet. The whole of the single cylinder installation therefore composed an area about five feet square and ten feet long. Furthermore, only the parts listed here, plus the piston rod and guides for the connecting rod, were, of necessity, iron. The engine was secured to the hull on a wooden framework and the pitman rod itself was usually hickory, with iron strapping for strength.

As to the boilers, these were simple also and were generally cylindrical flue-type. Usually, around three to four feet in diameter and from thirty to forty feet long, each had three flues and two or three furnaces. Exhaust steam was trunked into two smokestacks. Because these boilers used water directly from the streams and rivers, a "mud drum" was necessary. This was a tank-shaped container below the boilers where mud from the water settled. Boiler accessories included some type of pressure gauge and a device for monitoring the water level in the boilers, plus a safety valve. By the Civil War era, there was usually a "doctor" or donkey engine installed. This was separate from the propulsion machinery and pumped feedwater to the boilers as well as operated other auxiliary equipment.

Of course the boilers were the most dangerous parts of these steam installations. A series of horrendous boiler explosions in the 1830s led to a federal government inspection program as well as requirements that the boats have the monitoring instruments noted above. However, quality control in the boiler construction industry was not particularly stringent and the danger inherent in 150psi pressures being restrained by riveted ¼-inch wrought iron plates was palpable. It will be remembered that the 1865 destruction of the riverboat *Sultana* with its massive fatality list was the result of a boiler explosion. It should also be noted that these engines and boilers were, in peacetime practice, mounted in the open air, on the main deck.

There were two main varieties of river steamers: side-wheel and stern-wheel vessels. Stern-wheel steamers were generally more oriented towards cargo carrying, in that, on a given hull width, their cargo capacity was larger; they were not hampered by the width of the side wheeler's paddle housings and resulting overhang. This was a particular advantage in narrow streams. Their major disadvantage was lack of maneuverability due to the stern-mounted wheel impeding rudder operations.

The side-wheel steamer, on the other hand, usually had independent engines: a skilled operator could reverse one wheel and run the other forward, turning the boat in its own length. Another unusual capability came with the side wheels: in extremely shallow water and given sufficient power, the vessel could literally "walk" across the shoal river bottom on its wheels – though not without some obvious damage to wheels and hull.

To answer another obvious question, the screw propeller was tried and discarded on the rivers early on. The rivers in these years were essentially wild and filled with hazards. (Probably the best source on the subject of river operations is *Life on the Mississippi*, Mark Twain's narrative written from the standpoint of his years as a skilled river pilot.) The most common fate for a river steamer was "snagging" – running into an unmarked tree stump or even a sunken riverboat. Thus, the screw propeller was a prime candidate for fowling and damage. Additionally, the paddle wheel worked equally well forward or in reverse, an advantage in narrow rivers where many stops were normal practice whether at river communities or at wood yards.[533]

Thus, it can be seen that the typical riverboat of this era was a peaceable, somewhat eccentric piece of folklore, but hardly a boat suitable for warfare. From a defensive standpoint, the whole of the hull and superstructure was wood. And the cabins were actually less substantial than most clapboard houses of the era. The engine and boilers were either entirely or partly in the open air and well-placed projectiles could easily derange the hog chain system ending the vessel's structural integrity.

Offensively, their wide decks invited the mounting of ordnance, and adding iron armor was a matter of simply plating the sides. However, there was a structural limit inherent in the boats that made overloading far too easy. A second positive factor was that their simple machinery made them relatively speedy and, with their tonnage and momentum, rendered them candidates for the latest fashion in naval warfare of the era: the ram.

One of the major varieties of river steamers was the towboat, which shared most of the river packet boat's characteristics: shallow draft, low freeboard, high-pressure engines and "open air" location of both engines and boilers. (It should be noted here that the Civil War era vessel type termed a "towboat" here would in modern terms be called a tugboat – that is, a harbor towing-vessel, in contradistinction to the long-haul, barge traffic, river vessel now known as a towboat). The towboat/tug however, was usually significantly shorter than the cargo-passenger packet or riverboat, with much less cabin superstructure. Less tonnage, but utilizing the same basic engine size, resulted in significantly higher power-to-weight ratio, a characteristic particularly appropriate for fitting them out as rams). As will be seen, the Confederacy used many of these in the Mississippi River Defense Force in 1862.

A large number of the riverboats, both side- and sternwheelers were converted to the famous "tinclads" in the Union river fleet. Thus, the otherwise innocuous boats were parts of Lincoln's "web feet," as well as those of Jeff Davis's navy.

The majority of the riverboats in Confederate naval service during the conflict were used in utilitarian roles: for cargo or personnel transportation, and a great number were chartered for military use. It appears that the closest the Confederate navy came to a riverboat converted to a full-fledged ironclad was the *Baltic* at Mobile, though that vessel had been a towboat. The general structure, however, was similar, with hog chains and shallow draft (see pages 30-31). Another riverboat-ironclad conversion was to be the *Eastport*, at Nashville, which was never completed for the Confederacy. When the Union navy finished and armored the vessel, her longitudinal weakness was evident when her hull bent "double" at one point and she had to be strengthened before going into commission.

General Polk

In August 1861, Lt. J.H. Carter was detailed to take command of the steam packet boat *Ed Howard* and fit her out as an armed warship. The vessel had been built at New Albany, Indiana, in 1852, and was 280-feet in length, a thirty-five-foot beam with an eight-foot draft. She was one of the larger river steamers, at 390-tons, and had been on the Nashville to New Orleans route. Her pre-war activities included accidentally ramming and sinking two other steamers, the *Henry Lewis* and *Swallow*.[534]

Riverboat J.A. Cotten (sometimes rendered J.A. Cotton), in civilian life. A typical passenger/cargo packet built in 1861 and converted to an iron-protected gunboat. The steamer was 229-feet in length with a seven-foot depth of hold. University of Wisconsin at Lacrosse, Murphy Library Steamboat Collection

Carter promptly went to work, removing all unnecessary superstructure, cabins and passenger accommodations, reducing her to a "mere shell." He wrote that he intended to cover her already-lethal bows "with bar iron." In fact, he ordered 77,305-pounds (thirty-five tons) of railroad iron for the vessel, and spent over $50,000 on alterations

in addition to the $8,000 original cost of the vessel to the navy.[535]

The vessel went into the water sometime before the end of September and drew less than four feet. The steamer was commissioned October 22, 1861 and was renamed *General Polk*, for Confederate General Leonidas Polk. She was armed with two thirty-two-pounder rifles and one thirty-two-pounder smoothbore.[536]

She was sent to New Madrid, Missouri, in December 1861 and participated in operations there as part of Flag Officer Hollins' command. After the fall of Island No.10 in 1862, the *General Polk* was evacuated up the Yazoo River where she and two other Confederate vessels were burned to prevent capture.[537]

J.A. Cotton

Another typical river steamer altered for war was the *J.A. Cotton*, (sometimes spelled Cotten) built at Jeffersonville, Indiana, in 1861 for the New Orleans and Bayou Sara Mail Line Company. She was constructed at the Howard shipyards, a long time and prolific producer of riverboats. Jeffersonville is on the Ohio River opposite Louisville, Kentucky. This vessel is not to be confused with the *Mary T.*, a later and smaller riverboat that was also known as *J.A. Cotton* or *Cotton, Jr.* The latter vessel was surrendered to Federal forces in June 1865.[538]

This vessel was 229- by thirty-six-feet with a seven-foot depth of hold, and measured 549-tons. No specifics are known about her machinery,

CAPTURE OF THE HARRIET LANE.

River packet Bayou City at left. This vessel was commandeered by Confederate authorities in Galveston and attacked and captured the U.S. steamer Harriet Lane (shown at right). Cotton bales provided protection for the Bayou City. Naval Historical Center

but a period illustration shows her with "Low Pressure" above her name on the paddle housings.[539] If this is true, she was one of the very few non-high-pressure steamers on the rivers. Her captain and part owner, E.W. Fuller, a long time riverboat skipper, determined to convert her into an iron-protected gunboat. Consulting with Confederate army advisors, Fuller first built a timber and plank casemate on her main deck. Cotton bales, probably compressed, formed a second layer on the outside of this structure, and this was in turn plated with railroad iron. This staunch barricade did not extend far enough aft to completely protect the engines and boilers. Three smoothbore guns were mounted in the casemate, one thirty-two-pounder and two twenty-fours. Another source indicates she had four rather than two twenty-fours, plus two six-pounder rifles.[540]

It is noteworthy that Fuller was a civilian while supervising this conversion, and in fact his crew was composed of Confederate army volunteers, in addition to a few naval personnel employed to train the gunners. Fuller was not nominated for a naval commission until January 1863, and the steamer itself was not a commissioned naval vessel.[541]

J.A. Cotton went into combat in November 1862 around Berwick Bay and Bayou Teche, Louisiana, and the opposing Union naval officers found her to be an effective combatant. One commented that her superior speed, in one instance, enabled her to escape, and also noted that she must have been "casemated" because Union artillery projectiles glanced off her sides.[542]

Secretary of State Judah P. Benjamin wrote Secretary of War Seddon in December, forwarding a report on Fuller and the *J.A. Cotton*. He praised Fuller who, with "an artillery company on board a small steamer, successfully repulsed four gunboats carrying twenty-seven guns, and thus secured control of that important stream [Bayou Teche]."[543]

After a renewed battle with several Union gunboats in January 1863, the *J.A. Cotton* was destroyed by her crew in order to prevent capture.

Bayou City

This side wheel steamer was built at the Howard shipyard at Jeffersonville, Indiana, in 1859. She was built for J.H. Starrett, for the Houston-Galveston mail route. In this era, the Buffalo Bayou channel, which leads from Galveston Bay into Houston, was less than six feet deep, therefore the *Bayou City* was built with a three-foot draft and five-foot depth of hold. Her length was 165-feet and breadth, twenty-eight-feet, without paddle wheel housings.[544]

Period illustrations of the vessel show her to have been a typical river sidewheeler, with lofty stacks and possibly two decks above the main and open fore deck. The number of decks is obscured by the cotton bales on her sides.

The steamer was chartered by the Confederate government at Galveston in September 1861, as part of the Texas Marine Brigade, and the steamer was armed with one thirty-two-pounder gun. Along with the steamer *Neptune,* the *Bayou City* attacked the Union flotilla at Galveston on the early morning of January 1, 1863. Both vessels prepared for the encounter by stacking cotton bales high on their sides. One observer said the cotton on *Bayou City* was twenty-five feet high from her waterline. In the battle, *Bayou City* first collided with the Union ex-Revenue Cutter *Harriet*

Lane, then the *Neptune* rammed her, unsuccessfully. A second ram, this time by *Bayou City*, struck the *Harriet Lane* on the port side, under her paddle wheel guard, and was effective enough to lock the vessels together. This allowed the Confederate army contingent – about 200 strong – on *Bayou City* to board and capture the Union steamer.[545]

After the Confederate re-capture of Galveston, the *Bayou City* remained on duty on the coast. Further information on the fate of the vessel has not been found.[546]

Dollie Webb

This vessel is one of the few stern-wheel riverboats in Confederate armed service. She was built at Wheeling, West Virginia, in 1859. She was relatively small, at 125- by twenty-seven-feet, with a 4.5-foot depth, and at 139-tons.

The steamer was enrolled at New Orleans in February 1860, but later pressed into Confederate service. In July 1862, a Union officer reported that she was on the Red River, along with another Confederate steamer. His informers indicated she had five pieces of artillery mounted on board, as well as a complement of 200 men.

There is disagreement about this vessel, with one source indicating she was burned in Louisiana in 1861, whereas the Union naval officer reports her on the Red River in 1862. She may have been confused with the *W.H. Webb*, the converted towboat associated with the ironclad *Arkansas* and covered in a previous chapter.[547]

Pontchartrain (Lizzie Simmons)

The river steamer *Lizzie Simmons* was built in 1859 at New Albany, Indiana, near the falls of the Ohio River. The sidewheeler was 204-feet long with a 36½-foot beam, a 6½-foot depth of hold, and measured 454-tons. Her original route was between New Orleans and the Ouachita River.[548]

In November 1861, she was purchased by the Confederate Navy, renamed *Pontchartrain*, and was one of several vessels being fitted out for the defense of New Orleans. The contractor, Francis Vallette, used yellow and white pine, cypress, poplar, and oak knees in re-configuring the vessel. Over 79,000 board feet of pine was utilized, plus about 800-feet each, of oak and cypress. The work was done from December 1861 to February 1862. The pine was probably for planking a casemate, in layers, and the oak and cypress for attaching the casemate to the existing structure. Protected by the casemate were two thirty-two-pounder rifles and, later, four to five additional guns.[549]

In March 1862, the steamer was commissioned and sent to join the fleet at Island No.10. One Union officer reported later (June 1862) that the steamer was armored with cotton and had iron around the engines.[550] The gunboat may well have had both, added on an ad hoc basis while in service.

The vessel participated in the actions around Island No.10 and New Madrid, Missouri, and in June, was at the Battle of St. Charles, Arkansas. At the latter location, two of her guns were transferred to the fort and her crew joined the army contingent defending the area.[551]

Afterwards, *Pontchartrain* was moved to Little Rock where she remained until October 1863. A Union report of July of that year, based on unknown sources, indicated that she was pierced for seven guns, though these were not on board, and that her engines were protected by iron, but did not mention cotton. The expectation was that she was to be "sheathed as a ram."[552]

The truth of these reports was never confirmed, however. The steamer was burned in October 1863 to prevent capture.[553]

Maurepas (Gross Tete)

Another merchant vessel purchased for the defense of New Orleans, *Gross Tete* (translated "big head") had been built at New Albany, Indiana, in 1858. Measuring 180- by thirty-four- by seven-feet, and at 399-tons, she was in merchant service prior to the war, possibly serving Bayou Gross Tete and the town of the same name. A rare photograph exists of the sidewheel steamer, showing a rather unusual cabin structure. Rather than the "standard" two-tier cabin arrangement with passenger accommodation on the second level, there is only a single-story cabin, running from stern forward past the wheel housings. A Texas cabin appears to be placed on this, forward of the wheels, with the pilothouse in the usual place atop the Texas structure. The result is a standard riverboat, minus the second deck.[554]

The vessel was listed as one of the small fleet intended to defend the city, but she was at one point mislabeled "Grotesque." She was re-configured for naval use and armed with six or seven guns.[555] Renamed *Maurepas*, she was sent to join Hollins' flotilla at Island No.10 and participated in the actions there and at New Madrid, Missouri. Her career ended on June 16, 1862, when she was sunk as an obstruction near St. Charles, Arkansas.[556]

Queen of the West

Probably the most famous vessel of the river fleets, Union and Confederate, this vessel is included because she was used by both sides. Also, the steamer is one of the few for which there exists contemporary illustrations of the vessel, both before conversion and after.

The sidewheeler was built in Cincinnati in 1854, and measured 181- by thirty-six- by six-feet depth, at 406-tons. She was a typically ornate riverboat carrying passengers and freight between Cincinnati and New Orleans before the war. The vessel was one of several purchased by Col. Charles Ellet, with a commission in the Union army, to form his ram fleet.[557]

The river steamer Gross Tete was later converted to gunboat Maurepas for the defense of New Orleans. It is shown here before the war, on the left of the photo. Note the atypical cabin structure with a single deck the length of the vessel. Aft were cabins, and the area forward of the wheels would have been open for cargo and machinery. The vessel was armed with six or seven guns in Confederate service. University of Wisconsin at Lacrosse, Murphy Library Steamboat Collection

to cover the sides, and the pilothouse was shielded against musketry. A single thirty-pounder was mounted on the *Queen of the West*.[558]

At the Battle of Memphis, in June 1862, Ellet's structure proved itself: *Queen of the West* immediately plowed into the Confederate ram *Colonel Lovell*, and nearly cut her in two. Later in the engagement, one of the steamer's paddle wheels was damaged and she was forced ashore to prevent her sinking. Later raised, the Union used her on the rivers until she was sunk by Confederate forces on the Red River in February 1863.

The steamer was again raised from the bottom by the Confederates. Later, the steamer, along with the ram *Webb*, forced the surrender of the Union ironclad *Indianola*. The Confederate career of the steamer ended when she was attacked by three Union vessels on the Atchafalaya River in April 1863. A round from the USS *Calhoun*, former Confederate privateer and blockade runner, set fire to the cotton cladding on the *Queen of the West* and resulted in her destruction.[559]

The Mississippi River Defense Force

On January 9, 1862, the Confederate Congress voted $1-million for "floating defenses" for the Western waters. The funding was to be applied via the Secretary of the Navy or the Secretary of

Designed to use the vessel's momentum and, when possible, the force of the current, to deal deadly blows into the enemy vessels' hulls, Ellet made use of heavy longitudinal bulkheads, each 12-15-inches thick, running the length of each boat. The center timber was directly on the keelson and the outer two were braced on the sides of the hull. All the timbers were cross-braced, as were the engines and boilers, to withstand the shock of collision. The machinery and boilers were protected by two feet of oak. Externally, all the cabins were removed, heavy timbers were secured

Queen of the West was a large, ornate Cincinnati to New Orleans passenger steamer before the war. Note the three decks, Texas cabin and pilothouse. University of Wisconsin at Lacrosse, Murphy Library Steamboat Collection

"ROUNDING A BEND" ON THE MISSISSIPPI.
The parting Salute

the Army, and was to fund a "corps" of no more than 6,000 men as well as steam vessels for "temporary and special service." Pursuant to this authorization, Secretary of the Army Judah P. Benjamin directed Major General M. Lovell at New Orleans to procure vessels for this service.

Secretary Benjamin wrote that the intended flotilla was to be a "peculiar" one, and not part of the navy. The vessels were to be commanded and manned by western river steamboat men, under command of the appropriate army department. Each captain was to fit out his vessel essentially as a ram: with "iron casing at the bows" for running down and sinking Union gunboats and mortar boats. The main offensive weapon was to be the ram, though one gun was to be mounted in the event any of the enemy gunboats showed its vulnerable stern aspect.[560] At this point in the war on the western rivers, the Union was converting river steamers into "timberclads" and were building the Eads-designed "turtles": the *Cairo* and others of her class. The latter were slow and unwieldy, and their iron plating was concentrated on their forward casemates, leaving their sterns, including the paddle wheels, relatively vulnerable.

Queen of the West as she appeared after conversion to a Union navy ram, and part of Charles Ellet's ram fleet. Substantial timbers ran the length of the vessel and formed the ram, and, after her cabins were removed, the machinery and pilothouse were protected with heavy timbers. The steamer rammed and sank a Confederate steamer at the Battle of Memphis. She was later captured and used by Confederate forces, assisting in capturing the Union steamer Indianola. Naval Historical Center

Mississippi River Defense Force steamer General Bragg. Originally, the coastal merchant steamer Mexico, this vessel was the largest of the defense force flotilla and rammed and sank the Union ironclad Cincinnati in May 1862. This photo was taken after her capture at the Battle of Memphis. Naval Historical Center

The ship was 1,206 gross tons (1058 20/95 registered tons) and measured 210- by thirty-two-feet, with a sixteen-foot depth of hold. She was of sufficient draft for oceangoing coastal work and was part of Charles Morgan's Southern Steam Ship Company. She was described in her 1851 enrollment as having one deck, a billet head, three masts, and a round tuck stern. Her machinery was a low-pressure walking beam engine, with a cylinder fifty-six-inches in diameter and having a ten-foot stroke. A single boiler provided steam and she was capable of ten-knots.[563]

The steamer was impressed into Confederate service on January 15, 1862, along with thirteen others at New Orleans. Eventually the government paid the owners for the vessels. It is assumed that the ship was given the timber and cotton cladding described above, around her engines and boilers, plus an inch of iron on her bows. Union reports indicate the vessel had three guns mounted on her decks.[564] However, her armor configuration would have been significantly different than that of the converted towboats, given her vertical cylinder and enclosed boiler spaces. Contemporary views of the vessel show that she was reduced to a two-mast, schooner rig, and she had another deck added and a substantial cabin structure.

The *General Bragg* proved a formidable adversary early on. She was described as "strongly built" and "superior" to any of the Ellet rams. At the action near Fort Pillow in May 1862, her commanding officer immediately ran her into the Union ironclad gunboat *Cincinnati*, punching a

The upshot of Benjamin's directive was to be the Mississippi River Defense Force, which met and was soundly defeated off Memphis in June 1862.[561] The steamers' bows were protected by one-foot-square timbers and a layer of four-inch oak planking plus the one-inch iron casing mentioned by Secretary Benjamin. Foot-square timbers, bolted every eighteen inches, also protected the engines and boilers. The latter was to be the inner layer, with an outer bulkhead composed of six-by-twelve timbers. The space between these was to be filled with compressed cotton.[562]

Eight steamers of the Defense Force participated in the action at Memphis. These were: *Colonel Lovell, General Beauregard, General Bragg, General Earl Van Dorn, General Jeff Thompson, General Sterling Price, General Sumter,* and *Little Rebel.* Of these, only one – *General Earl Van Dorn* – escaped, and four were taken into the Union navy: *General Bragg,*

General Sterling Price, General Sumter, and *Little Rebel.*

Presenting a detailed description of any of these vessels is fraught with difficulties. Very few plans of river vessels of the era exist, and few formal plans were necessary to facilitate their conversions. Contemporary illustrations depart from accuracy in favor of drama or sometimes depict all the vessels as identical to each other. Furthermore, period photos were almost exclusively taken after the vessel was captured by the Union.

General Bragg

While six, possibly seven of the steamers at the battle of Memphis were converted Mississippi river towboats, *General Bragg* was unique. The vessel was a coastal steamer, built by Westervelt and McKay at New York in 1850, and originally named *Mexico*.

Two views of the ram General Sterling Price after capture by Union forces. Confederates strengthened her bows, built cotton and wood "barricades" around her machinery, and armed her with four guns. The steamer's hog frames can be seen above the casemate structure aft of the funnels. Naval Historical Center

six- by twelve-foot hole in her starboard quarter and her momentum was such that she ran one of her paddle wheels up the side of the ironclad, threatening to capsize the huge vessel. The damage done by the *General Bragg*'s ram resulted in the first of two sinkings of that ironclad.[565] A severed tiller rope then put *General Bragg* out of the action, leaving her drifting down with the current.

In June 1862, at Memphis, she was much less effective: a large Union projectile burst her cotton cladding and she ran aground on a sand bar. Her crew escaped over the sides and she was captured by Union forces.

The vessel was active with Union naval forces on the river campaigns through June of 1864, when her walking beam was damaged in an action with Confederate army artillery. After repairs, she remained in riverine combat until

sold at the close of the war.[566]

General Sterling Price

Another of the Mississippi River Defense Force vessels captured at Memphis, and which then served in the Union fleet, *General Sterling Price* began as the side-wheel towboat *Laurent Millaudon*. This vessel was built at Cincinnati in 1856, and powered by two twenty-four-inch by eight-foot stroke cylinders and four boilers, and used at New Orleans by the Good Intent Towing Company. She was 182-feet long by thirty-feet by 9.2-feet, and measured 483-tons.[567]

The steamer was acquired for Confederate service and conversion began in January 1862. Four inches of oak was installed on her bows as well as an inch of iron. To protect her machinery and boilers, a double timber casemate or barricade was built, with compressed cotton between the two layers. According to a Union report, she was armed with four guns. The steamer's ram, combined with her speed, which was reported to be 12mph (10.6-knots), and size made her a formidable adversary, particularly to slower, less agile, or stationary enemy vessels.[568]

The ram joined Confederate forces at Memphis, and then was part of the contingent that took on Union ironclads near Fort Pillow, on May 10, 1862. The steamer added her ram to that of the *General Bragg* in disabling Union ironclad *Cincinnati*, which later sank. Immediately after, *General Sterling Price* silenced a Union mortar boat that had been harassing them with low angle fire, sending shrapnel and grape over her decks. When the Union vessels went into waters too shallow for their adversaries, the engagement ended. The ram sustained substantial damage to her upper works and steam supply pipes.

In the engagement off Memphis, in June 1862, *General Sterling Price* again charged one of the Union gunboats, with intent to ram. Unfortunately, she instead collided with the Confederate ram *General Beauregard*, rendering both vessels vulnerable to Union fire. The *Price* had one wheel disabled and was victim to yet another collision with the Union ram *Queen of the West*, leaving the Confederate vessel sinking on a sand bar.[569]

The *General Sterling Price* was raised, repaired, renamed *General Price* and put into Federal service. The steamer was given four nine-inch Dahlgren smoothbores and was active for the balance of the war, participating in the actions around Vicksburg, Steele's Bayou, and the Red River Expedition. The vessel was sold in October 1865.[570]

It should be noted that one photograph and an illustration by F. Muller of the *General Sterling Price* based on that image in volume 23 (after page 54) of the *Official Records* have been determined to be erroneous. Four wartime photographs of the vessel exist and these are obviously not the same as the vessel shown in these two images. The photo is NH53868 in the Naval Historical Center collection.[571]

Little Rebel

Easily the smallest Confederate vessel at the Battle of Memphis, the *Little Rebel* was also unique in being the sole screw-propelled Southern ram in the Defense Force. The vessel had been built in 1859

at Belle Vernon, Pennsylvania, on the Monongahela River, and was originally named *R.E. & A.N. Watson* or otherwise called *R. & J. Watson*, the latter being the coal company for which it was built.[572]

The only statistics known of the vessel are a tonnage of 151 and a draft of twelve-feet, deeply loaded. The engine was a single cylinder, eighteen-inches in diameter, and with a twenty-four-inch stroke. With two boilers driving a single screw, she reportedly made ten-knots. The size of the vessel can only be a matter of speculation, but at 151-tons, she was less than a third of the size of any other steamer in the squadron, and may have been around 100-feet in length.

The vessel was acquired by the Confederates in 1861, a date which is an anomaly in that it precedes all the other vessels procured for the Army as a result of Secretary Benjamin's directive that resulted in the river defense force. She underwent a conversion that included the requi-

site iron and timber on the bows as well as double wood barricades and compressed cotton between the side timbers. All sources indicate the steamer was armed with three twelve-pounder guns.[573]

The *Little Rebel* was made flagboat of the Confederate flotilla at Memphis and she can be seen in several period illustrations of the fight. She had a simple rectangular casemate-like structure with sides and ends angled slightly inwards, a small pilothouse, and a single funnel. One engraving shows her with five gunports on each side, plus another forward, and, presumably, yet another aft. Obviously, the number of guns shown does not correlate with the number she officially carried.

The steamer was present but was not able to add her ram to that of the other vessels involved at the fight near Fort Pillow in May 1862, but only supported with her guns. At the Battle of Memphis, the steamer attempted to ram the Union tinclad *Monarch*. The *Monarch* turned the tables on *Little Rebel* and chased her towards the shore. Under fire from the Union *Carondelet* and rammed by the *Monarch*, the under-armed boat was beached and fell into Union hands.

In Union service, the vessel retained the same name and, at first, the same armament, though later she was given two twenty-four-pounders in addition to a pair of twelve-pounders. She participated in the Red River Expedition and the capture of the ironclad *Missouri*,

View of the Battle of Memphis, June 1862. To the left is the Little Rebel, one of the smaller rams. The small screw steamer is shown with significantly more guns than the three twelve-pounders that were her official battery. General Beauregard is on right. www.clipart. com (public domain)

and then was sold after the end of the war. In peacetime she was enrolled as the steamer *Spy* until 1874.[574]

Colonel Lovell

Another New Orleans towboat, generally used to bring sailing vessels up from the Passes to the city, was originally named *Hercules*. The steamer was built in 1843 at Cincinnati, and belonged to the Ocean Towing Company until the Civil War.

The vessel was a sidewheeler measuring 162-feet by thirty-feet ten-inches, with an eleven-foot draft. She appears to have had a single funnel and prominent hog frames, as usually seen on coastal steamers. The vessel was acquired by the Confederate army (Maj. General Lovell) in 1862 and converted to a ram, to counter Union forces, including timberclads and Eads ironclads, descending the Mississippi. As with the other converted towboats, the ex-*Hercules* received timber strengthening the bows and covered with one inch of iron, plus timbers and cotton cladding around the engines and boilers. According to later Union reports, the steamer mounted four heavy guns.

Colonel Lovell participated in the actions around Fort Pillow in May 1862, and was then at the Battle of Memphis the next month. In the latter engagement, the Union ram *Queen of the West* rammed her with such force that she sank immediately.[575]

General Beauregard

This former towboat was dimensionally nearly identical to *Colonel Lovell*, at 161-feet eight-inches, by thirty- by ten-feet, and 454-tons. The vessel had been the towboat *Ocean* when built at Algiers, Louisiana, in 1847, and operated by the Ocean Towboat Company and the Union Towboat Company before the Civil War.[576]

The sidewheel steamer was converted into a ram in early-1862, with iron-plated bows and timber and-compressed cotton built up around her machinery. The steamer is shown front and center in a period illustration of the battle at Memphis, and shows her with an angled, armored, forward bulkhead, but apparently vertical side bulkheads, forward of the wheel housings, obviously protecting the boilers. No gun ports are seen in these bulkheads, only one gun on the fore deck and a second directly aft. She was supposedly armed with four eight-inch guns and one forty-two-pounder (the latter probably an army piece). The steamer was commissioned April 5, 1862.[577]

General Beauregard participated at the battle of Plum Point Bend, near Fort Pillow, in May 1862, adding gunfire support to the engagement, while under heavy fire from the Union vessels. In June, at the Battle of Memphis, both the *General Beauregard* and the *General Price* attempted to ram the Union gunboat *Monarch*, coming at the vessel from both sides. The *Monarch* slid from between them and *Beauregard* instead severed one wheelhouse and side wheel from the *General Price*. She then was under fire from the USS *Benton*. The latter sent a shell that exploded one of the *Beauregard*'s boilers, killing many of her crewmen and leaving her sinking. The commander of the *Monarch* sent a line to her and attempted unsuccessfully to tow the stricken vessel to shore. After she settled to the bottom, the Union steamer sent boats to rescue the surviving crew – some of whom were clinging to the vessel's two funnels, still protruding from the river waters.[578]

General Sumter

There is disagreement among the sources on the origin of this sidewheel steamer. Some sources indicate the *General Sumter* was the towboat *Junius Beebe* before her conversion to a ram, others say the latter vessel became the *General Earl Van Dorn*. Dimensionally, they were very nearly alike: *General Sumter* was 182-feet by twenty-eight-feet four-inches, with a ten-foot eight-inch depth, at 525-tons. The other vessel was the same length, but differed by only an inch in the other two major dimensions. The *Beebe* had been built at Algiers, Louisiana, in 1853.

One distinguishing characteristic of the *General Sumter* was her low-pressure machinery – highly unusual for a river steamer. No information about the *Junius Beebe*'s machinery has been found. However, the vessel had been inspected by Confederate authorities in June 1861, in search of suitable vessels for the service. Three Confederate naval officers deemed her "unfit" for conversion to a gunboat.[579]

This evaluation was later ignored and the steamer was converted at the James Martin yard at Algiers and gained iron shielded bows as well as timber and cotton cladding around her machinery. Given a single, thirty-two-pounder on her fore deck, she was dispatched north in April 1862.[580]

At the Plum Point, Fort Pillow engagement in May 1862, a Confederate steamer, assumed to be the *General Sumter,* came within sixty feet of "Mortar Boat 16" and fired two projectiles and a volley of musketry into that vessel. None were wounded on the Union boat.[581]

At the Battle of Memphis *General Sumter* rammed the Union steamer *Queen of the West*, but was seriously damaged by Union gunfire. Her commanding officer ran her ashore and she was later re-floated and used by the Union forces. Her career in the Union navy ended in August 1862 when the steamer went hard aground near Bayou Sara, Louisiana. The stranded hulk was raided for spare machinery parts and was later burned by the Confederates.[582]

General Earl Van Dorn

As noted above, the *General Earl Van Dorn* may have been the side wheel steamer *Junius Beebe* before being taken into Confederate service in early-1862. The vessel was 182-feet, by twenty-eight

Battle of Memphis, showing the ramming of General Beauregard in the foreground. Little Rebel is the small steamer seen to left of General Beauregard. At far left is General M. Jeff Thompson, sinking, and General Sterling Price is in the mid-background. General Bragg is aground directly behind stern of Beauregard, and Colonel Lovell is shown sinking to the right of General Bragg. Only one Confederate steamer survived the fight. Unexplained is the single funnel shown on General Sterling Price. Naval Historical Center

feet three-inches, by ten-feet seven-inches.[583] The steamer was given the standard re-configuration including iron and timbers at the bows and wood and compressed cotton around the engines and boilers.

Armed with a single thirty-two-pounder on the bow, the steamer was engaged with Union forces off Plum Point near Fort Pillow. The attack on the Union mortar boat mentioned above may have been the work of this vessel rather than the *General Sumter*. During the action, the *Van Dorn* rammed the Union Eads gunboat *Mound City*, leaving that vessel with her bow "pretty much wrenched off," according to one Union officer. The *Mound City*'s commanding officer was obliged to run her onto the bank to prevent her sinking. However, the Union vessel was pumped out, afloat within twenty-four hours, and sent north for repairs.[584]

The Confederate steamer was engaged at Memphis the next month, and was the only Confederate ram to escape, being pursued by two Union steamers. Three weeks later, the Union rams arrived at Yazoo City, where they found the Confederates burning the *General Van Dorn* as well as the *General Polk* and *Livingston* to prevent their capture.[585]

General M. Jeff Thompson

The origins of the *General M. Jeff Thompson* are not recorded, nor are her measurements or tonnage. The sidewheel vessel was selected for the Mississippi River Defense Force in January 1862, after which she was converted and given iron and timbers on her bows as well as well as a timber and compressed cotton bulkhead around her machinery. A Union source indicated the vessel was armed with four guns.[586] The ram participated in the battle at Plum Point, near Fort Pillow, in May 1862. Though unable to bring her ram into the action, the steamer supported the Confederate flotilla with her guns. At the Battle of Memphis, the ram was severely mauled by Union fire from the ironclads and ran aground. After being abandoned by her crew, fires reached her magazine and the steamer blew up.[587]

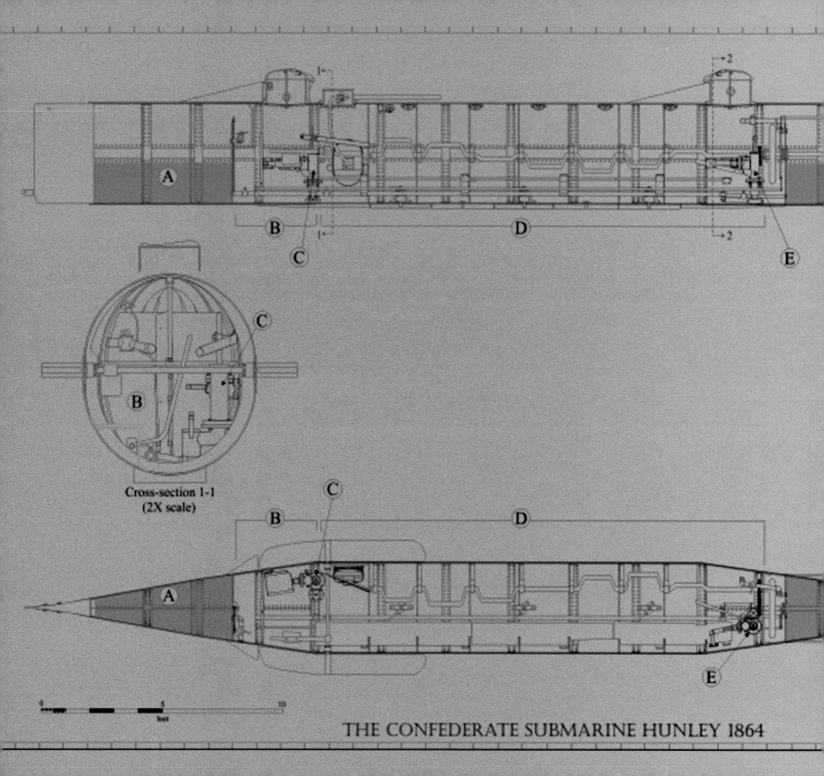

A

B

C

D

E

1

1

2

2

C

Cross-section 1-1
(2X scale)

B

C

D

A

E

0   5   10

feet

THE CONFEDERATE SUBMARINE HUNLEY 1864

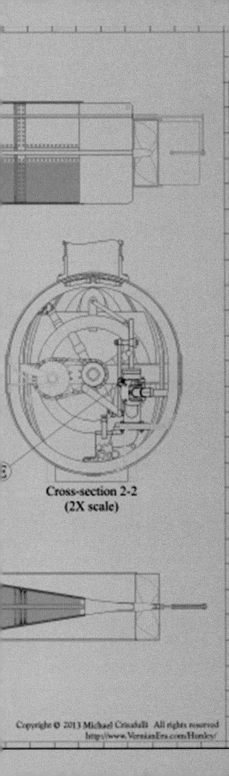

**Cross-section 2-2
(2X scale)**

TORPEDO CRAFT AND SUBMARINES

The American Civil War was marked by the extensive use of the "torpedo," that is the underwater or floating mine. Though the floating mine had seen some use in the Crimea, the South systematically set out hundreds of these devices in their vulnerable harbors and rivers to impede enemy activities. Their efforts were not without fruit. One authority calculated that forty-three Union vessels were damaged or sunk by Confederate torpedoes. Two of the most notable were the sinking of the Eads ironclad gunboat *Cairo* in December 1862 – the first warship to be sunk by a mine – and that of the monitor *Tecumseh* at the Battle of Mobile Bay.

The mine as an offensive weapon is the subject that is applicable in this naval history. The Confederacy was enamored of the explosive-on-a-stick concept of the spar torpedo, a weapon with obvious dangers both to the attacker as well as the attacked. Ironically, the most significant use of this delivery system was the sinking of the Confederate ironclad *Albemarle* in 1864 by a Union picket boat armed with a spar torpedo. The Confederate Navy, however, put much effort into this weapon, for the most part by developing various types of vessels on which it was to be mounted and delivered. Though many of the service's ironclads were equipped with spar torpedoes, the explosive device was not their primary weapon. Vessels whose sole offensive weapon was the torpedo ranged from open vessels, rowboats or steam launches, to low-profile "torpedo boats," to submersible craft or submarines capable of limited underwater operation. The latter two categories will be covered here.

Francis D. Lee's "Torpedo Ram"

In October 1862, Captain Francis D. Lee, of the engineering corps of the Confederate army, presented a plan for a "torpedo ram" to General P.G.T. Beauregard, commanding army forces at Charleston, and tasked with defending that port and breaking the Union blockade. Since the floating torpedoes could hardly affect the Union blockaders unless they entered the mined areas, Lee determined to take the torpedo to the prey. His vehicle for the purpose was, necessarily, based on stealth – if one was to literally ram an explosive device into an enemy hull, the approach was the critical factor. Lee's vessel was designed to operate with most of its hull under water, leaving only the pilot's cockpit, stack and armored upper part of the hull exposed. Powered by a steam engine and screw propeller, the vessel was equipped with a long, wooden spar projecting from the bow, on which was an explosive charge intended to be rammed against the enemy vessel's hull. The spar was elevated and lowered by a windlass, devised to place the charge well below the adversary's waterline.

A very large "David" photographed at Charleston, most likely the vessel built by Francis D. Lee, that measured 160-feet in length, and which made one unsuccessful attack on Union ironclad New Ironsides. National Archives

The distinguishing characteristic of the vessel Lee designed was its circular cross section and tapering, conical ends. This cigar shape was to be repeated in the smaller "Davids" built at Charleston later in the war. Lee may have had a double-ended version of the *Manassas* as his inspiration, or possibly the incredibly modern appearing "cigar ship," a spindle-shaped steamer built by Ross Winans in Baltimore in 1858, that was 180-feet long and still under testing at this time.

After Lee gained General Beauregard's approval – the general wrote that it would be "worth several gunboats" – the state of South Carolina funded the project with $50,000. Lee gained little assistance from the navy, but eventually support from army sources. It is generally believed that the basic hull was originally to have been the wooden Maury gunboat *Torch*, begun at the F.M. Jones yard in Charleston, and an engine was provided from the tug *Barton*.

After the fall of Charleston, a Union officer surveyed the "Davids" at various wharfs around the Cooper and Ashley Rivers and reported on six such vessels, five of which were about fifty feet in length, but one was 160-feet long and eleven-feet seven-inches in breadth. It was described as generally in good condition with a complete boiler and most of the engine in place.[588] A photo which is probably this vessel shows a nearly circular hull cross-section and longitudinal, shelf-like protrusions resembling bilge keels running for about eighty feet of her length and ending about where the hull begins to taper to a point.

Lee's efforts to construct the vessel were hampered by some inter-service wrangling, as well as significant shortages of materials. He had requisitioned oakum, spikes, 10,500-pounds of ¾-inch iron plates, sixty-tons of cast iron bars, and ten-tons of 1½-inch bars. The commanding naval officer at Charleston responded negatively, indicating that their supplies had already been depleted in the process of building ironclads. Lee was forced to resort to scouring the local neighborhood and in this way obtained about twenty-five-tons of iron in the form of railings, axles, skillets, etc.

Late in the year, yet another obstacle arose: the workers struck for higher pay. Once that was settled, the navy again became obstreperous, having taken over the ironworks at Charleston and imposing time-consuming bureaucratic stipulations on all orders and work to be done. Then, in the spring of 1863, work came to a complete halt due to lack of iron plates.

The process finally was completed in July 1863, with the mounting of a spar on the vessel's bows. The spar was tipped with three fork-like "tines," each of which was supplied with a torpedo. This duplication was to ensure that the failure of any one or two of the three would not abort the mission.

After a shakedown cruise on August 1, 1863, the vessel set out on her first mission on August 20. Casting off after dark, the vessel was burning anthracite coal to keep smoke and sparks at a minimum. At Fort Sumter, a squad of soldiers was taken on, then the vessel made for the USS *New Ironsides*, the most powerful Union ironclad in existence. The attack was bungled, however, with the steersman misconstruing a key helm order and the engine malfunctioning at a critical juncture. By the time the engine was re-started, the tide had swept the torpedo-ram away from the target and the Yankees were on alert and firing at the intruder, ending the mission.

The vessel's commanding officer was not pleased with the outcome and expressed his condemnation of the "vessel and engine," recommending that a "transport be made of her." Long afterwards, a contemporary wrote that the vessel had a "second-hand and much worn engine" and she could only be kept afloat "by bailing." Thus the product of much work and effort was docked and never saw service again.[589]

David

The beginning of 1863 saw the buildup of Union naval forces Charleston, which foreshadowed a

The project was under the direction of David C. Ebaugh, who superintended Ravenel's plantation nitre works. Ebaugh later wrote: "I laid out the boat full size under a niter shed ... It was 5 feet in diameter and 48½ feet long, 18 feet of the middle of the boat was the same size tapering to a point at each end. The ends were made of large pine logs turned off with a groove to receive the ends of the planking."[590]

Richard Maury later described the vessel: "The boiler was forward, the miniature engine, aft, and between them a cubby hole for captain and crew ... A two bladed propeller drove the craft at a six or seven knot rate ... nothing was visible save the ... smokestack, the hatch combing, and the stanchion upon which the torpedo line was brought aft."[591]

As to the engine itself, in January 1864, a Confederate deserter reported that the boat was powered by two cylinders, each five-inches with a stroke of eight-inches. This would make her cylinders smaller than a typical locomotive of the era. A contemporary, longitudinal, inboard plan shows a horizontal cylinder with a connecting rod operating a vertical gear. The beveled gear teeth turned a second gear that rotated the propeller shaft.[592]

The vessel made several trial trips around the harbor, then, in October 1863, set out to attack the *New Ironsides*. Other than the sixty-five-pounds of black powder being pushed along some fourteen feet ahead of the little steamer, the only other offensive weapons on board were four shotguns, with buckshot, and .36 caliber Navy pistols. At around 9:00pm, the quarry was within sight and the vessel's commander, William T. Glassell, ordered full speed. He rammed the charge into

major attack on the port city, which materialized in April of that year. Observers noted in particular the arrival of newly built Ericsson monitors as well as the hulking broadside, ironclad *New Ironsides* – the most heavily armed and armored vessel in the Union fleet. The public clamor was such that Lee's torpedo ram grew in popular importance and, indeed, attracted imitators – men whose impatience with the seemingly leisurely

construction pace of that vessel impelled them to take matters into their own hands. Dr. St. Julien Ravenel, a prominent Charlestonian, undertook to build a smaller version of the Lee torpedo-ram at his Cooper River plantation. The vessel was designed in consultation with both Lee and Matthew Fontaine Maury, the latter a major figure in Confederate torpedo warfare early in the war.

Plan sketch of Confederate "David." Note the small geared one-cylinder steam engine aft. Length was fifty-four feet, plus a spar about fourteen feet long for the explosive charge. Official Records

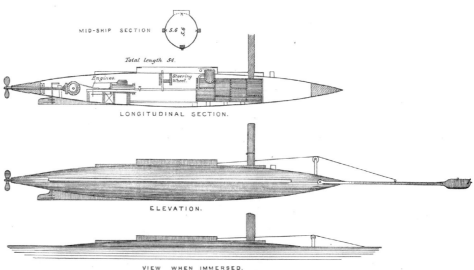

MID-SHIP SECTION

Total length 54.

Engines.   Steering Wheel.

LONGITUDINAL SECTION.

ELEVATION.

VIEW WHEN IMMERSED.

No. 13.—Sketch showing torpedo boats as constructed at Charleston, S. C.   Scale 10 feet to an inch.

the hull of the ironclad, about six feet beneath the waterline. The detonation severely shook the torpedo craft and stopped her engines, but she remained afloat. The *New Ironsides* was damaged but not seriously. Two men were wounded and a third – the deck officer who had been shot while hailing the intruder – died. The ironclad remained on station inside the bar off Charleston and steamed north for repairs, until June 1864.[593] The ironclad was back on duty and part of the attack on Fort Fisher, in December 1864.

In March 1864, the *David* made a second attack on a Charleston blockader: the steamer *Memphis*. In this instance, the charge was rammed into the stern quarter of the Union vessel, but failed to explode. F.D. Lee later wrote that he had informed the officers of the *David* that the torpedo in question had been in service overlong and was liable to misfire. He also offered to prepare a new explosive charge to replace it. His advice was ignored.[594]

Another "David" of note was the *St. Patrick*, of the usual fifty-foot length, equipped with water ballast pumps to raise and lower the steamer in the water. She was built near Mobile by John P. Halligan. The explosive was a copper-jacketed charge at the end of a twelve-foot spar. In January 1865, the vessel steamed out to attack the U.S. gunboat *Octorara*. At 2:00am, she was approaching the intended victim's stern and a bluejacket lookout

"David" at Charleston after the war. Note the torpedo spar extending from bow and damaged propeller at stern. Over a dozen "Davids" were built or under construction by the end of the war. Naval Historical Center

The Pioneer, predecessor to the H.L. Hunley. The hand-cranked vessel had a circular cross section and ballast tanks for submersion. It was never used against an enemy vessel and was scuttled at the approach of Union forces towards New Orleans. National Archives

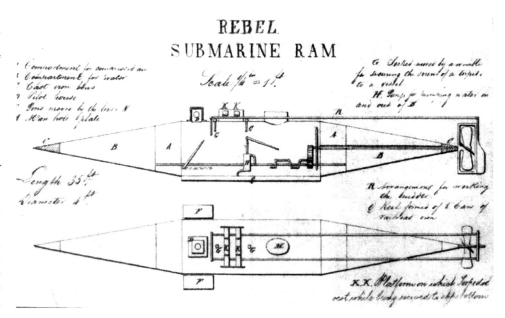

hailed, thinking the craft was the ship's cutter. The truth dawned only as the boat scraped against the *Octorara*'s hull. With amazing presence of mind, the captain of the guard simply reached out and grabbed the intruder's smokestack and shouted for a rope to tie her down. This audacity was short lived, as the Confederate crew opened fire and he was forced to release his arm lock on the funnel. The *St. Patrick* wrenched away and escaped relatively unharmed. The torpedo apparently was a dud.[595] This could well have been the only instance in history where one man nearly captured an enemy warship.

At least four more "Davids," of about the same dimensions as the original were subsequently built for Charleston waters, plus one other about 100-feet in length. Eight others were built or were a-building by the end of the war: five in Savannah, two in Wilmington, and another in Houston.[596] None achieved the results of the first of the type.

The "Davids" were in sharp contrast to the more conventional torpedo boats that were built elsewhere in the South. These were open-deck launches ranging from 30- to 50-feet with drafts from three- to less than five-feet. *Squib, Hornet, Wasp,* and *Scorpion* served on the James River, with the first of these attacking and damaging a Union steam frigate off Newport News, Virginia. In 1864, the navy ordered a dozen fifty-foot boats built, all of which were to have foreign-built machinery, which was to be brought in through the blockade. Towards the end of the conflict, the department ordered another dozen boats built in their entirety overseas. Only one, the *General Whiting,* is known to have actually arrived on Southern shores.[597]

H.L. Hunley and Predecessors

On August 8, 2000, the most famous Civil War underwater warship was brought to the surface, after nearly 136 years resting unfound in the waters near Charleston, South Carolina. The *H.L. Hunley,* a hand-cranked, iron-hulled craft with an eight-man crew had been the first submarine (or submersible) to sink a warship, the blockader USS *Housatonic,* on August 17, 1864.

The origins of this unique vessel can be traced to New Orleans in 1861. J.R. McClintock and Baxter Watson, later joined by Horace L. Hunley, began the project with the intention to make the vessel a privateer. They applied for a letter of marque on April 1, 1862, calling the vessel a "submarine boat," measuring thirty-four-feet in length and four-feet broad, and four-tons. The vessel, named *Pioneer,* had "round conical ends" and was painted black.[598]

Much of what is known about the *Pioneer* comes from drawings made after the vessel's recovery in 1863, by Union forces. The structure itself was composed of boiler iron plates riveted to an iron framework. Cast iron "points" formed the bow and stern, with a propeller shaft aperture in the latter, and two water tanks were formed by the tapered ends. Diving and surfacing "fins" were mounted on each side and a rudder overhung the propeller and was operated by rods running from amidships. Atop the cylindrical center section was a small pilothouse, an entry port for the two- or three-man crew, and a "cradle" for the torpedo. Beneath this cradle was a mechanism to secure the torpedo to a vessel. (The concept of attaching the explosive to the enemy vessel's hull had been used by David Bushnell in his Revolutionary War era "Turtle.") A detachable ballast "keel" was mounted along the bottom and was formed by five bars of railroad iron. Propulsion was provided by a crank operated by the crew rotating the propeller, and water allowed in the tanks to bring the vessel down could be pumped out to bring the vessel to the surface. Though one of the plans shows tanks for compressed air, other documentation indicates that the crew was limited to ambient air only.[599]

The vessel was tested on Lake Pontchartrain and proved to be – at least according to post-war claims – "seaworthy." However, there were difficulties in maintaining an even keel and in determining her direction while underwater. It is worth noting that the tests were not carried out in the strenuous currents of the Mississippi river or in the open Gulf.[600]

The *Pioneer* was never tested against an enemy vessel, though it was said that the boat blew up a barge in one of her trial runs. On the approach of Farragut's Union fleet, the builders scuttled the little vessel in the New Basin Canal in April 1862. It was recovered by Union forces in 1863, and auctioned for scrap in 1868.[601]

McClintock and his fellow entrepreneurs moved to Mobile following the loss of the *Pioneer* and proceeded to build a new version of the original. Very little contemporary information is available on this vessel, sometimes called *Pioneer II* or *American Diver*. Much of the information comes from McClintock's recollections in the early-1870s, as well as from his diagram drawn at the same time. Admiral Franklin Buchanan was the navy's commanding officer at Mobile during this time and his papers provide some – however scant – information on the vessel.

McClintock wrote that the new vessel dispensed with the circular hull cross-section and made it elliptical, and lengthened the hull by a foot. The result was sufficient room for a five-man crew. He also attempted to introduce an engine to replace the manpower propulsion. Admiral Buchanan mentioned a "man from New Orleans" with the "Magnetic Engine," as well as a steam engine that was "a failure," in connection with McClintock's "submarine boat."[602] Of course, the idea of utilizing electric power in a submarine predated its actual introduction by many decades, and in this era the technology was simply too primitive for the purpose.

In the end, McClintock reverted to the crank system. As to the torpedo delivery arrangement, the explosive was to be towed on a line behind the boat. The vessel then dived beneath the target and dragged the torpedo under the enemy ship's hull, where it was to be exploded remotely.

Testing the new vessel was begun late in 1862. During trials in Mobile Bay, the crew was unable to make the boat exceed two-knots, and, of course the air too quickly turned foul, and the telltale candle would too soon flicker signaling the time was right to surface. Then, in early-February, the vessel set out to attack the nearest blockader and encountered choppy waters. Hatches left open for ventilation were wide avenues for bay water and, despite frantic bailing, the boat sank, with the crew making a narrow escape. Buchanan wrote Secretary Mallory that he had, "considered the whole affair as impractical from the Commencement."[603]

Almost immediately, McClintock, Hunley and Watson again began a replacement boat. With an additional $15,000 of investors' money on hand, the new vessel was begun, utilizing forty-two wrought iron plates to form the basic elliptical, cross-section hull. To gain interior height, an eight-inch iron strake formed the horizontal longitudinal center, running the length of the boat. Externally, all the plates were butt fitted, rather than overlapped, using butt straps to which each plate was riveted. Cast iron caps formed the ends of the structure and the total length of the new vessel was forty-feet, with a width of 3½-feet and height of four-feet. It was designed for a crew of eight: one captain and seven to crank the propeller.

On the top of the hull were two crew hatchways, each beneath a tower with a hinged top, which had a rubber gasket to prevent leakage. From fore end to aft, there was the cast iron cap, a seven-foot-long, water-ballast tank, the shelf-like captain's station, with dive plane and steering lever, a pump for expulsion of water from the tanks, then the main chamber with the zig-zag propeller crank and the seven man crew bench, running about

fifteen feet on the port side. Aft of this was another pump for ballast, an aft ballast tank, the cast iron cap, the propeller and, overhanging that, the rudder. The structure had view ports and deadlights for light, and a twenty-foot long, iron ballast-keel. The latter was in seven sections, three of which could be jettisoned if necessary.

The interior of the vessel was nightmarishly cramped. The narrowness of the crew chamber prevented any movement by the men, other than to operate the crank, or, in the case of the most forward and most aft sailors, to man the ballast pumps. The seven crankers were permanently hunched over the crank – a position that actually helped maintain the center of gravity of the vessel.

Bulkheads divided the central chamber from the ballast tanks. These were riveted to the walls of the vessel, but were not watertight, and in fact ended some eight inches from the top of the hull. This gap was purposely left to allow air to escape from the tanks as they filled with water for each dive. McClintock also devised an additional air source for the crew. This consisted of a bellows and pipes just aft of the forward conning tower.[604]

Within the hull was a barometer and a compass, as well as a set of gears, which multiplied the crankers' revolutions to the propeller. Externally, there were two diving planes and a shroud to prevent any floating debris from fouling the propeller.[605] Originally the vessel, at this stage referred to as the 'Fish Boat,' was to employ the towed method of torpedo delivery.

Trials of the vessel began in the spring of 1863, and the crew gradually became accustomed to this strange little vessel. The climax came in July, when a public demonstration was given, with dignitaries in attendance. The vessel first descended to a level where only the towers were above water, then the captain took bearings on the target – an old coal flat. The vessel submerged completely, dived beneath the target, blew it up and resurfaced four hundred yards beyond the wreckage. Even Admiral Buchanan was impressed.

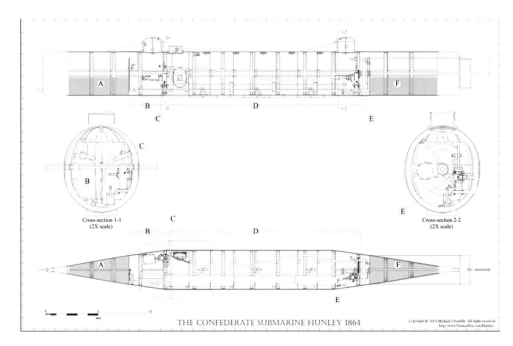

THE CONFEDERATE SUBMARINE HUNLEY 1864

Cross-section 1-1
(2X scale)

Cross-section 2-2
(2X scale)

Submarine H.L. Hunley, modern plan by Michael Crisafulli based on the vessel now preserved near Charleston. From fore to aft: (A) forward ballast tank, (B) Pilot's station, (C) Ballast pump for forward tank, (D) Crew compartment with crank, (E) aft ballast pump, (F) aft ballast tank. The vessel was originally designed to attack under water: diving beneath the target towing an explosive charge against the enemy's hull, then resurfacing beyond the target vessel. The technique had been successfully demonstrated in Mobile. The famous sinking of the Union sloop of war Housatonic, however, was effected instead by a spar torpedo rammed into the steamer's hull, while the H.L. Hunley remained only semi-submerged. Michael Crisafulli (copyright)

Shortly after this demonstration, Admiral Buchanan made arrangements to transfer the entire submarine operation to Charleston. The ostensible reason for this was that the relatively shallow waters of Mobile Bay were not appropriate for the deep-diving operations of the craft. At Charleston, the vessel gained the name *H.L. Hunley*, and also gained a deadly reputation. Two training accidents claimed the lives of Hunley himself and most of two crews.

Another freak accident at Charleston further marred these months of intense training in 1863-64. At one point, the towed torpedo became tangled in the *David*'s propeller (the little steamer was being used to tow the *Hunley*), and an explosion was barely averted. This incident as well as an earlier event, in which the towed torpedo was caught in a following sea and had to be cut loose to prevent it from hitting the sub, made the authorities

re-think the concept of the towed explosive. These two incidents convinced General Beauregard to order the vessel equipped with a spar torpedo, and to discontinue use of the tethered torpedo.[606]

The spar torpedo was on a seventeen-foot, iron spar, which was mounted on a yoke attached to the bottom of the vessel's bow – therefore about four feet below the water if the craft was running with only the towers above the surface. At the end of the spar the torpedo was mounted, just behind a barbed blade. The blade was to be rammed into the enemy's hull, and hold the explosive in place for detonation. A lanyard operated from the vessel pulled the trigger, setting off the explosion.[607]

Though the *Hunley*'s crew continued to practice complete submersion and diving, it was now obvious that the craft would operate in the same manner as the "Davids" and other torpedo boats: simply ram the charge into the enemy's

hull and hope to back away before the explosion damaged the torpedo vessel. Submersion was counterproductive and in fact would put the explosive farther from the target.

In this configuration, the *H.L. Hunley* made her last voyage. On February 17, 1864, the eight men set out to destroy a blockader, in this instance, the U.S. steam sloop *Housatonic*, a 207-foot cruiser, armed with at least nine guns. The latter were useless, however, when the *Hunley* rammed the ninety-pound black powder charge into her wooden hull. The explosion demolished the steamer's port quarter, killing five sailors and sinking the ship in less than five minutes.

This was the first time a submarine vessel had sunk a warship. However, it should be noted that the *Hunley* was not submerged during the event, and was being operated as a torpedo boat at the time.

The fate of the *Hunley* was for many years simply unknown: she never returned from this historic mission. One possibility was that the explosion had also destroyed the submarine. The mystery was not solved until an expedition under author Clive Cussler located her on the bottom, not far from the spot where her victim went down. The doughty little craft, with her crew still in place, was raised and is now under conservation at Charleston.

Confederate floating battery, ex-ironclad, Georgia. Though equipped with screw propulsion, the vessel's poor performance and constant leakage relegated her to a Savannah wharf for most of the war. She was called the "Mud Tub" and "not a fit command for a sergeant of marines." Naval Historical Center

THE CONFEDERATE IRONCLAD RAM "GEORGIA."

FLOATING BATTERIES

The Confederacy resorted to building numerous floating batteries throughout the war. These ranged from elaborate to improvised and in some instances were simply default utilizations for otherwise unsuccessful, engine-powered, war vessels. One of the latter is included here, as well as the formidable Charleston harbor battery associated with the outbreak of the war. A listing of other batteries follows.

Georgia

What became the floating battery *Georgia* was unusual and somewhat controversial from its inception. The project originated as the result of a "ladies' gunboat society" initiative in Savannah, in mid-1861. From the outset, there was a difference of opinion within the society: some wanted an ironclad steamer; others simply wanted a floating battery to defend the city. The actual construction was begun at Harding's shipyard and the initial work was by a unit of the Georgia militia under General Henry Rootes Jackson. The simplicity of the work was apparent in that the construction went forward "without plans" and that, when the society's steering committee suggested a keel, they were turned down.

The vessel was launched on May 19, 1862, and measured, by one estimate, 250- by sixty-feet. The casemate was heavily timbered with three layers of pine and oak, and was then covered by two layers of railroad t-rail. Unlike most of the other Confederate ironclads, there were no open decks either fore or aft of the casemate. Though pierced for ten guns, only six were initially on board. The vessel also had no wardroom or berth deck.[608]

At the time of her launch, there was no steam engine on board. But an unknown type of steam engine, two propellers and a locomotive type boiler eventually powered the battery. When the vessel attempted to move under her own steam, the controversy about her identity re-asserted itself. The *Georgia* could "not stem the current." The ladies' committee complained that she was "supposed to be a floating battery" and the builders dissembled a bit, calling it a "floating battery with propellers."

In July she was towed to Fort Jackson on the Savannah River and again was deemed "unsatisfactory" – she leaked so badly that the pumps barely stemmed the rising water. More leaks appeared in the casemate when it rained. She gained the local pejorative, "The Mud Tub."[609]

It was not difficult to determine the opinions of the men who served on the "battery." One officer called her an "iron box (for she is not a vessel)," and deemed her, "not a fit command for a sergeant of marines."[610]

The vessel was relegated to a pier and became the source of guns for other vessels more likely to be in combat. Her career ended on December 21, 1864, when she was burned and scuttled by her crew as Sherman's forces approached Savannah.[611]

The remains of the *Georgia* were discovered in 1969 near Old Fort Jackson where she had been scuttled in 1864. In the years since, the U.S. Army Corps of Engineers dredged the channel and some

Charleston floating battery, built specifically for use against Fort Sumter in early-1862, and mounting four guns. Miller's Photographic History

damage was done to the site. However, funding was recently approved to raise the wreck and thus remove it from the path of further dredging. At the date of this writing, some substantial sections of the *Georgia*'s casemate have been recovered.

The Charleston Floating Battery

As war clouds loomed over the nation in early-1861, the position of Union facilities in southern harbors became increasingly tenuous. In Charleston, it was obvious that Fort Sumter would soon be the focus of conflict, if President Lincoln persisted in maintaining the Federal presence in the seceded state. In addition to batteries at Fort Moultrie and Johnson, it was determined that a floating battery would be useful to bring more guns to bear on Sumter.[612]

To accomplish this $12,000 was appropriated by the South Carolina Executive Committee, with the stipulation that the structure be completed in less than a month. The upshot was a "remarkably ugly, ungainly craft" resembling a two-story building with the back and part of its roof cut off. There are two versions of its dimensions: 100- by twenty-five-feet, and eight-by forty-feet, with an eight-foot draft. Designed specifically to face the Federal fort, only one side was complete, with four gunports and an angled roof overhead. The fore wall sloped forward and was composed of timbers layered for a total of four feet thickness, covered with two layers of railroad iron. The opposite side was open over the guns, two forty-two- and two thirty-two-pounders. Powder and shot were stored below the gun positions.[613]

To counterbalance the tremendous weights on the fore side, thousands of sandbags were placed on the "aft" side, along with the munitions. When towed into firing position, the battery was secured in place by "giant wedges," and further protection was afforded by mooring it behind a stone breakwater. When the bombardment of the fort began, the battery was some 2,100-yards distant from the target. A floating hospital was moored directly behind the battery.

The latter was proved unnecessary, as only one Union projectile penetrated the front wall, injuring no one. In contrast, about 470 shots were fired from the four guns before the fort surrendered.[614]

The New Orleans Floating Batteries

From mid-1861 to the fall of the city in April 1862, two floating batteries were built at New Orleans, both converted from floating drydocks. Records indicate that one was the "Pelican Dock," which became the *New Orleans*, which was lost near Island No.10. The second battery was the *Memphis*, which remained part of the city defenses until Farragut and his fleet arrived.[615]

No dimensions are available for the *New Orleans* but construction invoices indicate about 70,000 feet of pine lumber was used in the process, as well as approximately sixteen-tons of iron for sheathing the "bomb proof."[616] To accommodate the typical ocean-going steamer of the era, the drydock itself would have been over 250-feet long and perhaps over 100-feet wide, providing a substantial basis for a gun platform. The floating drydocks each had a steam engine used to pump water in and out, as needed to dock a vessel. As of January 1862, the converted vessel mounted twenty-one guns: seventeen eight-inch shell guns, two thirty-two-pounders, and one nine-inch Dahlgren.[617]

A contemporary description described her: "The pumping engine in her hold enabled her to be lowered or raised in the water, and a slanting

Rear view of the Charleston floating battery. The guns were in the open and sandbags were used to counter the weight of the siege guns. The vessel was penetrated by only one projectile fired from the Federal fort. Wikimedia Commons

cover of timbers surmounted by a coating of sheet iron, erected over her, protected her pumping engine from shot and shell. Her deck was flush, without bulwarks, except a single sill around it, corresponding to the port sill on a ship." It is unfortunate that no illustrations have been found of this vessel.[618]

The vessel was towed upriver and participated in the actions around Island No.10, for the most part tethered to the bank as well as to the Confederate steamer *Red Rover*. In this position, the guns were removed from the shore side of the dock and used on shore. She was later scuttled as the Confederates retreated. A Union officer surveyed the wreck and noted that she had iron sheathing on the engine house and was pierced for twenty-two guns, eleven on each side. But by this time only six guns remained, five eight-inch guns and a single thirty-two-pounder.[619]

The *Memphis* may have been converted from the "Gulf Line dock" by the Vallette and Gerard firm. Invoices suggest that a similar amount of

timber and iron went into this conversion as was used on the *New Orleans*: 80,000-feet of pine and oak, plus about 40,000-pounds of iron for the "bomb proof."[620]

In January 1862, the "Memphis battery" was listed by Confederate authorities as capable of mounting eighteen guns. However, as of that date, no guns had been mounted on the vessel.[621]

North Carolina Batteries

On December 1, 1862, the firm of Martin and Elliot, who were then building the ironclad *Albemarle*, contracted to construct a four-gun "stationary floating battery" downriver from Halifax, North Carolina. The cost was to be $26,000 and the iron plating was to be supplied by the government. Delivery of the completed vessel was to be the first day of February 1863.[622]

Sixty days would seem to be a very optimistic deadline for completing the work, and it proved so. However, a government inspector approved

payments for the project on January 26, 1863. Severe weather provided another delay, but did not prevent another payment being made in early-February.[623]

In March, an informant brought Union naval authorities a description of the floating battery in its almost-completed state. The battery was, at this point already in the water and was described as being built "of pine sills, 14 inches square … The roof of the battery and all parts exposed are to be covered with 5 inches of pine, 5 inches of oak, and then plated with railroad iron, so say the workmen." A diagram was drawn to accompany the description. It showed that to top, slanting sides and under side of a four-foot overhang were to be plated, and that a hatch was planned on the sixteen-foot square upper deck.[624]

The work was delayed by lack of iron, as well as by an accident that occurred while it was being towed. When Union forces approached, the battery was towed again to Halifax. Though significant amounts of iron were eventually delivered to the Elliots, it is not clear from the records what proportion was actually installed on the floating battery, as opposed to being used to complete the *Albemarle*.[625] For obvious reasons, the latter vessel had the priority.

Little is known about the battery until nearly the end of the war. A Union officer located the floating battery up the Roanoke River, sunk on a sand bar with only two feet exposed above water. The reporter wrote: "I found it to be a four-sided box, 20 feet square at the top, with

Diagram of a floating battery found on the Roanoke River, North Carolina at the end of the war. Six gunports were cut into the sides. When found, semi-submerged, the structure had neither guns nor iron armor. Official Records

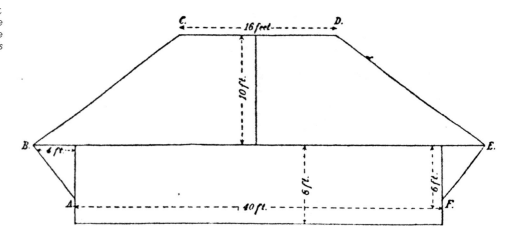

sides sloping at an angle of about 45 degrees. Height between decks, 8 feet, the box composed of heavy timber frames with a layer of yellow pine 1½ feet thick. On two of the sides this pine was covered with 6-inch oak, bolted athwartship. I found two ports on either side."[626] Note that there is no mention of any iron plating. The vessel may well have never been plated, or plating could have been installed and later removed for other purposes. After his inspection, the officer set fire to the battery.

If these descriptions are accurate, the battery's hull was forty-feet square and the overhanging sides brought this measurement to forty-four-feet total. The hull was eight-feet deep and casemate was ten-feet high. Two sides of the casemate had two gunports each, and there was a single port on each of the other sides.[627]

A second floating battery in North Carolina was the *Arctic*, described in the *Official Records* as "iron plated" and mounting three guns.[628]

The iron-hulled vessel, which may have previously been a lightship, was located by Captain Samuel Barron in July 1861, who wrote Secretary Mallory requesting permission to purchase the hull, which measured 115-120-feet long by a 23½-foot beam, and seven- to 7½-feet depth of hold. It was two years old and was available for $10,000. Two months later, William F. Lynch reported back to Mallory that the vessel was "admirably fitted to be a floating battery."[629]

The vessel was stationed in the Cape Fear River from at least August of 1862 to December 1864. The vessel was a receiving ship for the North Carolina Defense Force and was reported as mounting three thirty-two-pounder guns and having a crew of thirty-nine. When Union forces approached Fort Fisher in late-1864, the vessel was sunk as a channel obstruction.[630]

Floating Batteries at Mobile

In May 1861, an insurance company representative wrote Secretary Gideon Welles inquiring about the seizure of the ship *Danube* supposedly by a Confederate privateer in Mobile waters. The sailing ship had been built in Bath, Maine, in 1854, was registered in Portsmouth, New Hampshire, and was a 980-ton vessel measuring 170-feet four-inches by thirty-feet eleven-inches.[631]

In fact, the Confederate authorities had seized the vessel and had incarcerated her crew.[632]

The vessel was converted to a floating battery mounting four guns. The ship was stationed at the Apalachee Battery on Mobile Bay and was sunk by the Confederates as an obstruction in the Spanish River gap in November 1864.[633]

A second floating battery at Mobile, late in the war, was the ironclad *Phoenix*. It had been built in 1863 and mounted six guns. The vessel was sunk as an obstruction prior to Farragut's entry into Mobile Bay in August 1864.[634]

The Confederate Navy was very effective for its size, particularly considering that it was a force created in a short time from few resources. Of course, one of the major factors in its fight against the Union was the willingness to employ new technology to negate, or at least stymie, some of Lincoln's navy.

A few major arenas where the South's navy took advantage were in the use of iron for ship construction and armor, torpedo warfare and submarine vessels. The latter two facets were essentially defensive in nature, and the Union navy did little to counter these threats. On the other hand, the use of iron armor forced the Union navy to respond in kind.

Ultimately, once the technological stakes were laid out, the superior industrial infrastructure of the Union not only negated but overwhelmed the Confederacy. However, during the middle years of the conflict, it is obvious that the Confederate ironclads exerted an influence that far exceeded their actual value as fighting vessels. It was not unusual for Union leaders (both army and navy) to hold back and delay actions on the mere rumor of the existence of a Confederate ironclad in the area. It might be argued that this ironclad "phobia," in addition to some generally ineffective (or non-existent) Union strategic planning, may well have contributed to lengthening the war. At any rate, it appears that more could have been done, had more effective use been made, of the Confederate domestically built ironclads.

On the negative side, the Confederate commerce raiders probably did little to effect the outcome or length of the conflict. Rather, it appears that a more coordinated effort to produce armored warships overseas would have been of more direct use to the fledgling nation. One of James Bulloch's suggestions was to avoid international neutrality considerations by having components of ironclad warships, rather than the ships themselves, produced overseas. These would be run in through the blockade, then assembled at Southern ports. These vessels might have effected a serious breach in the blockade, and thus have enabled an offensive move on major northern ports and possibly thereby brought in an overseas ally. It is noteworthy that Bulloch indeed attempted to do this on a small scale very late in the conflict, by which time the Union blockade had become effective enough to prevent fulfillment of this plan. Therefore, it can be said that the Confederate navy was effective in its operations, but was an instrument that was not utilized to its full potential.

NOTES ON 19TH CENTURY SHIPBUILDING
AND STEAM ENGINE TECHNOLOGY

Ship builders used the term, "length between perpendiculars," that measured the hull on a horizontal line running from the inner side of the stem to the inner side of the sternpost, where these two intersected with the main deck. Other common length measures were "length over all," "length on deck," and "length on waterline," which were self explanatory, with the exception that "over all" did not include bowsprit.

Breadth dimensions were either "moulded beam" or "extreme beam." The former measured the width of the ship's frame at the midship point, not including thickness of the hull planking. The latter measure included the planking on both sides. On sidewheel vessels, the width of the paddles and paddle wheel guards was not included in the beam, unless otherwise noted as breadth "over guards."

The distance between the centerline of each frame to the centerline of the next frame is termed "room and space" and is somewhat analogous to the distance between centers on the frame of a house. The term "ceiling" on a ship hull referred to the planking on the inside of the ship's frames.

Wooden hull parts included futtocks, floors, keel, keelsons, and floors. Each of the hull's transverse members was called a frame, and each frame was composed of sections termed futtocks, which grew narrower from the lowest part of the hull upward to the gunwales. The floors were the lowest sections of the frames, which met the ship's keel. The keel ran the length of the hull and keelsons ran along the keel for extra strength. Treenails (or "trunnels") were wooden "pins" driven through, fastening parts of the hull. On naval vessels iron or copper through bolts were used in lieu of trunnels.

Oakum was old rope picked apart and driven between planks to make watertight seams. Tar was used to "paint" rigging to preserve and waterproof it.

The term "depth of hold" was not synonymous with "draft." The former was a construction term, the distance between the bottom of the lowest complete deck and the top of the keel – in other words the hold of the vessel. The vessel's draft was an operational term meaning how deep in the water the ship rode. Often the latter was given in fore and aft terms if the vessel was "down at the head" or otherwise unequally loaded. Another common descriptor of a hull is the "deadrise" which is angle of the ship's floors up from the keel to the bilges: a vessel with little deadrise would be nearly flat-bottomed. A great deal of deadrise would mean the bottom would form a deep "v."

There were at least three types of "tonnage" measures. "Register" tonnage or "custom house measure" was an arbitrary formula calculated to determine customs duties. It was often expressed in unusual fractions: American merchant vessels sometimes measured "690 94/95 tons," for instance, with the legal ton equal to ninety-five-cubic feet.

Gross tons or "tons burthen" was simply a type of cubic measure of the ship's cargo capacity. Displacement tonnage measured the actual weight of the water displaced by the ship.

Sailing, and sail and steam vessels were usually identified by their rig. A ship-rigged vessel had three masts, all of them square-rigged. The same vessel with the mizzen-mast fore and aft rigged was termed a barque (bark). If two of the three were fore and aft rigged, it was a barquentine. If the vessel had two masts, both of which were square rigged, it was a brig. A brigantine was square rigged on the foremast only. A schooner was fore and aft rigged on both masts and became a "topsail schooner" if a square sail was on her fore mast. A fore and aft rigged single mast vessel was a sloop.

Naval vessel types were based on number of gun decks: a frigate usually had her main battery on a single deck, but with guns fore and aft on the quarterdeck and forecastle. A vessel with two or more complete gundecks plus guns on the forecastle and quarterdeck was a ship-of-the-line. A sloop of war mounted her main battery on a one deck, usually the weather deck. "Corvette" was the French term for the sloop of war.

Early marine steam engine terminology is sometimes confusing. It was common to call each cylinder an "engine." Horsepower measures were usually "nominal" horsepower or "indicated" horsepower. The former was a calculation simply based on the diameter of the cylinder. The actual measured horsepower was the "indicated" horsepower.

There were two major types of marine steam engines: condensing and non-condensing. The condensing engine had a condensing chamber where exhaust steam was reduced to water for re-use in the boilers. On the other hand, the exhaust steam from the non-condensing engine vented to the atmosphere. The latter type was common in fresh water vessels where the water did not have the corrosiveness of seawater. Sea-going ships re-used the fresh water supply. Condensing engines utilized the vacuum effect to assist in engine operation, and typical condensing engines were "low pressure" – with steam usually less than 20psi. High-pressure engines ranged from around 80psi upward. (The land-based high-pressure engine was the steam locomotive, which had a large source of fresh water).

There were two basic types of boilers. In the fire tube, or flue boiler, the heated gases passed through a central tube that was surrounded by water. The gases heated the water to steam, which then passed through piping to the cylinders.

The water tube boiler consisted of many small tubes that ran through the center of the boiler. The heated gases surrounded the tubes and the steam emanated from the tubes for use.

Water tube boilers were more complicated, expensive to produce and to maintain, but were more efficient. Consequently, most of the converted merchant riverboats used their original fire tube (flue) boilers, whereas navy-built vessels were, for the most part, provided with water tube units.

In this era, steam engines were simple expansion units. That is, the steam generated passed to the cylinders and was exhausted. The concept that steam could continue to expand and, therefore, be used a second time was the subject of much controversy. The earliest "compound" steam engines would emerge during this decade. These would use the steam first in a high-pressure cylinder, then use it again in a low-pressure cylinder before being exhausted.

It should also be noted that steam engine technology was at this point limited by the drawbacks inherent in the use of iron. Whether wrought iron or cast iron, the material was not as ductile or strong as steel. Consequently, iron-steam engine components were highly susceptible to dislocation and fracture. The weakest points were the engine's journals, or bearings, where the moving parts physically joined each other: particularly where the connecting rod operated the paddle wheel or screw propeller's crankshaft. Another factor in play was that the technology was not yet available to create tight tolerances between moving surfaces. In consequence, when marine steam engines were run at high-speed and were mounted on relatively non-rigid wooden hulls, journals easily overheated and seized. Thus, steam powerplants, that had fewer moving parts, were obviously more reliable and less likely to break down in, for instance, high-speed chase operations. This explains much of the difference between the speed and reliability of paddle wheel vessels in contrast to screw-propelled ships. In the former types of vessels, the piston operated a connecting rod that was acting directly on the paddle wheel shaft. In contrast, to make a navy screw steamer's steam engine fit in a confined location below the waterline (as well as operate the propeller at relatively high rpm), some mechanical contrivance, whether with gears, levers, or other instrumentalities, was necessary. Screw steamships – particularly naval steamers – were therefore notoriously unreliable in this era. Also it was general practice to make screw steam engine parts as solid and large as possible to further enhance reliability. This practice resulted in very heavy engines and components. These problems would not fade away until steel came into more general use. In particular, when steel became the standard for the machine tools necessary to produce smaller, lighter and more efficient steam engines.

1. Lyon, David, and Rif Winfield, *The Sail and Steam Navy List*, p.240-1.

2. Conway's *All the World's Fighting Ships*, p.7-8, 286-7.

3. Canney, Donald L., *The Old Steam Navy*, Vol.2, The Ironclads, p.3-6.

4. Canney, Donald L., *The Old Steam Navy*, Vol.1, Frigates, Sloops and Gunboats.

5. Soley, J. Russell, *The Blockade and the Cruisers*, p.11-12; Conway's, p.114-5.

6. Scharf, J. Thomas, *History of the Confederate States Navy*, p.68; and Still, William N., Jr., *Confederate Shipbuilding*, p.x.

7. Still, p.48-9.

8. Scharf, p.32-3; Soley, p.8-10.

9. Soley, p.22; Coski, John M., *Capital Navy*, p.7.

10. Scharf, p.28-9; Still, William N., Jr., *Iron Afloat*, p.6; Durkin, Joseph D., *Stephen R. Mallory*, p.133-137.

11. Baughman, James P., *The Mallorys of Mystic*, p.105.

12. *Official Records of the Union and Confederate Navies in the War of the Rebellion*, Ser.2, Vol.2, p.47.

13. Semmes, Raphael, *Memoirs of Service Afloat*, p.83-8; Baughman, p.105.

14. Durkin, p.149; Scharf, p.24-5; *Civil War Naval Chronology*, VI, p.283.

15. Scharf, p.263; "Investigation of the Navy Department," ORN, Ser.2, Vol.2, p.791.

16. Robinson, *The Confederate Privateers*, p.30; CWNC, VI, p.7; Jones, Virgil Carrington, *The Civil War at Sea*, Vol.1, p.84.

17. Report of the Secretary of the Navy, July 18, 1861, ORN, Ser.2, Vol.2, p.79; Jones, Vol.1, p.180.

18. Ltr, Mallory to North, May 17, 1861, ORN, Ser.2, Vol.2, p.70-1.

19. Still, *Shipbuilding ... p.12-3*.

20. Robinson, William Morrison, Jr., *The Confederate Privateers*, p.155.

21. Canney, Donald L., *The Old Steam Navy: Vol.2, The Ironclads*, p.20, 25, 137.

22. Scharf, J. Thomas, *The Confederate Navy*, p.264; Robinson, 156.

23. Scharf, p.264-5; Robinson, 156; Jones, Vol.1, p.241-3; Ltr, March 31, 1904, Capt. Littlepage, Asst Eng., NARS Subject File of the Confederate Navy, M1091 Reel 7.

24. Robinson, 157; Silverstone, *Civil War Navies*, 152.

25. *Official Records of the Union and Confederate Navies ...*, Ser.I, Vol.18, pps.154, 195, 198, 337, 340, 344; Scharf, p.264-5; *Battles and Leaders of the Civil War*, Vol.2, p.69.

26. Scharf, 265.

27. ORN, Ser.1, Vol.16, p.703-5, 712, 718, 730a; Jones, Vol.1, p.243-7.

28. ORN, Ser.1, Vol.18, p.182, 198, 205-6, 336-7; Melton, Maurice, *Confederate Ironclads*, p.100.

29. Park, Carl D., *Ironclad Down*, 54-61; Scharf, p.146-8; Still, *Iron Afloat*, p.12-13.

30. Still, p.14.

31. Scharf, p. 148-151; Park, p.61-2.

32. Canney, *Old Steam Navy*, Vol.1, p.47-59; Journal of the Franklin Institute, Vol.61, Apr. 1856, p.274-78. "Trial Trip of the United States Steam Frigate Merrimac."

33. Board Report on Engines for six Steamers, Sept. 20, 1854. NARS RG 45, Entry 224, Letters from Constructors.

34. Ibid.

35. Ibid.

36. Isherwood, Benjamin F., *Experimental Researches in Steam Engineeering*, Vol.1, p.160-2.

37. Ibid; and JFI, *Trial Trip ...*, p.277

38. Canney, Vol.1, p.47-8, 50; Isherwood, p.160-2.

39. Canney, Vol.1, p.48, 50.

40. Flanders, Alan B., *The Merrimac*, p.13.

41. Flanders, p.58.

42. Park, p.136-7.

43. Park, p.147-9, 154-6.

44. Park, p.108-9.

45. Park, p.150-1.

46. Park, p.136, 158, 162.

47. Park, p.174; and Flanders, p.63.

48. Flanders, p.61.

49. Ltr, Porter to R.L. Page, May 11, 1874, NARS M625 Area File; Park, p.91-2, 172.

50. Ltr, Mallory to F. Buchanan, Feb. 24, 1861 (ORN Ser.1 Vol.6, p.777.)

51. NARS RG19 Plan 3-4-20.

52. Ibid; Park, p.143, 158; *Dictionary of American Fighting Ships* (DANFS), Vol.3, p.815.

53. DANFS, Vol.3, p.815.

54. Park, p.165.

55. Scharf, p.189.

56. Flanders, p.87

57. Ltr, Buchanan to Mallory, Mar. 19, 1862, Franklin Buchanan Notebook; Ltr, Buchanan to J. Tatnall, Apr. 4, 1862, Tatnall Papers; Scharf, p.190, 207-8.

58. NARS RG365, Confederate Treasury Dept. Records; Campbell, R. Thomas, *Confederate Naval Forces in Western Waters*, p.54-5.

59. Specifications by Joseph Pierce, NC, Sept. 1861, RG 365; Scharf, p.283.

60. Ibid.

61. Specifications, Pierce, RG 365.

62. Ibid; Way, Frederick, *Way's Packet Directory*, p.224.

63. Ibid; ORN, Ser. 2, Vol.2, Investigation of Navy Department, p.760; Campbell, p.35; Diagram of Louisiana in J.K. Mitchell Papers. Virginia Historical Society.

64. Campbell, p.58-63; Melton, Maurice, *The Confederate Ironclads*, p.75.

65. Ltr. Wilson Youngblood to J.K Mitchell, Aug. 1, 1862, J.K. Mitchell Papers.

66. J.K. Mitchell, quoted in Scharf, p.281.

67. Report, John K. Mitchell, ORN, Ser.1, Vol.18, p.312; Abstract of log of *Iroquois*, ORN Ser.1, Vol.18, p.800; Scharf, p.298; Mahan, A.T., *The Gulf and Inland Waters*, p.79.

68. Durkin, p.34, 232-8; Campbell, p.52.

69. Campbell, p.52-3; Stephen R. Mallory, Diary, Sept. 1, 1861, p.33.

70. ORN, Ser.2, Vol.2, (Investigation of Navy Dept.,) Ltr., Tift to Mallory, Oct. 10, 1861, p.575, 540-1, 547; Scharf, p.268-9; Campbell, p.53-5; Melton, *Confederate Ironclads*, p.75-8.

71. ORN, Ser.2, Vol.2, Investigation of Navy Department, p.533, 535, 540-1, 547, 572, 575, 583; Scharf, p.268-9.

72. NARS M1091, Reel 4, Invoice for Leeds & Co., Apr. 25, 1862.

73. ORN, Ser 2, Vol.2, p.533; Campbell, p.57.

74. Melton, Maurice, *Confederate Ironclads*, p.75-6.

75. Campbell, p.58, 62-3; ORN, Series 2, Vol.2, p.580; Manuscript, "Miscellaneous File," unsigned, Museum of the Confederacy.

76. Smith, Myron, Jr., *The CSS Arkansas*, p.30-7.

77. Specification, Aug. 24, 1861, NARS M365, Confederate Treasury Records.

78. Smith, p.47, 50-1, 54-7; Scharf, p.303-4.

79. Smith, p.52; Report, J.J. Guthrie, CSN to T. Jordan, CSA, Apr. 10, 1862. NARS M1091.

80. Guthrie Report.

81. Smith, p.80-1; Scharf, p.306.

82. Smith, p.90; Campbell, p.105; Scharf, p.306; Melton, *Confederate Ironclads*, p.117.

83. Smith, p.96, 101-2; Campbell, p.108. (There is no general consensus on the types of guns on the vessel, only that there were 10).

84. Smith, p.53-4; Specifications, Aug. 24, 1861, RG365; Report, J. Guthrie, Apr. 10, 1862, M1091.

85. *Civil War Naval Chronology*, VI, p.200.

86. Ibid; Smith, p.100.

87. Smith, p.120-2.

88. Stern, p.104-6; Mahan, p. 99-106; Scharf, p.312-21.

89. Report, T.A. Jenkins, Jan.15, 1864, ORN, Ser.1, Vol.21, p.35; CWNC, VI, p.202.

90. *Baltic File*, Alabama Department of Archives and History.

91. Ibid; Jenkins Rpt., ORN, Ser.1, Vol.21, p.35.

92. Ltr, P. Crosby et al, June 19, 1865,

ORN, Ser.1, Vol.22, p.226; Hunter, Louis C., *Steamboats on the Western Rivers*, p.139-41.

93. Rpt., ORN Ser.1, Vol.22, p.226; *Baltic* File, ADAH; Hunter, p.97-9.

94. CWNC, VI, p.202.

95. Symonds, Craig L., *Confederate Admiral*, p.184; 207.

96. Rpt. June 19, 1865, ORN, Ser.1, Vol.22, p.226.

97. Loeffler, Mark Dallas, "Sea King." *Handbook of Texas Online*.

98. Mahan, p.24-5.

99. Coski, p.77.

100. Holcombe, Robert, "Notes on the Classification of Confederate Ironclads," p.3, 7-8.

101. Way, p.137.

102. Ltr, S.L. Phelps w/endorsement of A.H. Foote, Feb. 18, 1862, ORN, Ser.1, Vol.22, p.615.

103. Ltr. Phelps to D.D. Porter, Feb. 5, 1863, S.L. Phelps, Ltr, Book. Mo. Hist. Soc.

104. Ltr. Porter to Phelps, Jan. 18, 1863, ORN, Ser.1, Vol.24, p.178.

105. Canney, *The Old Steam* Navy, Vol.2, The Ironclads, p.105.

106. Wilson, Walter C., and Gary L. McKay, *James D. Bulloch*, p.52; Graham, Eric J., *Clyde Built*, p.29.

107. Graham, p.28-9, 209.

108. Ibid.

109. Ibid, Graham, p.29.

110. Melton, Maurice, *The Best Station of them All*, p.138.

111. Melton, p.168, 177.

112. Scharf, 641-4; Ltr, E.S. Scott to J.K. Albro, June 17, 1863, Atlanta File, Museum of the Confederacy; Rpt., W.R. Taylor, et al, to DuPont, June 22, 1863, ORN Ser.1, Vol.14, p.273-6.

113. Melton, p.173; 206.

114. McBlair Papers, Ltr, Oct. 16, 1862; J.W. Alexander to W. Hoke, Apr. 14, 1863, Hoke Collection.

115. Scharf, p.641-2.

116. Ibid, p.643-4.

117. Ltr. Webb to Mallory, Oct. 19, 1864, ORN, Ser.1, Vol.14, p.291; Stern, p. 139; Scharf, p.643-4; Melton, p.229.

118. Scharf, p.642; Melton, p.153.

119. Ltr. T.S. Seybolt to Seward, Aug.3,

1862, ORN Ser.1, Vol.13, p.625; Coski, p.204-10.

120. Ltr. G.B. Davids to C. Wilkes, July 22, 1862, ORN Ser.1, Vol.7, p. 589-90; Ltr. John H. Burroughs, Nov. 10, 1862, ORN. Ser.1, Vol.8, p.207.

121. Peebles, Martin D., "The History and Archeology of a Civil War Ironclad on the Cape Fear River," (MA Thesis), p.10-11.

122. Coski, p.80; Heyl, Vol.4, p.13.

123. Rpt., E.H. Williams, Gunner, May 26, 1864, Minor Papers.

124. Stern, p.240-1; Rpt., J.M. Kell, to J.K. Mitchell, Jan. 26, 1865, ORN Ser.1, Vol.11, p.673-4.

125. In Scharf (p.671) Porter is quoted, taking credit for designs of the two vessels in Charleston as well as the two being built at Wilmington, NC.

126. Scharf, p.670-2; Still, p.80-2; Coker, p.224-5; Holcombe, Robert, "The Richmond Class Confederate Ironclads," Confederate Historical Association of Belgium (chab-belgium.com.)

127. Still, p.81.

128. Still, p.81-2, 87.

129. Ibid; Scharf, p.670; Charleston *Mercury*, Oct. 13, 1862 (www.cw-chronicles.com)

130. Coker, p.224-5.

131. Scharf, p.670; ORN, Ser.2, Vol.1, p.262.

132. Scharf, p.672.

133. Ltr., Abbott et al to Stellwagen, Feb.2, 1863, ORN, Ser.1, Vol.13, p.596.

134. Scharf, p.670-1; Silverstone, *Warships…*, p.238.

135. Coker, p.225; Ltr, Minor to A.F. Warley, Dec. 25, 1862, Minor Family Papers.

136. Melton, p.66, 120; Contract dated Mar. 31, 1862, NARS M365.

137. Melton, p.132.

138. Melton, p.150-1.

139. Melton, p.150-1, 64.

140. Turner, Maxine, *Navy Gray*, p.68; Melton, p.133, 199.

141. Melton, p.199; Plan, Stern section, CSS Savannah.

142. Ltr, W.W. Hunter to Mallory, June 29, 1863, ORN, Ser.1, Vol.14, p. 713-4; Melton, p.244-5.

143. Ltr., W.W. Hunter to Gilmer, Jan.

12, 1864, ORN, Ser.1, Vol.15, p.702-3; Melton, p.388-90.

144. Peebles, p.91-3.

145. Ibid, p.96.

146. Ibid, p.98.

147. Ibid, p.41.

148. Ibid, p.39-40.

149. Rpt. J.T. Wood to Jefferson Davis, Feb. 14, 1863, ORN Ser.1, Vol.8, p.859.

150. Peebles, p.53, 35.

151. Report, Apr. 30, 1864, Sec. Navy Mallory, ORN Ser.1, Vol.9 p.809; Peebles, p.42.

152. Ltr, W.A. Parker to S.P. Lee, May 7, 1864, ORN Ser.1, Vol.10, p.19; Peebles, p.67; CWNC, IV, p.56-7.

153. Peebles, p.59.

154. Peebles, p.36, 39, 66.

155. Peebles, p.59.

156. Holcombe, "Classification...," p.3, 9, 11, 14.

157. Ibid.

158. Coski, p.81-3.

159. Coski, p.82-3; Scharf, p.726-7.

160. Coski, p.84-6.

161. Canney, *Old Steam Navy*, Vol.2, The Ironclads, p.76-7; 138.

162. Ltr, J.T. Wood to Catesby Jones, Feb. 26, 1864, ORN Ser.1, Vol.9, p.800-1.

163. Ibid; Scharf, p.671.

164. J.K. Mitchell to Mallory, Sept. 21, 1864, ORN, Ser.1, Vol.10, p.745.

165. Still, William, ed., *The Confederate Navy*, p.54; Scharf, p.671.

166. Scharf, p.671.

167. Coker, p.231-2.

168. Scharf, p.671.

169. Holcombe, p.11-12.

170. Melton, p.182, 240, 268, 373.

171. Ltr, Tatnall to W.W. Hunter, Oct. 19, 1864, W.W. Hunter Papers; Ltr, Tatnall to S.S. Lee, Jan. 17, 1865, ORN, Ser.1, Vol.16, p.502.

172. Symonds, Craig L., *Confederate Admiral*, p.184-5

173. Still, *Iron Afloat*, p.190; Lewis, Herbert J., "Selma Ordnance and Naval Foundry," www.Encyclopedia of Alabama.org.

174. Holcombe, p.20; Still, *Confederate Navy*, p.54.

175. NARS RG 19, plan, 41-5-10;

Plan, CSS *Columbia*, NARA M1091; CWNC, VI, p.314.

176. Symonds, p.185-7; 193.

177. Ibid, p.190-1.

178. Ltr, Buchanan to Mallory, July 17, 1863, and April 6, 1863, Buchanan Papers (UNC).

179. Ltr, Buchanan to Mallory, Sept. 20, 1863, Buchanan Papers (UNC).

180. Symonds, p.201-2; Stuart, Charles B., *Naval Dry Docks of the United States*, Part II, p.16-7.

181. Mahan, *The Gulf and Inland Waters*, p.221.

182. Rpt, T.A. Jenkins et al, to Farragut, Aug. 13, 1864, ORN, Ser.1, Vol.21, p.547-8; Speech, James D. Johnston, 1882, Transcript in Museum of the Confederacy.

183. Rpt, Sept. 12, 1864, ORN, Ser.1, Vol.21, p.551.

184. Ibid.

185. Way, p.16; Still, *Iron Afloat*, p.191-2; Ltr, Buchanan to Mallory, Apr.6, 1863, Buchanan Papers, UNC.

186. Johnston speech; Still, p.201; Maclay, Edgar S., *History of the Navy*, Vol.2, p.447-8.

187. Maclay, p.448; Still, p.201.

188. Rpt., Jenkins, et al; Schneller, Robert J., *Farragut*, p.89-91; Scharf, p.564; Canney, *The Old Steam Navy*, Vol.1, p.102; Stern, p.207-11; Still, p.207-11.

189. Still, *Confederate Shipbuilding*, p.26; CWNC, VI, p.229.

190. Coski, p.85-6.

191. Ibid, p.86-7.

192. Ibid, p.153-4; Secretary of the Navy Report, Apr.30, 1864, ORN, Ser.1, Vol.9, p.809.

193. Ltr. C.H. Gormley, gunner, to R.D. Minor, May 26, 1864, Minor Papers, Va. Hist. Soc.

194. Ltr, T.R. Rootes to J.K. Mitchell, Oct. 22, 1864, ORN Ser.1, Vol.10, p.588-9.

195. Still, *Shipbuilding...* p.38; Ltr Mallory to Seddon, May 19, 1864, ORN, Ser.1, Vol.10, p.645; CWNC, VI, p.229.

196. Ltr. T. Rootes to J.K. Mitchell, Oct. 22, 1864, ORN Ser.1, Vol.10, p.588-9.

197. Contract, May 1, 1862, NARS M 365.

198. Ltr, C.J. McRae to Mallory, Aug.1,

1862, ORN, Ser.2, Vol.2, p.230-2; CWNC, VI, 251, 318.

199. CWNC, VI, p.251; Invoice for engines, Apr. 20, 1863, W.R. Brown, NARS M 1091; Way, p.85.

200. Symonds, p.189-90; Ltr, F. Buchanan to Mallory, April 6, 1863 and Buchanan to J.K. Mitchell, May 13, 1863, in Buchanan Papers, UNC.

201. CWNC, VI, 251, 318; Symonds, p.189-90.

202. CWNC, VI, 251, 318; Melton, Confederate Ironclads, p.212.

203. NARS M365, Contracts, dated Aug.12 and 15, 1862; Still, ed., Confederate Navy, p.107.

204. Ltr, Buchanan to Mallory, Nov. 18, 1863, Buchanan Papers. UNC.

205. Still, Iron Afloat, p.91.

206. NARS M365 (Contract).

207. Ltr, Mallory to S. Barron, Oct. 2, 1862, ORN, Ser.1, Vol.23, p.704.

208. Symonds, p.189; Ltr, Buchanan to Mallory, Sept. 20, 1863, Buchanan Papers, UNC; Ltr, Buchanan to C. Jones, Apr. 14, 1864, ORN, Ser.1, Vol.21, p.892.

209. Ltr, J.M. Brooke to C. Jones, Jan. 15, 1864, NARS Area File M625; Ltr., McCorkle to C. Jones, Jan. 25, 1864, ORN, Ser.1, Vol.21, p.869; Ltr., C. Jones to Buchanan, Apr.12, 1864, ORN, Ser.1, Vol.21, p.892.

210. Report, H.K. Thacther, June 30, 1865, ORN Ser.1, Vol.22, p.225.

211. Ibid.

212. Melton, Confederate Ironclads, p.225-30.

213. Elliot, Robert G., Ironclad of the Roanoke, p.62; Ltr, J.W.Cooke to Martin, Oct. 10, 1862, W.F. Martin Papers, UNC.

214. Elliot, p.62-3.

215. Ltr w/enclosures, S.P. Lee to Foster, Aug. 18, 1863, ORN, Ser.1, Vol.9, p.164. (Enclosure statement by Michael Cohen, plumber.)

216. Elliot, p.92-6.

217. Elliot, p.96.

218. Ibid, p.102.

219. Ibid, p.112.

220. Ibid, p.114-6.

221. Ibid, p.121-9.

222. Ibid, p.141-3, 99.

223. Ibid, p.149, 167-9.

224. Elliot, p.63; "The Life of the CSS Neuse," www.nchistoricsites.org/Neuse/history/htm.

225. "The Life of the CSS Neuse."

226. Ibid.

227. Ibid; Ltr. B.P. Loyall to R. Minor, Apr. 7, 1864, Minor Papers.

228. Ltr. Loyall to Minor, Apr. 16, 1864, Minor Papers.

229. Contract, Nov. 1, 1862, NARS M365; Jeter, Katherine Brash, A Man and His Boat, p.ix-xi.

230. Jeter, p.xiv.

231. Ibid, p.xvi.

232. Ibid, p.xix-xxv.

233. Rpt., E.P. Lull et al, June 14, 1865, ORN, Ser.1, Vol.27, p.241-2; Melton, p.149.

234. Melton, p.152.

235. Turner, p.159-60.

236. Holcomb, p.21; Silverstone, Warships..., p.207; Still, ed., p.108-10.

237. Turner, p.169-70; Still, ed., p.108.

238. Ibid, p.172.

239. Ltr, McLaughlin to C. Jones, (n.d.), NARS Area File, M625; Still, ed., p.108.

240. Turner, p.182.

241. Ibid, p.186.

242. Ibid, p.204-5.

243. Ltr., G. Gift to C. Jones, Jul. 13, 1864, NARS M625.

244. Ltr, McLaughlin to C. Jones, Dec. 24, 1864 (1865), NARS M625; Turner, p.214.

245. Ltr, McLaughlin to Jones, Dec.22, 1864, NARS M625.

246. Turner, p.236-7.

247. From National Civil War Naval Museum web site. (www.portcolumbus.org).

248. Turner, p.161; Holcombe, p.20; Still, Confederate Shipbuilding, p.60-1.

249. Turner, p.164, 202.

250. Holcombe, p.10-11.

251. Ltr., J.A. Dahlgren to Welles, June 1, 1865, ORN Ser.1, Vol.16, p.388.

252. ORN, Ser 2, Vol.1, p.251.

253. Coker, p.232.

254. Coski, p.87; Holcombe, p.20.

255. Coski, p.78; ORN, Ser.2, Vol.1, p.222, 268.

256. Still, ed., Confederate Navy, p.67.

257. ORN, Ser.2, Vol.1, p.222, 268.

258. Coski, p.87; Ltr. Mallory to J. M.Bulloch, Sept. 5, 1864, ORN, Ser.2, Vol.2. p.718-9; Still, Iron Afloat, p.99.

259. Still, Iron Afloat, p.99.

260. Ltr., Warner to C. Jones, Jan. 28, 1865, NARS M625.

261. Semmes, Raphael, Memoirs of Service Afloat, p.94.

262. Ltr, Mallory to C.M. Conrad, May 9, 1861, NARS M625 (Area 7).

263. Scharf, p.782-3.

264. Scharf, p.36; Semmes, p.93.

265. Reaney Book, courtesy Bob Holcombe; Heyl, Vol.1, p.201.

266. Ibid; Brooks, William Param, papers, (MSS 499, Emory Univ.)

267. Reaney Book; Semmes, 217, 273.

268. Semmes, p.98, 106-7; Tucker, p.232.

269. Semmes, p.98-104.

270. Semmes, p.118, 138-9, 202, 217, 265, 275, 281, 298, 342.

271. Owsley, Frank, The CSS Florida, p.17-18.

272. Ibid, Bennett, John D., The London Confederates, p.30.

273. Owsley, p.19-21.

274. Owsley, p.18-19; Bulloch, James D., The Secret Service of the Confederate States in Europe, p.40-2.

275. Preston, Anthony and John Major, Send a Gunboat, p.156-7; Bulloch, p.41; Lyon, David and Rif Winfield, The Sail and Steam Navy List, p.221-2.

276. Bulloch, p.41-2.

277. Owsley, p.21-4; Bulloch, p.41-2.

278. Owsley, p.42, 190; Silverstone, Civil War Navies, p.159; Panamerican Consultants, "Documentation of the Civil War Vessels CSS Florida and USS Cumberland, Hampton Roads Virginia" (U.S. Army Corps of Engineers, 1994.), p.47-9 (Plans of CSS Florida)

279. Lyon, p.221-3.

280. Ibid.

281. Owsley, p.22-4.

282. Hoole, William Stanley, Four Years in the Confederate Navy, p.30.

283. Owsley, p.36-40; Jones, Vol.2, p.259-71; Stern, p.114-6.

284. Ltr, M. Sicard to G.H. Preble, Oct. 8, 1862, ORN, Ser.1, Vol.2, p.443; Ltr F.C. Dade (Chief Engineer), to Preble, Oct. 9, 1862, ORN Ser.1, Vol.2, p.445.

285. Ltr, Buchanan to Maffitt, Jan. 6, 186(3?), Buchanan Notebook, UNC; Ordnance Instructions, USN, 1866, Part 3, p.84.

286. Owsley, p.43-8.

287. Ltr, G.F. Emmons to R. B. Hitchcock, Mar. 12, 1863, ORN, Ser.1, Vol.2, p.30-1; Owsley, p.48-9.

288. Ltr, T.H. Stevens to C. Wilkes, Feb. 9, 1863, ORN. Ser.1, Vol.2, p.69-70; Owsley, p.53-4; Canney, Old Steam Navy, Vol.1, p.109-13.

289. Owsley, p.54-5; Scharf, p.792.

290. Owsley, p.61-2.

291. Canney, Donald L., U.S. Coast Guard and Revenue Cutters, 1790-1935, p.23-4.

292. Owsley, p.73-5.

293. Ltr, G.D. Lining, (Engineer), to Maffitt(?), Sept. 9, 1863, NARS M625 Area File. Florida deck plans do not show the stern pivot gun. The original plans may well have omitted guns, for security reasons, and Maffitt, at sea, was free to mount pivot rails and guns where he saw fit.

294. Owsley, p.92-7.

295. Owsley, p.98-103.

296. Owsley, p.97.

297. Owsley, p.128-34.

298. Owsley, p.158-9.

299. Summersell, Charles G., CSS Alabama: Builder, Captain and Plans, p.9.

300. Ibid, p.12

301. Lyon, p.218; 228.

302. Bowcock, Andrew, CSS Alabama, p.18-25.

303. Ibid, p.25.

304. Ibid, p.9-12; Summersell, p.15-6.

305. Ibid, p.34-5.

306. Ibid, p.83-8; 58-9.

307. Bennett, p.431.

308. Bowcock, p.24; 139-42; 173-9.

309. Semmes, p.402-3; Bowcock, p.81-3.

310. Bowcock, p.83.

311. Bowcock, p.76-80; 136.

312. Semmes, p.403.

313. Summersell, p.36-9; Semmes, p.423; Stern, p.119.

314. Semmes, p.474-7.

315. Silverstone, *Warships of the Civil War Navies*, p.209-10.

316. ORN, Ser.2, Vol.1, p.200; Stern, p.119.

317. Semmes, p.536.

318. Stern, p.126-7; Soley, p.195-9.

319. Silverstone, p.210; Semmes, p.590.

320. Summersell, p.56.

321. Summersell, p.54.

322. Semmes, p.56.

323. Semmes, p.667.

324. Semmes, p.709, 749.

325. Canney, *Old Steam Navy*, Vol.1, p.76; ORN, Ser.1, Vol.3, p.63.

326. Semmes, p.753.

327. Ltr., Mallory to Bulloch, Aug. 1, 1864, and Enclosure: Memorandum from J.M. Brooke, ORN Ser.2, Vol.2, p.708-9.

328. Ibid, (Memorandum).

329. Horan, James D., ed., *C.S.S. Shenandoah*, p.98.

330. Ltr, Bulloch to Mallory, Sept. 16, 1864, ORN, Ser.2, Vol.2, p.723-4; Specifications from Denny Files, Univ. of Glasgow; Silverstone, *Civil War Navies*, p.161; MacGregor, David, *Fast Sailing Ships*, p.189, 249-51; Chaffin, Tom, *Sea of Gray*, p.50; Horan, Ed., p.98.

331. Stern, p.250; Chaffin, p.54, 67.

332. Stern, p.250.

333. Chaffin, p.90.

334. Jones, p.385; Stern, p.252-3.

335. Chaffin, p.216, 317.

336. Stern, p.253.

337. Bennett, John D., *The London Confederates*, p. 105; Canney, *The Old Steam Navy,* Vol.1, p.86.

338. J. Bennett, p.105.

339. Foster, Kevin, "Phantoms, Banshees, Will-of-the-Wisps and the Dare: or The Search for Speed under Steam…," p.173; J. Bennett, p.105; McKenna, Joseph, *British Ships in the Confederate Navy*, p.175; CWNC, VI, p.309.

340. ORN, Ser.2, Vol.1, p.268.

341. Ltr, S.P. Lee to Welles, Sept. 9, 1864, ORN, Ser.1, Vol.10, p.445.

342. Jones, Vol.3, p.265.

343. Ltr, J.L. Davis to D.D. Porter, Nov. 9, 1864, ORN, Ser.1, Vol.3, p.324-7.

344. Ltr, T.A. Harris to D.D. Porter, Nov. 9, 1864, ORN, Ser.1, Vol.3, p.327-8.

345. Wise, p.202.

346. Wilkinson, John, *The Narrative of a Blockade Runner*, p.233.

347. Wilkinson, p.210.

348. Graham, Eric J., Clyde *Built*, p.134-5.

349. ORN, Ser.2, Vol.1, p.254; "Register of the Georgia," in NARS M1091; NARS RG19 Plan "SS Japan Deck and Cabin Arrangement."

350. Noirsain, Serge, *La Flotte Europeenne de la Confederation Sudiste*, p.201.

351. Heyl Collection, "CSS Georgia"; Heyl, Vol.5, p.125.

352. Graham, p.134-5.

353. Morgan, James Morris, *Recollections of a Rebel Reefer*, p.115, 161; Abstract of Log of CSS *Georgia*. ORN, Ser.1, Vol.2, p.811.

354. Morgan, p.143.

355. Morgan, p.147, 153, 157.

356. Morgan, p.178; Stern, p.187.

357. Morgan, p.180.

358. Ibid.

359. Morgan, p.180; Scharf, p.803.

360. Wise, p.297.

361. Wilkinson, p.209.

362. Ibid, p.210.

363. Ibid, p.225; Journal of *Chickamauga*, ORN, Ser.1, Vol.3, p.710-713.

364. Graham, p.154; J. Bennett, p.73; Preston, p.149; Lyon, p.220-1.

365. Milton, David H., *Lincoln's Spymaster*, p.81.

366. Wilson, Walter E., and Gary L. McKay, *James D. Bulloch*, p.106, 118,123; Stern, p.166-7; Graham, p.153.

367. J. Bennett, p.68; Silverstone, *Civil War Navies*, p.162; *Conway's All the World's Fighting Ship, 1860-1905*, p.383; CWNC, VI, p.314.

368. Graham, p.142-6.

369. Graham, p.147-9.

370. Conway's AWFS, p.383; Silverstone, p.162. CWNC, VI, p.314.

371. Bulloch, p.344.

372. Spencer, p.148-9.

373. Bulloch, p.335; Spenser, p.153.

374. Bulloch, p.342-3.

375. Conway's AWFS, p.250, 418; Silverstone, *Civil War Navies*, p.163.

376. Bulloch, p.476; Foster, p.180-2.

377. Ltr, Bulloch to J. Low, Jan. 8, 1865, ORN Ser.2, vol.2, p.787-8; Silverstone, *Civil War Navies*, p.162.

378. Bulloch, p.476; Ltr., Mallory to Bulloch, Aug. 19, 1864, ORN, Ser.2, Vol.2, p.707.

379. "Specifications of 2 Twin screw Tug Steamers," Denny Papers; Foster, p.183-5; Silverstone, *Civil War Navies*, p.163.

380. Silverstone, p.163.

381. Still, *Iron Afloat*, p.10-11

382. *Conway's AWFS*, p.7-8, 286-7.

383. *Conway's AWFS*, p.286.

384. McKenna, Joseph, *British Ships in the Confederate Navy*, p.165.

385. Ltr, Bulloch to Mallory, July 21, 1862, ORN, Ser.2, Vol.2, p.223-6.

386. Ibid.

387. Ibid; Ltr., Bulloch to Mallory, July 8, 1863, ORN, Ser.2, Vol.2, p.453.

388. Baxter, James Phinney, *The Introduction of the Ironclad Warship*, p.190-5.

389. Canney, *Old Steam Navy*, Vol.2, p.137; *Illustrated London News*, Mar. 29, 1862 (Vol.40, No.1137, p.305); Ltr., Bullloch to Mallory, Sept. 10, 1862, ORN, Ser.2, Vol.2, p.265.

390. Ltr., Bulloch to Mallory, Dec. 18, 1862. ORN, Ser.2, Vol.2, p.310; McKenna, p.166; Bulloch, p.269.

391. Wilson and McKay, p.109.

392. Ltr., Bulloch to Mallory, July 8, 1863, ORN, Ser.2, Vol.2, p.453-4; Conway's AWFS, p.19; Lyon, p.182.

393. Ltr., Bulloch to Mallory, July 8, 1863, ORN, Ser.2, Vol.2, p.453.

394. Ltr., Dudley to Seward, Jan. 28, 1863 (NARS M1091); Still, ed., p.57.

395. Lyon, p.252-3.

396. *Conway's AWFS*, p.20.

397. Bulloch, p.282-4.

398. Gardiner, Robert, ed., *Steam, Steel & Shellfire*, p.79.

399. Bulloch, p.266.

400. Contract, specifications and alterations, ORN, Ser.2, Vol.2, p.193-204.

401. Ltr, G. Thomson to North, Jul. 17, 1862, Thomson Letters, U. of Glasgow.

402. Contract, etc. p.193-204.

403. Spencer, Warren F., *The Confederate Navy In Europe*, p.74-5.

404. Spencer, p.74-5, 120.

405. *Conway' AWFS*, p.364; Silverstone, *Civil War Navies*, p.151; Still, ed., p.56.

406. Bulloch, p.337-8; Spencer, p.160-1.

407. Bulloch, p.358.

408. Ltr, Bulloch to Mallory, Nov. 26, 1863, ORN, Ser.2, Vol.2, p.525.

409. Ibid; Contract, Arman and Bulloch, July 16, 1863, ORN, Ser.2, Vol.2, p.464-5.

410. Spencer, p.200-2; Bulloch, p.345-53.

411. Spencer, p.200-6; Bulloch, p.373-81.

412. Page, Thomas Jefferson, Papers: "The Cruise of the Stonewall."

413. ORN, Ser.2, Vol.1, p.160, 196.

414. Report of Court Martial, T.T. Craven, RG125, M125 No.4071, Vol.143.

415. *Conway's AWFS*, p.219, 242.

416. Wise, p.285-328.

417. Foster, p.32-7; Wise, p.27, 221.

418. Ridgely-Nevitt, Cedric, *American Steamships on the Atlantic*, p.257-61.

419. Ibid.

420. Ibid; Heyl, Vol.1, p.277.

421. Ridgely-Nevitt, p.162, 174; Heyl, Vol.1, p.277.

422. Ridgely-Nevitt, p.261-3; CWNC, Vol.III, p.35-6; Jones, Vol.2, p.378-80.

423. Wise, p.50-3.

424. Heyl, Vol.1, p.163; Foster, p.129; Bradlee, Francis, *Blockade Running During the Civil War*, p.21.

425. Foster, p.129.

426. ORN, Ser.2, Vol.1, p.45.

427. Silverstone, *Civil War Navies*, p.81.

428. Silverstone, *Civil War Navies*, p.50; Heyl, Vol.1, p.361; Foster, p.57.

429. Wilkinson, p.105.

430. Heyl, Vol.1, p.361; Foster, p.57; Scharf, p.468; Wilkinson, p.116, 120.

431. Wilkinson, p.128-9, 164-8; Ltr., A.L. Case to S.P. Lee, Aug. 20, 1863, ORN, Ser.1, Vol.9, p.158-9; Ltr., S.P. Lee to Case, Sept. 4, 1863, ORN, Ser.1, Vol.9, p.191.

432. Heyl, Vol.1, p.361-2; Wise, p.99-

100; ORN, Ser.2, Vol.2, p.85; Foster, p.63; CWNC, VI, p.294; Scharf, p.468.

433. Foster, p.59-61.

434. Carr, Dawson, *Gray Phantoms of the Cape Fear*, p.170-2.

435. Heyl, Vol.3, p.154.

436. *Official Records of the Union and Confederate Navies in the War of the Rebellion*; Still, ed. p.245 (n.10).

437. Foster, p.60; ORN, Ser.2, Vol.1, p.88; Heyl, Vol.3, p.154.

438. Carr, p.178-80.

439. CWNC, VI, p.189.

440. ORN, Ser.2, Vol.1, p.88.

441. Foster, p.134-6; Jones, Quiggin Specification Book #146.

442. Foster, p.136; Wise, p.113.

443. McKenna, p.232-3; Ridgely-Nevitt, p.184.

444. Silverstone, *Civil War Navies*, p.47.

445. Foster, p.156-8.

446. Ibid.

447. Ltr, Prioleau to Welsman, May 9, 1863, Prioleau Letterbook.

448. Ltr, Prioleau to Welsman, July 21, 1863, Prioleau Letterbook.

449. Ltr, J.J. Almy to S.P. Lee, Sept. 23, 1864, ORN, Ser.1, Vol.9, p.216.

450. Wise, p.147-50; Foster, p.136-9.

451. Silverstone, *Civil War Navies*, p.195; Ltr., Bulloch to Mallory, Sept. 15, 1864, ORN Ser.2, Vol.2, p.720.

452. Ltrs., Prioleau to McRae, May 12, 1864 and Prioleau to Welsman, Apr. 8, 1864, Prioleau Letterbook.

453. Wise, p.315; McKenna, p.248-9.

454. Silverstone, *Civil War* Navies, p.48; Foster, p.206.

455. Wise, p.162-4; 216-7; 327.

456. Wise, p.306.

457. Specifications for Paddle Steamer Hope, Merseyside Maritime Museum.

458. Wise, p.204; Foster, p.152-3; Specifications for Paddle Steamer Hope, Merseyside Maritime Museum.

459. Ltr., Prioleau to Welsman, Apr. 8, 1864, Prioleau Letterbook.

460. Wise, p.205.

461. Wise, p.204; Silverstone, *Civil War Navies*, p.195.

462. Still, ed., *The Confederate Navy*,

p.43-4.

463. Invoices/Receipts, "Appropriations for 10 Gunboats," Oct. 25, 1861, Nov. 16, 1861, Dec. 21, 1861, Jan. 8, 1862, Jan. 15, 1862, Feb. 2, 1862. NARS M1091 Reel 3.

464. ORN, Ser.2, Vol.1, p.253, 260.

465. Still, *Confederate Shipbuilding*, p.14.

466. Ltr, P. Crosby et al, to H.K. Thatcher, May 29, 1865, ORN, Ser.1, Vol.22, p.227-8; CWNC, VI, p.230.

467. Ltr, P. Crosby et al to H.K. Thatcher, May 29, 1865, ORN, Ser.1, Vol.22, p.228.

468. Contract, w/J. Hughes, Sept. 15, 1861, NARS M1091.

469. NARS M1091; Investigation of Navy Department, ORN, Ser.2, Vol.1, p.455; Silverstone, *Civil War Navies*, p.165.

470. NARS M1091, Invoices, Sept. 19, 1861, Nov. 12, 1861; Investigation of Navy Dept. ORN, Ser.2, Vol.1, p.454; Silverstone, *Civil War Navies*, p.165; Extract of Proceedings of Court of Inquiry, Jun. 4, 1863, ORN, Ser.1, Vol.18, p.354.

471. CWNC, Vol.II, p.45; Silverstone, *Civil War Navies*, p.165.

472. Contract, Oct. 14, 1861, NARS M1091; Turner, p.53.

473. Turner, p.57-59.

474. Ltr., McLaughlin to Baker, June 22, 1862, (Baltic File, Alabama Dept. of Archives and History); Ltrs, Sept. 27 and Oct. 13, 1862, Minor Papers, Virginia Hist. Soc.; "An Investigation of the Remains of the Confederate Gunboat CSS *Chattahoochee*," East Carolina University, 1990, p.13.

475. Turner, p. 66-8; "An Investigation…," p.45.

476. ORN, Ser.2, Vol.1, p.250.

477. Turner, p.81-2, 94-5.

478. Turner, p.98-9; Silverstone, *Civil War Navies*, p.164.

479. "An Investigation…," p.39-40.

480. Ibid.

481. "An Investigation…," p.42-5.

482. Melton, p.66, 268; Invoice, A.N. Miller, Dec.12, 1862, NARS, M1091; Ltr, S.S. Lee to W.W. Hunter, Oct. 14, 1864, W.W. Hunter Papers.

483. Melton, p.66; Invoice, Dec. 12,

1861, NARS M1091.

484. Melton, p.403; Report to Hunter, Jan. 9, 1865, ORN, Ser.1, Vol.16, p.496-8; Silverstone, *Civil War Navies*, p.164.

485. Scharf, p.669; Invoice, Dec. 18, 1862, NARS M1091.

486. Silverstone, *Civil War Navies*, p.164.

487. Web site: csnavy.org.

488. Still, ed., *The Confederate Navy*, p.44; Coski, p.92; Conversation, 9/25/2013 w/Kevin Foster.

489. Ordnance Returns, *Hampton* and *Nansemond*, May 19, 1864 and June 1864, Minor Papers, Va. Hist. Soc.

490. Drawing, Naval Historical Center, NH73908; Melton, (Holcombe drawing), p.181; Ltr, W. Butt to J.K. Mitchell, Jan. 26, 1865, ORN, Ser.1, Vol.11, p.682.

491. CWNC, Vol.VI, p.246, 275.

492. Ltr, Maury to Mallory, Oct. 27, 1861, ORN Ser.2, Vol.2, p.99; Williams, Frances Leigh, *Matthew Fountaine Maury: Scientist of the Sea*, p.383-6.

493. Ibid.

494. Ibid; Brooke, George M., ed., *Ironclads and Big Guns: the Journal and Letters of John M. Brooke. Jr.*, p.53;

495. Still, ed., *The Confederate Navy*, p.46-7.

496. "Specifications," Navy Department, Va. Hist. Soc.

497. Melton, p.182, 262; Invoice, Apr. 17, 1863, NARS M1091.

498. Still, ed., *The Confederate Navy*, p.47.

499. Robinson, William Morrison, Jr., *The Confederate Privateers*, p.37-9; Wise, p.291.

500. Heyl, Vol.3, p.43-5.

501. CWNC, Vol.6, p.207.

502. Two officers on the *Calhoun* "saw the shot as it left the gun and traced its trajectory and saw it strike the *Queen*." "… the shot … struck her roof, exploded, cut a steam pipe, and set fire to the cotton [cladding]." Diary, Eng. Baird, USS *Calhoun*, Apr. 14, 1863, ORN, Ser.1, Vol.20, p.138.

503. Heyl, Vol.3, p.45.

504. Heyl, Vol.1, p.465; "Particulars of the Steamer Yorktown," *Journal of the Franklin Institute*, July 1859, p.139.

505. Scharf, p.141-2.

506. Ltr., H. Clark, Engineer, to J.R. Tucker, July 23, 1861, ORN, Ser.1, Vol.6, p.711.

507. Scharf, p.195.

508. "Webb Book" reprinted in Nautical Research Journal, June 1969, p.90-1; Ridgely-Nevitt, p.169; ORN, Ser.2, Vol.1, p.271.

509. CWNC, Vol.VI, p.323; Ltr, J.P. Benjamin to Lovell, Jan. 14, 1861, ORN, Ser.1, Vol.17, p.159.

510. Ltr., Lovell to Pemberton, Feb. 28, 1863, ORN, Ser.1, Vol.24, p.398.

511. Jones, Vol.2, p.389-90.

512. Ltr, Read to Mallory, Apr. 22, 1865, ORN, Ser.1, Vol.22, p.168.

513. Scharf, p.366-7; Allan Pinkerton Report, Apr. 25, 1865, ORN, Ser.1, Vol.22, p.153.

514. Canney, *U.S. Coast Guard and Revenue Cutters, 1790-1935*, p.28; ORN, Ser.2, Vol.1, p.99.

515. Wise, p.187-90, 308.

516. Canney, *U.S. Coast Guard and Revenue Cutters*, p.28.

517. Canney, *The Old Steam Navy,* Vol.1, p.41-2.

518. Jones, Vol.3, p.206-12.

519. ORN, Ser.2, Vol.1, p.89.

520. ORN, Ser.2, Vol.1, p.220, 268.

521. Scharf, p.728; Stern, p.108-9; Perry, Milton F., *Infernal Machines*, p.18.

522. ORN, Ser.2, Vol.1, p.220.

523. *Annual Report* of the Secretary of the Navy, 1860, p.12; Silverstone, *Civil War* Navies, p.172.

524. ORN, Ser.2, Vol.1, p.259; Invoice, Jun. 11, 1861, NARS M1091; *Journal of the Franklin Institute,* Feb. 1853, p.140.

525. CWNC, VI, p.269; Jones, Vol.2, p.108-113.

526. CWNC, VI, p.300; From Richmond Dispatch, Dec. 14, 1861 (reprinted from Mobile Evening News), ORN, Ser.1, Vol.16, p.809; ORN, Ser.2, Vol.1, p.266.

527. Ibid.

528. Hughes Proposal, June 28, 1861, NARS M1091.

529. ORN, Ser.2, Vol.1, Investigation of the Navy Department, p.756; CWNC, VI, p.262-3.

530. CWNC, VI, p.262-3.

531. Throm, Edward L., ed., *Picture History of American Transportation*, p.4.

532. Hunter, Louis C., *Steamboats on the Western Rivers*, p.141.

533. Hunter, p.141-175.

534. Way, p.140.

535. Ltr, Carter to L. Polk, Sept. 19, 1861; Oct. 28, 1861, NARS M1091.

536. Ibid; Silverstone, *Civil War Navies*, p.187.

537. CWNC, VI, p.234.

538. Way, p. 228; CWNC, VI, p.252.

539. Image #8648, U. of Wisconsin Steamboat Collection.

540. Way, p.228; Melton, p.143; Ltr, T.M. Buchanan to B.F. Butler, Nov.4, 1862, ORN Ser.1, Vol.19, p.330-1.

541. Melton, p.228-9.

542. Ltr, T.M. Buchanan to B.F. Butler, Nov. 4, 1862, ORN, Ser.1, Vol.19, p.330-1.

543. Ltr, Benjamin to Seddon, Dec.2, 1862, ORN, Ser. 1, Vol.19, p.334.

544. Way, p.40; CWNC, VI, p.203.

545. Stern, p.124-5; Ltr, Burt to Banks, n.d., ORN, Ser.1, Vol.19, p.456; Newspaper article, ORN, Ser.1, Vol.19, p.468-9.

546. Silverstone, *Civil War Navies*, p.175.

547. Way, p.131; CWNC, VI, p. 222; Ltr, Preble to Farragut, July 22, 1862, ORN, Ser.1, Vol.19, p.83.

548. Way, p.291.

549. Invoices/Receipts, Dec. 12, 1861, Jan. 4 and 6, and Feb. 21, 1862, NARS, M1091.

550. Ltr, C.H. Davis to Welles, June 19, 1862, ORN, Ser.1, Vol.23, p.171.

551. CWNC, VI, p.288.

552. Ltr, G.M. Bache to D.D. Porter, July 17, 1863, ORN, Ser.1, Vol.25, p.311.

553. CWNC, VI, p.288.

554. Way, p. 201; Photograph #15058, Univ. of Wisconsin, Lacrosse, Steamboat Collection.

555. Scharf, p.267.

556. CWNC, VI, p.268-9.

557. Way, p.382.

558. Warren, Daniel Crandall, and Isaac Dennison Jewell, *The History of the Ram Fleet and the Mississippi Marine Brigade in the War for the Union on the Mississippi and Its Tributaries...*, p.28-9;

Jones, Vol.2, p.157.

559. CWNC, VI, p.289; Stern, p.102.

560. Ltr., J.P. Benjamin to M. Lovell, Jan. 19, 1862, ORN, Ser.1, Vol.17, p.160-1.

561. It should be noted that Secretary Judah's first directive was for the seizure of fourteen vessels at New Orleans, and the names of those vessels were listed. Later, fourteen vessels were in the Mississippi River Defense Force, but the only vessel on both lists is the *Mexico* (which became *General Bragg*). The majority of the initial fourteen ships were not suitable for conversion to rams and many were used to run the blockade. See ORN, Ser.1, Vol.17, pps.159-161.

562. Jones, Vol.2, p.172-3.

563. "Mexico" File, Heyl Collection, Bowling Green State University; Silverstone, *Civil War Navies*, p.122.

564. Porter, D.D., *Naval History of the Civil War*, p.171.

565. Porter, p.172; Miles, Jim, *A River Unvexed*, p.58.

566. Silverstone, *Civil War Navies*, p.122.

567. Way, p.280; CWNC, VI, p.235.

568. Ibid; Silverstone, *Civil War Navies*, p.122; Porter, p.171.

569. CWNC, VI, p.235-6.

570. ORN, Ser.2, Vol.1, p.92-93; Silverstone, *Civil War Navies*, p.122.

571. Website: www.history.navy.mil (Naval Historical Center).

572. Way, Frederick, *Way's Steam Towboat Directory*, p.185.

573. CWNC, VI, p.262; Silverstone, *Civil War Navies*, p.134, 169; ORN, Ser.2, Vol.1, p.128, 258.

574. Ibid; Way, *Towboat...*, p.211.

575. CWNC, VI, p.213; Porter, p.171; ORN, Ser. 2, Vol.1, p.251; Stern, p.102.

576. Way, p.179.

577. Silverstone, *Civil War Navies*, p.168.

578. Miles, p.70-1; CWNC, VI, p.230-1.

579. Ltr, W.W. Hunter et al to Rousseau, June 27, 1861, ORN, Ser.1, Vol.16, p.828.

580. CWNC, VI, p.236-7; Way, *Towboats...*, p.136; ORN, Ser.2, Vol.1, p.216; ORN, Ser.1, Vol.23, p.379.

581. Ltr, Gregory to Maynadier, May 10, 1862, ORN, Ser.1, Vol.23, p.15-66.

582. CWNC, VI, p.237.

583. Way, *Packet Directory*, p.180.

584. Ltr, Phelps to Foote, May 11, 1862, ORN, Ser.1, Vol.23.

585. CWNC, VI, p.233.

586. CWNC, VI, p.233; Silverstone, *Civil War Navies*, p.169; Porter, p.171.

587. CWNC, VI, p.233; Porter, p.171.

588. Ltr, Chaissaing to Dahlgren, Mar. 29, 1865, ORN, Ser.1, Vol.16, p.378-9.

589. Perry, Milton, *Infernal Machines*, p.63-80; Still, *Iron Afloat*, p.115-6; Still, ed., *The Confederate Navy*, p.46-7; CWNC, VI, p.316.

590. Quoted in Campbell, R.Thomas, ed., *Engineer in Gray*, p.68; Still, ed., *The Confederate Navy*, p.62.

591. Maury Papers, Museum of the Confederacy.

592. From diagram in Campbell, p.69; Information from deserters, Jan. 7, 1864, ORN, Ser.1, Vol.15, p.228.

593. Perry, p.85; Roberts, William H., "The Neglected Ironclad," *Warship International*, No.2, 1989, p.132; Various reports, and Ltr. Dahlgren to Rowan, June 8, 1864, ORN, Ser.1, Vol.15, p.512.

594. Ltr, F. Lee to Gen. Jordan, Mar. 8, 1864, ORN, Ser.1, Vol.15, p.358.

595. Perry, p.183-4; CWNC, VI, p.296.

596. Still, ed., *The Confederate Navy*, p.62.

597. Ibid, p.63.

598. ORN, Ser.2, Vol.1, p.399-400.

599. Chaffin, Tom, *The H.L. Hunley*, p.70-72. McClintock claimed they could remain below for two hours (Chaffin, p.71).

600. Chaffin, p.72-76.

601. Ibid, p.207.

602. Ltr, F. Buchanan to Mallory, Feb. 14, 1863, Buchanan Papers, UNC.

603. Ibid, p.89-97; Simonds, p.188; Perry, p.96-7.

604. Chaffin, p.107-111, and end papers (plans of *Hunley*).

605. Ibid.

606. Chaffin, p.165.

607. Ibid, p.166-7.

608. Melton, p.126, 134, 141.

609. Melton, p.153, 158.

610. Ltr, C.F.M. Spotswood to Minor, Apr. 14, 1863, Minor Papers, Va. Hist. Soc.

611. Ltr, W.W. Hunter to Mallory, Sept. 3, 1863, ORN, Vol.14, p.766.

612. Coker, p.207.

613. Smith, *CSS Arkansas*, p.12-13.

614. Ibid.

615. Invoices, construction of floating batteries, Aug.-Dec. 1861, NARS M1091.

616. Invoices, Aug. 31, Oct. 11, Nov. 7, 1861, NARS, M1091.

617. Rpt, ORN, Ser.1, Vol.17, p.163.

618. Scharf, p.245.

619. Ltr, Sanford to Pennock, June 16, 1862, ORN, Ser.1, Vol.23, p.212.

620. Invoices, Oct. 16, Nov. 7, Nov. 28, 1861, NARS M1091.

621. ORN, Ser.1, Vol.17, p.163; "Investigation of Navy Dept...," ORN, Ser.2, Vol.2, p.472.

622. Contract, Dec. 1, 1862, NARS RG 365.

623. Elliot, p.78, 83.

624. Ltr, Flusser to S.P. Lee, June 8, 1863, ORN, Ser.1, Vol.9, p.66.

625. Elliot, p.129.

626. Ltr, J. Franklin to J. Frebiger, Apr. 9, 1865, ORN, Ser.1, Vol.12, p.108.

627. Ltr, Flusser... ORN, Ser.1, Vol.9, p.66.

628. ORN, Ser.2, Vol.1, p.248.

629. Ltr, Barron to Mallory, July 26, 1861, ORN, Ser.1, Vol.6, p.714; Ltr, Lynch to Mallory, Sep. 12, 1861, ORN, Ser.1, Vol.6, p.727. The hull dimensions given for this vessel are roughly those of the exploring ship/lightship *Arctic*, (Heyl, Vol.4, p.13) but that vessel was wooden hulled. Apparently, the engines from the old *Arctic* were still at Norfolk navy yard and were used in the ironclad *Richmond*.

630. CWNC, VI, p.198.

631. Ltr, J. Jones to Welles, May 28, 1861, ORN, Ser.1, Vol.4, p.186; CWNC, VI, p.218.

632. Ltr, M. Smith to W. McKean, Nov.29, 1861, ORN, Ser.1, Vol.16, p.794.

633. CWNC, VI, p.218.

634. CWNC, VI, p.282-3; Silverstone, *Civil War Navies*, p.178.

Bibliography

Unpublished Sources

Baltic Files: Alabama Department of Archives and History

Brooke, J.M., Collection, University of North Carolina

Brooks, William Param, Papers, Emory University

Buchanan, Franklin, Notebook, University of North Carolina

Foster, Kevin, "Phantoms, Banshees, Will-of-the-Wisps and the Dare, or: The Search for Speed under Steam, the Design of Blockade Running Steamships." MA Thesis, East Carolina U., 1991.

Forrest, French, Notebook, University of North Carolina

Grimball, T., Papers, Duke University

Heyl, Eric, Papers, Bowling Green State University, Bowling Green, Ohio

Hoke, W.A., Collection, University of North Carolina

Holcombe, Robert, "Notes on the Classification of Confederate Ironclads", Paper submitted to U.S. Army Corps of Engineers, Savannah District, 1980.

Hunter, W.W., Papers, Duke University

Johnston, James D., "Speech to the Georgia Historical Society, 1880, (Museum of the Confederacy. Richmond. VA)

Jones, Quiggin Specification Book, Merseyside Maritime Museum, Liverpool, UK

Mallory, Stephen, Diary, University of North Carolina

Martin, W.F., Papers, University of North Carolina

McBlair, Myers Papers, Emory University, Atlanta, GA

Minor Papers, Duke University

Minor Family Papers, Virginia Historical Society

National Archives, Cartographic Branch, RG 19, U.S. Navy, Ship Plans.

NARS RG 45 Navy Department Records, Entry 225, Letters from Constructors

NARS RG 125, Records of Courts Martials, T.T.Craven, Vol. 143, No. 4071.

NARS M365, Confederate Navy Department, Contracts.

NARS M625, Area File, Naval Records, 1775-1910.

NARS M1091, Subject File, Confederate States Navy

Page, Thomas Jefferson, Papers: "The Cruise of the Stonewall", Duke University Library

Peebles, Marlon D., "The History and Archeology of a Civil War Ironclad on the Cape Fear River", MA Thesis, East Carolina University, Greenville, NC, 1986.

Phelps, S. L., Papers, Missouri Historical Society

Porter, John L., Papers, Museum of the Confederacy, Richmond, VA.

Prioleau Letterbooks, Merseyside Maritime Museum, Liverpool

Savannah Squadron Papers, Emory University

Specification, Blockade Runner "Hope", #159, Merseyside Maritime Museum, Liverpool.

Specifications, 116' Gunboat, Virginia Historical Society

Tatnall, Josiah, Papers, Duke University

Thomson, J. & G., Letterbook, University of Glasgow

Tomb Papers, University of North Carolina

Willink Papers, Emory University

Published Sources

"An Investigation of the Remains of the Confederate Gunboat CSS *Chattahoochee*", by Gordon P. Watts, et al, The Program in Maritime History and Underwater Research, East Carolina University, Greenville, SC, 1990.

Battles and Leaders of the Civil War, 4 vols., (Reprint), Castle.

Baughmann, James P., *The Mallorys of Mystic*, Wesleyan University Press, Middletown, CT, 1972.

Baxter, James Phinney, *The Introduction of the Ironclad Warship*, (Reprint), Archon, 1968.

Bennett, Frank M., *The Steam Navy of the United States*, Warren & Co., Pittsburgh, 1896.

Bennett, John D., *The London Confederates*, McFarland, Jefferson, North Carolina, 2008.

Bowcock, Andrew, *CSS Alabama*, Chatham Publishing, London, 2002.

Bradlee, Francis B.C., *Blockade Running During the Civil War*, The Essex Institute, Salem, MA, 1925.

Brooke, George M., Jr., *John M. Brooke, Naval Scientist and Educator*, University Press of Virginia, Charlottesville, VA, 1980.

Bulloch, James Dunwoody, *The Secret Service of the Confederate States in Europe,* (Reprint), Thomas Yoseloff, New York, NY, 1959.

Campbell, R. Thomas, *Confederate Naval Forces in Western Waters*, McFarland, Jefferson, NC, 2005.

—, *Engineer in Grey: Memoirs of Chief Engineer James H. Tomb.* McFarland, Jefferson, NC, 2007.

Canney, Donald L., *The Old Steam Navy*: Vol.1, Frigates, Sloops and Gunboats, Naval Institute Press, Annapolis, MD, 1990.

—, *The Old Steam Navy*: Vol.2, The Ironclads, Naval Institute Press, Annapolis, MD, 1993.

—, *U.S. Coast Guard and Revenue Cutters, 1790-1935*, Naval Institute Press, Annapolis, MD, 1995.

Carr, Dawson, *Grey Phantoms of the Cape Fear*, John F. Blair, Publishers, Winston-Salem, NC, 1998.

Chaffin, Tom, *The H.L. Hunley,* Hill & Wang, New York, NY, 2008.

—, *Sea of Grey,* Hill & Wang, New York, NY, 2006.

Civil War Naval Chronology, Naval History Division, Navy Department, Washington, DC, 1971.

Coker, P.C., III, *Charleston's Maritime Heritage, 1670-1865*, Cokercraft Press, Charleston, SC, 1987.

Conway's *All the World's Fighting Ships*, 1860-1905, Mayflower Books, New York, NY, 1979.

Coski, John M., *Capital Navy*, Savas Beatie, New York, NY, 2005.

Dictionary of American Naval Fighting Ships, 8 vols., Naval History Division, Navy Department, Washington, DC.

"Documentation of the Civil War Vessels CSS Florida and USS Cumberland, Hampton Roads, Virginia." Panamerican Consultants, for U.S. Army Corps of Engineers, U.S. Navy Atlantic Division Naval Facilities Engineering Command, May 1994.

Durkin, Joseph T, *Stephen R. Mallory, Confederate Navy Chief*, University of North Carolina Press, Chapel Hill, NC, 1954.

Elliot, Robert, *Ironclad of the Roanoke*, White Mane Publishing Co., Inc., Shippensburg, PA, 1994.

Flanders, Alan B., *The Merrimac*, Scribner's, New York, NY, 1982.

Gardiner, Robert, ed., *Steam, Steel, and Shellfire*, Conway Press, London, UK, 1992.

Graham, Eric J., *Clyde Built*, Birlinn, Edinburgh, UK, 2006.

Heyl, Erik, *Early American Steamers*, 6 vols., 1953-1967.

Holcombe, Robert, "The Richmond Class Confederate Ironclads", Confederate Historical Association of Belgium, (www.chab-belgium.com).

Hoole, William Stanley, ed., *Four Years in the Confederate Navy*, University of Georgia Press, Athens, GA, 1964.

Horan, James D., ed., *CSS Shenandoah: The Memoirs of James I. Waddell,* Crown Publishers, New York, NY, 1960.

Hunter, Louis C., *Steamboats on the Western Rivers*, Dover, Reprint, 1993.

Isherwood, Benjamin F., *Experimental Researches in Steam Engineering*, 2 vols., W. Hamilton, Philadelphia, PA, 1863-5.

Jeter, Katherine Brash, ed., *A Man and His Boat*, Center for Louisiana Studies, Lafayette, LA, 1996.

Jones, Virgil Carrington, *The Civil War at Sea*, 3 vols., Holt, Rinehart & Winston, New York, NY, 1962.

"Journal of the Franklin Institute," Philadelphia, PA, Various Issues, 1847-1862.

King, W.W., *Lessons and Practical Notes on Steam*. Van Nostrand, New York, NY, 1864.

Kinnaman, Stephen Chapin, *The Most Perfect Cruiser*, Dog Ear Publishing, Indianapolis, IN, 2009.

Lester, Richard I., *Confederate Finance & Purchasing in Great Britain*, University of Virginia Press, Charlottesville, VA, 1975.

Lewis, Herbert J., "Selma Ordnance and Naval Foundry", www.encyclopediaofalabama. Org.

Lyon, David and Rif Winfield, *The Sail and Steam List*, Chatham Publishing, UK, 2004.

MacGregor, David R., *Fast Sailing Ships*, Naval Institute Press, Annapolis, MD, 1988.

Maclay, Edgar S., *History of the Navy*, 2 vols., D. Appleton, New York, NY, 1897.

Mahan, Alfred Thayer, *The Gulf and Inland Waters*, (Reprint), The Archive Society, Harrisburg, PA, 1992.

Marvel, William, *The Alabama and the Kearsarge*, The University North Carolina Press, Chapel Hill and London, 1996.

McKenna, Joseph, *British Ships in the Confederate Navy*, McFarland, Jefferson, NC, 2010.

Melton, Maurice, *The Confederate Ironclads*, Thomas Yoseloff, New York, NY, 1968.

—, *The Best Station of them All*, University of Alabama Press, Tuscaloosa, AL, 2012.

Miles, Jim, *A River Unvexed*, Rutledge Hill Press, Nashville, TN, 1954.

Milton, David Hepburn, *Lincoln's Spymaster*, Stackpole, New York, NY, 2003.

Morgan, James Morris, *Recollections of a Rebel Reefer*, Houghton & Mifflin, Boston and New York, 1917.

Musicant, Ivan, *Divided Waters*, Harper Collins, New York, NY, 1995.

Noirsain, Serge, *La Flotte Europeene de la Confederation Sudiste*, Editions de la C.H.A.B, Bruxelles, 2000.

Official Records of the Union and Confederate Navies in the War of the Rebellion, 30 Vols. Government Printing Office, Washington DC, 1894-1922.

Ordnance Instructions for the U.S. Navy, Government Printing Office, Washington, DC, 1866.

Owsley, Frank Lawrence, Jr., *The CSS Florida*, University of Alabama Press, Tuscaloosa & London, 1987.

Park, Carl D., *Ironclad Down*, Naval Institute Press, Annapolis, MD, 2007.

Peebles, Martin, "CSS Raleigh: Site Survey," North Carolina Department of Cultural Resources, Kure Beach, NC, 1996.

Perry, Milton F., *Infernal Machines*, Louisiana State University Press, Baton Rouge and London, 1965.

Porter, David Dixon, *Naval History of the Civil War*, (Reprint), Castle, Secaucus, NJ, 1984.

Preston, Anthony, and John Major, *Send a Gunboat*, Conway, London, UK, 2007.

Report of the Secretary of the Navy, Bowman, Washington, DC, 1860.

Ridgely-Nevitt, Cedric, *American Steamships on the Atlantic*, Associated University Presses, New Brunswick, NJ, 1981.

Roberts, William H., "The Neglected Ironclad: A Design and Constructional Analysis of the USS New Ironsides", *Warship International*, No.2, 1989, 109-134.

Robinson, William Morrison, Jr., *The Confederate Privateers*, Yale University Press, New Haven, CT, 1928.

Scharf, J. Thomas, *History of the Confederate States Navy*, (Reprint), The Fairfax Press, 1977.

Semmes, Raphael, *Memoirs of Service Afloat*, (Reprint), The Blue and Grey Press, Secaucus, NJ, 1987.

Silverstone, Paul, *Civil War Navies*, Naval Institute Press, Annapolis, MD, 2001.

—, *Warships of the Civil War Navies*, Naval Institute Press, Annapolis, MD, 1989.

Smith, Myron, Jr., *The CSS Arkansas*, McFarland, Jefferson, NC, 2011.

Soley, James Russell, *The Blockade and the Cruisers*, (Reprint), The Archive Society, Harrisburg, PA, 1992.

Spencer, Warren F., *The Confederate Navy in Europe*, University of Alabama Press, Tuscaloosa, AL, 1983.

Steam, Steel, & Shellfire: The Steam Warship, 1815-1905, Conway Press, UK, 1992.

Stern, Philip Van Doren, *The Confederate Navy*, Bonanza, New York, NY, 1962.

Stuart, Charles Beebe, *Naval Drydocks of the United States*, Baker, Godwin Co., New York, NY, 1852.

Still, William N., Jr., *The Confederate Navy*, Naval Institute Press, Annapolis, MD, 1997.

—, *Confederate Shipbuilding*, University of Georgia Press, Athens, GA, 1969.

—, *Iron Afloat*, University of South Carolina Press, Colombia, SC, 1985

Summersell, Charles Grayson, *CSS Alabama*, The University of Alabama Press, Tuscaloosa, AL, 1985.

Symonds, Craig, *Confederate Admiral*, Naval Institute Press, Annapolis, MD, 1999.

"The Life of the CSS Neuse", www.nchistoricsites. org/Neuse/history/htm.

Throm, W.L., ed., *Picture History of American Transportation*, Simon & Schuster, New York, NY, 1952.

Tucker, Spencer, *Arming the Fleet*, Naval Institute Press, Annapolis, MD, 1989.

Turner, Maxine, *Navy Grey*, The University of Alabama Press, Tuscaloosa and London, 1988.

Vandiver, Frank, ed., *The Civil War Diary of Josiah Gorgas*, The University of Alabama Press, Tuscaloosa and London, 1947.

—, *Ploughshares into Swords*, University of Texas Press, Austin, TX, 1952.

Warren, Daniel Crandall, and Isaac Dennison Jewell, *The History of the Ram Fleet and the Mississippi Marine Brigade in the War for the Union on the Mississippi River and its Tributaries: The Story of the Ellets and their Men*. Buschart Brothers, St. Louis, MO, 1907.

Way, Frederick, Jr., *Way's Packet Directory, 1848-1994*. (Revised Edition), Ohio University Press, Athens, OH, 1983.

Way, Frederick, Jr., and Joseph W. Rutter, *Way's Steam Towboat Directory*, Ohio University Press, Athens, OH, 1990.

Webb, William H., *Plans of Wooden Vessels…*, William H. Webb, 1895. Reprinted in "Nautical Research Journal", Vol.34, No.2, June 1989.

Wilkinson, John, *Narrative of a Blockade Runner*. Sheldon, New York, NY, 1877.

Williams, Frances Leigh, *Matthew Fontaine Maury*: *Scientist of the Sea*. Rutgers University Press, New Brunswick, NJ, 1963.

Wilson, Walter E., and Gary L., McKay, *James D. Bulloch*, McFarland, Jefferson, NC, 2012.

Wise, Stephen R., *Lifeline of the Confederacy*, University of South Carolina Press, Columbia, SC, 1988.

www.hunley.org.

Index

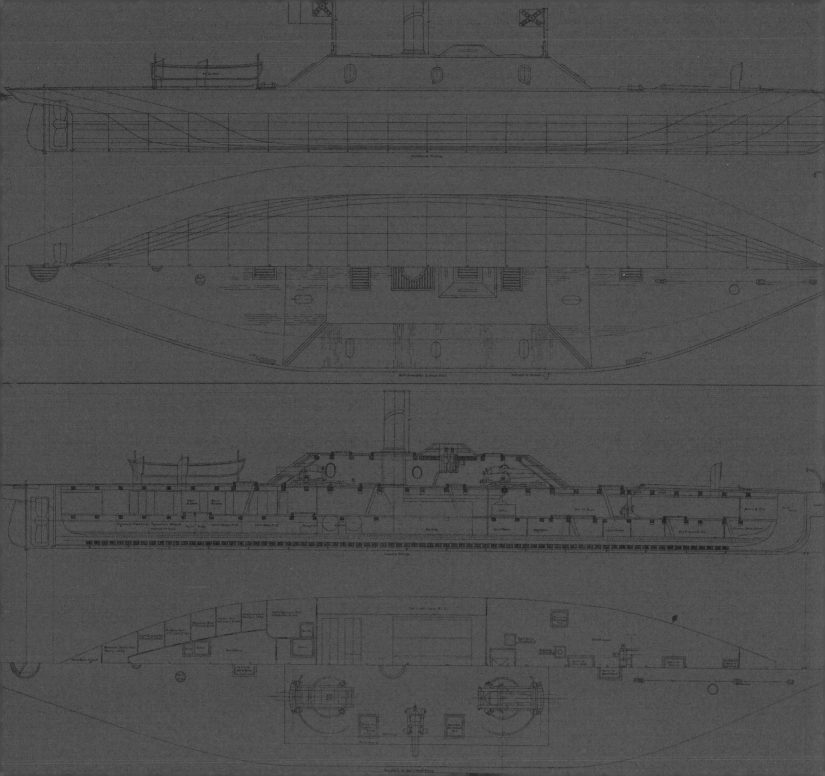